AF148739

Sustainable Management, Wertschöpfung und Effizienz

Series Editors

Gregor Weber, Breunigweiler, Germany

Markus Bodemann, Warburg, Germany

René Schmidpeter, Köln, Germany

In dieser Schriftenreihe stehen insbesondere empirische und praxisnahe Studien zu nachhaltigem Wirtschaften und Effizienz im Mittelpunkt. Energie-, Umwelt-, Nachhaltigkeits-, CSR-, Innovations-, Risiko- und integrierte Managementsysteme sind nur einige Beispiele, die Sie hier wiederfinden. Ein besonderer Fokus liegt dabei auf dem Nutzen, den solche Systeme für die Anwendung in der Praxis bieten, um zu helfen die globalen Nachhaltigkeitsziele (SDGs) umzusetzen. Publiziert werden nationale und internationale wissenschaftliche Arbeiten.

Reihenherausgeber:
Dr. Gregor Weber, ecoistics.institute
Dr. Markus Bodemann
Prof. Dr. René Schmidpeter, Center for Advanced Sustainable Management, Cologne Business School

This series is focusing on empirical and practical research in the fields of sustainable management and efficiency. Management systems in the context of energy, environment, sustainability, CSR, innovation, risk as well as integrated management systems are just a few examples which can be found here. A special focus is on the value such systems can offer for the application in practice supporting the implementation of the global sustainable development goals, the SDGs. National and international scientific publications are published (English and German).

Series Editors:
Dr. Gregor Weber, ecoistics.institute
Dr. Markus Bodemann
Prof. Dr. René Schmidpeter, Center for Advanced Sustainable Management, Cologne Business School

More information about this series at http://www.springer.com/series/15909

Claudia Lemke

Accounting and Statistical Analyses for Sustainable Development

Multiple Perspectives and Information-Theoretic Complexity Reduction

 Springer Gabler

Claudia Lemke
Berlin, Germany

Dissertation Technische Universität Berlin, 2020

ISSN 2523-8620   ISSN 2523-8639   (electronic)
Sustainable Management, Wertschöpfung und Effizienz
ISBN 978-3-658-33245-7   ISBN 978-3-658-33246-4   (eBook)
https://doi.org/10.1007/978-3-658-33246-4

Planung/Lektorat: Carina Reibold
This Springer Gabler imprint is published by the registered company Springer Fachmedien Wiesbaden GmbH part of Springer Nature.
The registered company address is: Abraham-Lincoln-Str. 46, 65189 Wiesbaden, Germany

Preface

Claudia Lemke's dissertation addresses the aim to develop a sustainable development indicator set that

1. includes the economic, environmental, and social domains and maps their interrelations into a composite measure;

2. incorporates the so-called "multilevel perspective", i.e. it is applicable to economic units of different size; and

3. overcomes critical conceptual and methodological deficiencies identified in index construction for sustainable development.

To meet this objective, Claudia Lemke derives a profound conceptual framework of sustainable development. Theoretical principles for the assessment of contributions to sustainable development are outlined and an overview of assessment methodologies is provided. Because the thesis identifies indicator sets and composite indicators (i.e. indices) derived from them as an expedient method to meet conceptual requirements and assessment principles, the methodology of a novel index, the Multilevel Sustainable Development Index (MLSDI), is derived subsequently.

Weighting and aggregation are crucial steps in index construction. In terms of weighting, the thesis identifies statistical procedures as expedient to yield the most promising results, because they are able to account for the correlations of underlying variables from the environmental, economic, and social domains. Three specific techniques are identified and tested against each other: Principal Component Analysis (PCA), Partial Triadic Analysis (PTA), and the information-theoretic Maximum Relevance Minimum Redundancy Backward (MRMRB) algorithm. For aggregation purposes, geometric aggregation is identified as the only method that accounts for non-comparable and ratio-scaled indicators.

The methodology is applied to a sample of the German economy for the years 2008 to 2016 in the empirical part of the dissertation. A comparable assessment of different branches is performed within each of the three domains and the aggregated MLSDI is derived for selected branches of the German economy.

This work has far-reaching implications for research and practice. With regards to sustainable development research, major contributions include the inclusion of the multilevel perspective. A wide range of indicators from all three domains of sustainable development are integrated and the analysis of their interconnections is performed in the statistical procedure of the innovative MRMRB algorithm. The thesis further uses open source data and makes all methodological choices transparent. Its Implications for practice include the support of policy-level decisions, because a methodologically sound and comparable tool is proposed to assess the sustainability performances of different units of account. The MLSDI is further proposed as an alternative to the Gross Domestic Product (GDP) as a measure of societal wellbeing at the policy level, because economic growth is limited and the additional dimensions of environmental protection and social development need to be considered when assessing societal wellbeing.

Claudia Lemke's dissertation therefore represents an important contribution to the research field of how a comparable evaluation of sustainability performances of units of different size can be performed. The results are equally important for science and practice. I wish Claudia Lemke's work the attention it certainly deserves.

Berlin, July 2020   JProf. Dr. Karola Bastini

Foreword

After submitting her dissertation to Technische Universität Berlin, Claudia Lemke joined the Beiersdorf AG as a Supply Chain Sustainability Manager. Since 1882, the name Beiersdorf stands for innovative skin care. We continuously develop our products and brands to win consumers' loyalty and trust through best-in-class quality. Nowadays, quality and trust do not only refer to the use phase of a product, but the consumers of today – and even more the consumers of tomorrow – demand products with a reduced environmental impact as well as an increased value for society. Innovative value creation goes beyond improving the consumer's experience of product application. Sustainable production and consumption are one of the great challenges of the 21st century, and especially global corporations have to take on the responsibility to contribute to societal wellbeing by taking the entire value chain and life cycle of their products into account. Beiersdorf meets the needs of these increased demands and has publicly pledged to improve its environmental footprint and social impact at global level.

Beiersdorf quantifies its sustainable development performances according to the Global Reporting Initiative (GRI) and allocates its contributions to the Sustainable Development Goals (SDGs). These two guiding frameworks are the foundation of Claudia Lemke's dissertation. By aligning the corporate GRI framework and the societal SDG framework at indicator level, Claudia Lemke enables the *measurement* of corporate contributions to societal sustainable development. Moreover, by developing a methodologically sound sustainable development index from this newly aligned indicator base, Claudia Lemke facilitates benchmarking throughout all aspects of sustainable development. Benchmarking in turn facilitates decision making in modern-day corporations, often dealing with several competing priorities.

By co-funding the open access publication of Claudia Lemke's dissertation, Beiersdorf supports the public accessibility of this excellent theoretical and methodological research. Knowledge and education should not be exclusive, but inclusiveness is part of sustainable development and Beiersdorf's vision. We are proud to care beyond skin.

Hamburg, November 2020

Jean-François Pascal
Vice President Sustainability
Beiersdorf AG

Acknowledgement

The present dissertation was developed during my occupation as a (senior) research associate at the economic research institute WifOR and later in the Field of Sustainability Accounting and Management Control at the Technische Universität Berlin under the supervision of JProf. Dr. Karola Bastini. This dissertation is submitted to acquire the academic degree of Doctor of Business and Economic Sciences (Dr. rer. oec.) at the Technische Universität Berlin. Parts of the dissertation are published in Lemke and Bastini (2020). I state my deepest recognition to everyone who has supported me during my time as a doctoral student.

First, I am grateful to JProf. Dr. Karola Bastini for her supervision and far-reaching feedback. Her eager willingness and engaged passion for scientific debates contributed considerably to the successful completion of my dissertation project. I also thank Prof. Dr. Maik Lachmann, Chair of Accounting and Management Control at the Technische Universität Berlin, for being the secondary referee of my dissertation.

I am grateful to Prof. Dr. Dennis A. Ostwald for supporting my dissertation project during my tenure at WifOR with his stimulating visions and encouraging leadership. I am also thankful for fruitful methodological debates with Dr. Marcus Cramer. I thank Rita Bergmann for her secondary authorships of the first two working papers of my dissertation project as well as her strengthening joy and ease in life. I appreciate the permission to include data on the German health economy by Jochen Puth-Weissenfels, Federal Ministry for Economic Affairs and Energy (BMWi).

Furthermore, I thank Fares Getzin for exchanging valuable thoughts and mutual motivations on progresses of our dissertations throughout my time at the Technische Universität Berlin. I also appreciate the fruitful debates and the motivating moments with all other colleagues at the Technische Universität Berlin and WifOR.

Last but foremost, I thank my partner Alexander Andor for never-ending encouragement, tolerance, and patience in both good and bad times of my dissertation. I am also thankful to my friend Cordula Klaus for her long-lasting support and cheering spirits. I am grateful to my parents Soon Boon and Bernd Lemke as well as my sister Susanne Lemke for providing a network of safety throughout all ups and downs of my entire academic career.

Berlin, February 2020   Claudia Lemke

To Clea and all future generations to come

The publication of this work was funded by the Open Access Publication Fund of Technische Universität Berlin and the Beiersdorf AG.

Table of contents

List of abbreviations

A4S	Prince's Accounting for Sustainability Project
aHC	average Headcount
AIChE	American Institute of Chemical Engineers
ARIMA	Autoregressive Integrated Moving Average
BA	Federal Employment Agency
Bellagio STAMP	Bellagio Sustainability Assessment and Measurement Principles
BLI	Better Life Index
BMJV	Federal Ministry of Justice and Consumer Protection
BMWi	Federal Ministry for Economic Affairs and Energy
CBS	Centre for Bhutan Studies
CEFIC	European Chemical Industry Council
CEPI	Composite Environmental Performance Index
CIS	Compass Index of Sustainability
CIT	Corporate Income Tax
CO$_2$	Carbon Dioxide
CO$_{2e}$	Carbon Dioxide Equivalents
CPA	Classification of Products by Activity
CRAN	Comprehensive R Archive Network
Destatis	Federal Bureau of Statistics
DJSI	Dow Jones Sustainability Indices
EC	European Commission
EDP	Eco Domestic Product
EEA	European Environment Agency
EPI	Environmental Performance Index
ESA	European System of Accounts

ISO	International Organization for Standardization
ISSC	International Social Science Council
IT	Information Technology
IW	Inclusive Wealth Index
KMO	Kaiser-Meyer-Olkin
LPI	Living Planet Index
MAR	Missing at Random
MCAR	Missing Completely at Random
MDG	Millennium Development Goal
MISD	Mega Index of Sustainable Development
MLSDI	Multilevel Sustainable Development Index
MNAR	Missing Not at Random
MRMRB	Maximum Relevance Minimum Redundancy Backward
n/a ·	not applicable
NACE	Statistical Classification of Economic Activities in the European Community
NEF	New Economic Foundation
NDP	Net Domestic Product
NNI	Net National Income
OAT	One-at-a-Time
OECD	Organisation for Economic Co-operation and Development
p.c.	per capita
PC	Principal Component
PCA	Principal Component Analysis
p.h.	per hour
PTA	Partial Triadic Analysis
R&D	Research and Development
SASB	Sustainability Accounting Standards Boards
SDG	Sustainable Development Goal
SDGI	Sustainable Development Goal Index
SDI	Sustainable Development Index
SNBI	Sustainable Net Benefit Index
SSI	Sustainable Society Index

UN	United Nations
UNCED	United Nations Conference on Environment and Development
UNCHE	United Nations Conference on the Human Environment
UNCSD	United Nations Conference on Sustainable Development
UNDP	United Nations Development Programme
UNEP	United Nations Environment Programme
UNFCCC	United Nations Framework Convention on Climate Change
UNGA	United Nations General Assembly
UNGC	United Nations Global Compact
VAT	Value Added Tax
WBCSD	World Business Council for Sustainable Development
WCED	World Commission on Environment and Development
WI	Wellbeing Index
WSSD	World Summit on Sustainable Development
WTO	World Trade Organization
WWF	World Wide Fund for Nature

List of figures

List of tables

List of equations

List of symbols

α	Outlier coefficient
β	Outlier rate
c_1	Overall Multilevel Sustainable Development Index (MLSDI)
c_2	Set of sustainable development subindices
c_3	Set of sustainable development key components
c_4	Set of sustainable development key indicators
c_{4s}	Set of rescaled sustainable development key indicators
c_5	Set of sustainable development key figures
c_5^{NACE}	Set of sustainable development key figures in Statistical Classification of Economic Activities in the European Community (NACE)
χ_n	Number of bins of equal frequency discretisation for the Maximum Relevance Minimum Redundancy Backward (MRMRB) algorithm
χ_s	Bin size of equal frequency discretisation for the Maximum Relevance Minimum Redundancy Backward (MRMRB) algorithm
d	Subindex of a contentual domain
D	Number of subindices
δ_{max}	Maximum of the rescaling range
δ_{min}	Minimum of the rescaling range
ε	Random noise in a basic structural time series model
η	Relative efficiency in convergence of an estimate in multiple imputation
γ	Seasonal component in a basic structural time series model
I	Identity matrix
λ	Rate of missing values
m	Number of imputations in multiple imputation
M_T	Technology matrix
μ	Trend component in a basic structural time series model

n	Economic object
N	Number of economic objects
ω	Weight of a sustainable development key indicator
ω^{MRMRB}	Weight of a sustainable development key indicator derived by the Maximum Relevance Minimum Redundancy Backward (MRMRB) algorithm
ω^{PC}	Weights of a sustainable development key indicator derived by the Principal Component (PC) family
ω^{PCA}	Weight of a sustainable development key indicator derived by the Principal Component Analysis (PCA)
ω_t^{PCA}	Weight of a sustainable development key indicator derived by the Principal Component Analysis (PCA) in a time period
ω^{PTA}	Weight of a sustainable development key indicator derived by the Partial Triadic Analysis (PTA)
Ω^{PTA}	Weight of a time period derived by the Partial Triadic Analysis (PTA)
p	Sustainable development key component
P	Number of sustainable development key components
ψ	Importance factor of a sustainable development key indicator
ψ^{MRMRB}	Importance factor of a sustainable development key indicator derived by the Maximum Relevance Minimum Redundancy Backward (MRMRB) algorithm
ψ^{PC}	Importance factor of a sustainable development key indicator derived by the Principal Component (PC) family
ψ^{PCA}	Importance factor of a sustainable development key indicator derived by the Principal Component Analysis (PCA)
ψ^{PTA}	Importance factor of a sustainable development key indicator derived by the Partial Triadic Analysis (PTA)
q	Interquartile Range (IQR)
Q_1	25th percentile of a distribution
Q_3	75th percentile of a distribution
r	Geographical region
R	Number of geographical regions
S	Supply table
t	Time period
T	Number of time periods
θ	Outlier thresholds
θ_{max}	Upper outlier threshold

θ_{min}	Lower outlier threshold
x	Sustainable development key figure
x^{CPA}	Sustainable development key figure in Classification of Products by Activity (CPA)
x^{NACE}	Sustainable development key figure in Statistical Classification of Economic Activities in the European Community (NACE)
x_{std}	Standardising sustainable development key figure
X	Number of sustainable development key figures
ξ	Effective direction of a sustainable development key indicator
ξ^+	Positive effective direction of a sustainable development key indicator
ξ^-	Negative effective direction of a sustainable development key indicator
y	Sustainable development key indicator
y_g	Sustainable development growth indicator
y_{gs}	Rescaled sustainable development growth indicator
y_{max}	Maximum of a sustainable development key indicator in the sample
y_{min}	Minimum of a sustainable development key indicator in the sample
y_o	Outlying sustainable development key indicator
y_r	Sustainable development ratio indicator
y_{rs}	Rescaled sustainable development ratio indicator
y_s	Rescaled sustainable development key indicator
y_z	Z-score scaled sustainable development key indicator
Y	Number of sustainable development key indicators
Y_g	Number of sustainable development growth indicators
Y_{gs}	Number of rescaled sustainable development growth indicators
Y_o	Number of outlying sustainable development key indicators
Y_r	Number of sustainable development ratio indicators
Y_{rs}	Number of rescaled sustainable development ratio indicators
Y_s	Number of rescaled sustainable development key indicators
Y_z	Number of z-score scaled sustainable development key indicators

Chapter 1

Introduction

"The world has enough for everyone's need, but not enough for everyone's greed."
Mohandas K. Gandhi

1.1 Background and motivation

The Atlantic hurricane season terminated for this term with category-5 hurricanes such as Dorian (National Weather Service, 2019). Because of climate change, intense and damaging hurricanes are three times more frequent nowadays than 100 years ago (Grinsted, Ditlevsen & Hesselbjerg, 2019; McGrath, 2019). Likewise, scientific evidence suggests that climate change made Europe's major heatwave in 2018 more than twice as likely to occur (Schiermeier, 2018; World Weather Attribution, 2018). Less dominant in public but at higher and more alarming risk than climate change is the genetic biodiversity of the biosphere (Steffen et al., 2015). Extinction rates may be 100 to 1,000 times higher than corresponding natural background rates (Ceballos et al., 2015; de Vos, Joppa, Gittleman, Stephens & Pimm, 2015). These examples demonstrate the abandonment of the Holocene and the entering of the Anthropocene, a new geological era that is characterised by threatening human activities towards fundamental Earth system dynamics (e.g. Griggs et al., 2013; Rockström et al., 2009b; Sachs, 2012). In addition to that, humanitarian crises persist. The number of people living in extreme poverty is declining, but projections estimate that 479 million people will remain in extreme poverty in 2030 (Roser & Ortiz-Ospina, 2019) – 479 million people too many.

Sustainable development and sustainability consist of three contentual domains: environmental protection, social development, and economic prosperity. Today's and tomorrow's human needs should be satisfied subject to respecting present and future environmental limits (Holden, Linnerud & Banister, 2017; WCED, 1987). Economic prosperity serves this purpose (UNCED, 1992). Traditionally, the satisfaction of needs is enabled by economic growth at the expense of the environment and social justice (A. B. Atkinson, 2015; Holden et al., 2017; Piketty, 2014). Decoupling the nexus of economic

© The Author(s) 2021
C. Lemke, *Accounting and Statistical Analyses for Sustainable Development*, Sustainable Management, Wertschöpfung und Effizienz, https://doi.org/10.1007/978-3-658-33246-4_1

growth and environmental degradation or social deprivation is a current challenge for decision makers (Holden, Linnerud & Banister, 2014). Human-nature interactions in a complex socio-ecological system (Clark, van Kerkhoft, Lebel & Gallopín, 2016; Hall, Feldpausch-Parker, Peterson, Stephens & Wilson, 2017; WCED, 1987) are studied in sustainability science, with the objective to develop a solution-oriented agenda (Kates, 2015) for sustainable development and sustainability. Generally, sustainable development and sustainability are characterised by complexity, which might be held liable for our unsustainable world. From an economic theory perspective, unsustainable outcomes are present due to market failures. Environmental and social externalities are not internalised (Patterson, McDonald & Hardy, 2017; Sala, Ciuffo & Nijkamp, 2015), and governmental regulation is demanded for correction. At the moment, sustainable development and sustainability are visions of future (White, 2013), and the goal is to turn the sustainable future into the present as soon as possible. Pursuing this goal is widely referred to be the major and the most difficult challenge of today's society (van Poeck, Læssøe & Block, 2017).

To take up the challenge of making our world environmentally and socially sustainable, measurement and assessment of sustainable development performances are inevitable. Only what is measured can be managed (e.g. Parris & Kates, 2003). Indicator sets are central for sustainable development measurement because they are able to capture complexity: Indicator sets can cover a wide range of aspects of the three contentual domains (Almássy & Pintér, 2018), multiple objects of investigations, large time series, and diverse geographical regions. Including an index or a composite measure in an indicator set yields further advantages. An index is a compressed description of a multidimensional state (Ebert & Welsch, 2004) and hence reduces complexity (Bell & Morse, 2018). The important focus in measurement is recaptured (Griggs et al., 2014), combating the disadvantage of a rich indicator set to potentially cause more confusion than understanding (Wu & Wu, 2012). Several scholars even argue that a sustainable development index is necessarily required because such complexity cannot be mapped by standalone indicators (Almássy & Pintér, 2018; Costanza, Fioramonti & Kubiszewski, 2016; Hanley, Moffatt, Faichney & Wilson, 1999; Nardo et al., 2008; Ramos & Moreno Pires, 2013). Moreover, sustainable development indices have the potential to replace the Gross Domestic Product (GDP) as a measure of societal wellbeing (Costanza, Fioramonti & Kubiszewski, 2016; Costanza et al., 2014). GDP has been heavily criticised for being an insufficient measure of wellbeing because it only quantifies the size of an economy in terms of final goods and services (Costanza et al., 2014; Giannetti, Agostinho, Villas Bôas de Almeida & Huisingh, 2015; van den Bergh, 2009). In contrast, sustainable development indices are metrics that fulfil the ambitions of measures of wellbeing as they comprehensively describe environmental, social, and economic aspects. A further major advantage of sustainable development indices is their capability to explore interactions of individual sustainable development elements

(Costanza, Fioramonti & Kubiszewski, 2016; T. Hahn & Figge, 2011). Knowledge
about these interactions are prerequisites for the effectiveness of coordinated actions
and thus for maximising progress on sustainable development (Costanza, Fioramonti
& Kubiszewski, 2016; ICSU & ISSC, 2015; Spaiser, Ranganathan, Swain & Sumpter,
2017; Weitz, Carlsen, Nilsson & Skånberg, 2018).

Several weaknesses and gaps are present in the field of sustainable development
indicators and indices, which motivate this research. First, conceptual frameworks of
sustainable development lack multiple perspectives (e.g. Baumgartner, 2014; Boron
& Murray, 2004; Chofreh & Goni, 2017; Griggs et al., 2014; Maletič, Maletič, Dahlgaard, Dahlgaard-Park & Gomišček, 2014), such that previous sustainable development
indicators and indices can only be applied to economic objects of the same aggregational size. However, a comparable multilevel assessment of economic objects of any
aggregational size is crucial because sustainable development is a society level concept
(T. Hahn, Pinkse, Preuss & Figge, 2015; Jennings & Zandbergen, 1995), and effects on
the planet (macro level) are the cumulative results of individuals (micro level) (Dahl,
2012). Sustainable development and sustainability can only be achieved if micro and
meso objects contribute (Griggs et al., 2014; Sachs, 2012). A positive side effect of
this mandatory requirement of multilevel comparability is the provision of objective
macro-economic benchmarks that prevent meso-economic objects such as corporations
from greenwashing their sustainable development performances. The micro-to-macro
connection is seen as the major challenge that scholars from business and economics
face (McGregor & Pouw, 2017). The management literature calls for a meso-to-macro
connection in order to stop missing the "big picture" (Whiteman, Walker & Perego,
2013). To the best of the author's knowledge, multilevel indicators and indices that address this perspective gap by being comparably applicable to micro (individuals), meso
(organisations such as corporations), and macro objects (conglomerates of organisations
such as industries or overall economies) are absent in the academic literature. This
work is motivated by this call and will make significant contributions to this challenge.
Second, sustainable development and sustainability is mostly integrated at operational
tiers while lacking strategic and normative tiers (Baumgartner & Rauter, 2017; Tseng,
Lim & Wu, 2018). This operational-to-normative gap is a further reason for deficiencies
in the progress towards sustainability. The conceptual part of this work will address
the operational-to-normative gap. Third, a knowledge gap on interactions of individual
sustainable development elements is present (see above), and generating insights about
synergies and trade-offs of individual sustainable development elements is a subject of
current research (e.g. Allen, Metternicht & Wiedmann, 2019; Nilsson, Griggs & Visback,
2016; Pradhan, Costa, Rybski, Lucht & Kropp, 2017; Spaiser et al., 2017; Weitz et al.,
2018). This work is motivated by the knowledge gap and will contribute new methodological and empirical understandings. Fourth, bottlenecks in the science-practice
linkage persist (Agyeman, 2005; Christie & Warburton, 2001; Hall et al., 2017; Sala,

Farioli & Zamagni, 2013), further harming the progress towards sustainability. The empirical part of this work will contribute to this knowledge-to-action or sustainability gap. Fifth and last, previous sustainable development indices such as the Dow Jones Sustainability Indices (DJSI) (e.g. RobecoSAM, 2018a), Composite Sustainable Development Index (ICSD) (Krajnc & Glavič, 2005), Sustainable Development Goal Index (SDGI) (e.g. Schmidt-Traub, Kroll, Teksoz, Durand-Delacre & Sachs, 2017a), or the Sustainable Society Index (SSI) (e.g. van de Kerk, Manuel & Kleinjans, 2014) feature methodological shortcomings, such that decisions based on these metrics may be misled (Böhringer & Jochem, 2007; Mayer, 2008). This study is motivated by making methodological contributions to the (sustainable development) index literature.

The following section, Section 1.2, explains how the present work will take up these challenges and fill the five identified research gaps, setting the research question and aim of this dissertation.

1.2 Research question and aim of the dissertation

Against this background, the present dissertation aspires to contribute to the science and practice community to accelerate progress in sustainable development. In doing so, it addresses the call that sustainable development demands performance measurement by an indicator set that includes a composite measure to replace GDP as a measure of wellbeing (see Section 1.1; e.g. Costanza, Fioramonti & Kubiszewski, 2016). It further acknowledges that multiple perspectives must be comparably captured (see Section 1.1; e.g. Dahl, 2012) in a methodologically sound manner to avoid misled decision making (see Section 1.1; e.g. Böhringer & Jochem, 2007). As multilevel sustainable development indices are not represented in the literature (see Section 1.1), the aim of the dissertation is to develop a sustainable development indicator set that includes a composite measure, with the following features: First, the indicator set should include environmental, social, and economic indicators as well as a composite measure; second, it should be applicable to multiple levels meaningfully; and third, it should be constructed in a methodologically sound manner. The newly derived index will be called the "Multilevel Sustainable Development Index (MLSDI)". Because of the multilevel applicability, the MLSDI will be able to support taking up the challenge of managing decoupling economic growth and environmental degradation or social deprivation (see Section 1.1; Holden et al., 2014) at corporate, industry, and national levels.

This work will draw on prior research and will contribute to existing studies. First, Rotmans, Kemp and van Asselt's (2001) multilevel perspective is incorporated in the conceptual framework to tackle the perspective gap. Sustainable development indicators and indices will be identified as the most suitable multilevel assessment method, and a multilevel indicator set will be contributed. Second, the conceptual framework is amplified by the St. Gallen management model (Ulrich, 2001) for decision making at operational, strategic, and normative tiers. Third, this work will address the knowledge gap and contribute insights about interconnections of individual sustainable development elements. These interconnections will be investigated by three different, sophisticated weighting methods from the fields of multivariate statistics and information theory. The three weighting methods will be compared against each other, and the methods' sensitivities will be analysed. This procedure enhances previous studies in several ways: Compared to indices that apply equal weighting (e.g. the SDGI; Schmidt-Traub et al., 2017a), interconnections are studied; by contrast with indices that rely on expert elicitation (e.g. the ICSD; Krajnc & Glavič, 2005), objectivity, which is a critical sustainable development assessment principle (Sala et al., 2015), is ensured; in comparison with indices that do not study sensitivities, transparency and robustness, which are further central assessment principles (e.g. Pintér, Hardi, Martinuzzi & Hall, 2018; Sala et al., 2015), are improved. Fourth, this work contributes to the sustainability gap by delivering a sustainable development index that can be re-built and re-used, given the full transparency in its methodology, data sources, and empirical findings. The present work will contribute 44 sustainable development indicators of the environmental, social, and the economic domains that originate in an alignment of the meso Global Reporting Initiative (GRI) and the macro Sustainable Development Goal (SDG) frameworks (GRI, 2016; UN, 2018), three subindices for each contentual domain and an overall index, the MLSDI. The sample consists of 62 industries and five aggregated branches (Eurostat, 2008b), including the cross-sectional health economy (Gerlach, Legler & Ostwald, 2018), in the German economy from 2008 to 2016. Thereby, this study contributes objective benchmarks that may prevent greenwashing (see Section 1.1). The application is expected to be more useful than previous indices because a wider, multilevel scope of decisions can be covered: management decisions, national industry policy, and international affairs. Fifth and last, this work will contribute profound methodological knowledge to the (sustainable development) index literature. Methodological shortcomings of existing sustainable development indices will be highlighted by a systematical evaluation based on sustainable development assessment principles. The MLSDI will overcome these deficits by profound methodological research. It will further contribute to the (sustainable development) index literature by making use of methods from further disciplines that are neither common in sustainability science nor in business statistics yet. Identified lacks of previous sustainable development indices will involve insufficient data cleaning, weighting of the indicators, and aggregation into the composite measures as well as a lack in sensitivity analyses. The MLSDI is further expected to be more accurate for decision making because of its overall methodological soundness.

The next section, Section 1.3, outlines the procedure of this dissertation.

1.3   Procedure

To investigate and tackle the research gaps as presented in Section 1.2, this work is structured as follows. The next chapter, Chapter 2, will derive a conceptual framework of sustainable development. Definitions of sustainable development and sustainability will be reviewed and adopted for this work. The conceptual framework will provide a guiding structure throughout the remainder of this dissertation. It will consist of six dimensions, thereof two major ones that require detailed examinations. First, the three contentual domains of sustainable development – environmental protection, social development, and economic prosperity – will be explored and integrated into the framework. The contentual domains will constitute the topics and aspects of sustainable development that are aimed to be mapped quantitatively. Second, the three major change agent groups of sustainable development – business, policy, and science – will be examined. The change agent group business will form the objects of investigation.

Chapter 3 will focus on measurement and assessment methods of sustainable development. Sustainable development measurement and assessment principles will be reviewed and harmonised in order to systematically evaluate diverse measurement methods and previous indices. An overview on sustainable development assessment methods will be given and the most suitable method for comprehensive multilevel sustainable development assessment will be determined. Previous meso and macro indices of sustainable development will be analysed.

In Chapter 4, profound methodological research on sustainable development index construction will be accomplished. First, an overview on the calculation steps will be given, and the assessment principles and further criteria will be allocated to the calculation steps they are relevant to. A systematic assessment of the reviewed indices' methodological approaches by means of the assessment principles and further criteria will follow. Last, the methodology for the new sustainable development index – the MLSDI – will be researched and explained.

In Chapter 5, the MLSDI will be applied to a sample of 62 industries as well as five aggregated branches, including the cross-sectional health economy, in the German economy from 2008 to 2016. The empirical findings will be described and analysed. This chapter will be structured according to the calculation steps of a sustainable development index.

The dissertation will terminate with a discussion of the research results and an overall summary and conclusion (see Chapter 6).

Chapter 2

Conceptual framework of sustainable development

In this chapter, a conceptual framework of sustainable development is elaborated by an extensive literature research. Along with this, the first four research gaps are uncovered. Jabareen (2009) defines a *"conceptual framework* as a network [...] of interlinked concepts that together provide a comprehensive understanding of a phenomenon or phenomena". Therefore, a conceptual framework is a result of a theorisation, and it is required to understand soft facts and enable interpretations (Jabareen, 2009). Furthermore, it helps to navigate complexity (Pope, Bond, Hugé & Morrison-Saunders, 2017) and thereby supports decision makers during the implementation phase of sustainable development (Chofreh & Goni, 2017).

Among existing sustainable development frameworks (e.g. Baumgartner, 2014; Boron & Murray, 2004; Chofreh & Goni, 2017; Griggs et al., 2014; Maletič et al., 2014), comprehensive approaches are rare, and there is a lack of conflation of various aspects. Hence, a synthesis and integration of multiple sustainable development dimensions is accomplished in this chapter. Established fragments are adopted, and novel elements are added.

Constructing the conceptual framework, this chapter is structured as follows. Section 2.1 discusses distinct definitions of sustainable development and sustainability and adopts one for the remainder of this work. The underlying concepts of the three contentual domains of sustainable development – environmental protection (see Section 2.2.1), social development (see Section 2.2.2), and economic prosperity (see Section 2.2.3) – as well as their linkages (see Section 2.2.4) are presented in Section 2.2. Stakeholders and change agents of sustainable development are introduced in Section 2.3. Multilevel perspectives are present (see Section 2.3.1), and the change agent groups business, policy, and science are debated in Section 2.3.2 to Section 2.3.4. The chapter ends with a summary (see Section 2.4).

© The Author(s) 2021
C. Lemke, *Accounting and Statistical Analyses for Sustainable Development*, Sustainable Management, Wertschöpfung und Effizienz, https://doi.org/10.1007/978-3-658-33246-4_2

2.1   Definition of sustainable development and sustainability

The modern debate on sustainable development is led by the United Nations (UN), who has held world summits for more than 40 years and released the most elaborated concept of sustainable development (Lock & Seele, 2017). The start of their global agenda for a change was the United Nations Conference on the Human Environment (UNCHE), which took place in Stockholm in 1972. In this conference, the foundation of the concept of sustainable development was clarified as the alignment of human development and the planet's environmental limits (Kates, 2015; UNCHE, 1972). 26 principles on the capacity of the Earth, social as well as economic development for a favourable living, and an action plan with 69 recommendations were worked out (UNCHE, 1972). Further elaborating on the concept of sustainable development, the World Commission on Environment and Development (WCED), also known as the Brundtland Commission, defined *sustainable development* as a development "that meets the needs of the present without compromising the ability of future generations to meet their needs" (WCED, 1987). To this day, the definition is contemporary and even referred to as an "ethical standard" (Baumgartner, 2014). Centrepiece of this definition is the intergenerational justice (Jerneck et al., 2011) of today's and tomorrow's generation regarding two concepts: needs and limits (WCED, 1987). Intergenerational justice spans the first *dimension* of the sustainable development space: the *temporal horizon*. The second dimension of sustainable development deals with intragenerational justice of the two concepts. The United Nations Conference on Environment and Development (UNCED) subdivided this second dimension into three *contentual domains*: environmental protection (given the concept of limits), social development (given the concept of needs), and economic prosperity (UNCED, 1992).[1] These first two dimensions are visualised in Figure 2.1. In spite of the splitting into the three contentual domains, each of them is not a separate crisis, but they are interdependent and mutually reinforcing, requiring a simultaneous and integrated consideration (see Section 2.2.4; WSSD, 2002). Furthermore, sustainable development is a collective responsibility at local, national, regional,[2] and global levels (WSSD, 2002). This notion constitutes the third sustainable development dimension, the *geographical region*, depicted in Figure 2.2.

Despite the fact that the UN's approach to sustainable development and sustainab-

---

[1]Some authors, e.g. Jesinghaus (2018), interpret the Agenda 21 to subdivide sustainable development into four domains: environment, society, economy, and institutions (UNCED, 1992). As institutions deal with the three contentual domains, a separation at the same level is not systematic, and is thus not adopted in this work. Confirming this view, the SDG 17, "Partnerships for the goals", does not clearly span its own, institutional domain (see Figure 2.12b).

[2]The term "regional" may also refer to an area smaller than the national level (e.g. Ramos & Caeiro, 2010). However, the WSSD's (2002) classification is adopted in this work.

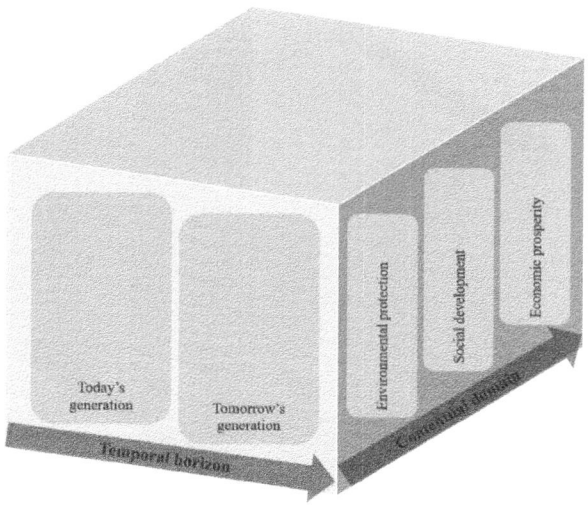

Figure 2.1 The first two dimensions of the sustainable development space (based on Witjes et al., 2017; with friendly permission of © 2017 The Authors)

ility now represents a global consensus (Costanza, Fioramonti & Kubiszewski, 2016; Vermeulen, 2018), both terms are controversially discussed in the academic literature. On the one hand, scholars such as T. Hahn et al. (2015); Lozano (2008); Sala et al. (2013); Shaker (2015); and Reid (1997) are in line with the UN's approach, interpreting sustainable development not as a steady state but as a journey or a process of change, adaption, and learning. Contrasting, *sustainability* is the ideal, dynamic state to achieve. In this case, the pathway of sustainable development ought to be pursued in order to obtain the long-term goal of sustainability (Dragicevic, 2018). On the other hand, authors such as Clark et al. (2016); Holden et al. (2014); and Waas et al. (2014) use both terms interchangeably. Further scholars such as P. James, Magee, Scerri and Steger (2015) argue vice versa: Sustainability is the capacity to persist over time, and therefore, it is a process to achieve the goal sustainable development (Dragicevic, 2018). An overview of different approaches to sustainable development can be found in, e.g. Hopwood, Mellor and O'Brien (2005). Arising from the numerous existing definitions, other works intend to capture the terminology by generating a tag cloud of commonly-used elements in peer-review-published definitions (White, 2013). This approach might be questionable because, for example, in highly subjective areas such as the social domain of sustainable development (see Section 2.2.2), a larger group than the science community should be consulted. However, for merely identifying the main research domains, this reflective method might be legitimate (Kajikawa, Ohno, Takeda, Matsushima & Komiyama, 2007).

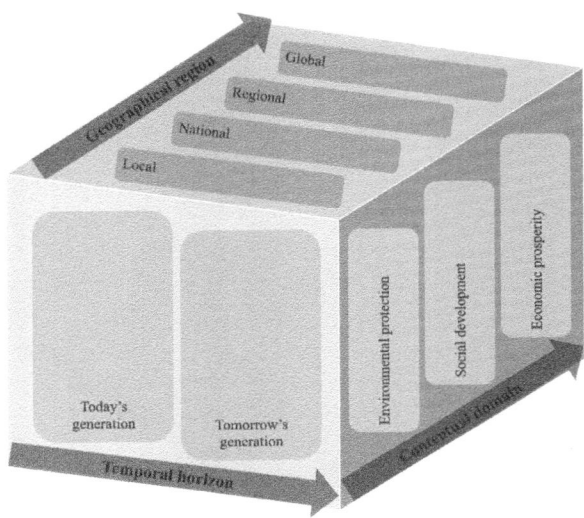

Figure 2.2 The first three dimensions of the sustainable development space (based on Witjes et al., 2017; with friendly permission of © 2017 The Authors)

The UN's approach to sustainable development is adopted for this work because it is most profound and comprehensive (Biermann, Kanie & Kim, 2017; Lock & Seele, 2017) and agreed on by world leaders, awarding it with a high degree of accordance. Sustainable development is interpreted as a process that requires change and transformation (Lock & Seele, 2017; Sala et al., 2013) to a desired development path (T. Hahn et al., 2015) in order to reach the ideal, dynamic state of sustainability (Lozano, 2008; Reid, 1997), which is a long-term goal (Shaker, 2015). If sustainable development and sustainability can be both referred to simultaneously, for brevity, the term sustainable development is preferred in the remainder of this work because sustainability has not yet been reached.

Dealing with sustainable development consists of two modes: first, a descriptive-analytical mode that aims to understand the human-nature interaction in a complex socio-ecological system; and second, a transformational mode that addresses the societal transition required to achieve sustainability (Clark et al., 2016; Hall et al., 2017; McGreavy & Kates, 2012; Schaltegger, Beckmann & Hansen, 2013; Spangenberg, 2011; Wiek, Ness, Schweizer-Ries, Brand & Farioli, 2012). The next section, Section 2.2, sheds light on the first mode and investigates the contentual domains of sustainable development, whereas the other two, already spanned dimensions (temporal horizon and geographical region) do not require further theoretical analysis due to their straight-forwardness; they are directly incorporated in the methodological and empirical part (see Chapter 4 et seq.). Subsequently, Section 2.3 addresses the second mode, the stakeholders and change agents of the transition process, expanding the three-dimensional to a six-dimensional sustainable development space. The six-dimensional space is the final conceptual framework of sustainable development, required to adequately measure and assess sustainable development. In turn, the adequate assessment is the prerequisite for sustainable development management and its transition (see Chapter 3; e.g. Parris & Kates, 2003).

2.2 The three contentual domains of sustainable development

The UNCED (1992) classified sustainable development into three contentual domains: environmental protection, social development and economic prosperity (see Section 2.1). The following sections, Section 2.2.1 to Section 2.2.3, review and analyse the academic literature of these domains. Other segmentations such as the natural capital approach by Costanza and Daly (1992), the five capital approach by Porritt (2007), or the place-permanence-persons approach by Seghezzo (2009) are not further considered because these attempts "explain the composition of the cake by cutting it into thinner [or different] slices" (Hacking & Guthrie, 2008). The last section, Section 2.2.4 integrates the three domains to a unified dimension of sustainable development.

2.2.1 Environmental protection

In the academic literature of sustainable development, the use of the terms environment and ecology is not precise (e.g. Costanza, Fioramonti and Kubiszewski, 2016; Kates, 2015; and T. Hahn et al., 2015 vs. Hall et al., 2017; and Holden et al., 2014). *Ecology* is defined as "the branch of biology that deals with the relations of organisms to one another and to their physical surroundings" (Oxford Dictionaries, 2018a). In contrast, the *environment* is defined as (1) "the surrounding or conditions in which a person, animal, or planet lives or operates", or as (2) "the natural world, as a whole or in a particular geographical area, especially being affected by human activity" (Oxford Dictionaries, 2018b). Ecology refers to the relationship between an organism and its natural environment, whereas the environment as of definition (1) is something an organism possesses (Mebratu, 1998). In the context of sustainable development, the term ecology is too narrow because only the human-nature interaction would be regarded. The first definition of the term environment is too wide since it would include, in addition to the natural environment, the economic, political, and cultural environment (Mebratu, 1998). These aspects are already assigned to the other two domains – social development (see Section 2.2.2) and economic prosperity (see Section 2.2.3). Finally, the second definition of the environment suits the sustainable development context: The natural environment itself and the human-nature interaction are referred to simultaneously. It follows that, in this work, *environmental protection* is defined as the path to *environmental sustainability*, a state in which the natural world is not harmed nor degraded by human activity, such that needs of today's generation are met without compromising needs of tomorrow's generation.

For highly anthropocentric reasons, the natural world is pointed at: The environmental system of the Earth is intended to remain stable because it provides life-supporting services to humans and is thus a prerequisite for thriving societies (Griggs et al., 2013; Kates, 2015; Steffen et al., 2015). Scientific insights deduced by the natural science community are in the centre of the environmental domain. The main focus is on limits or threshold values as well as interdependences of ecological and Earth system processes (Holden et al., 2017; Patterson et al., 2017; Sala et al., 2015). Especially the research group around Rockström spreads new knowledge in this field. Their concept of planetary boundaries (Rockström et al., 2009a, 2009b; Steffen et al., 2015) perfectly reflects the UN's concept of limits (see Section 2.1). *Planetary boundaries* are threshold values of life-supporting Earth system processes above which an unacceptable global environmental change might not be possible to be avoided. This zone is the *zone of high risk*. The threshold itself lies in the *zone of uncertainty* that features an increasing risk. Below the boundary, the *zone of safe operating space for humanity* is located. *Core boundaries* are boundaries "each of which has the potential on its own to drive the Earth system into a new state should they be substantially and persistently transgressed" (Steffen et al., 2015). Nine planetary boundaries, thereof two core boundaries (climate change and biosphere integrity), are identified. Figure 2.3 displays the nine planetary boundaries and their current statuses of exploitation.[3] The planetary boundaries stratospheric ozone depletion, ocean acidification, and freshwater use are currently operating in the safe zone. Climate change and land system change are in the zone of uncertainty, while the boundaries biochemical flows and the biosphere integrity's subboundary genetic diversity are in the zone of high risk. For novel entities, atmospheric aerosol loading, and the subboundary functional diversity, thresholds could not be quantified yet.

Despite the derivation from natural science, the concept of planetary boundaries draws on both objective and subjective matters. Measuring thresholds is objective, but assessing and setting the level of the boundaries is highly subjective because it implies defining the acceptable risk. Therefore, boundary setting is eventually a social decision (Griggs et al., 2014; Leach, Raworth & Rockström, 2013) that requires political decision making (see Section 2.3.3).

---

[3]Detailed descriptions of the planetary boundaries, their functioning, and role in the Earth system are not further outlined but can be found in Rockström et al. (2009b).

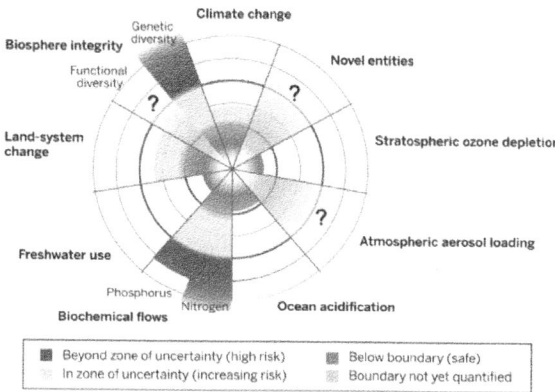

Figure 2.3 Nine planetary boundaries and current statuses of exploitation (from Steffen et al., 2015; with permission of © 2015, American Association for the Advancement of Science)

2.2.2 Social development

Of the three contentual domains, the social domain of sustainable development is least developed (Missimer, Robèrt & Broman, 2017a, 2017b). The concept remains open and contested (Boström, 2012), different meanings circulate, and there are difficulties in identifying purely social issues (Murphy, 2012). The literature is fragmented and limited (Ajmal, Khan, Hussain & Helo, 2018; Dempsey, Bramley, Power & Brown, 2011), such that a further development of this domain is required (see Section 6.3).

Murphy (2012) identifies four dimensions in the social domain of sustainable development: equity, awareness, participation, and social cohesion. Cuthill (2010) also points out four key concepts, though, slightly different: social capital, social infrastructure, social justice and equity, and engaged governance. Overviews and more detailed concepts of the social domain can be found in, e.g. Ajmal et al. (2018); Boström (2012); Missimer et al. (2017a); Missimer et al. (2017b); and Murphy (2012). Core concepts include, among others, quality of life, wellbeing, subjective welfare, happiness, life satisfaction, social inclusion, dignity, affection, freedom, and safety (Harangozo, Csutora & Kocsis, 2018; Vavik & Keitsch, 2010). These involve material as well as non-material aspects and their achievement is highly subjective and individually determined (McGregor & Pouw, 2017). Especially the former concepts rather refer to the developed world, where basic needs have been successfully addressed and higher order needs are focused (Vallance, Perkins & Dixon, 2011).[4] Vallance et al. (2011) subdivide the social domain into three categories: development sustainability, bridge sustainability, and

---

[4]Vallance et al. (2011) neither specify basic nor higher order needs. The concept of needs adopted in this work follows shortly.

maintenance sustainability. *Development sustainability* addresses basic needs, justice, and equity, whereas *bridge sustainability* covers the changes in behaviour to achieve environmental sustainability. *Maintenance sustainability* aims to preserve socio-cultural patterns. In this work, the social domain is understood as development sustainability. Bridge sustainability and the notion of changes in behaviour is the underlying process of sustainable development in general, not only a means of obtaining environmental sustainability. Furthermore, social conditions correlate with environmental protection, but this linkage is not the focal point of the social domain. Maintenance sustainability is disregarded as the preservation of socio-cultural patterns is not necessarily desired. Thus, maintenance is not an overriding principle, but it is actively and explicitly governed. Further authors agree on the notion of development sustainability by Vallance et al. (2011): In view of Ajmal et al. (2018); Holden et al. (2017); Stumpf, Baumgärtner, Becker and Sievers-Glotzbach (2015); and Stumpf, Becker and Baumgärtner (2016), social development is characterised by moral principles and philosophy on needs, equity, and justice. *Needs* are in-born requirements of humans to be physically, emotionally, and mentally healthy (Missimer et al., 2017a). *Equity* regards "situations in which the claimant is equally off" (Young, 1995), whereas *justice* is concerned with the "fair balance of mutual claims and obligations within a community" (Stumpf et al., 2015). *Equality* also appears frequently in the context of social development and deals with equal considerations as a claim holder or equal shares in distribution (Stumpf et al., 2015). Because equity and equality are principles of justice (Stumpf et al., 2015; Stumpf et al., 2016; Young, 1995), they become obsolete in working out the overarching concepts of the social domain. The guiding principle is justice on its own, supporting the concept of needs. Satisfaction of needs must be fairly balanced across regions (intragenerational justice) and time (intergenerational justice) (Dower, 2004; Stumpf et al., 2015). A definition of social development might therefore read: *Social development* is the path to *social sustainability*, a state in which human needs of today's generation are satisfied in a just manner without compromising the human needs of tomorrow's generation.

Because the core of the social domain are human needs (see Section 2.1), concepts of human needs ought to be adduced in theorising this domain. The most well-known concept of human needs is the hierarchy of needs by Maslow (1943).[5] He points out that humans are motivated by in-born needs that are ordered hierarchically and can be visualised in a pyramid (see Figure 2.4). At the bottom of the pyramid are needs that humans first seek to satisfy. After their satisfaction, needs from a higher layer are desired to be met, until the top of the pyramid is reached. Physiological needs at the bottom consist of homeostasis and appetite needs. Safety needs include, among others, the need for security, protection, freedom of fear and chaos, as well as structure and law. Belongingness and love needs are the third step on the hierarchy of needs

---

[5]Other works on human needs include, e.g. Max-Neef, Elizalde and Hopenhayn (1991), but are not further examined.

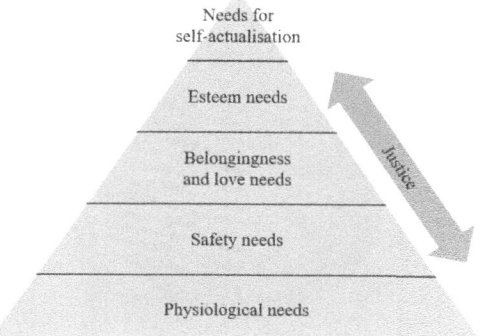

Figure 2.4 Maslow's hierarchy of needs and the principle of justice (Maslow, 1943, 1987)

and refer to relations with other people to get and receive affection. Esteem needs can be categorised into two parts: first, self-esteem such as the desire for strength, achievement, competence, and confidence; and second, esteem of others such as desire for reputation, fame, recognition, attention, and dignity. The last stage consists of needs for self-actualisation, which Maslow (1987) described as the "desire to become [...] what one idiosyncratically is". In other words, humans desire self-fulfilment and seek to become actualised in what they potentially are (Maslow, 1943, 1987).[6] The principle of justice is applicable to every hierarchy level: justice among physiological needs at the bottom and justice among needs to self-actualisation at the top.

The concept of social boundaries is designed in analogy to the concept of planetary boundaries. *Social boundaries* represent thresholds above which basic conditions are met and below which critical human deprivations occur (Raworth, 2012, 2017). These boundaries count water, food, health, education, income and work, peace and justice, political voice, social equity, gender equality, housing, networks, and energy (see Figure 2.5). Water, for example, is measured as the "population without access to improved drinking water [and sanitation]", or food quantifies the "population undernourished" (Raworth, 2017). The setting of the threshold values and current statuses of achievement as of Raworth (2017) are also displayed in Figure 2.5.[7] Although referencing to the UN's approach, in particular the SDGs (see Section 2.3.3), Raworth's social boundaries are mainly applicable to the developing world, which is not in line with the UN suggesting a universally applicable approach. A merger of Maslow's hierarchy of needs, which includes needs of the developed and the developing world, with Raworth's concept of social boundaries yields a valuable conceptual framework of the social domain of sustainable development. In this connection, Maslow's hierarchy is dissolved to a

---

[6]Maslow (1972) added self-transcendence at the top of the pyramid. However, since he did not include it in his work in 1987, it is also disregarded in this work.

[7]Worldwide data set; in the majority of cases one year of calculation between 2008 and 2015.

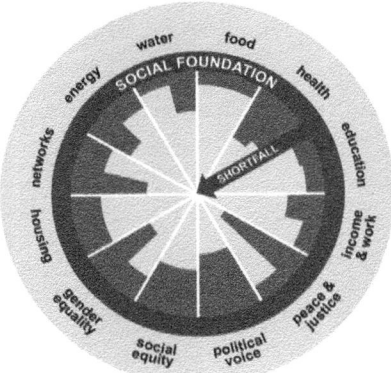

Figure 2.5 12 social boundaries and current statuses of achievement (from Raworth, 2017;
with friendly permission of © The Author)

circle of boundaries. The dissolution is legitimate because the hierarchy might not be
significant, but needs might be independent of each other (Tay & Diener, 2011). An
illustrative example is an artist not having satisfied all material needs but being rich in
terms of self-actualisation.

2.2.3   Economic prosperity

Economic growth or profits are often incorporated in the economic domain. However,
neither economic growth nor profits are key to sustainable development, nor are they
required for a broader conception of it (Jackson, 2009; McGregor & Pouw, 2017;
Vermeulen, 2018). Even happiness does not necessarily require economic growth.
Empirical evidence suggests diminishing marginal happiness in the course of a rising
GDP per capita (p.c.) (Jackson, 2009). The misconception of economic growth or profits
being key to sustainable development can be traced back to Elkington (1997) and the
triple bottom line of *people, planet, profit* (Vermeulen, 2018).[8] This misconception is
carried forward, and only 8% of reviewed corporate sustainable development literature
negatively invoke the term triple bottom line (Isil & Hernke, 2017). Economic prosperity
is the third contentual domain of sustainable development, and economic growth is only
needed in places where human needs are not met in order to bring people out of poverty
(Holden et al., 2014, 2017; McGregor & Pouw, 2017; WCED, 1987). In other words,
the production of resources is only required to maintain a reasonable standard of living
(Bansal, 2002). *Prosperity* is defined as the state of being successful in material and
financial terms (Oxford Dictionaries, 2018c, 2018d). In contrast, Jackson (2009) does

---

[8]Elkington (2018) himself requested to revise his framework of the triple bottom line. It was not
designed to be an accounting tool that balances financial, environmental, and social aspects, but it
intended to induce reflections about capitalism and its future.

Literature stream	Assumption, description	Example references
Degrowth economy, negative growth economy	The throughput of an economy can be reduced by political and social transitions while increasing quality of life and wellbeing.	Buch-Hansen, 2018; Harangozo et al., 2018; Kallis et al., 2018; Latouche, 2009; Magee and Devezas, 2017; Schneider, Martinez-Alier and Kallis, 2011
Zero growth economy, steady state economy	The throughput of an economy, capital stocks, and population remain constant at a desired maintenance rate to stay within the planetary [and social] boundaries. Economic growth is not required for increasing wellbeing.	H. E. Daly, 1977, 1991, 1996; Harangozo et al., 2018; Kallis et al., 2018; Kerschner, 2010
A-growth economy	Environmental effectiveness is the central point and an a-growth economy is indifferent about economic growth.	van den Bergh, 2011
Positive growth economy, green growth economy	Economic growth can be decoupled from environmental usage and is based on efficiency as well as environmental-friendly technologies.	Harangozo et al., 2018; Schneider et al., 2011; UNEP, 2011
Green economy	Economic growth is not explicitly addressed, but the improvement of human wellbeing and social equity is focused as well as the reduction of environmental risks and ecological scarcities.	Harangozo et al., 2018; UNEP, 2010, 2011

Table 2.1 Overview of (post-)growth literature streams

not define prosperity based on only material success, but prosperity further includes social and psychological aspects. However, as these aspects are already subsumed in the social domain (see Section 2.2.2), economic prosperity in this work follows the Oxford Dictionaries' definition: *Economic prosperity* is the path to *economic sustainability*, a state in which material and financial success is achieved, such that today's environmental limits and social (or human) needs are met without compromising future generations' limits and needs.

The effect of economic growth on sustainable development is ambiguous. On the one hand, economic growth might contribute to sustainable development because first, it might induce technological advancement required to mitigate environmental degradation (Holden et al., 2017; Stern, 2015; van den Bergh, 2011), and second, it might lift people out of poverty, improve social welfare, and satisfy human needs. On the other hand, economic growth might harm sustainable development as it typically entails environmental damages and might reduce social equality (A. B. Atkinson, 2015; Holden et al., 2017; Piketty, 2014) and justice. Because of this ambiguity, various streams of (post-)growth literature have emerged. These are presented in Table 2.1. Degrowth, negative growth, zero growth, steady state, positive growth, and green growth economies are disregarded by definition since the concept of sustainable development purports that economic growth is merely a means to an end. In contrast, an a-growth economy and a green economy comply with this notion: Economic growth is not a driving force, but human needs and environmental limits are centred.

Economic growth can be understood in terms of GDP, employment, consumption, production and further measures (EC, IMF, OECD, UN & World Bank, 2009). The most widely used economic performance measurement is the *GDP*, which is defined as the "monetary market value of all final goods and services produced in a country" (Giannetti et al., 2015; van den Bergh, 2009). GDP receives severe criticism for its construction and its use, while its founder, Kuznets (1934a, 1934b), was well aware of its shortcomings – or rather its pointedness. For instance, he was aware of the fact that GDP cannot measure economic welfare because the distribution of income and means of earning the income remain unknown. He even warned not to equalise GDP growth and economic or social wellbeing (Costanza, Hart, Kubiszewski, Posner & Talberth, 2018; Costanza et al., 2014; Kuznets, 1934a, 1934b). Moreover, GDP does not differentiate between desirable and undesirable activities but positively accounts all expenditures. For example, undesired clean-up costs of an oil spill lead to an increase in GDP (Cobb, Halstead & Rowe, 1995; Giannetti et al., 2015; Kubiszewski et al., 2013). GDP gives an incomplete picture by only including priced goods. Social costs such as environmental damages are known as *negative externalities* and remain unpriced with the result that GDP encourages the depletion of natural resources faster than their renewal rate (Costanza et al., 2018; Costanza et al., 2014; Giannetti et al., 2015; van den Bergh, 2009). Further limitations and examples can be found in, e.g. Cobb et al. (1995); Costanza et al. (2014); Giannetti et al. (2015); Kubiszewski et al. (2013); Stiglitz, Sen and Fitoussi (2009); and van den Bergh (2009). Even the argument that GDP positively correlates with wellbeing indicators such as life expectancy or literacy rate is not enough for GDP being utilised as a measure of wellbeing because a correlation does not attest causality (van den Bergh, 2009). However, GDP is not a wrong measure, but it is wrongly used (Giannetti et al., 2015; Stiglitz et al., 2009). Instead of attempting to measure welfare or progress, ending up with wrong conclusions, GDP's original purpose should be stuck to: GDP quantifies the size of an economy in monetary terms of final goods and services.

2.2.4   Integration of the three contentual domains

In the previous sections, Section 2.2.1 to Section 2.2.3, it has come to light that a strict separation of the three domains is not feasible, but the three domains are deeply interlinked (WSSD, 2002). To investigate the demanded synchronisation and coordination of the three subsystems nature, society, and economy (Bossel, 1998; Spangenberg, 2011), cross-disciplines such as *environmental sociology, economic sociology*

(Boström, 2012), or *ecological economics* (e.g. Costanza & Daly, 1992) have emerged. The interlacing is driven by the socio-economic subsystem's embeddedness in and dependence on the global biophysical system (Griggs et al., 2014; Patterson et al., 2017; Sala et al., 2015). Changes in environmental circumstances (environmental domain) have resulted in economic gains (economic domain) but not for all people (social domain) (Kates, 2015; Turner II et al., 1990). The principles of limits and needs are combined, and clear cuts between the domains are challenging. Environmental pollution that pushes people back below the social foundation (Raworth, 2012) might be interpreted as an environmental-economic or environmental-social issue. Also, environmental pollution that arises from higher living standards (typically leading to pollution at global level) or environmental pollution that originates in poverty (mostly resulting in pollution at local level (WCED, 1987)) may be classified as environmental-economic or environmental-social problems. This example further evokes thoughts about environmental justice, and it illustrates the ambiguous correlation of income and environmental degradation: Higher living standards but also poverty can lead to environmental degradation. However, it is certain that people only take up with environmental protection if their basic needs are met (Bansal, 2002; Vallance et al., 2011). Similarly, corporations are more likely to engage with sustainable development if they feature a strong financial performance (Campbell, 2007). A more clear-cut example of the linkage of the environmental and the social domains is the discussion whether an environmental tax should be a fixed or progressive tax. Furthermore, the social and economic domains are closely intertwined as income and prosperity brings people out of poverty, ensuring a minimum wellbeing and typically enhancing social cohesiveness (Dragicevic, 2018). Here, ambiguities are also present because economic prosperity at a macro level might reduce social equality, a setback in social development (A. B. Atkinson, 2015; Holden et al., 2017; Piketty, 2014). The relationship of the three domains are illustrated in Figure 2.6. The arrows symbolise the direction of the relationship. Environmental protection and social development are both focal points and mutually dependent, whereas economic prosperity only serves the other two domains and should be adjusted according to their requirements.

On the conceptual side of integrating the three domains, the concepts of planetary and social boundaries are combined, obeying the UN's core concepts limits and needs. The result is the so-called *safe and just space for humanity* or *doughnut for the Anthropocene* (see Figure 2.7a; Raworth, 2012, 2017). The outer boundary represents the environmental ceiling and should not be exceeded. The inner boundary expresses the social foundation and should not be deceeded. Critical natural thresholds are located above the outer boundary, and critical deprivations of human needs occur below the inner boundary. As a result, the safe and just space for humanity is located below the planetary and above the social boundaries, respectively (O'Neill, Fanning, Lamb & Steinberger, 2018; Raworth, 2012, 2017). The current status of the safe and just operating space is

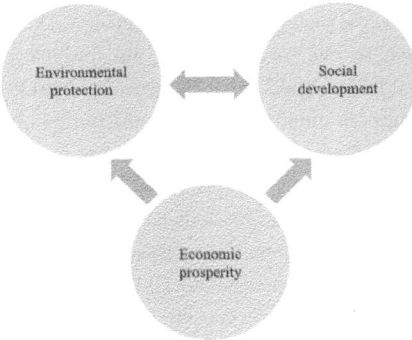

Figure 2.6 Relationship of the three contentual domains

displayed in Figure 2.7b.[9]

Within the safe and just space, a range of possible pathways that could yield sustainability can be mapped. The preferred trail is highly subjective because it is a function of, among others, cultures, visions, values, costs, risks, and distribution of power (Leach et al., 2013). The existence of a range of possible pathways makes sustainable development a deeply political topic. The role of policy and their current goal setting will be further discussed in Section 2.3.3. Moreover, the range of possible pathways implies that weak sustainability can be applied. The notion of *weak sustainability* originates from capital theory and assumes substitutability of the different types of capital. Natural and manufactured capital can be reduced individually as long as the overall level of capital passed to future generations remains constant or grows (Cabeza Gutés, 1996; Figge & Hahn, 2004; Neumayer, 2010; Pearce & Atkinson, 1993; Pope et al., 2017; Sala et al., 2013). This type of sustainability is often represented in a Venn diagram (see Figure 2.8a), the most common graphical representation of sustainability (Dragicevic, 2018; Lozano, 2008; Mebratu, 1998). On the contrary, *strong sustainability* assumes that the different types of capital are complements and need to be preserved for future generations (Costanza & Daly, 1992; H. E. Daly, 1990; Dragicevic, 2018; Figge & Hahn, 2004; Neumayer, 2010; Sala et al., 2013). Therefore, the capital with the shortest supply is a limiting factor (H. E. Daly, 1990; Dragicevic, 2018). The graphical representation of strong sustainability is often a concentric diagram (see Figure 2.8b; Dragicevic, 2018; Griggs et al., 2013; Lozano, 2008; Mebratu, 1998), with the environmental domain on the outside and the economic domain on the inside because the socio-economic subsystem is embedded in the global biophysical system (see above; Patterson et al., 2017; Sala et al., 2015).[10] Strong sustainability is in line with most

---

[9]Denotations and statuses of the boundaries slightly differ from Steffen et al. (2015; see Figure 2.3).

[10]Lozano (2008) suggests further graphical representations grounded in a critical review of the existing visualisations. Major criticism includes compartmentalisation of the linked domains and the missing representation of dynamics.

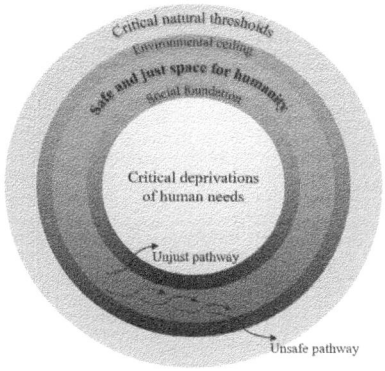

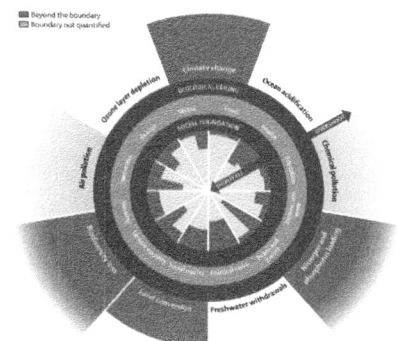

(a) The concept of the safe and just operating space for humanity

(b) Current statuses of the nine planetary and 12 social boundaries

Figure 2.7 The safe and just operating space for humanity (based on/from Leach et al., 2013; Raworth, 2012, 2017; with friendly permissions of © ISSC, UNESCO 2013; © Oxfam International February 2012; © 2017 The Author)

ecological economists (e.g. Costanza & Daly, 1992; H. E. Daly, 2005; Holden et al., 2014; Isil & Hernke, 2017). The reasons behind are twofold. First, the anthropocentric, natural science perspective recognises that human outcomes depend on the functioning of the Earth system (O'Neill et al., 2018) and acknowledges that the limiting factor has become exactly this system (Costanza & Daly, 1992; H. E. Daly, 2005). Second, from an economic perspective, strong sustainability is required as natural and manufactured capital are often complements by their nature (Costanza & Daly, 1992). Synthesising Leach et al.'s (2013) and the ecological economists' viewpoints, weak sustainability, which is allowed within the safe and just operating space for humanity, should be accompanied by minimised substitutability to respond to both factor limitations and complementarity. However, outside the safe and just space, strong sustainability must be applied because factors of the environmental or the social domain are exhausted and thus become limiting factors. The environmental and the social boundaries must be known to determine whether weak or strong sustainability should be in use.

After dealing with the descriptive-analytical mode of sustainable development by analysing the three contentual domains and their linkages, the next section, Section 2.3, examines stakeholders and change agents of sustainable development. These are prerequisites for the second, transformational mode of sustainable development that aims to put the normative concept of sustainable development into practice (see Section 2.1; Wiek et al., 2012).

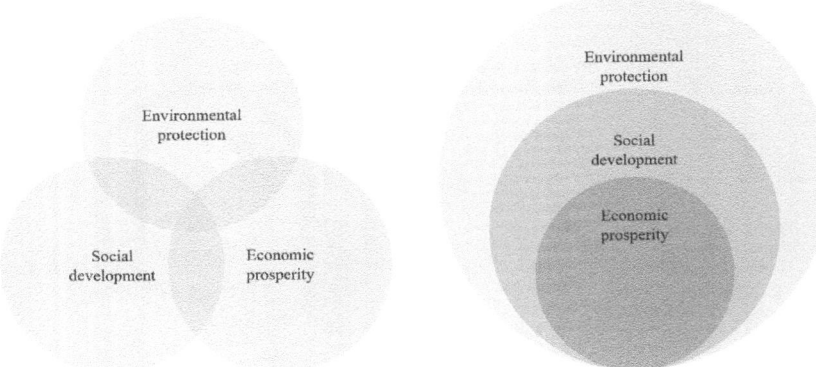

(a) Venn diagram of the contentual domains, visualising weak sustainability

(b) Concentric diagram of the contentual domains, visualising strong sustainability

Figure 2.8 Venn and concentric diagrams of weak and strong sustainability (based on Dragicevic, 2018; Griggs et al., 2013; Lozano, 2008; Mebratu, 1998; with friendly permissions of © 2018 John Wiley & Sons, Ltd and ERP Environment; © 2013 Macmillan Publishers Limited. All rights reserved; © 2008 Elsevier Ltd. All rights reserved; © 1998 Elsevier Science Inc. All rights reserved)

2.3 Stakeholders and change agents of sustainable development

At the start of the UN's debate on sustainable development in the 1970s, the UNCHE (1972) recognised that citizens, communities, enterprises, and institutions at any level should share equitable efforts in the sustainability transition. Groups or individuals that can affect or be affected by actions are *stakeholders* (Freeman, 1984, 2010; Hörisch, Freeman & Schaltegger, 2014). *Change agents* are defined as "internal or external actors that play a significant role in initiating, managing, or implementing change" (Caldwell, 2003; van Poeck et al., 2017). Because sustainable development requires change and transformation (see Section 2.1; e.g. Lock & Seele, 2017), it is desired that all stakeholders become change agents who devote actions, behaviour, decision making, and solutions (Hall et al., 2017) towards sustainable development. Thus, the *change agent group* builds the fourth dimension of the sustainable development framework and can be arranged into four clusters: *business, policy, society* (Hajer et al., 2015), and *science* (Lock & Seele, 2017).[11] Each group acts on every sustainable development dimension. To facilitate the visualisation of the sustainable development space, the

---

[11]Lock and Seele (2017) divide change agents into several categories: companies, governments, Intergovernmental Organisations (IGOs), private citizens, non-governmental organisations, charitable organisations or non-profit organisations, grassroot organisations, media, future generations (though, being passive stakeholders), and academia. For this work, this granularity is not required but the general structure is adopted.

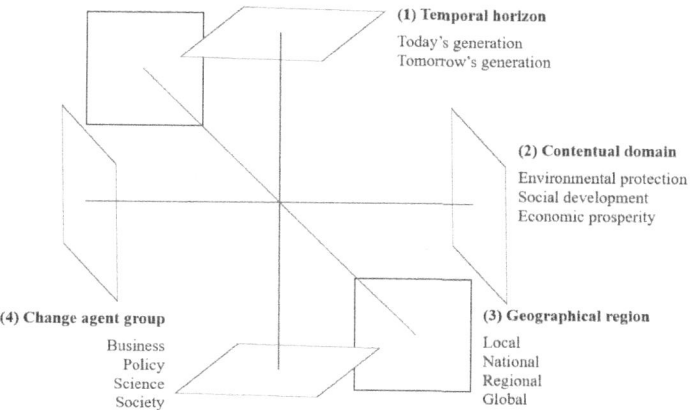

Figure 2.9 The first four dimensions of the sustainable development space

previously displayed cube is now disassembled into its six squares; each represents one sustainable development dimension. Figure 2.9 shows the visualisation of the first four dimensions of the sustainable development space: the temporal horizon, contentual domain, geographical region, and the change agent group. The fifth and sixth dimension will follow in Section 2.3.1 and Section 2.3.2.

In the following section, Section 2.3.1, the *multilevel perspective* is discussed. It is a framework that conflates the different change agents into one, unified framework. Hereafter, the main change agent groups business, policy, and science are examined (see Section 2.3.2 to Section 2.3.4). The group society is not further investigated as deeper insights from sociology or further disciplines are beyond the scope of this work. However, society remains an indispensable change agent group in the sustainability transition as, for instance, private citizens can influence corporations by their consumer behaviour (Kucuk & Krishnamurthy, 2007) and politics by their election decision.

2.3.1 The multilevel perspective

In sustainable development, multiple perspectives are present (Lock & Seele, 2017; Seyfang & Haxeltine, 2012) for two reasons. First, various types of stakeholders exist and have myriad demands (Perez-Batres, Miller & Pisani, 2011). Second, sustainable development, which is a society level concept (see Section 2.3.2; e.g. T. Hahn et al., 2015), requires change and transformation (Lock & Seele, 2017) at multiple scales and across all sectors (Griggs et al., 2014) because effects on the planet are the cumulative results of individuals (Dahl, 2012). Both sustainability transition frameworks – the multilevel perspective and transition management – organise these multiple perspectives into three levels: micro, meso, and macro (e.g. Geels, 2002; Kemp, 1994; Köhler et al., 2019; Loorbach, 2010; Markard, Raven & Truffer, 2012; Rip & Kemp, 1998; Rotmans et al., 2001; Smith, Voß & Grin, 2010). By doing so, the big picture and the broader problem framing can be captured (Smith et al., 2010), which is in turn necessary for a successful transition to sustainability. Only if multiple actors cooperate, their actions can intensify each other, leading to a successful transition (Loorbach, 2007). On the one hand, the multilevel perspective regards technological change for sustainable development and organises the analysis into niches (micro), regimes (meso), and landscapes (macro) (e.g. Geels, 2002; Kemp, 1994; Loorbach, 2007; Rip & Kemp, 1998; Smith et al., 2010). *Niche* is the level of innovation inside which novelties are created, tested, and diffused. A *regime* is the "dominant culture, structure and practice embodied by physical and immaterial infrastructures", whereas a *landscape* is defined as the overall societal setting (e.g. social values, political cultures, or economic trends), in which a process of technological change occurs (Loorbach, 2007).[12] Given its focus on technological change, this framework is not further regarded in this work. On the other hand, the transition management framework by Rotmans et al. (2001) is of relevance for this work because it is a decision-oriented framework that sorts the *aggregational size* of stakeholders and change agents of sustainable development into micro, meso, and macro. A *micro object* comprises individuals and individual actors, a *meso object* is composed of networks, communities, or organisations, whereas a *macro object* is a conglomerate of institutions or organisations. Because this framework also addresses micro, meso, and macro levels, it is also referred to as the *multilevel perspective*. Every stakeholder can be divided to the three aggregational sizes. For example, business may be an individual economic agent (micro), a corporation (meso), or a branch or an overall economy (macro); policy may be a single politician (micro), a single national government (meso), or an IGO (macro); and so on ad nauseam. Figure 2.10 illustrates this novel dimension within the sustainable development space, which is disregarded in existing sustainable development frameworks (see Chapter 2; e.g. Chofreh & Goni, 2017). This *perspective gap* is closed by the present framework. The sixth and last dimension follows in the next section, Section 2.3.2, which deals with the change agent group business.

2.3.2 Corporate sustainability

Without dedication and leadership by corporations to sustainable development, sustainable development will not be reached (Sachs, 2012). Sustainable production and consumption are the major challenges of sustainable development (Sala et al., 2013; Weitz et al., 2018), and corporations represent the productive sources of the economy, producing and consuming resources (Bansal, 2002; T. Hahn & Figge, 2011).

---

[12]Further definitions of landscapes, regimes, and niches exist and can be found in, e.g. Geels (2002); and Rip and Kemp (1998).

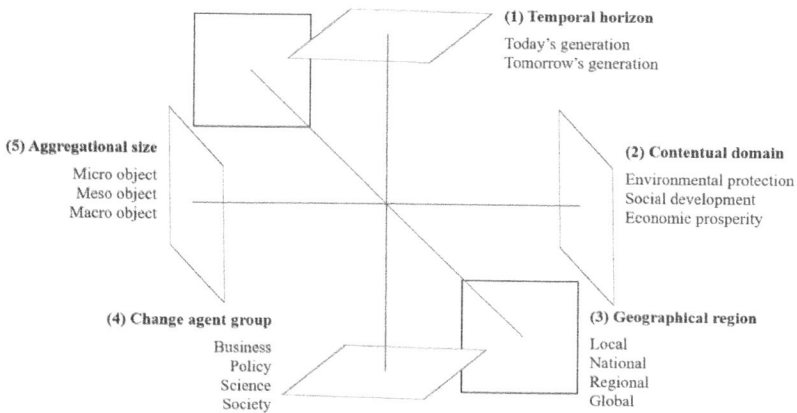

(1) Temporal horizon
Today's generation
Tomorrow's generation

(5) Aggregational size
Micro object
Meso object
Macro object

(2) Contentual domain
Environmental protection
Social development
Economic prosperity

(4) Change agent group
Business
Policy
Science
Society

(3) Geographical region
Local
National
Regional
Global

Figure 2.10 The first five dimensions of the sustainable development space

Analysing corporations with respect to sustainable development, T. Hahn and Figge (2011) developed three conceptual principles: instrumental finality, teleological integration, and practicability. First, *instrumental finality* is concerned with the determinateness of corporate sustainability and can be either organisational or societal (G. D. Atkinson, 2000; T. Hahn & Figge, 2011). *Organisational* sustainable development targets the long-term survival of the firm (G. D. Atkinson, 2000; T. Hahn & Figge, 2011), advancing financial performance by means of environmental and social issues (Dyllick & Hockerts, 2002). In other words, environmental and social issues only enter the equation to the degree of an opportunity for business success (T. Hahn & Figge, 2011). Sustainable development is seen as a source of value creation (Baumgartner, 2014; McWilliams & Siegel, 2011). To this end, *corporate sustainability* is defined as meeting the needs of a firm's direct and indirect stakeholders, without compromising its ability to meet the needs of future stakeholders as well (Dyllick & Hockerts, 2002). *Societal* sustainable development of the firm postulates corporate contributions to sustainable development at society level. The firm should only exist to the degree it contributes (G. D. Atkinson, 2000; T. Hahn & Figge, 2011). Societal instrumental finality is demanded because sustainable development is a society level concept (T. Hahn, Figge, Pinkse & Preuss, 2010; T. Hahn et al., 2015; Jennings & Zandbergen, 1995). Corporate sustainability must be about transposing the notion of sustainable development to the business level (Dyllick & Hockerts, 2002), such that corporate sustainability is conceptually linked to the Brundtland definition of sustainable development (Montiel & Delgado-Ceballos, 2014). Consequently, businesses themselves cannot become sustainable (T. Hahn et al., 2015; Jennings & Zandbergen, 1995), but their contribution at society level is haunted. The triple bottom line of people, planet, profit by Elkington (1997) is not only a misconception in the society level concept of sustainable development but also in corporate sustainability. In the society level concept, economic prosperity and not economic growth is key to sustainable development (see Section 2.2.3; e.g. Vermeulen, 2018); for corporate sustainability, also economic prosperity and not profit is key as societal instrumental finality is required (see above). Furthermore, the defensive approach of *corporate social responsibility* is not enough because it only addresses corporations' responsibility to society and regards the moral obligation of managers (Bansal & Song, 2017). Only negative impacts of businesses on society are eliminated (Baumgartner, 2014; Carpenter & White, 2004), but contributions to sustainable development must be tackled by a scientific system perspective (Bansal & Song, 2017). This perspective is pursued by corporate sustainability and societal instrumental finality.

Second, *teleological integration* deals with the integration of environmental, social, and economic aspects (T. Hahn & Figge, 2011). This integration is seen as a major challenge in post-modern society and thus in corporate sustainability (Gladwin, Kennelly & Krause, 1995; T. Hahn & Figge, 2011; Taylor, 1989) as the interlinkages include tensions (T. Hahn et al., 2015). Tensions may arise along each sustainable development dimension visualised in Figure 2.10, forthcoming in Figure 2.11.[13] Four management approaches are identified that cope with tensions. The *win-win perspective* regards situations in which the three domains are in harmony, such that economic, social, and environmental objectives can be reached simultaneously (T. Hahn et al., 2010). The *business case for sustainable development* is realised (Dyllick & Hockerts, 2002; T. Hahn et al., 2010) by avoiding tensions through alignment of the three domains. This typically implies an economic bias, which is referred to as *bounded instrumentality* (T. Hahn & Figge, 2011; T. Hahn et al., 2010; van der Byl & Slawinski, 2015). The triple bottom line leads to bounded instrumentality. By limiting itself to profit maximisation, this perspective is likely to dismiss potential positive corporate contributions to sustainable development (T. Hahn et al., 2010). The *trade-off perspective* recognises that there are situations in which the three domains cannot be obtained simultaneously. Owing to the multidimensionality of sustainable development, these situations are rather the rule than the exception,[14] and thus, corporate sustainability is required to conceptually be able to deal with trade-offs (T. Hahn & Figge, 2011; T. Hahn et al., 2010). In this management perspective, tensions are avoided by choosing one sustainable development element over the other. Typically, profits are sought to be maximised (van der Byl & Slawinski, 2015). Thinking "beyond the business case" is required (Dyllick & Hockerts,

---

[13]According to T. Hahn et al. (2015), tensions may only arise along three dimensions: levels, process of change, and context. *Levels* refer to the aggregational size and can be individuals, organisations, or systems. This view is in line with the multilevel perspective by Rotmans et al. (2001) (see Section 2.3.1). *Process of change* regards the three contentual domains, and *context* refers to the temporal and spatial context (i.e. intergenerational and intragenerational aspects, respectively).

[14]Opposing, Pradhan et al. (2017) conclude in their empirical study that there are typically more synergies than trade-offs. Nonetheless, conceptual ability to deal with trade-offs remains essential because they have to be managed regardless of their relative frequency.

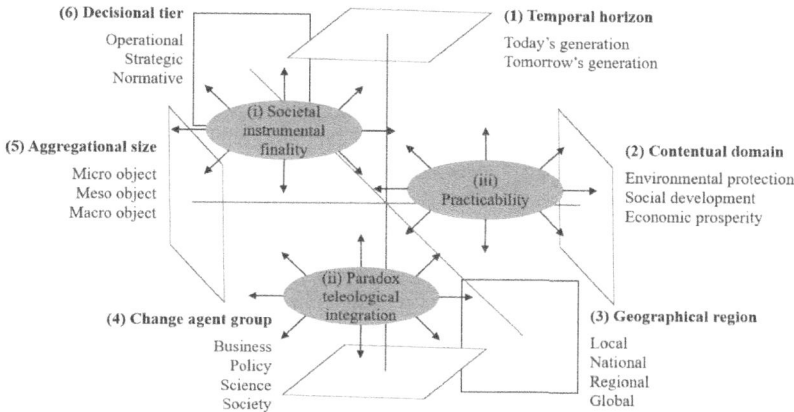

Figure 2.11 The six-dimensional sustainable development space and the three conceptual principles of its management

2002; T. Hahn & Figge, 2011; T. Hahn et al., 2010, 2018; T. Hahn et al., 2015), and businesses should not have any a priori economic superiority (T. Hahn & Figge, 2011) but simultaneously address the three, interconnected sustainable development domains (T. Hahn et al., 2015). The *integrative perspective* requests managers to pursue different sustainable development aspects at once even if they are oppositional (T. Hahn et al., 2015). The focus is shifted from economic to environmental and social issues (van der Byl & Slawinski, 2015), and solutions for the entire system of interrelated elements are looked for (Gao & Bansal, 2013). Last, the *paradox perspective* explicitly acknowledges tensions (T. Hahn et al., 2018) by coexistence of oppositional elements (Clegg, Vieira da Cunha & Pina e Cunha, 2002; T. Hahn et al., 2015; Lewis, 2000). These situations are managed by first accepting the contradictions and second exploring them (van der Byl & Slawinski, 2015), such that managers are able to achieve competing objectives (T. Hahn et al., 2018). T. Hahn et al. (2018); T. Hahn et al. (2015); and van der Byl and Slawinski (2015) agree that in terms of teleological integration, the paradox perspective must be implemented. Notwithstanding, Landrum and Ohsowski (2018) find that the dominating mindset is the business case for sustainable development, which neither acknowledges the paradox theory nor tensions in general.

Third, *practicability* refers to the need of effectively informing and guiding decision makers (Boron & Murray, 2004; T. Hahn & Figge, 2011). These three conceptual principles do not only apply to their original field of corporate sustainability but can be transferred to the management of sustainable development in general. Therefore, they enter the conceptual framework of sustainable development (see Figure 2.11).

The three conceptual principles – societal instrumental finality, paradox teleological integration, and practicability – are urged to be embedded into all decisional tiers

(Engert, Rauter & Baumgartner, 2016; Galbreath, 2009; R. Hahn, 2013), opening the sixth and last dimension of the sustainable development space. The *decisional tier* can be divided into three levels: normative, strategic, and operational (Baumgartner, 2014; Ulrich, 2001). The *normative tier* deals with the management philosophy and basic beliefs as well as values of the corporation that influence behaviours and decisions of management and employees (Baumgartner, 2014; Ulrich, 2001). The *strategic tier* is responsible for the effectiveness of the sustainability strategy. The process of planning, implementing, and evaluating effects is dealt with in order to achieve the long-term goals (Baumgartner, 2014; David, 2009). The *operational tier* is concerned with efficiency and implements normative and strategic goals (Baumgartner, 2014; Ulrich, 2001). This model is known as the *St. Gallen management model* (Ulrich, 2001). Similar to the conceptual principles, the decisional tiers are not only of relevance for corporate sustainability but for sustainable development management in general, entering the conceptual framework. The final version of the framework, with its six dimensions and three conceptual principles, is pictured in Figure 2.11. Despite the need to address all three decisional tiers, many corporations only integrate corporate sustainability at the operational tier (Engert et al., 2016; Galbreath, 2009; R. Hahn, 2013). This *operational-to-normative gap* is seen as the major reason in the lack of progress towards (corporate) contributions to sustainable development (Baumgartner & Rauter, 2017; Tseng et al., 2018) and is hence taken into consideration in the selection process of the sustainable development measurement method (see Section 3.1 to Section 3.2).

Generally, corporations need an incentive to engage in corporate contributions to sustainable development (T. Hahn & Figge, 2011; Husted & de Jesus Salazar, 2006). Incentives and drivers can be of internal or external nature (Lozano, 2015), and several theories exist to explain engagements in corporate sustainability. An overview on literature streams, their main assumptions, and example references from theory-building, summarising, or empirical studies are given in Table 2.2. The last column of Table 2.2 evaluates the fulfilment of the respective theory with the conceptual principles of societal instrumental finality and paradox teleological integration (see Figure 2.11). Practicability is not meaningful to be evaluated in this context but will be taken up on in Chapter 3. The natural resource-based view focuses on competitive advantage and maximisation of the firm, such that bounded instrumentality is present. The win-win or the trade-off perspective might be the managing view. Institutional, legitimacy, and stakeholder theories are driven by stakeholders and therefore may fit the criteria of instrumental finality and teleological integration if stakeholders desire or enforce these. Stewardship theory and sustaincentrism are the only theories that conceptually include societal instrumental finality and paradox teleological integration at any time. Consequently, corporations are encouraged to take actions to employ stewards and implement sustaincentrism in their organisation. Further studies on drivers of corporate sustainability include Engert et al. (2016); and Lozano (2015). Eccles, Ioannou and

Literature stream	Assumption	Example references	Societal instrumental finality and paradox teleological integration
Natural resource-based view, agency theory	Corporations depend on natural and manufactured resources and regard their scarcity to gain competitive advantage. Managers are rational agents and maximise profits.	T. Hahn and Figge, 2011; Hart, 1995; Hart and Dowell, 2011; Jensen and Meckling, 1976; McWilliams and Siegel, 2011; Montiel and Delgado-Ceballos, 2014	No
Stakeholder theory	Corporations keep the interest of their stakeholders in mind in order to achieve a superior performance.	Freeman, 1984, 2010; R. Hahn and Kühnen, 2013; Laplume, Sonpar and Litz, 2008; Montiel and Delgado-Ceballos, 2014; Perez-Batres et al., 2011; Shevchenko, Lévesque and Pagell, 2016	Only if stakeholders desire
Legitimacy theory	Corporations require a *licence to operate*, granted by their stakeholders.	Bansal and Clelland, 2004; Baumgartner, 2014; Deegan, 2002; DiMaggio and Powell, 1983; Dowling and Pfeffer, 1975; R. Hahn and Kühnen, 2013; Perez-Batres et al., 2011; Schaltegger and Hörisch, 2017; Suchman, 1995	Only if stakeholders desire
Institutional theory	Institutional culture of the corporation enables and constrains behaviour.	Campbell, 2007; DiMaggio and Powell, 1983; Egels-Zandén and Wahlqvist, 2007; Galbreath, 2010; Linnenluecke and Griffiths, 2010; J. W. Meyer and Rowan, 1977; Montiel and Delgado-Ceballos, 2014	Only if regulations or stakeholders enforce and institutionalise
Stewardship theory	Managers receive a higher utility from pro-organisational, collectivistic than self-serving behaviour and actively shape pathways of social and environmental change.	Davis, Schoorman and Donaldson, 1997; Folke, Biggs, Norström, Reyers and Rockström, 2016; Godos-Díez, Fernández-Gago and Martínez-Campillo, 2011; Tseng et al., 2018	Yes
Sustaincentrism	Managers are guided by an environmental and moral compass.	Gladwin et al., 1995; Montiel and Delgado-Ceballos, 2014; Valente, 2012	Yes

Table 2.2 Overview of literature streams of corporate sustainability drivers

Serafeim (2014) investigate vice versa and tackle the impact of corporate sustainability on organisational processes and performances.

2.3.3   Political goal setting: The United Nations's (UN) Sustainable Development Goals (SDGs)

Policy making and the involvement of governments are inherent in sustainable development (Meadowcroft, 1997, 2011). The subjective nature of sustainable development means going beyond efficiency and deciding upon one of the multiple pathways (see Section 2.2.4; Leach et al., 2013), requiring negotiations in a democratic system (McGregor & Pouw, 2017). Moreover, governments exercise control by launching laws or regulations and by providing public goods such as infrastructure (Clarkson, 1995; Hood & Margetts, 2007; Lock & Seele, 2017). IGOs frame political interactions (Meadowcroft, 2011), and in this vein, the UN has released the most elaborated concept of sustainable development (see Section 2.1; Lock & Seele, 2017). Further international organisations such as the Organisation for Economic Co-operation and Development (OECD) and International Labour Organization (ILO) spread advices on political landscapes and legal frameworks for sustainable development in documents such as ILO (2013); and OECD (2016).[15] However, as in previous sections, this work continues to concentrate on the UN's approach to sustainable development. Section 2.1 has dealt with the normative concept of the UN's approach, whereas this section regards the strategic level and the release of development goals.

The first development goals were the Millennium Development Goals (MDGs). The MDGs are an integrated framework adopted by 189 countries around the world in the 2000s, aiming at social development and improved living standards of the world's poor (Glaser, 2012; Griggs et al., 2014; Sachs, 2012; UNGA, 2000). With the MDGs, measurable and timebound objectives were set, promoting global awareness, political accountability, social feedback, and public pressure for sustainable development (Sachs, 2012). In 2015, the MDGs were replaced by the SDGs. The SDGs do not only embrace developing countries but are universally applicable to all countries and geographical regions (Glaser, 2012; Sachs, 2012). Given the third dimension of the sustainable development space (see Figure 2.11), an essential improvement is realised. The SDGs promote social development and economic prosperity in harmony with nature for all nations and are globally accepted as the content and meaning of sustainable development (Dahl, 2018; UNCSD, 2012; UNGA, 2015). There are 17 SDGs with 169 targets and 232 indicators in total. The goals and targets are agreed on by international negotiation, whereas the indicators are worked out and annually refined by an expert group (UN, 2018, 2019a; UNGA, 2015). With the numerous, quantitative indicators, progress can be monitored, policy may be informed, and accountability of all stakeholders can be

---

[15]The ILO focuses topics of labour and thus only regards the social or economic domain.

ensured (UN, 2019a). The SDGs are, similar to the MDGs, voluntary, time-bounded targets (Glaser, 2012) and can be summarised to poverty elimination, sustainable lifestyles for all, and a stable resilient planetary life-supporting system (Griggs et al., 2014). In detail, the 17 SDGs read (UN, 2018):

- SDG 1:   End poverty in all its forms everywhere.
- SDG 2:   End hunger, achieve food security and improved nutrition, and promote sustainable agriculture.
- SDG 3:   Ensure healthy lives and promote wellbeing for all at all ages.
- SDG 4:   Ensure inclusive and equitable quality education and promote lifelong learning opportunities for all.
- SDG 5:   Achieve gender equality and empower all women and girls.
- SDG 6:   Ensure availability and sustainable management of water and sanitation for all.
- SDG 7:   Ensure access to affordable, reliable, sustainable, and modern energy for all.
- SDG 8:   Promote sustained, inclusive, and sustainable economic growth; full and productive employment; and decent work for all.
- SDG 9:   Build resilient infrastructure, promote inclusive and sustainable industrialisation, and foster innovation.
- SDG 10: Reduce inequality within and among countries.
- SDG 11: Make cities and human settlements inclusive, safe, resilient, and sustainable.
- SDG 12: Ensure sustainable consumption and production patterns.
- SDG 13: Take urgent action to combat climate change and its impacts.
- SDG 14: Conserve and sustainably use the oceans, seas, and marine resources for sustainable development.
- SDG 15: Protect, restore, and promote sustainable use of terrestrial ecosystems; sustainably manage forests; combat desertification; halt and reverse land degradation; and halt biodiversity loss.
- SDG 16: Promote peaceful and inclusive societies for sustainable development; provide access to justice for all; and build effective, accountable, and inclusive institutions at all levels.
- SDG 17: Strengthen the means of implementation and revitalise the global partnership for sustainable development.

Figure 2.12a displays the 17 SDGs and Figure 2.12b shows their allocation to the three contentual domains. Four goals are assigned to the environmental domain, eight goals belong to the social domain, another four goals make up the economic domain and

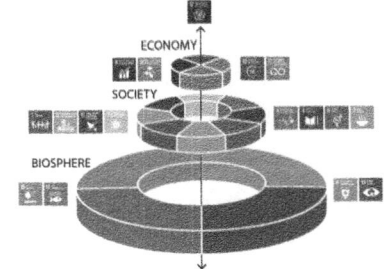

(a) Overview of the Sustainable Development Goals (SDGs) (UN, 2019b)

(b) Assignment of the Sustainable Development Goals (SDGs) to the three contentual domains (from/based on Folke et al., 2016; Rockström and Sukhdev, 2014; with friendly permission of © 2016 by the authors)

Figure 2.12 The Sustainable Development Goals (SDGs)

one goal, SDG 17 on partnership for the goals, cannot be assigned to any but affects all contentual domains.

The SDGs are critically discussed in the academic literature. On the positive side, they open the door to a unified framework of sustainable development (Griggs et al., 2014), and the level of ambition and comprehensiveness are the greatest so far in the history of political goal setting for sustainable development (Biermann et al., 2017). Similar to the MDGs, the SDGs place this goal setting at the centre of political agendas and generate worldwide commitments and actions (Glaser, 2012). The novel bottom-up, non-legally-binding approach is a key success factor as, among others, moral and practical commitments feature lower transaction costs as well as fewer delays than the classical top-down approach (Biermann et al., 2017; Hajer et al., 2015; Sachs, 2012). Nonetheless, the SDGs are explicit in the endpoint and may therefore clarify pathways to necessary end outcomes (Vermeulen, 2018). The SDGs are universally applicable (Glaser, 2012; Griggs et al., 2013; Sachs, 2012), and the small number of goals as well as their simplicity are essential for focus and effectivity (Griggs et al., 2014; Sachs, 2012). Yet, the goals and targets are comprehensive (Pradhan et al., 2017). Besides, they are practicable (Sachs, 2012), measurable (Griggs et al., 2013), and science provides guidance on their framing (Glaser, 2012; Griggs et al., 2014), such that the important science-practice interlinkage is realised (see Section 2.3.4). To sum up, advocates claim major requirements of the sustainable development framework are met.

However, opponents of the SDGs do not interpret the bottom-up approach as a success factor but claim that an obligation for target fulfilment should be established. Otherwise, counterproductive drivers are supported, and only easily achievable targets might be chosen with the result that the full potential of the SDGs might be forfeited (Allen et al., 2019; Spangenberg, 2017). Furthermore, the global goals and targets must be translated into corresponding efforts at the national level (Dahl, 2018). In addition, the SDGs are said to be vague, weak, or meaningless (Holden et al., 2017; Stokstad, 2015). 54% of the targets require further work and need to be strengthened by, for instance, determining endpoints and time frames for an accurate measurement. 17% of the targets are non-essential and can be disregarded (ICSU & ISSC, 2015; Stokstad, 2015). Spaiser et al. (2017) reinforce these qualitative assertions by empirical evidence derived by several multivariate techniques. They conclude that the economic domain is valid, the social domain is well represented, but the environmental domain is poorly defined and incoherent. Scholars generally agree that further research is demanded in the environmental domain, among others, the planetary boundaries must be linked to the SDGs and broken down to national or corporate level (see Section 2.2.1 and Section 6.3; e.g. O'Neill et al., 2018; Whiteman et al., 2013). Further criticism involves that there are repetitions and that the environmental goals 12 to 15 are not quantifiable (Holden et al., 2017).[16] The author of this work does not agree on this criticism as the UN (2018) lists numerous solid, quantitative indicators. Nonetheless, the author agrees on Holden et al.'s (2017) criticism that the SDGs rest on wrong premises by balancing the three dimensions. The UN (2018) includes economic growth as a sustainable development indicator but does not specify a threshold above which economic growth is not required anymore. Further criticism includes having too many goals results in not having a goal at all. Therefore, only relevant indicators should be chosen (see Section 3.1; Hák, Janoušková & Moldan, 2016; Holden et al., 2017; Janoušková, Hák & Moldan, 2018; Reyers, Stafford-Smith, Erb, Scholes & Selomane, 2017). Reyers et al. (2017) offer an approach to monitor the SDGs with only essential variables. Moreover, prioritisation of the SDGs is a prerequisite for effectiveness of actions. The SDGs are individually straight forward but the system as a whole, its dynamics, synergies, and trade-offs have to be understood (Allen et al., 2019; Nilsson et al., 2016; Pradhan et al., 2017; Sachs, 2012; Spaiser et al., 2017; Weitz et al., 2018). This *knowledge gap* must be solved for maximising progress on the SDGs (Costanza, Fioramonti & Kubiszewski, 2016; ICSU & ISSC, 2015; Spaiser et al., 2017; Weitz et al., 2018), critically determining the selection process of the sustainable development assessment method (see Section 3.1 to Section 3.2). If decision makers ignore the interlinkages and overlaps, important contributions to sustainable development may be missed. However, decision makers require science-based assistance for complexity reduction and prioritisation. First works on SDG prioritisation include, for instance, Allen et al. (2019); Pradhan et al. (2017); and Weitz et al. (2018). New insights on the system dynamics, synergies, and trade-offs will be contributed by the empirical part of this work (see Chapter 5).

To sum up, the SDGs entail both risks and opportunities: The SDGs bear the risk of

---

[16]Folke et al. (2016); and Rockström and Sukhdev (2014) assign SDG 12 on responsible consumption and production to the economic domain. The author of this work rather agrees with Holden et al. (2017) and the SDG 12 being an environmental goal (see Section 5.3.1).

creating a huge bureaucratic burden with failure of practical results, and they have the potential to transform the globe towards sustainable development. To reduce the risk of failure, the knowledge gap must be closed. This is a task for the science community (including this work), which is characterised in the next section, Section 2.3.4.

2.3.4   Sustainability science

Last, the science community is fundamental in the process of sustainable development because it crafts knowledge, facilitates the transition with the new knowledge, passes the knowledge on to young people in institutions of higher education, and publishes the information for the public (Bachmann, 2016; Barth, 2016; Clark, 2007; Clark et al., 2016; Folke et al., 2016; Lock & Seele, 2017). The discipline sustainability science was initiated by Kates et al. (2001), decades after the start of the intergovernmental debate headed by the UN (see Section 2.1 and Section 2.3.3). Kates (2015); and Kates et al. (2001) raised seven core questions to be answered by the discipline, drawing on both the descriptive-analytical and the transformational mode (see Section 2.1; Wiek et al., 2012). The dual mission of sustainability science (Hall et al., 2017; McGreavy & Kates, 2012) shapes this discipline, always seeking solutions to real world problems and being teleologically directed towards sustainable development (Spangenberg, 2011). Most importantly is the connection of science (knowledge) and practice (societal action and informed decision making) between which sustainability science creates a dynamic bridge (Clark, 2007; Kates, 2015; Sala et al., 2015; Turner II et al., 2003). To manage both the descriptive-analytical and the transformational mode, sustainability science needs to be transdisciplinary (Jahn, Bergmann & Keil, 2012; Lang et al., 2012; Schaltegger et al., 2013; Spangenberg, 2011). Transdisciplinary research is not only characterised by science-practice collaborations that focus on societally relevant problems and seek for real-world solutions, but also by methodological pluralism and collaborations of various disciplines (Lang et al., 2012; Schaltegger et al., 2013; Spangenberg, 2011).[17] In sustainability science, pluralism is required to handle the complexity arising from the multidimensionality of the framework. A conceptual agenda for transdisciplinary research can be found in Jahn et al. (2012); and Lang et al. (2012) and is reproduced in Figure 2.13. Societal and scientific practice work hand in glove. During the first phase (Phase A), a societal problem is identified and triggers the scientific research question. Herefrom, the joint problem is framed, and collaborative teams from academia and practice are built, such that mutual learning among researchers and practitioners is enabled. In Phase B, solution-oriented and transferable knowledge is generated and disclosed. Subsequently, this knowledge is reintegrated and applied, leading to useful and relevant results for social and scientific practice in Phase C. This in turn loops

---

[17] A detailed differentiation of disciplinary, multidisciplinary, interdisciplinary, and transdisciplinary research can be found in Schaltegger et al. (2013).

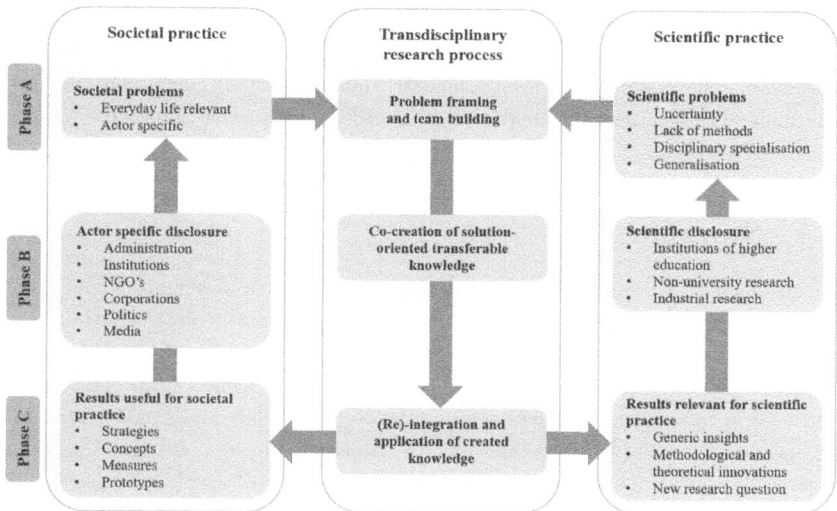

Figure 2.13 Conceptual agenda of a transdisciplinary research processes (based on Jahn et al., 2012; Lang et al., 2012; with friendly permissions of © 2012 Elsevier B.V. All rights reserved; © Springer 2012)

back into Phase B and Phase A.

Taking into account the research reviewed for this work, the discipline sustainability science has accomplished Phase A to the point of being on hold for further feedback loops. Societal and scientific problems are framed, which, for example, resulted in the SDGs (see Section 2.3.3). The development of a sustainable development indicator set demands scientific knowledge production as well as political norm creation (Rametsteiner, Pülzl, Alkan-Olsson & Frederiksen, 2011). The SDGs successfully draw this line from science to practice first by the process itself (see Section 2.3.3) and second by providing results of the goals, targets, and indicators for political decision making as well as scientific analysis. Actor specific and scientific disclosure (Phase B) has been performed. Examples include corporations that disclose sustainability reports in accordance with the standard of the GRI (see Section 3.3.1; GRI, 2016) and the growing number of academic publications (Kates, 2015). Phase C has been entered but it is not finalised yet, such that sustainable development remains a vision of future (White, 2013). Useful and relevant results for society and science have been generated but are not completed. On the scientific side, not all planetary boundaries have been quantified, the concept of social boundaries demands further refinement, and the corresponding economic system has to be designed (see Section 2.2). On the societal side, for instance, practicability and effectiveness of the SDGs have to be tested and concluded on. Future research will be discussed in Section 6.3. In spite of having entered Phase C, there are bottlenecks in the science-practice linkage (Castellani, Piazzalunga & Sala, 2013; Sala et al., 2015), also called the *knowledge-to-action gap* (Sala et al., 2013) or the *sustainability gap* (Agyeman, 2005; Christie & Warburton, 2001; Hall et al., 2017). This work aims to contribute to closing this fourth research gap by easily applicable measurement methods, which will be discussed and selected in Section 3.2 et seq.

2.4   Summary

In this chapter, a six-dimensional framework of sustainable development has been developed, and three central conceptual principles of the management of sustainable development have been identified. The finalised framework includes both the descriptive-analytical and the transformational mode of sustainable development. The dimensions (1) to (3) in Figure 2.11 primarily refer to the descriptive-analytical mode, whereas dimensions (4) to (6) primarily bear upon the transformational mode. The temporal horizon (1) implies that present and forward-looking time series analysis instead of single points in time should be incorporated. The contentual domain (2) consists of several concepts. Environmental protection rests on the concept of limits, represented by the planetary boundaries. Social development is theorised by the concept of needs, captured by the social boundaries, within which the principle of justice should be applied. Combining these concepts, the safe and just operating space for humanity results, for which the green economy should be calibrated. This ideal system should be applied around the whole globe and at every regional scope (3). Sustainable development is a vision of future, which is aimed to become the present as soon as possible. Necessary to this end is change and transition, managed and guided by change agents (4) of every aggregational size (5), who take decisions at normative, strategic, and operational tiers (6). By including the multilevel perspective on the aggregational size of change agents and the St. Gallen management model for the decisional tiers, the perspective and the operational-to-normative gaps are closed, respectively. The conceptual management principles of societal instrumental finality (i), paradox teleological integration (ii), and practicability (iii) ought to be obeyed with regard to every dimension of the framework. Sustainable development requires a transdisciplinary working agenda, whose main characteristic is the connection from science to practice. The SDGs are a successful transdisciplinary result. Nonetheless, a knowledge gap of the individual sustainable development elements and their dynamic interactions as well as a sustainability gap concerning the application of crafted scientific knowledge to political, entrepreneurial, and societal practice is present.

The next chapter, Chapter 3, deals with the measurement and assessment of contributions to sustainable development. Any pursued method should comply with the conceptual framework of sustainable development and is critically determined by the ability to address the knowledge and the sustainability gaps.

Chapter 3

Measuring and assessing contributions to sustainable development

Measurement and assessment of sustainable development must be executed to reduce the risk of failure in the transition to sustainability. The old axiom "what gets measured gets managed" (e.g. Parris & Kates, 2003) or its reverse "what is not measured often gets ignored" (e.g. Giljum, Burger, Hinterberger, Lutter & Bruckner, 2011) prevails. Measurement and assessment address both the descriptive-analytical and the transformational mode of sustainable development (see Section 2.1; Wiek et al., 2012): They generate and structure information to serve decision making (Waas et al., 2014).

The measurement of contributions to sustainable development can involve the measurement of practices or performances (e.g. Gjølberg, 2009). Practice measurement quantifies activities, but it does not include a practice's result and is therefore unrelated to a practice's success (Gjølberg, 2009; Wood, 1991) or effectiveness. In contrast, performance measurement quantifies results that allow for inferences back to performed practices despite the absence of direct information about these practices (Searcy, 2012; Tangen, 2005). Hence, performance measurement supports managing, controlling, planning, implementing, and evaluating practices and activities (Ramos & Moreno Pires, 2013; Searcy, 2012; Tangen, 2005) that are directed towards sustainable development (Bond, Pope & Morrison-Saunders, 2015; Hacking & Guthrie, 2008). Because of this superior property, performance measurement and not practice measurement is adopted for the remainder of this work.

Besides the overarching objective to support both modes of sustainable development, several reasons for measurement and assessment of sustainable development are present. Measurement helps to better understand and interpret the current situation as well as the desired end state (Searcy, 2012; Waas et al., 2014) by enabling evaluation of progress towards goals (Kates, 2015; Searcy, 2012; Spangenberg, 2015; Vermeulen, 2018),

© The Author(s) 2021
C. Lemke, *Accounting and Statistical Analyses for Sustainable Development*, Sustainable Management, Wertschöpfung und Effizienz, https://doi.org/10.1007/978-3-658-33246-4_3

adherence of standards (Ramos, Caeiro & Joanaz de Melo, 2004), or derivations from baselines and principles (Hacking & Guthrie, 2006, 2008). Quantification further facilitates comparison of performances (Esty, 2018; Waas et al., 2014), policy appraisal, and identification of superior regulatory approaches (Esty, 2018). Eventually, measurement serves as a basis for efficient decision making (Baumgartner, 2014; de Villiers & Hsiao, 2018; Parris & Kates, 2003; Ramos et al., 2004; Waas et al., 2014; Wu & Wu, 2012) and is thus required for goal achievement (Almássy & Pintér, 2018). Moreover, measurement and assessment results can be reported to stakeholders for reduction of information asymmetries (R. Hahn & Kühnen, 2013; Maroun, 2018). *Asymmetric information* are present when "different people know different things" (Spence, 1973; Stiglitz, 2002), and in signalling theory, asymmetric information are sought to be reduced by "high quality firms" to increase their payoff (Connelly, Certo, Ireland & Reutzel, 2011). Above average sustainable development performances may be signalled to stakeholders for image enhancement; building relationships, legitimacy, and accountability with stakeholders (see Section 2.3.2; Landrum & Ohsowski, 2018; Maroun, 2018). However, only effective green practices and not *greenwashing*, which is the overstatement of environmental commitments, is positively correlated with the firm value (Testa, Miroshnychenko, Barontini & Frey, 2018). Underperformance might lead to shame, which is the origin of the power of monitoring (Kelley & Simmons, 2015). To be in line with societal instrumental finality (see Section 2.3.2; e.g. T. Hahn & Figge, 2011), an increased payoff should not be the ultimate goal but a byproduct.

Criticism on measurement and assessment of contributions to sustainable development is scarce. One objection could be that sustainable development might be immeasurable (Bell & Morse, 2008; Böhringer & Jochem, 2007). The measurement of sustainable development depends on the body performing it, and hence, subjectivity is inevitable. Sustainable development becomes defined when measured by quantifiable variables, instead of being defined before measuring it (Bell & Morse, 2008). This finding comes into effect in the methodological choices (see Section 4.3.7.1). In contrast, the temperature is an example for a measurable, pre-defined variable. In spite of this possible objection, sustainable development should be measured as benefits dominate.

The chapter is structured as follows. In the next section, Section 3.1, principles of sustainable development measurement and assessment methods are summarised and harmonised. Hereafter, an overview on quantitative assessment methods is given in Section 3.2. The various assessment methods are evaluated against the conceptual framework (see Figure 2.11) and assessment principles (see Section 3.1) to derive the most suitable method for addressing the first four identified research gaps: First, the assessment method must be able to address the perspective gap (see Section 2.3.1), second tackle the operational-to-normative gap (see Section 2.3.2; e.g. Baumgartner & Rauter, 2017), third, give indication on the interlinkages of the individual sustainable development elements (knowledge gap) (see Section 2.3.3; e.g. Weitz et al., 2018), and fourth, be easily applicable in practice to close the sustainability gap (see Section 2.3.4; e.g. Hall et al., 2017). Section 3.3 gives an overview on micro, meso, and macro sustainable development indicators (see Section 3.3.1) and indices (see Section 3.3.2 and Section 3.3.3). A summary is provided in Section 3.4.

3.1 Principles of sustainable development measurement and assessment methods

In 1997, a group of practitioners from the International Institute for Sustainable Development (IISD) developed principles for the measurement of sustainable development (IISD, 1997). These principles became known as the Bellagio Sustainability Assessment and Measurement Principles (Bellagio STAMP) and were updated by Pintér, Hardi, Martinuzzi and Hall (2012, 2018). The Bellagio STAMP consist of eight principles: guiding vision; essential considerations of the underlying subsystems' environment, society, and economy, including implications of synergies and trade-offs for decision making; adequate temporal and geographical scope; framework and standardised indicators that enable comparisons;[18] transparency of data, methods, and results; effective communication to attract a broad audience; broad stakeholder participation for legitimacy; and last, continuity and capacity of and for measurement.

Hacking and Guthrie (2008) identify the following principles in sustainable development assessment: comprehensiveness of theme coverage; integratedness of themes and techniques; and strategicness of goals, benchmarks, scales, and scope, including alternatives, cumulative impacts, and uncertainties. Sala et al. (2015) add to Hacking and Guthrie's (2008) principles boundary orientedness, stakeholder involvement, scalability, transparency, as well as objectivity and robustness in measurement.

According to Esty (2018), benchmarking must be possible across all scales and issues (i.e. along the temporal horizon, contentual domain, geographical region, and aggregational size) for understanding and judging relative performances. Benchmarking and multilevel comparability is essential to enable quantification of micro-level and meso-level contributions to the society level concept of sustainable development (see Section 2.3.2; e.g. T. Hahn et al., 2015). Establishing a micro-to-macro connection is essential because effects on the planet (macro level) are the cumulative results of individuals (micro level) (Dahl, 2012), such that sustainable development can only be achieved if micro and meso objects contribute (Griggs et al., 2014; Sachs, 2012). Furthermore, benchmarking is important because rankings are rendered possible, preventing greenwashing, forcing objects of investigation to question their own performance, facilitating the detection of underperformance and thereby creating social pressure

---

[18]Indicators play a crucial role in the assessment of sustainable development and therefore entered the Bellagio STAMP. Section 3.3 will reveal the reason for their centrality.

Bellagio STAMP (IISD, 1997; Pintér et al., 2012, 2018)	Hacking and Guthrie, 2008; Sala et al., 2015	Further authors	Summary and harmonisation
Guiding vision, adequate scope, framework, continuity	Comprehensiveness, strategicness of scales and scope, scalability		Compliance with framework
Indicator comparison	Strategicness of benchmarks and alternatives	Benchmarking (Becker et al., 2017; Esty, 2018; Kelley & Simmons, 2015), multilevel comparability	Comparability
Essential considerations	Integratedness of themes	Interconnection of goals (Costanza, Fioramonti & Kubiszewski 2016), synergies and trade-offs (Griggs et al., 2014; T. Hahn & Figge, 2011)	Synergies and trade-offs
	Strategicness of cumulative impacts	Efficiency and effectiveness (Figge & Hahn, 2004)	Efficiency and effectiveness
	Strategicness of goals, boundary orientedness		Target and boundary orientedness
Continuity and capacity		Practicability (T. Hahn & Figge, 2011)	Practicability
Stakeholder participation	Stakeholder involvement	Salience, legitimacy (Cash et al., 2003; Parris & Kates, 2003)	Stakeholder involvement
Effective communication			Effective communication
Transparency	Transparency		Transparency
	Integratedness of techniques, strategicness of uncertainties, objectivity, robustness	Credibility (Cash et al., 2003; Parris & Kates, 2003), relevance, validity, reliability (Janoušková et al., 2018)	Methodological soundness

Table 3.1 Overview of principles of sustainable development measurement and assessment methods

towards stakeholders (see above; Kelley & Simmons, 2015). Therefore, benchmarking and rankings are interpreted as drivers of behaviour and change (Becker, Saisana, Paruolo & Vandecasteele, 2017; Kelley & Simmons, 2015) by triggering motivation (Dahl, 2018), which eventually leads to progress (Esty, 2018). Interconnection of goals is necessary because individual sustainable development elements depend on each other and contribute to the overarching objective of sustainability in an unequal manner (Costanza, Fioramonti & Kubiszewski, 2016; Griggs et al., 2014; T. Hahn & Figge, 2011). Synergies and trade-offs are present. *Synergies* are interactions that favour each other, whereas *trade-offs* are interactions that hinder each other (Pradhan et al., 2017). Figge and Hahn (2004) postulate the inclusion of both relative and absolute measurement to project efficiency as well as effectiveness, necessary to control for rebound effects (Berkhout, Muskens & Velthuijsen, 2000; Dyllick & Hockerts, 2002; Harangozo et al., 2018; Schneider et al., 2011). T. Hahn and Figge (2011) press for practicability of measurement tools.[19] For Cash et al. (2003); and Parris and Kates (2003), assessment principles are salience, credibility, and legitimacy. *Salience* refers to relevance of the measurement to decision makers, *credibility* regards the scientific and technical adequacy of measurement, and *legitimacy* is concerned with the stakeholders' views. Closely related are Janoušková et al.'s (2018) principles: relevance, validity, and reliability. *Relevance* is "the importance of something" or "the relationship of something to the matter at hand" (Janoušková et al., 2018). It functions as a selective criterion, and only relevant, important, and useful information gets observed. Hence, relevance and its maximisation is key to human cognition (Janoušková et al., 2018; Sperber & Wilson, 1999), and it has become a major area in information science (Cosijn & Ingwersen, 2000; Janoušková et al., 2018). With regard to sustainable development, relevance represents the importance of the contentual domains and their individual elements (Janoušková et al., 2018). In Chapter 4 et seq., it will be revealed that this work is also shaped by information-theoretic relevance. *Validity* refers to the "degree to which the measurement tool measures what it claims to measure" (Janoušková et al., 2018), and *reliability* regards the consistency of measurement. Methodological soundness is crucial for policy or management conclusions to be accurate and non-misleading (Böhringer & Jochem, 2007; Nardo et al., 2008). Holden et al. (2017); and Spangenberg (2015) list the same principles with slightly different wording. An overview on the presented assessment principles is given in Table 3.1. The last column of Table 3.1 summarises and harmonises the various principles into one structure, which is then utilised to evaluate a quantification method's aptitude to measure and assess contributions to sustainable development by micro, meso, and macro objects of investigation. An evaluation of quantitative assessment methods follows in the next section, Section 3.2.

---

[19]Practicabiliy entered the sustainable development framework as a conceptual principle (see Section 2.3.2). Due to its inherent conceptual and practical relevance, it is also incorporated in the assessment priniples.

3.2 Overview of quantitative sustainable development assessment methods

Quantitative sustainable development measurement and assessment methods can be categorised by their temporal focus (e.g. Ness, Urbel-Piirsalu, Anderberg & Olsson, 2007), methodological approach (e.g. Sala et al., 2015), or measurement unit (e.g. Gasparatos & Scolobig, 2012). Because this work aims to implement the multilevel perspective (see Section 2.3.1; Rotmans et al., 2001), a categorisation by the aggregational size of an object of investigation is expedient. Figure 3.1 gives an overview on micro, meso, macro, and multilevel assessment methods.

As only multilevel methods are relevant, single level assessment methods are not further explained but only listed.

At the micro level, products or projects might be assessed. Major techniques for product assessment include life cycle costing, life cycle assessment, and contingent valuation. Details on these methods can be found in, e.g. Curran (1996); Finnveden et al. (2009); Finnveden and Moberg (2005); Finnveden and Östlund (1997); McWilliams and Siegel (2011); Ness et al. (2007); and Patterson et al. (2017). Projects can be appraised by cost benefit analysis or various impact assessment methods, such as environmental impact assessment or integrated sustainability assessment (e.g. Finnveden & Moberg, 2005; Ness et al., 2007; Petts, 1999a, 1999b; Pope et al., 2017; Sala et al., 2015; Weaver & Rotmans, 2006). Assessment tools for corporations include, for example, the sustainable value added and measures for relative sustainable performance (Cubas-Díaz & Martínez Sedano, 2018; Figge & Hahn, 2004; T. Hahn & Figge, 2011). Policy, plans, and programmes can be evaluated by the strategic environmental impact assessment (e.g. Finnveden & Moberg, 2005; Ness et al., 2007; Partidário, 1999; Therivel & Partidário, 1996). Probably the most prominent example of macro-level measurement is the ecological footprint by Wackernagel and Rees (1996).[20] Other macro-level environmental accounting or green accounting methods include the adjusted national accounts, in which key figures such as the GDP or the Net Domestic Product (NDP) and the Gross National Income (GNI) or the Net National Income (NNI) are greened (e.g. Bartelmus, 2018; Finnveden & Moberg, 2005; Hanley, 2000; Hueting & de Boer, 2018; Singh et al., 2012). Input-output analysis as well as system assessment and modelling, including vulnerability analysis, multiagent simulation models, Bayesian network models, and system dynamic models, are further macro tools (e.g. Boulanger & Bréchet, 2005; Costanza, Daly et al., 2016; Finnveden & Moberg, 2005; Ness et al., 2007; Patterson et al., 2017; Todorov & Marinova, 2011; Turner II et al., 2003).

Multilevel methods comprise, for instance, regression analysis, full cost accounting,

---

[20]The ecological footprint is often listed as an index (e.g. Saisana & Philippas, 2012; Singh, Murty, Gupta & Dikshit, 2012). However, Wackernagel et al. (2018) clarify it to be an environmental accounting system.

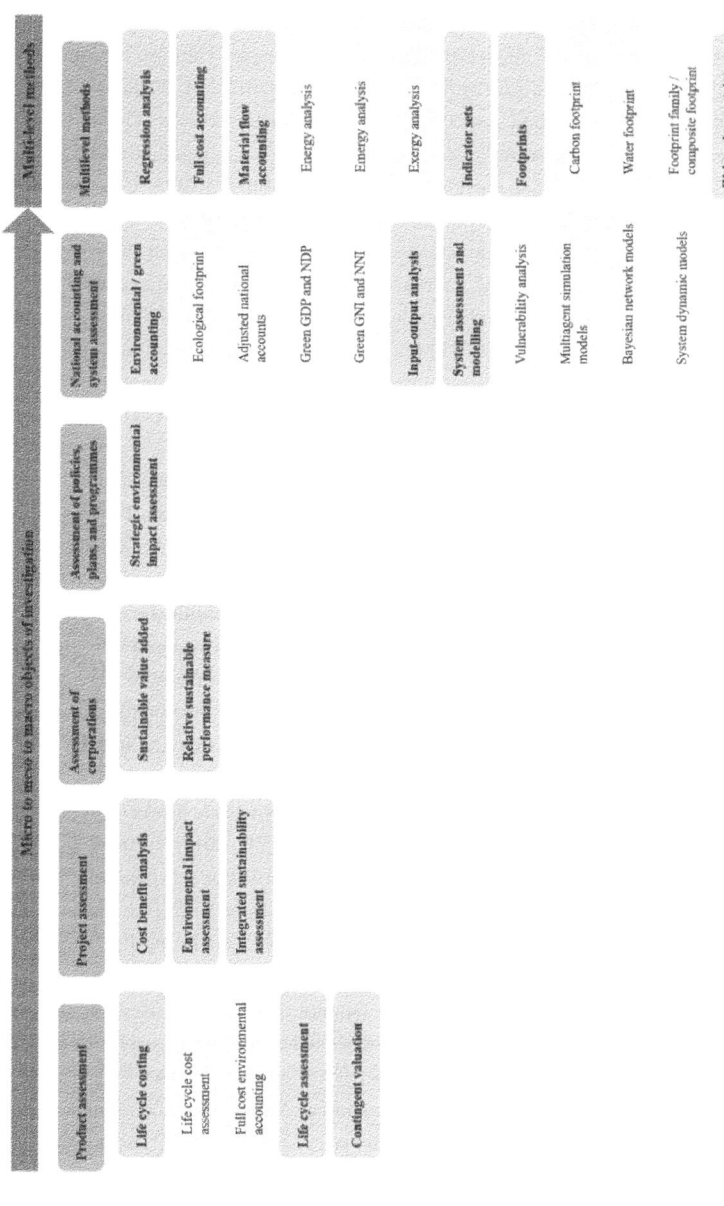

Figure 3.1 Overview of sustainable development assessment methods by the aggregational size of an object of investigation; GDP, Gross Domestic Product; GNI, Gross National Income; NDP, Net Domestic Product; NNI, Net National Income

material flow accounting, indicator sets, footprints, as well as risk and uncertainty analysis. Regression analysis studies the relationship of variables. Typically, there is one dependent variable and one or more independent variables. Examples in the field of sustainable development involve Aşıcı (2013); dos Santos Gaspar, Cardoso Marques and Fuinhas (2017); Gao and Bansal (2013); Godos-Díez et al. (2011); M. V. López, Garcia and Rodriguez (2007); Menegaki and Ozturk (2013); Menegaki and Tiwari (2017); and Testa et al. (2018). Because regression analysis requires a dependent variable and focuses on the relationship of few variables, it is not suitable nor able to capture the multiple facets of sustainable development. However, investigating relationships of variables (i.e. their synergies and trade-offs) remains important in closing the knowledge gap (see Section 2.3.3; e.g. Weitz et al., 2018). Full cost accounting is the assessment of costs arising from all three contentual domains. This method generally complies with the conceptual framework (see Figure 2.11) but involves the conversion of non-monetary units, such as physical units stemming from the environmental domain, to monetary units (e.g. G. D. Atkinson, 2000; Ness et al., 2007). Reasons for avoidance of this procedure will be discussed in Section 4.3.4. Material flow accounting deals with the flow of materials in production processes. Energy analysis, emergy analysis, and exergy analysis are examples of this method (e.g. Finnveden & Moberg, 2005; Finnveden & Östlund, 1997; Ness et al., 2007; Odum, 1996; Patterson et al., 2017; Wu & Wu, 2012). Due to its focus on materials, other elements of sustainable development are disregarded, and thus, a comprehensive picture of sustainable development cannot be drawn.

Indicator sets have played an important role in the debate on sustainable development assessment.[21] Practitioners as well as scientific scholars demanded the deployment of sustainable development indicators for a solid base for decision making since the 1990s (e.g. Antonini & Larrinaga, 2017; Baumgartner, 2014; Böhringer & Jochem, 2007; Cabeza Gutés, 1996; Costanza, Fioramonti & Kubiszewski, 2016; Eurostat, 2018; Kelley & Simmons, 2015; Nardo et al., 2008; Parris & Kates, 2003; Ramos & Moreno Pires, 2013; Singh et al., 2012; Spangenberg, 2015; UNCED, 1992; UNEP, 2011; Vermeulen, 2018; Wu & Wu, 2012). The reasons for this urge are manifold. Indicator sets generally have a high potential to comply with the sustainable development framework (see Figure 2.11) and the assessment principles (see Table 3.1). Indicators can be easily computed for a time series, the multiple facets of the contentual domains can be represented by individual indicators, an indicator set can be repetitively computed for diverse geographical regions, and indicators are – when designed accordingly (see Section 4.3.2 and Section 4.3.4) – capable of applying the multilevel perspective (see Section 2.3.1; Rotmans et al., 2001), ensuring object comparability. Moreover, each change agent group can contribute to the establishment and the use of indicators. Businesses may be objects of investigation and change agents simultaneously. On behalf of society, policy and science may decide upon the design of the indicator set or compute the set to

---

[21]Technical terms and definitions of indicators will be introduced in Section 3.3.

draw conclusions for management and policy making. Indicators further serve the last dimension of the sustainable development space: With indicators, the (often-forgotten) strategic tier can be addressed in addition to the operational tier (Baumgartner, 2014) because indicators can measure distances to strategic goals. Thereby, the operational-to-normative gap (see Section 2.3.2; e.g. Baumgartner & Rauter, 2017) is tackled. The normative tier does not need to be managed by the measurement because sustainable development indicators are inherently normative (Bakkes et al., 1994; Waas et al., 2014). The normative tier is a prerequisite dealt with in the conceptual phase (see Section 2.3.2) and later on reflected by the methodology (see Chapter 4). Indicator sets can follow societal instrumental finality by linking indicator targets to societal targets. For instance, thresholds of the planetary boundaries can be broken down into thresholds for micro, meso, or macro objects of investigation (e.g. O'Neill et al., 2018; Whiteman et al., 2013). However, further research is needed in this field (see Section 4.3.6.2) and will be discussed in Section 6.3. In fact, Section 3.3 will reveal that the possible linkage to reference values (i.e. targets and boundaries) is the defining feature of indicators. Paradox teleological integration and the acknowledgement of the coexistence of oppositional elements can be managed by individually pursuing targets of the indicators. Exploring sustainable development elements' synergies and trade-offs can be reached by including a composite measure in an indicator set (Costanza, Fioramonti & Kubiszewski, 2016; T. Hahn & Figge, 2011). Portraying both efficiency and effectiveness is feasible by incorporating relative as well as absolute values. With relative measures, relative decoupling of economic growth and environmental degradation (see Section 2.2.3) can be managed, a major challenge for decision makers (Holden et al., 2014). Enclosing absolute, non-standardised measures implies to sacrifice comparability and may therefore be only realised to some extent. Section 4.3.4 will further discuss this conflict. Given indicators' simplicity, they are practicable in computation, viable in stakeholder participation and consensus building (Parris & Kates, 2003), and effective in communication with the public at large (Spangenberg, 2015). A closure of the sustainability gap (see Section 2.3.4; e.g. Hall et al., 2017) can thus be yielded. Transparency and methodological soundness can be in place for any measurement method.

The main advantage of including a composite measure in an indicator set is the exploration of synergies and trade-offs, thereby addressing the knowledge gap (see Section 2.3.3; e.g. Weitz et al., 2018). Furthermore, comprising various indicators in an index implies presenting complexity in simple ways (Bell & Morse, 2018): A composite measure is a compressed description of a multidimensional state (Ebert & Welsch, 2004), providing a simple summary picture (Becker et al., 2017). Thereby, the important focus in measurement is recaptured (Griggs et al., 2014), such that a better understanding of the data is obtained (Jesinghaus, 2018), combating the disadvantage of a rich indicator set to potentially cause more confusion than understanding (Wu & Wu, 2012). Almássy and Pintér (2018); Costanza, Fioramonti and Kubiszewski (2016); Hanley et al. (1999);

Nardo et al. (2008); and Ramos and Moreno Pires (2013) even argue that sustainable development necessarily requires an index because it is a multifaceted concept that cannot be captured by standalone indicators, and GDP as a measure of wellbeing needs to be replaced. Moreover, an index further facilitates benchmarking (Almássy & Pintér, 2018; Ebert & Welsch, 2004), decision making (Bolis, Morioka & Sznelwar, 2017), and communication with policy, management, and the public (Becker et al., 2017; Moldan & Dahl, 2007; Ramos & Moreno Pires, 2013; Schmidt-Traub et al., 2017a).

Despite the manifold benefits, indicators and indices are critically discussed in the literature. First, (composite) indicators may not always be objective, precise, or certain. Subjectivity is inevitable (see Chapter 3; Bell & Morse, 2008) because it originates in the choices taken over the indicator computation method (Bondarchik, Jabłońska-Sabuka, Linnanen & Kauranne, 2016; Singh et al., 2012; Waas et al., 2014; Wu & Wu, 2012). Precision cannot be proven because sustainable development only becomes defined when measured (see Chapter 3; Bell & Morse, 2008). Uncertainty cannot be eliminated but only accounted for (see below). Second, indices are criticised for their defining characteristic: Aggregation implies weak sustainability, such that underperformance in one aspect can be compensated by overperformance in another aspect (Holden et al., 2017). This mechanism grants decision makers with mediating power, and they might be tempted to set low weights on underperforming elements and high weights on overperforming elements (Jesinghaus, 2018). Objections to this criticism are that on the one hand, non-compensatory aggregation functions that do not allow for compensation may be applied (see Section 4.3.8; Pollesch & Dale, 2015), and on the other hand, weak sustainability is permitted within the safe and just operating space in any case (see Section 2.2.4). Moreover, full freedom in weight definition should not be granted (Rogge, 2012), but weights should be set universally to minimise arbitrariness and subjectivity as well as to ensure comparability. Universal validity of weights (as well as, e.g. outlier handling) will be further discussed in Section 4.3.5 and Section 4.3.7. Third, given the complexity reduction, indices may invite narrow-minded pathways and simplistic management and policy conclusions (Nardo et al., 2008; Spangenberg, 2015). To counter this argument, conclusions should always be double checked with the subjacent layers. Finally, the computation of a meaningful, methodological sound index is difficult (Ebert & Welsch, 2004), and therefore, the computation of a sustainable development index might not be practicable for all change agent groups. Support might be required. A summary of the evaluation of indicator sets against the assessment principles is visualised in Figure 3.2a. Towards the interior of the radar chart, the assessment method is not capable of fulfilling the principle, and at the exterior, it is qualified to accomplish the principle.

A footprint is the quantification of direct and indirect effects of human activity on, for example, global warming (carbon footprint) or water reserves (water footprint) (e.g. Cucek, Klemes & Kravanja, 2012; Ewing et al., 2012; Galli, Weinzettel, Cranston

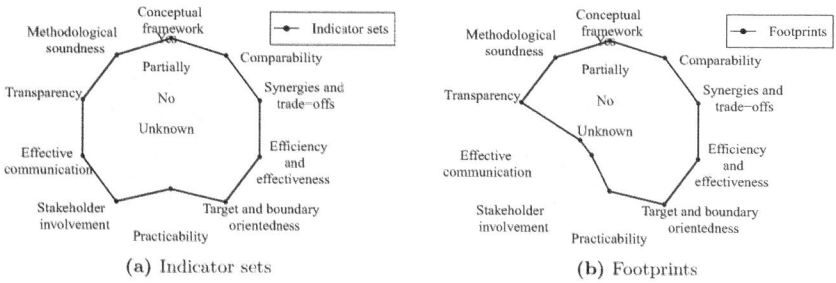

(a) Indicator sets   **(b)** Footprints

Figure 3.2 Capability evaluation of assessment principle compliance by indicator sets and footprints (based on Sala et al., 2015; with friendly permission of © 2015 The Authors)

& Ercin, 2013; Galli et al., 2012; Patterson et al., 2017). Given the possibility of computing a footprint for many variables and aggregating them into one composite measure, similar to indicator sets, footprints have a high potential of being in line with the conceptual framework (see Figure 2.11) and assessment principles (see Table 3.1). In contrast to indicators, footprints are informationally richer because they additionally include indirect effects. GRI (2016) sets the corporate standard to include upstream and downstream effects of direct suppliers and direct consumers (see Section 3.3.1). Though, to quantify total indirect effects of the entire value chain of upstream supply and downstream consumption, process methods or input-output analysis have to be applied and performed (Patterson et al., 2017). Similar to the computation of a sustainable development index, the computation of footprints might not be practicable for every change agent group. However, footprints do not produce easily understandable results as indices do, but outputs are rather complex. Stakeholders can neither be involved for acquiring legitimacy nor are footprints effective in communication. The analysis of footprints' compliance with the sustainable development assessment principles is shown in Figure 3.2b. Last, risk and uncertainty analysis are multilevel analyses, which can and should be performed after finalising any assessment in order to evaluate and minimise potential risks (Ness et al., 2007).

In conclusion, indicator sets that include a composite measure are the most successful assessment method in comprehensively quantifying sustainable development and tackling the first four identified research gaps: Comparability of micro, meso, and macro objects is ensured (perspective gap; see Section 2.3.1), each decisional tier can be addressed (operational-to-normative gap; see Section 2.3.2; e.g. Baumgartner & Rauter, 2017), synergies and trade-offs can be explored (knowledge gap; see Section 2.3.3; e.g. Weitz et al., 2018), and indicators are easily applicable (sustainability gap; see Section 2.3.4; e.g. Hall et al., 2017). In this respect, this work concentrates on sustainable development indicators and indices. The next section, Section 3.3, reviews previous indicator frameworks and indices. As a concluding remark, it is emphasised that the other presented methods are also valuable in the analysis of and transformation towards sustainable development. For instance, life cycle assessment is a crucial approach at micro level, indirectly supporting the macro SDG 12 on responsible consumption and production. Standalone micro, meso, and macro assessment approaches should complement multilevel methods.

3.3   Sustainable development indicators

An *indicator* is an operationalisation of a system characteristic (Gallopín, 1997; Waas et al., 2014; Wu & Wu, 2012), and an *indicator set* is a group of indicators used for a particular purpose (Wu & Wu, 2012). An indicator can be a *composite indicator*, also called *index*, which is a function of its underlying indicators (Saltelli et al., 2008; Waas et al., 2014). As already pointed out in Section 3.2, comparability to reference values is the defining feature of indicators: A variable becomes an indicator when it is linked to a reference value or a benchmark (Waas et al., 2014). These can be targets or thresholds, expressing a normal or a desired state. Consequently, an indicator can assess progress while a variable cannot. To determine useful reference values, system knowledge and understanding is necessary (Wu & Wu, 2012). Examples of such macro-level system knowledge are the planetary boundaries (see Section 2.2.1; Steffen et al., 2015) and industry benchmarks, enabling to judge and pin down a corporation's performance at meso level (Cubas-Díaz & Martínez Sedano, 2018; Figge & Hahn, 2004).

The next sections review meso (composite) indicators (see Section 3.3.1 and Section 3.3.2) and macro indices (see Section 3.3.3) and examine their conformity with the assessment principles (see Table 3.1). Reference to synergies and trade-offs is not made because they are inherent in indices (see Section 4.3.7). Methodological soundness will be investigated in Section 4.2. Macro indicator frameworks are not included in this section as the most elaborated framework – the SDGs – has been covered in Section 2.3.3. This section neither contains a section on micro nor multilevel indices. Micro indicator frameworks could not be identified, and only one micro index – the Better Life Index (BLI) (OECD, 2017) – could be detected. It is listed along with macro subjective indices in Section 3.3.3. Multilevel indices could not be traced at all; disregarding the multilevel perspective (see Section 2.3.1; Rotmans et al., 2001) is a general shortcoming of sustainable development measurement and assessment methods and consequently the main theoretical, methodological, and empirical contribution of this work.

3.3.1   Corporate indicator frameworks

Indicator frameworks can serve management control purposes (Parris & Kates, 2003) and are therefore used by corporations to integrate sustainable development into strategy (e.g. Bui & de Villiers, 2018; Gond, Grubnic, Herzig & Moon, 2012; Wijethilake, 2017; Witjes et al., 2017). The most widely used standard for corporate reporting on sustainable development indicators is the GRI framework, used by 63% of reporting companies in 2017 (KPMG, 2017).[22] The GRI standard was established in the 1990s with the goal to provide a trusted and credible framework (Ogata, Inoue, Ueda & Yagi, 2018) that "can be used by an organisation of any size, type, sector, or geographic location" (GRI, 2016) to quantify corporate contributions to sustainable development. The framework is divided into six disclosures: an organisation's reporting principles, reporting practices, management approach, and indicators of the three contentual domains. Details on the currently valid standard can be found in GRI (2016).[23] Given the large variety of topic coverage, the GRI framework can be considered as comprehensively picturing sustainable development contributions. Within the world of business, comparability is enhanced by creating a common language (GRI, 2016). However, the framework is criticised for following the business case of sustainable development (Landrum & Ohsowski, 2018) instead of engaging in societal instrumental finality and paradox teleological integration. The author of this work does not agree on this criticism because first, the GRI standard is a reporting standard that does not provide integrated information on the importance of the individually reported indicators, such that dominance of one aspect over the other is not a subject matter. Second, reports are released to guide business in their alignment with the societal level SDGs (GRI & UNGC, 2018a, 2018b; GRI, UNGC & WBCSD, 2015, 2017), which follow societal instrumental finality and paradox teleological integration by definition. Antonini and Larrinaga (2017) criticise GRI reports for not including boundary values. To set against, the science community is required to derive meaningful corporate boundaries from the macro level; first research exists, but more work is necessary to integrate boundaries into corporate practice (see Section 3.2 and Section 6.3; e.g. Haffar & Searcy, 2018; Whiteman et al., 2013).

Further sustainable development reporting standards for corporations involve, for instance, the Prince's Accounting for Sustainability Project (A4S), Integrated Reporting <IR> by the International Integrated Reporting Council (IIRC), and the Sustainability Accounting Standards Boards (SASB) (A4S, 2018; IIRC, 2013; Ogata et al., 2018; SASB, 2018). These are not further considered because of their deviating focus (e.g. on finance and investment). An overview of corporate reporting tools on sustainable development can be found in, e.g. Siew (2015).

---

[22]Sample: 4,900 top 100 companies in terms of revenues in 49 countries.
[23]Minor updates will become effective in 2021 (GRI, 2019).

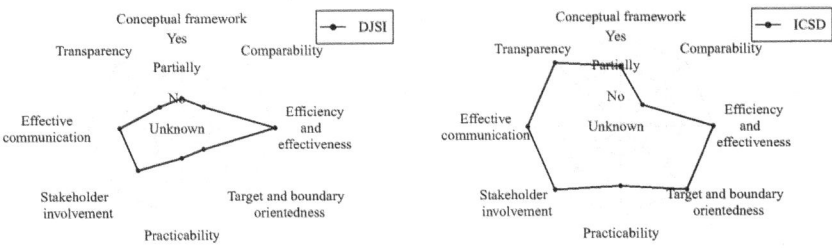

(a) Dow Jones Sustainability Indices (DJSI) (e.g. RobecoSAM, 2018a)

(b) Composite Sustainable Development Index (ICSD) (Krajnc & Glavič, 2005)

Figure 3.3 Evaluation of assessment principle compliance by meso-level indices of sustainable development

3.3.2   Meso-level indices

According to the multilevel perspective by Rotmans et al. (2001; see Section 2.3.1), meso-level indices are metrics for networks, communities, or organisations such as corporations. Two expedient meso-level indices for the assessment of sustainable development contributions by corporations are identified and discussed in the following.

The family of the DJSI aims to provide investors with benchmarks of corporate performances for "managing their sustainability investment portfolios" (S&P Dow Jones Indices, 2018). Aspects of sustainable development are widely covered (RobecoSAM, 2018a). However, the indices' objective misses the conceptual framework of sustainable development by definition: Societal instrumental finality is clearly not the purpose but management of investment is (RobecoSAM, 2019). The non-transparent presentation of the DJSI hampers its evaluation against the assessment principles. The methodology report (S&P Dow Jones Indices, 2018) as well as further documents available on the RobecoSAM website (RobecoSAM, 2018c) neither deliver a clear picture. Examining the available information, it seems that the DJSI involve both efficiency and effectiveness measures. However, it seems that the DJSI are neither comparable,[24] nor target oriented or practicable, but corporations can apply and are invited for an assessment. Therefore, stakeholder involvement is reduced. Effective communication may also be harmed, given the great number of indices and low transparency. In conclusion, the DJSI are inappropriate instruments in assessing corporate contributions to sustainable development. However, they may be valuable for investors. Figure 3.3a summarises the DJSI's properties, evaluated against the assessment principles.

In contrast, the ICSD was explicitly developed to monitor corporate contributions to sustainable development (Krajnc & Glavič, 2005). The data input of this index is based on the GRI framework, generally ensuring data quality and coverage of the

---

[24]This conclusion is drawn from the floating and industry-specific weights (see Section 4.2; RobecoSAM, 2018b; S&P Dow Jones Indices, 2018, 2019).

three contentual domains. However, the social domain is not sufficiently dealt with, for example, aspects concerning equality (SDG 5 on gender equality) are missing. Furthermore, profits enter the economic domain despite the fact that they are not key to sustainable development (see Section 2.2.3 and Section 2.3.2; e.g. Vermeulen, 2018). Comparability is not ensured because indicators are standardised to the unit of production, which is further discussed in Section 4.3.4. However, absolute as well as relative values are included, and targets are set. Given the ICSD's transparency and simple structure, this index is practicable (as far as possible, see Figure 3.2a), suitable for stakeholder involvement, and effective in communication. The appraisal of this index against the assessment principles is visualised in Figure 3.3b.

Several authors engage in the construction of corporate social responsibility indices (e.g. Amor-Esteban, Galindo-Villardón & García-Sánchez, 2018; Gjølberg, 2009; Ruf, Muralidhar & Paul, 1998; Skouloudis, Isaac & Evaggelinos, 2016). Such indices generally fail in complying with the conceptual framework because corporate social responsibility seeks to eliminate negative effects of businesses instead of actively contributing to sustainable development (see Section 2.3.2; e.g. Bansal & Song, 2017). Further indices can be found in, e.g. Singh et al. (2012). However, these indices are unrewarding for the comparable measurement of contributions to sustainable development by micro, meso, and macro objects and are thus not further investigated.

3.3.3 Macro-level indices

GDP plays a central role in macro-level measurement of sustainable development because GDP is the most widely used measure of macro-economic performances (see Section 2.2.3; Giannetti et al., 2015). Macro-level measures of sustainable development seek to replace GDP by going beyond economic performance and are thus called *GDP alternatives*. The SDGs might be a potential vehicle for GDP alternatives, which can be classified into three types: adjusted economic measures, subjective measures of wellbeing, and weighted composite indicators of wellbeing (Costanza et al., 2014). Adjusted economic measures are macro-economic measures in monetary units that are supplemented with environmental and social aspects. Examples include the Eco Domestic Product (EDP) (e.g. Hanley, 2000), Genuine Progress Indicator (GP) (e.g. Lawn, 2003), Genuine Savings Indicator (GS) (e.g. Pearce & Atkinson, 1993; Pearce, Hamilton & Atkinson, 2001), Index of Sustainable Economic Welfare (ISEW) (e.g. Beça & Santos, 2010; Costanza & Daly, 1992; H. E. Daly & Cobb, 1989), Inclusive Wealth Index (IW) (e.g. Dasgupta, 2010), and the Sustainable Net Benefit Index (SNBI) (e.g. Böhringer & Jochem, 2007; Mayer, 2008; Saisana & Philippas, 2012; Singh et al., 2012; van den Bergh, 2009). As this type of measure can only be applied at the macro level and quantifies sustainable economic welfare instead of sustainable development as a whole (Lawn, 2003), it cannot serve the research question of the present work. Subjective welfare measures are survey-based metrics and aspire to quantify subjective wellbeing. The BLI (e.g. OECD, 2017),[25] Compass Index of Sustainability (CIS) (e.g. Atkisson & Hatcher, 2001), Gross National Happiness (GNH) (e.g. CBS & GNH Research, 2016), and the Happy Planet Index (HPI) (e.g. Bondarchik et al., 2016; NEF, 2012) are examples of (at least partially) subjective welfare measures. Subjective wellbeing highly varies between societies and cultures. A universal and comparable measure is difficult to obtain (Costanza et al., 2014), which is not in line with the conceptual framework of being universally applicable (see Section 2.1; WSSD, 2002) and the assessment principle objectivity (see Table 3.1; Sala et al., 2015). Thus, subjective measures of welfare are not further considered. Last, weighted composite indicators of wellbeing give a comprehensive picture of sustainable societal wellbeing (Costanza et al., 2014), capturing the notion of sustainable development as a whole. A prerequisite for comprehensiveness is the inclusion of the three contentual domains. Indices that omit one domain are disregarded. Examples include the Composite Environmental Performance Index (CEPI) (e.g. García-Sánchez, das Neves Almeida & de Barros Camara, 2015), Environmental Performance Index (EPI) (e.g. Esty & Emerson, 2018), Environmental Sustainability Index (ESI), Environmental Vulnerability Index (EVI) (e.g. Dahl, 2018), and the Living Planet Index (LPI) (e.g. WWF, 1998). Moreover, the suggestion that both subjective and objective indicators should be integrated (Costanza et al., 2007; Costanza et al., 2014) is not followed because it would violate the assessment principle objectivity (see Table 3.1; Sala et al., 2015). In the following, seven macro-level indices that include the three contentual domains of sustainable development are examined: the Fondazione Eni Enrico Mattei Sustainability Index (FEEM SI), Human Sustainable Development Index (HSDI), Mega Index of Sustainable Development (MISD), SDGI, Sustainable Development Index (SDI), SSI, and the Wellbeing Index (WI). An overview on the mentioned GDP alternatives, sorted by their capability of capturing sustainable development, is displayed in Figure 3.4.

The FEEM SI is an index that projects future evolution of macro-economic contributions to sustainable development by being based on a general equilibrium model. It is able to generate scenarios under different policy assumptions (Carraro et al., 2013; Pinar, Cruciani, Giove & Sostero, 2014) and is therefore a macro-economic tool that supports target setting and policy making for the transition to sustainability. It can neither be transferred to micro nor meso objects but disregards the multilevel perspective (see Figure 3.5a). Because of the modelling complexity, it is neither practicable, effective in communication, nor can stakeholders be involved. On the positive side, the index includes efficiency as well as effectiveness and is transparent.

The HSDI is a composite measure that investigates the aggregate of four indicators: life expectancy at birth, years of schooling, purchasing power adjusted GDP p.c., and

---

[25]The BLI is a micro index quantifying "whether life is getting better for people" (OECD, 2017). It is listed in this section as it is the only identified micro index (see Section 3.3).

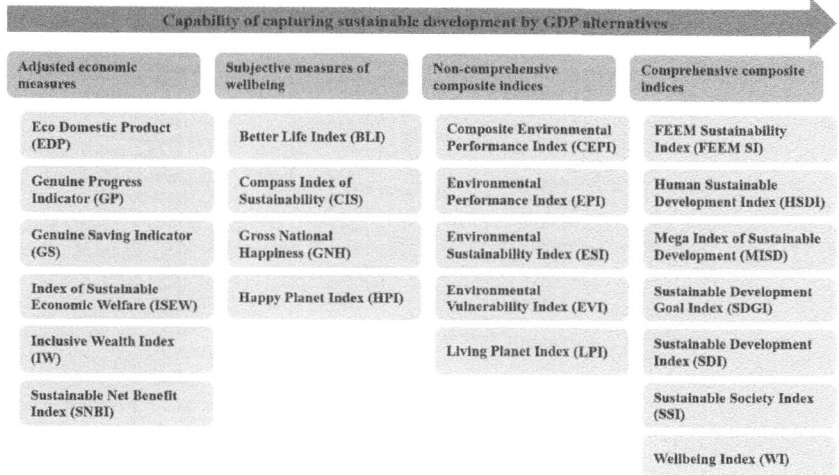

Figure 3.4 Overview of Gross Domestic Product (GDP) alternatives

Greenhouse Gas (GHG) emissions p.c. (Bravo, 2014, 2018; Singh et al., 2012; Togtokh, 2011; Togtokh & Gaffney, 2010; UNDP, 1990).[26] Given its few variables, this index is neither able to comprehensively map the environmental domain (Bravo, 2014, 2018) nor sustainable development as a whole (see Figure 3.5b). Furthermore, the index cannot be computed in a meaningful way for businesses. However, it can be universally applied to different regions, it includes absolute values (e.g. life expectancy at birth) and relative values (e.g. GHG emissions p.c.), and targets and boundaries are set (e.g. 100% literacy rate) (UNDP, 1990). Given the HSDI's simplicity, it is practicable (as far as possible, see Figure 3.2a), stakeholders can be involved, and results can be communicated effectively. Its methodology and data are transparent.

The MISD is a function of 31 known indices (Shaker, 2015, 2018), which makes an evaluation with the assessment principles difficult. Transparency is only given partially, and the principles comparability, efficiency and effectiveness, as well as target and boundary orientedness remain unknown (see Figure 3.5c). A mega index is not practicable because a huge variety of methods are implemented. The complexity also harms stakeholder involvement and effective communication.

Apart from the Global Burden of Disease Index (GBDI), which is a health-related index, the SDGI is the only index that is clearly linked to the SDGs (Lim et al., 2016; Schmidt-Traub et al., 2017a, 2017b). Therefore, it is a highly relevant candidate in comparably quantifying contributions to sustainable development. By definition, it maps the sustainable development domains well and is universally applicable to any

---

[26]The HSDI is a successor of the Human Development Index (HDI), which did not include GHG emissions p.c. (UNDP, 1990).

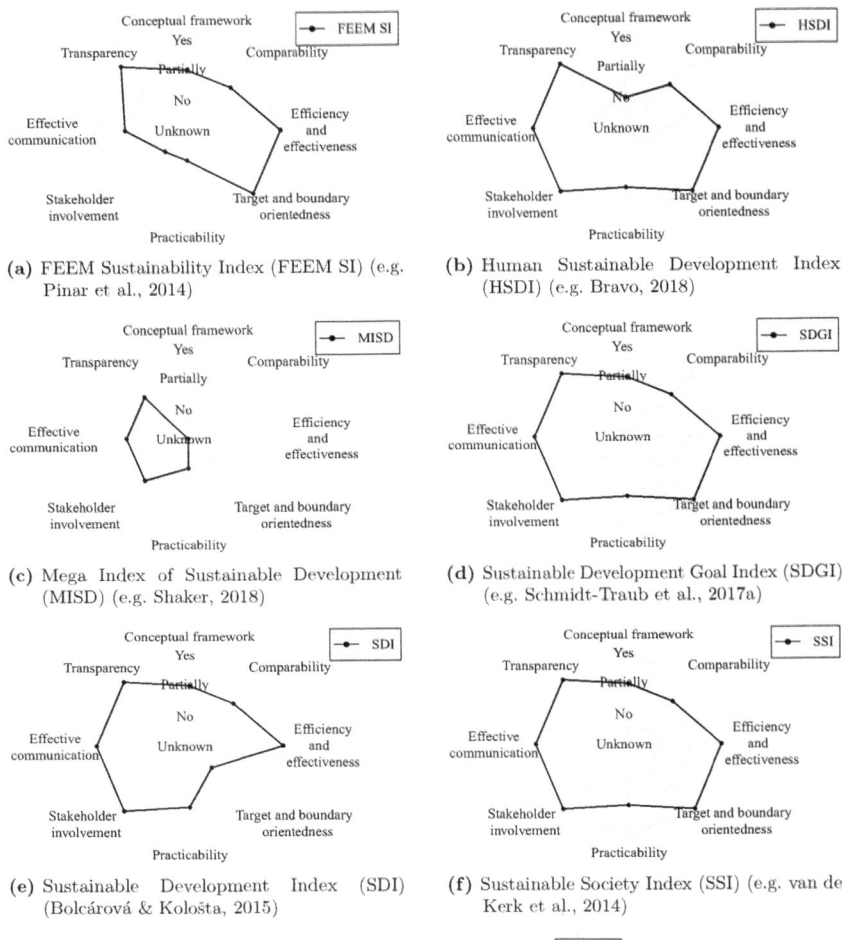

(a) FEEM Sustainability Index (FEEM SI) (e.g. Pinar et al., 2014)

(b) Human Sustainable Development Index (HSDI) (e.g. Bravo, 2018)

(c) Mega Index of Sustainable Development (MISD) (e.g. Shaker, 2018)

(d) Sustainable Development Goal Index (SDGI) (e.g. Schmidt-Traub et al., 2017a)

(e) Sustainable Development Index (SDI) (Bolcárová & Košta, 2015)

(f) Sustainable Society Index (SSI) (e.g. van de Kerk et al., 2014)

(g) Wellbeing Index (WI) (Prescott-Allen, 2001)

Figure 3.5 Evaluation of assessment principle compliance by macro-level indices of sustainable development

geographical region (see Figure 3.5d). However, its macro-economic focus and resulting indicator selection prevents it to be applicable to micro and meso objects. Efficiency as well as effectiveness are measured, targets are included in terms of the SDG agenda or top five performers, and the transparent presentation enables stakeholder involvement as well as effective communication.

The SDI aims to quantify a country's contribution to macro-level sustainable development. It includes 12 indicators in areas such as socio-economic development, sustainable consumption and production, social inclusion, demographic changes, public health, climate change and energy, sustainable transport, natural resources, and global partnership (Bolcárová & Kološta, 2015). The SDI maps the contentual domains of sustainable development well and is universally applicable to different countries (see Figure 3.5e). However, given its indicator selection, a computation for micro and meso objects is not possible, such that comparability across aggregational sizes is not enabled. Absolute and relative indicators are present, but targets and boundaries are not included. Its simplicity further ensures practicability (as far as possible, see Figure 3.2a), stakeholder involvement, and effective communication. The assessment principle transparency is complied with.

The SSI also aspires to measure macro-level sustainable development of countries, and contains 21 indicators in the categories basic needs, health, personal and social development, natural resources, climate and energy, transition, and economy (Saisana & Philippas, 2012; van de Kerk & Manuel, 2008; van de Kerk et al., 2014). It generally complies with the conceptual framework by depicting the contentual domains well and by being universally applicable; scores for 151 countries are computed (see Figure 3.5f). However, it is only computable for macro objects, and the multilevel perspective is dismissed. Data and methods are transparently disclosed; targets are included in terms of a sustainability value, and efficiency as well as effectiveness are included. Practicability, stakeholder involvement, and effective communication are ensured.

Last, the WI is an index that comprises 87 indicators, thereof 36 indicators that summarise human wellbeing and 51 indicators that aggregate into ecosystem wellbeing. Topics covered are health and population, wealth, knowledge and culture, community, equity, land, water, air, species and genes, and resource use (Mayer, 2008; Prescott-Allen, 2001). The contentual domains of sustainable development are mapped well, but this index features the same shortcomings as the previously mentioned indices: It is not compliant with the multilevel perspective, disabling comparability across aggregational sizes (see Figure 3.5g). However, the WI is in line with the further assessment principles.

Summarising, the review yields following conclusions:

1. Multilevel indices do not exist, and the reviewed indices' scopes and objectives disable multilevel applications.

2. If indices encompass the three contentual domains (a prerequisite of this review),

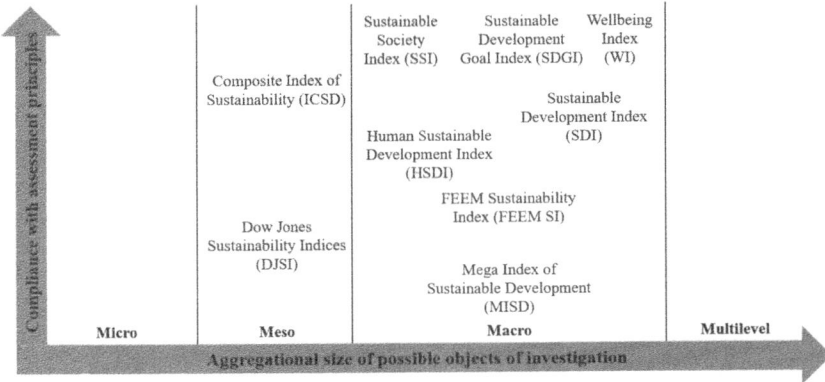

Figure 3.6 Ranking of sustainable development indices by assessment principle compliance

they are generally comprehensive.

3. Comparability within an aggregational level is generally ensured but benchmarking of micro, meso, and macro objects is not.

4. Efficiencies and effectiveness are mostly mapped.

5. Targets and boundaries are mostly included. However, these are subjective, corporate or policy targets. Their scientific derivation has emerged only recently, and further research is needed (see Section 6.3; e.g. O'Neill et al., 2018; Whiteman et al., 2013).

6. Practicability is mostly given (as far as possible) as well as stakeholder involvement, effective communication, and transparency.

Figure 3.6 ranks the investigated sustainable development indices by their compliance with the assessment principles, sorted by their aggregational sizes.

3.4 Summary

Measurement and assessment of sustainable development is inevitable; only what is measured can be managed. With measurement and assessment, both modes of sustainable development – the descriptive-analytical and the transformational mode – are addressed. Knowledge is generated to serve informed decision making. In search of suitable assessment methods, the first four identified research gaps provide guidance: First, a sustainable development assessment method is required to comparably measure contributions to sustainable development by micro, meso, and macro objects (perspective gap); second, it must be capable of supporting decisions at operational, strategic, and

normative tier (operational-to-normative gap); third, it is demanded to investigate
interlinkages of the individual sustainable development elements (knowledge gap);
and fourth, it must be easily applicable to put the crafted knowledge into practice
(sustainability gap). To be able to systematically determine a method's potential in
approaching these gaps, sustainable development assessment principles are reviewed first.
By summarising and harmonising this review, ten assessment principles are yielded:
compliance with framework; comparability in all sustainable development dimensions;
synergies and trade-offs of interconnected themes and goals; efficiency and effectiveness
of impacts; target and boundary orientedness of individual sustainable development
elements; practicability for decision makers; stakeholder involvement for legitimacy;
effective communication to stakeholders; transparency of data, methods, and results;
and methodological soundness. Second, multilevel assessment methods are evaluated
based on these principles. Indicator sets that include a weighted composite indicator
(i.e. a sustainable development index) result to be the most successful assessment
method in tackling the first four identified research gaps. Two meso-level and seven
macro-level indices are identified: the DJSI, ICSD, FEEM SI, HSDI, MISD, SDGI,
SDI, SSI, and the WI. Examining these indices, substantial lacks in the assessment
principles are ascertained. These involve, for instance, the non-comprehensive depiction
of sustainable development elements, the violation of societal instrumental finality,
and lacks in transparency. Moreover, multilevel indices could not be identified in
the literature despite their compelling necessity, demonstrating the expansion of the
perspective gap, which regards the conceptual framework, into methods and empirical
findings. The multilevel perspective is neglected in the conceptual framework, leading to
an absence of multilevel indices. This in turn results in a lack of multilevel comparable
empirical findings. Given these deficiencies, this work develops a new index – the
MLSDI – that comparably measures multilevel contributions to sustainable development,
supports decisions at all tiers, comprehensively studies interconnections of sustainable
development elements, and is applicable in practice. The MLSDI's methodology follows
in the next chapter, Chapter 4.

Chapter 4

Methodology

Because sustainable development only becomes defined when measured (see Chapter 3; e.g. Bell & Morse, 2008), sustainable development index construction is an unsupervised modelling task without a supervising output variable (G. James, Witten, Hastie & Tibshirani, 2013). Consequently, sustainable development measurement is diverse in methods and methodologies (see Section 3.2, Section 3.3, and Section 4.2) and hallmarked by subjectivity and arbitrariness (e.g. Böhringer & Jochem, 2007), such that sustainable development indicators are rather confusing and non-consensual (Pope et al., 2017; Ramos & Moreno Pires, 2013). To counteract this finding and to achieve objectivity in assessment (see Table 3.1; Sala et al., 2015), the previous theoretical research is coupled with a profound methodological research. The conceptual framework derived in Chapter 2 has resulted in assessment principles in Section 3.1, and these now guide the methodological choices to be made from a pool of alternative techniques for each index calculation step. Thereby, methodological shortcomings of previous indices are overcome, which constitute the fifth and last research gap. Moreover, methodological understanding of the interactions of the individual sustainable development elements will be established by the end of this chapter: The knowledge gap (see Section 2.3.3; e.g. Weitz et al., 2018) is addressed by the index computation (see Section 3.2).

The first part of this chapter, Section 4.1, introduces the calculation steps of a sustainable development index and establishes methodological requirements based on the assessment principles in Section 3.1. By means of these requirements, the methodological approaches of the indices identified in Section 3.3.2 and Section 3.3.3 are evaluated in Section 4.2. The main part of this chapter, Section 4.3, addresses the MLSDI's methodology. First, data are collected (see Section 4.3.1), prepared (see Section 4.3.2 and Section 4.3.4), and cleaned (see Section 4.3.3 and Section 4.3.5); second, the major index computation steps are executed (see Section 4.3.6 to Section 4.3.8); and third, sensitivities are investigated (see Section 4.3.9). This chapter ends with a summary and interim conclusion in Section 4.4 that conflate the theoretical investigation of Chapter 2 and Chapter 3 as well as the methodological research of this chapter.

© The Author(s) 2021
C. Lemke, *Accounting and Statistical Analyses for Sustainable Development*, Sustainable Management, Wertschöpfung und Effizienz, https://doi.org/10.1007/978-3-658-33246-4_4

4.1 Overview of sustainable development indices' calculation steps and methodological requirements

Sustainable development indices are typically constructed in nine steps. These are visualised in Figure 4.1, and a primer can be found in Nardo et al. (2008). The first calculation step comprises the *collection of sustainable development key figures* (see Section 4.3.1). Key figures are the raw data to collect. For transparency (see Table 3.1; e.g. Pintér et al., 2018), data acquisition should be open access. The *preparation of sustainable development key figures* is realised in the second calculation step (see Section 4.3.2) and is necessary because data from different aggregational objects (micro, meso, and macro) must be harmonised for multilevel object comparability (see Table 3.1; e.g. Hacking & Guthrie, 2008) and methodological soundness in terms of credibility, validity, and reliability (see Table 3.1; e.g. Cash et al., 2003; Janoušková et al., 2018). This step is typically not included in sustainable development index calculations because Rotmans et al.'s (2001; see Section 2.3.1) multilevel perspective is disregarded (see Section 3.3.2 and Section 3.3.3). *Imputation of missing values* is performed (see Section 4.3.3) to turn the key figures' incomplete data set into a complete one (van Buuren, 2012), reducing statistical biases (e.g. Little & Rubin, 2002) and ensuring the assessment principle methodological soundness (see step two). Imputation is deployed on key figures (i.e. the raw data) in order to prevent possible biases that would arise from afore-going calculations such as standardisation accomplished in the next step. *Standardisation to sustainable development key indicators* is realised with the complete sample of key figures (see Section 4.3.4). It accounts for different aggregational sizes of micro, meso, and macro objects of investigation and ensures the assessment principle multilevel object comparability (see Table 3.1; e.g. Hacking & Guthrie, 2008). Moreover, the key indicators are primarily in charge of the assessment principle compliance with framework (see Table 3.1; e.g. Pintér et al., 2018). For instance, the key indicators critically determine the comprehensiveness (e.g. Böhringer & Jochem, 2007) and capability of multilevel application of an index because the key indicators are an index's data input. Both key figures and key indicators are variables in terms of input data at certain stages of an index. In this context, Waas et al.'s (2014; see Section 3.3) finding that a variable becomes an indicator when linked to a reference value is disregarded. In order to prevent misunderstandings, the term "variable" is only used in general contexts of a method's input data, and when referring to input data of a sustainable development index, "key figure" or "key indicator" is quoted, respectively. Furthermore, a methodologically sound index only contains relevant key indicators (see Table 3.1; Janoušková et al., 2018) and maps both efficiencies and effectivenesses of sustainable development performances (see Table 3.1; e.g. Figge & Hahn, 2004).

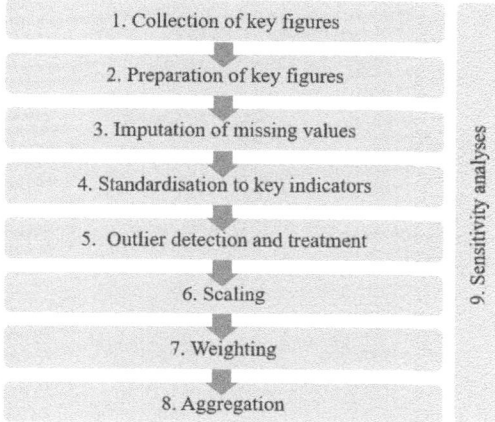

1. Collection of key figures

2. Preparation of key figures

3. Imputation of missing values

4. Standardisation to key indicators

5. Outlier detection and treatment

6. Scaling

7. Weighting

8. Aggregation

9. Sensitivity analyses

Figure 4.1 Calculation steps of a sustainable development index

In the fifth calculation step, *outlier detection and treatment* is conducted (see Section 4.3.5) to diminish statistical biases (Hadi, Rahmatullah Imon & Werner, 2009) and once more induce methodological soundness (see step two). Key indicators' instead of key figures' outliers are treated because outliers primarily impact scales, which are computed with the key indicators in the next step (see step six). For detection and treatment, a perspective of information loss should be adopted, and statistical bias should be balanced with distortion of the true picture (e.g. McGregor & Pouw, 2017; Zhou, Fan & Zhou, 2010). *Scaling* the key indicators (sixth step) harmonises the key indicators' diverse units (see Section 4.3.6). This step complies with the assessment principle indicator comparability (see Table 3.1; e.g. Pintér et al., 2018) and methodological soundness (see step two) because scaling is essential for a meaningful aggregation to be realised in the eighth calculation step (see step eight; e.g. Ebert & Welsch, 2004). Because different types of scales contain distinct degrees of information, the chosen scaling procedure should minimise loss of information (e.g. Zhou et al., 2010). Moreover, scales should empower compliance with the assessment principles target and boundary orientedness (see Table 3.1; e.g. Sala et al., 2015) as well as effective communication (see Table 3.1; e.g. Pintér et al., 2018). A further clarification of terminology is required: Both standardisation and scaling are concerned with transformation of different scales onto one common scale. "Normalisation" is a further synonym (Pollesch & Dale, 2016). To avoid misunderstandings between the fourth calculation step – standardisation of the key figures to the key indicators for multilevel object comparability (see Section 4.3.4) – and the sixth calculation step – scaling the key indicators for indicator comparability (see Section 4.3.6) – the terms "standardisation" and "scaling" are exclusively used for their respective purposes. The expression "normalisation" remains unused.

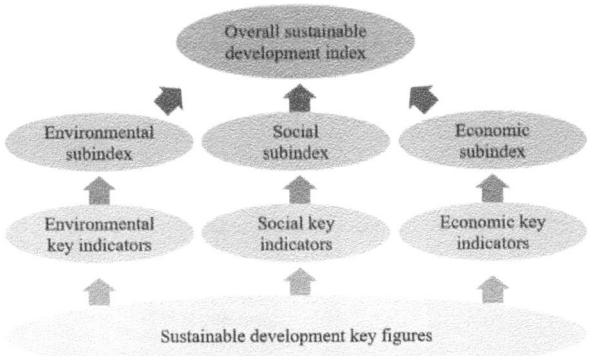

Figure 4.2 Layers of an overall sustainable development index

The seventh calculation step accomplishes *weighting* of scaled key indicators (see Section 4.3.7). This step is essential for assessing relationships among the data (e.g. Greco, Ishizaka, Tasiou & Torrisi, 2019) and accounting for synergies and trade-offs (see Table 3.1; e.g. Costanza, Fioramonti & Kubiszewski, 2016). Thereby, it is the substantive step in closing the knowledge gap (see Section 2.3.3; e.g. Weitz et al., 2018). In doing so, methodological soundness in terms of objectivity (see Table 3.1; Sala et al., 2015) and relevance should be guaranteed (see Table 3.1; Janoušková et al., 2018). The eighth step performs *aggregation* (see Section 4.3.8). First, scaled and weighted key indicators are aggregated into sustainable development subindices of each contentual domain. Second, these are combined to an overall sustainable development index. Figure 4.2 visualises the layers of an overall sustainable development index. The implemented aggregation function moderates the degree of substitutability (Grabisch, Marichal, Mesiar & Pap, 2009) and is hence guided by the allowance of weak sustainability with minimised substitutability within the safe and just operating space for humanity (see Section 2.2.4). Furthermore, the aggregation function must interplay meaningfully with the underlying scales for methodological soundness (see step six; e.g. Ebert & Welsch, 2004) and also minimise loss of information (e.g. Zhou et al., 2010). Last, *sensitivity analyses* are carried out for calculation steps that provide alternatives (see Section 4.3.9). The aim is to ensure methodological soundness in terms of credibility, validity, reliability, and robustness (see Table 3.1; e.g. Cash et al., 2003; Janoušková et al., 2018; Sala et al., 2015) and enhance transparency (see Table 3.1; e.g. Pintér et al., 2018). In case of the MLSDI sensitivities are tested for missing value imputation, outlier detection, and weighting. For the other calculation steps, the theoretical and methodological research points to one unique approach.

Methodological soundness is emphasised in individual calculation steps despite being effective in each step and the overall computation. Table 4.1 provides a summary of the

Calculation step	Guiding assessment principle and further criteria
1. Collection of key figures	Transparency
2. Preparation of key figures	Multilevel object comparability, methodological soundness (credibility, validity, reliability)
3. Imputation of missing values	Methodological soundness (see step two)
4. Standardisation to key indicators	Comprehensiveness, multilevel object comparability, methodological soundness (relevance), efficiency and effectiveness
5. Outlier detection and treatment	Methodological soundness (see step two), balanced information loss
6. Scaling	Indicator comparability, methodological soundness (see step two), minimum information loss, target and boundary orientedness, effective communication
7. Weighting	Synergies and trade-offs, methodological soundness (objectivity, relevance)
8. Aggregation	Weak sustainability with minimised substitutability, methodological soundness (see step two), minimum information loss
9. Sensitivity analyses	Methodological soundness (credibility, validity, reliability, robustness), transparency

Table 4.1 Assignment of the guiding assessment principles and further criteria to the calculation steps of a sustainable development index

assignment of the guiding assessment principles and further criteria to the calculation steps of a sustainable development index. Based on this assignment, methodological approaches of the nine identified sustainable development indices (see Section 3.3.2 and Section 3.3.3) are evaluated in the following section, Section 4.2. In contrast to the indices' evaluation in Section 3.3.2 and Section 3.3.3, methodological soundness and the assessment principles' connection to an index's major calculation steps – step six to step nine – are focused on.

4.2 Methodological evaluation of sustainable development indices

The first evaluated index in Section 3.3.2 is the family of DJSI (e.g. S&P Dow Jones Indices, 2018, 2019). It has been concluded that the DJSI are not presented transparently. In this vein, data cleaning (missing value imputation and outlier treatment), sensitivity

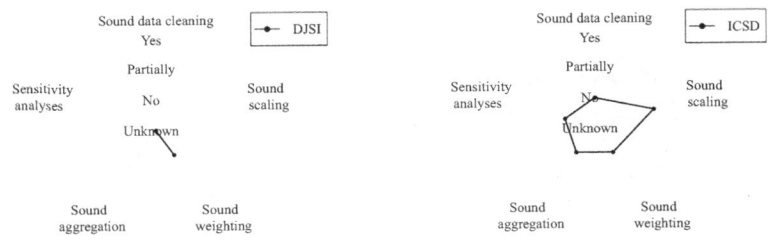

(a) Dow Jones Sustainability Indices (DJSI) (e.g.
S&P Dow Jones Indices, 2018)

(b) Composite Sustainable Development Index
(ICSD) (Krajnc & Glavič, 2005)

Figure 4.3 Evaluation of methodological soundness and linkage to assessment principles by
meso-level indices of sustainable development

analyses, scaling, and aggregation are unknown. Full information on weighting is not
provided, but it is announced that weights are floating and industry specific. Individual
weight adjustment should be refrained from because it disables comparability (see
Section 4.3.6.2; Nardo et al., 2008) and grants developers mediating power, setting
low weights on underperforming elements (see Section 3.2; Jesinghaus, 2018). The
evaluation of the DJSI's methodological soundness and major calculation steps' linkage
to assessment principles is portrayed in Figure 4.3a.[27]

The other identified micro-level sustainable development index is the ICSD (Krajnc
& Glavič, 2005). It does not impute missing values, treat outliers, nor does it test
sensitivities (see Figure 4.3b). Data cleaning might be superfluous because of the small
sample size, but a holistic methodological approach prepares for occasions in which data
cleaning becomes necessary (Nardo et al., 2008). Scaling is accomplished by ratio scaling
with target setting. Key indicators are divided by company targets, implementing the
assessment principle target and boundary orientedness. However, ratio scaling entails
mathematical inconsistencies (see Section 4.3.6.2; Pollesch & Dale, 2016), and scores
are difficult to interpret, such that effective communication is harmed. Weights are
determined by the analytical hierarchy process, which involves critical subjectivities
(see Section 4.3.7.1; Zhou, Ang & Poh, 2006). Arithmetic aggregation is applied, but
this aggregation function is not compatible with the underlying scales, leading to
meaningless results (see Section 4.3.8; e.g. Ebert & Welsch, 2004). Moreover, arithmetic
aggregation implements weak sustainability but does not minimise substitutability (see
Section 4.3.8; e.g. Pollesch & Dale, 2015).

Among the identified macro-level indices, the FEEM SI is the first index to be
examined (e.g. Pinar et al., 2014). Missing values are not imputed, but outliers are
treated with lower weights (see Figure 4.4a). Compared to a non-treatment, this
procedure is progressive, but biases remain (see Section 4.3.5.2; Rässler, Rubin & Zell,

---

[27]References and sources of the assessment principles are not repeated in this section but can be
found in Section 3.1, Section 4.1, and Section 4.3.

2013). Policy targets are included in the scaling procedure, which is performed by rescaling. The data range on a discrete interval from zero to one. Rescaling yields easily understandable scores, encouraging effective communication. However, scales should be continuous to minimise information loss (see Section 4.3.6 and Section 4.3.7.4; e.g. Yang & Webb, 2009; Zhou et al., 2010). Weights are determined by experts' elicitation, and aggregation relies on the Choquet integral, which allows for preference-based index construction. Both experts' elicitation and Choquet integral do not follow the assessment principle objectivity. Notwithstanding, sensitivities of experts' preferences are tested.

The HSDI does not clean data, nor does it test sensitivities (see Figure 4.4b; e.g. Bravo, 2018). Equal weights are applied, ignoring correlations of indicators. Equally weighted correlated variables entail double counting of the correlated information, implicitly upgrading their weights (see Section 4.3.7.1; Greco et al., 2019; Nardo et al., 2008). Hence, equal weights are "universally considered to be wrong" (see Section 4.3.7.1; e.g. Chowdhury & Squire, 2006). Data are scaled between zero and one and aggregated geometrically. Geometric aggregation implements weak sustainability with minimised substitutability (see Section 4.3.8; e.g. Pollesch & Dale, 2015). However, it obtains overall zero results when combined with a lower rescaling bound of zero. In other words, substitutability vanishes, and thus, the lower bound should be raised (see Section 4.3.6.2 and Section 4.3.8; Saisana & Philippas, 2012).

The MISD comprises 31 indices (e.g. Shaker, 2018). Therefore, an overall methodological evaluation is not feasible. Concentrating on the MISD, it does not treat outliers despite recognising issues in computation (see Figure 4.4c). However, it overcomes other indices' methodological shortcomings in terms of missing value imputation: The MISD fills missing values by multiple imputation, reducing statistical biases (see Section 4.3.3; e.g. Little & Rubin, 2002) and accounting for uncertainties in the imputation process (see Section 4.3.3.3; e.g. Schafer & Graham, 2002). Furthermore, it determines weights by multivariate statistical analysis, which is generally the preferred field of methods (see Section 4.3.7.1; Mayer, 2008). However, factor analysis is not suitable for sustainable development index construction because it is a top-down approach (see Section 4.3.7.1; Haerdle & Simar, 2012). Similar to the HSDI, rescaling between zero and one is combined with geometric aggregation. Sensitivities are not investigated.

The SDGI does not treat missing values on purpose in order to draw attention to missing data. Although, few exceptions carried out cold deck or mean imputation (see Figure 4.4d; Schmidt-Traub et al., 2017b). Both methods do not fully eliminate statistical biases (see Section 4.3.3.2; Rässler et al., 2013). The SDGI claims to follow Nardo et al.'s (2008)[28] recommendation "truncating the data by removing the bottom 2.5 percentile from the distribution" (Schmidt-Traub et al., 2017b). Replacing outliers

---

[28]Schmidt-Traub et al. (2017b) reference a 2016 publication. To the best of the author's knowledge, the here cited 2008 publication by Nardo et al. is the most recent one at the time of research.

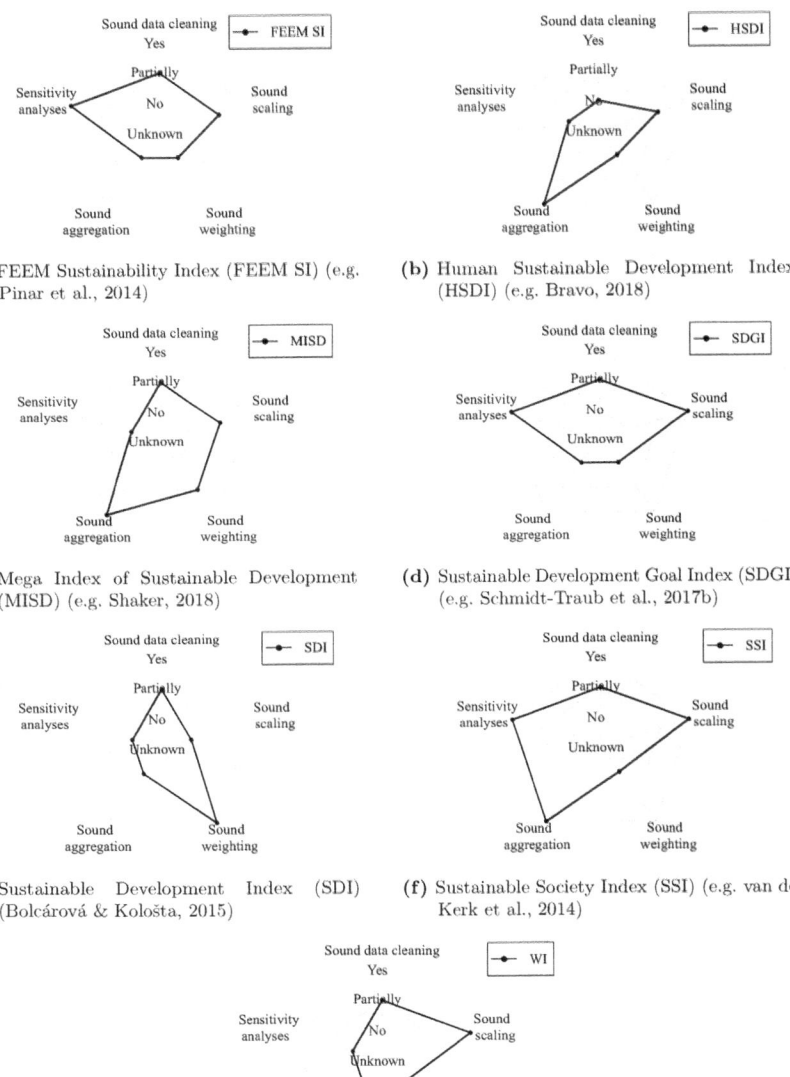

(a) FEEM Sustainability Index (FEEM SI) (e.g. Pinar et al., 2014)

(b) Human Sustainable Development Index (HSDI) (e.g. Bravo, 2018)

(c) Mega Index of Sustainable Development (MISD) (e.g. Shaker, 2018)

(d) Sustainable Development Goal Index (SDGI) (e.g. Schmidt-Traub et al., 2017b)

(e) Sustainable Development Index (SDI) (Bolcárová & Kološta, 2015)

(f) Sustainable Society Index (SSI) (e.g. van de Kerk et al., 2014)

(g) Wellbeing Index (WI) (Prescott-Allen, 2001)

Figure 4.4 Evaluation of methodological soundness and linkage to assessment principles by macro-level indices of sustainable development

with thresholds is methodologically sound, but Nardo et al. (2008) advises to shorten the bottom *and* top of a distribution; one-sided treatment is not reasonable (see Section 4.3.5.2). Rescaling between zero and 100 is appropriate in the context of arithmetic aggregation. However, the arithmetic mean should be avoided and likewise should equal weights (see above). Sensitivities are tested for outlier thresholds and the aggregation function.

The SDI does not treat outliers, nor does it investigate sensitivities (see Figure 4.4e; Bolcárová & Kološta, 2015). It imputes missing values, but the chosen mean imputation still leads to invalid inferences (see Section 4.3.3.2; Rässler et al., 2013). Sound weighting is executed by application of multivariate statistical analysis. In particular, the bottom-up Principal Component Analysis (PCA) is deployed (see Section 4.3.7.1 and Section 4.3.7.2; e.g. Mayer, 2008). Classical scaling and aggregation in PCA are z-scores (mean equal to zero and variance equal to one) and arithmetic aggregation. Both are retained in the SDI. Arithmetic aggregation does not fulfil the methodological criteria (see above). Z-scores are not favourable because they are difficult to interpret, and due to negative values, they cannot be combined with geometric aggregation (see Section 4.3.6.2; e.g. Field, 2009).

The SSI imputes missing values by expert judgement (e.g. van de Kerk et al., 2014). Compared to a non-imputation case, bias is reduced, but the assessment principle objectivity is violated (see Figure 4.4f). Outliers are identified with thresholds on skewness and kurtosis and treated by non-linear scale transformations. Both methods are not recommendable. First, skewness and kurtosis are not robust to outliers because outliers inflate these measures, such that outliers might not be detected as such (see Section 4.3.5.2; e.g. Aggarwal, 2017; Hadi et al., 2009). Second, non-linear transformation is particularly harmful in index calculation because it changes correlations between variables (see Section 4.3.5.2; Oh & Lee, 1994), while correlations should be investigated in statistical weighting procedures (see Section 4.3.7.1; e.g. Mayer, 2008). The SSI does not deploy statistical but top-down equal weighting. On the positive side, the non-linear transformations are not harmful because correlations are not investigated. On the other side, equal weights are not sufficient (see above). Furthermore, the justification of the SSI to implement equal weighting because "[t]here are no highly correlated indicators (all Pearson correlations coefficients are lower than 0.82)" (Saisana & Philippas, 2012) might be false: Correlation coefficients greater than 0.8 typically indicate very high correlations (Field, 2009). Apart from that, Pearson's coefficient might be inappropriate because it assumes normality (see Section 4.3.3.3; Field, 2009), which is not tested in the SSI. Nonetheless, sound scaling, sound aggregation, and sensitivity analyses are executed: Geometric aggregation is applied on the rescaled indicators, and sensitivities are tested for the weighting procedure. The rescaling range starts at one and ends at ten; substitutability is maintained throughout the entire range.

The WI partially deals with missing values, but the method remains unknown (see

Figure 4.4g; Prescott-Allen, 2001). Outliers are detected and replaced by respective threshold values. However, the detection is one-sided (at the top). Weighting is arbitrary, arithmetic aggregation is applied, and sensitivities are not tested. On the positive side, rescaling between zero and 100 is implemented.

In conclusion, previous sustainable development indices do not only lack compliance with the assessment principles (see Section 3.3.2 and Section 3.3.3) but fail to meet methodological and scientific requirements (see above; e.g. Böhringer & Jochem, 2007). This forms the fifth and last research gap. Major criticisms include non-comprehensive scope (das Neves Almeida, Cruz, Barata & García-Sánchez, 2017; Frugoli, Villas Bôas de Almeida, Agostinho, Giannetti & Huisingh, 2015; Singh et al., 2012); insufficient weighting, not addressing interconnections of indicators (i.e. knowledge gap; see Section 2.3.3; e.g. Weitz et al., 2018); meaningless aggregation; missing sensitivity analyses (Böhringer & Jochem, 2007; Singh et al., 2012); and statistical biases as a result of unsatisfactory data cleaning.

To overcome these conceptual and methodological shortcomings, the following section, Section 4.3, conducts profound methodological research on each calculation step of a sustainable development index. The MLSDI's methodology will be the result.

4.3 Methodology of the Multilevel Sustainable Development Index (MLSDI)

This section addresses each calculation step of a sustainable development index in detail and derives the MLSDI. On that account, broad methodological research is carried out, and a variety of methods are reviewed to make profound decisions. This section's structure follows the nine calculation steps (see Figure 4.1).

4.3.1 Collection of sustainable development key figures

The first step in the calculation process is the collection of sustainable development key figures. These are inferred from the sustainable development key indicators, and further information will follow in Section 4.3.4. Decisive in the key figure collection process is data availability: Data must be available by official statistics. Official statistics are open access and hence easily acquired (Zuo, Hua, Dong & Hao, 2017), addressing the sustainability gap (see Section 2.3.4; e.g. Hall et al., 2017) and ensuring the assessment principle transparency (see Table 3.1; e.g. Pintér et al., 2018).

The structure of the *set of sustainable development key figures* c_5 follows from the conceptual framework (see Chapter 2) and is formally denoted by:

$$c_5 = c_5(n, x, t, r), \tag{4.1}$$

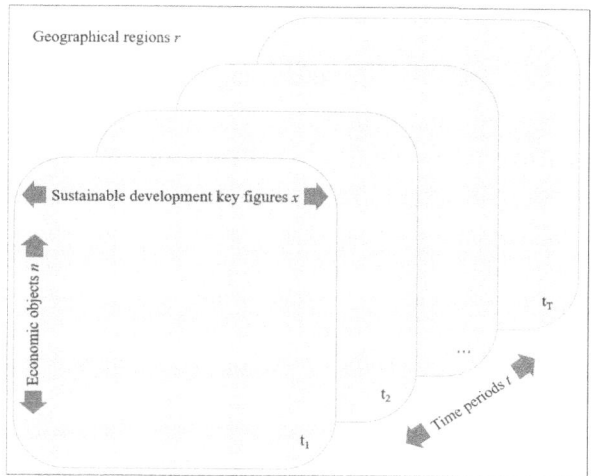

Figure 4.5 Structure of the sustainable development key figures' data set

where $n\epsilon[1, N]$ represents an *economic object* of the change agent group business of any aggregational size, $x\epsilon[1, X]$ portrays a *sustainable development key figure*, $t\epsilon[1, T]$ depicts a *time period*, and $r\epsilon[1, R]$ is a *geographical region*. The structure of the set of key figures c_5 is illustrated in Figure 4.5. Economic objects n are stored in rows, columns contain key figures x, tables represent time periods t, and geographical regions r constitute the fourth axis.

Neither society, policy, nor science are objects of investigation but participate in the transition to sustainability by, for instance, designing, performing, or drawing conclusions on the analysis (see Section 3.2). Moreover, as a consequence of the multilevel perspective, economic objects n are organised in an *inclusive hierarchy*: Multiple layers are nested within each other (Steenbergen & Jones, 2002), and higher ranked economic objects n contain lower ranked economic objects n. That is, macro-economic objects n such as conglomerates of institutions or organisations comprise meso-economic objects n such as networks, communities, or organisations, and these in turn encompass micro-economic objects n such as individuals and individual actors (see Section 2.3.1; Rotmans et al., 2001). In contrast, in an *exclusive hierarchy*, objects that are ranked lower are not included in objects that are ranked higher (Gibson, Ostrom & Ahn, 2000). To avoid complex multilevel methods, which implicitly account for double counts arising from the inclusive hierarchy, the inclusive hierarchical multilevel data structure is eliminated before the MLSDI's modelling process. Section 5.1 will reveal that the industry level is maintained, while potential corporations, aggregated branches, or overall economies are eliminated. Bias from the elimination is not expected because of the inclusiveness. Not potential corporations at the meso level but industries at the macro level are maintained because sustainable development is a macro-level concept (see Section 2.3.2; e.g. T. Hahn et al., 2015).

The following section, Section 4.3.2, describes the preparation of key figures x.

4.3.2   Preparation of sustainable development key figures

The key figures' preparation homogenises data formats to enable multilevel comparability and to accomplish the assessment principle methodological soundness in terms of credibility, validity, and reliability (see Table 3.1; e.g. Cash et al., 2003; Janoušková et al., 2018). With respect to multilevel comparability, meso-economic company data are transferred to macro-economic categories (see Section 4.3.2.1). A transfer from meso to macro and not vice versa is performed because economic objects n at the macro level (i.e. industries) are maintained (see Section 4.3.1). In Section 4.3.2.2, statistical classifications of macro-economic data are transformed because not all data are released in the same classification scheme. For both transformations, it is anticipated that Germany is the sample region r (see Section 5.1) and that data are acquired from the Statistical Office of the European Communities (Eurostat) and the Federal Bureau of Statistics (Destatis). The implemented transformation methods in this work are equivalent to the approaches by the statistical offices.

4.3.2.1   Meso-level transformation to macro-economic categories

Typically, corporations report revenues, costs, and profits, while the macro-economic Gross Value Added (GVA) is required for standardisation of the key figures x. This finding is derived in Section 4.3.4. To allow for the demanded standardisation, meso-economic data is transferred to the GVA, which "is a measure of the contribution to GDP made by an individual producer, industry or sector" (EC et al., 2009). It can be calculated in several ways. Computation via the gross and net output is shown in Table 4.2.[29] Another way of calculation is to first determine the intermediate consumption or input (marked with "†" in Table 4.2) and subsequently subtract it from the gross output. The *output* measures all goods and services produced and not used up by the same establishment, while the *intermediate consumption* or *input* comprises goods and services used up in the production process (EC et al., 2009). Further definitions can be found in Destatis (2019c); and EC et al. (2009).

4.3.2.2   Macro-level transformation of statistical classifications

This section deals with transformations of official statistical classifications. In the EU and hence in Germany, official macro-economic statistical data are released in Classification of Products by Activity (CPA) or Statistical Classification of Economic Activities in

---

[29]Publications in German from Destatis are utilised because, in contrast to methodological aspects, meso-economic data collection is decentralised in the European Union (EU).

+	Revenue of own production
+	Revenue of merchandise
+	Commission fees from trade intermediation
+	Revenue from other, non-industrial activities
−	Stock of unfinished and finished goods and services from own production at the beginning of a period
+	Stock of unfinished and finished goods and services from own production at the end of a period
+	Self-produced equipment
=	**Gross output**
−	Stock of raw materials and supplies at the beginning of a period[†]
+	Stock of raw materials and supplies at the end of a period[†]
−	Receipt of raw materials and supplies[†]
−	Stock of merchandise at the beginning of a period[†]
+	Stock of merchandise at the end of a period[†]
−	Receipt of merchandise[†]
−	Cost of subcontractors[†]
=	**Net output**
−	Costs of temporary agency workers[†]
−	Cost of other industrial services[†]
−	Costs of leases and rents[†]
−	Other costs[†]
=	**Gross Value Added (GVA)**

Table 4.2 Calculation of the Gross Value Added (GVA) with meso-economic data (Destatis, 2019c); [†], intermediate consumption

the European Community (NACE) (Eurostat, 2008a, 2008b). The first classification scheme classifies products, and the latter groups industries, which typically produce more than one product. For the analysis of sustainable development performances by macro-economic objects n, both classifications are valid. However, because companies usually produce various products that belong to more than one CPA class, meso-economic corporate data are generally classified according to NACE. A company's NACE assignment is accomplished according to its main field of activity (Destatis, 2019c). Therefore, data classified according to NACE are prerequisites for multilevel comparability (see Section 4.3.4) that is methodologically sound.

Some official macro-economic statistical data are released in CPA, such that transformations from CPA to NACE are necessary. This is undertaken by methods deployed in the calculation of input-output tables. *Input-output tables* are symmetric matrices that serve to present the process of production, use of goods and services, as well as the income generated (Eurostat, 2008a).[30] They are transformations of supply and use tables, and both contain products in CPA in their rows and industries in NACE in their columns. Transforming supply and use tables to input-output tables either yields industry-by-industry or product-by-product tables. Destatis computes product-by-product tables with the product technology assumption (Destatis, 2010a). This assumption states that "[e]ach product is produced in its own specific way, irrespective of the industry where it is produced" (Eurostat, 2008a). In the computation process, secondary products are relocated to industries, such that they become primary products. *Primary products* are products that are related to one industry by definition (Eurostat, 2008a). For input-output tables, these are diagonal elements, whereas secondary products are off-diagonal elements. The *technology matrix* M_T realises the transformation of classifications and reads:

$$M_T = \left((I \cdot S)^{-1} \cdot S\right)^t, \tag{4.2}$$

where I is an *identity matrix*, and S depicts a symmetric *supply table*. Due to the transposition, the technology matrix M_T contains industries in the rows and products in the columns. To complete the transformation, the technology matrix M_T is multiplied with a *sustainable development key figure in CPA* x^{CPA}, yielding the respective *sustainable development key figure in NACE* x^{NACE}:

$$x^{NACE}(n,t,r) = M_T \cdot x^{CPA}(n,t,r). \tag{4.3}$$

The *set of sustainable development key figures in NACE* c_5^{NACE} is represented by:

$$c_5^{NACE} = c_5^{NACE}(n, x^{NACE}, t, r). \tag{4.4}$$

For the remainder of this work, key figures in NACE x^{NACE} are regarded but simply denoted by "x". Their set is also simply quoted by "c_5".

On this data set, missing values are imputed as described in the following section, Section 4.3.3.

4.3.3   Imputation of missing values

Missing values or *missing data* are underlying but unobserved data (Rässler et al., 2013). Assuming that missing values are meaningful for the modelling and analysis process,

---

[30]Eurostat's (2008a) *Manual of supply, use and input-output tables* was released under the European System of Accounts (ESA) 1995. The currently valid standard is ESA 2010 (Eurostat, 2013). An updated manual has not been released at the time of research. However, the utilised method is expected to remain valid without changes under the updated standard.

they cause a bias if they remain untreated: The observed data dominate the result (Little & Rubin, 2002). As missing data frequently occur in sustainable development quantification (e.g. Schmidt-Traub et al., 2017a), dealing with them is an essential step, contributing to the methodological soundness of an index in terms of credibility, validity, and reliability (see Table 3.1; e.g. Cash et al., 2003; Janoušková et al., 2018). Generally, there are four approaches to address missing values, converting the incomplete sample to a complete one (van Buuren, 2012): complete case analyses, weighting procedures, model-based procedures, and imputation-based procedures. Complete case analyses ignore objects with missing data, weighting procedures weight non-response objects less, model-based procedures specify a model with the observed data, and last, imputation-based procedures estimate missing values (Little & Rubin, 2002; Rässler et al., 2013). Generally, only model-based and imputation-based procedures yield valid inferences (Rässler et al., 2013). Imputation is chosen to handle missing values because it does not require modelling that is specific to the missing data; this would lead to a loss of generality in application.

This section is structured as follows. First, missing values are characterised (see Section 4.3.3.1). Second, two imputation methods are presented: The MLSDI's single imputation method is derived in Section 4.3.3.2, and its multiple imputation method follows in Section 4.3.3.3. Last, statistical tests of model assumptions are outlined in Section 4.3.3.4.

4.3.3.1 Characterisation of missing values

Three characteristics of missing values are crucial in determining suitable imputation methods: the missing data pattern, degree of missingness, and the missing data mechanism. The *missing data pattern* describes the structure of observed and unobserved data in the data set and can be, for instance, *univariate*, *monotone*, or *general* (Little & Rubin, 2002). General missingness is also referred to as *non-monotone* (van Buuren, 2012) or *arbitrary* (Schafer & Graham, 2002). Figure 4.6 visualises these patterns. Further patterns can be found in, e.g. Little and Rubin (2002).

The *degree of missingness* can be analysed according to unit non-response and item non-response. *Unit non-response* refers to objects that do not deliver any information. *Item non-response* regards an object's missingness of one or more variables. The *rate of missing values* λ is the ratio of unobserved to total data and indicates the severity of the missing data problem (Rässler et al., 2013; van Buuren, 2012).

The relationship between observed and unobserved data is characterised by the *missing data mechanism*. The missing data mechanism can be classified into three types. First, if data are *Missing Completely at Random (MCAR)*, missingness is independent of the observed as well as the unobserved data. Second, *Missing at Random (MAR)* implies that missingness is independent of the unobserved but depends on the observed

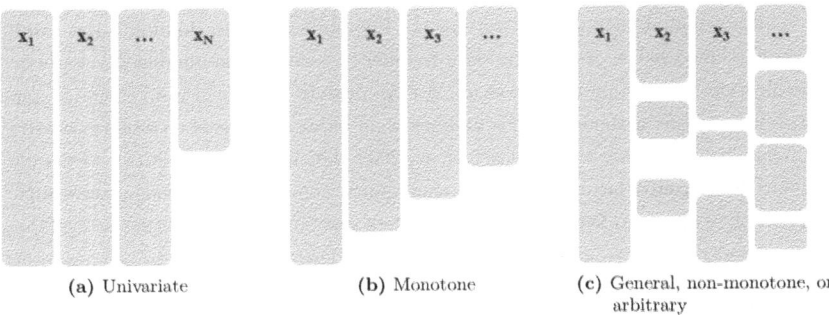

(a) Univariate   (b) Monotone   (c) General, non-monotone, or
                                                                  arbitrary

Figure 4.6 Examples of missing data patterns (based on Little and Rubin, 2002; with friendly permission of © 2002 by John Wiley & Sons, Inc. All rights reserved)

data. In both cases, distributions of variables are unaffected by inclusion of the missing data, such that the same modelling process can be performed. The non-response is *ignorable*. Third, *Missing Not at Random (MNAR)* means that missingness depends on both the observed and the unobserved data, and distributions are influenced by the missingness. In this *non-ignorable* case, the model for the complete data differs from the incomplete data's model (Little & Rubin, 2002; Rässler et al., 2013; Rubin, 1976; Schafer & Graham, 2002; van Buuren, 2012). Ignorability and MAR are typical in practice (Enders, 2010) and therefore assumed for the MLSDI, such that only MAR methods are researched.

4.3.3.2   Single time series imputation: Various methods depending on the missing data pattern

Generally, methods for missing value imputation can be divided into single and multiple imputation. Single imputation methods impute missing values only once, whereas multiple imputation methods are simulation techniques that compute several plausible values for the final fill (Rässler et al., 2013). Single imputation does not account for uncertainties in the imputation process, but multiple imputation does (Little & Rubin, 2002). The MLSDI makes use of both single and multiple imputation methods. Single imputation methods are expected to yield valid results because the uncertainty of the imputation process is assumed to be relatively low: Either further data in the time series or higher aggregational economic objects n of the inclusive hierarchy (see Section 4.3.1) are observed (see Section 5.2.1). In order to confirm or reject the expectation of uncertainties having a relatively low effect on the MLSDI's imputation process, single imputation is tested against multiple imputation (see Section 4.3.3.3).

Single imputation methods comprise hot deck imputation, substitution, cold deck imputation, imputation by mean, and (stochastic) regression imputation. In hot deck imputation, data from similar objects serve to impute missing values. Substitution replaces blanks with objects that are not in the initial sample, and cold deck imputation fills missing values with data from external sources (Little & Rubin, 2002; Nardo et al., 2008). Mean imputation uses the sample mean for estimating missing values. In regression imputation, observed data represent independent variable(s) to predict missing, dependent variable(s) (Little & Rubin, 2002). Hot deck and regression imputation are single imputation methods that are capable of correctly reflecting variability of the imputation process (Rässler et al., 2013) and are thus applied in the MLSDI.

Generally, a univariate time series point of view is adopted in the MLSDI's single imputation process for two reasons: First, key figures x show stable trends (see e.g. Figure 5.3), such that time periods t are expected to be reliable predictors; and second, each economic object n is assumed to feature distinct sustainable development characteristics with the result that cross sections are expected to be unreliable predictors. Kalman smoothing on a basic structural time series model fitted by the maximum likelihood method is the preferred single imputation method because it yields more stable results than further time series models such as Autoregressive Integrated Moving Average (ARIMA) models (Harvey, 1989; Kalman, 1960). Additionally, its application enables imputation of the first time period (Moritz, 2018).

A basic structural time series model regards an observation (i.e. a key figure x) as a permanent *trend component* μ, *seasonal component* γ, and an irregular *random noise* ε in time period t. The model is described by the following formula (Harvey, 1989):

$$x(t) = \mu(t) + \gamma(t) + \varepsilon(t). \tag{4.5}$$

On this model, the Kalman filter is applied. It is a recursive algorithm for estimating observations based on the available information (Harvey, 1989). The estimation is a maximum likelihood estimation, and parameters that maximise the likelihood function are searched for. The Kalman filter assumes normally distributed variables, stationarity (i.e. time invariant distributional properties) of data, and independent and identically distributed (i.i.d.) residuals (Greene, 2003; Harvey, 1989). However, Harvey (1989) asserts the Kalman filter to remain an optimal linear estimator that minimises the mean square error if the normality assumption is violated.

Kalman smoothing on a basic structural time series model is not applicable to any missing data pattern but requires a minimum of three observations in a time series. If there are only two observations, the Stineman algorithm is applied (Moritz, 2018). The Stineman algorithm features monotonical properties and thus gives smoother results as, for example, polynomial interpolations (Stineman, 1980). Once again, this property suits the key figures' stable trends (see e.g. Figure 5.3). If there is only one observation in the time series, this value is held constant, and a modified hot deck imputation is deployed: Data from the same economic object n but other time period t are imputed. If an economic objects' total time series is unobserved, the inclusive hierarchy (see Section 4.3.1) is taken advantage of: Key figures x of higher aggregational economic objects n are always observed, and their key indicators y (see Section 4.3.4) are computed back to the missing lower aggregational key figures x. This is essentially equivalent to imputing higher aggregational industry means. Rässler et al. (2013) do not approve mean imputation. However, the presented modified mean imputation is expected to obtain valid results because the inclusive hierarchy reduces uncertainty in the imputation process.

To summarise, the missing data pattern imposes limitations on the applicability of methods, and four single time series imputation techniques are implemented:

- ≥ 3 observations: Kalman smoothing on a basic structural time series model fitted by a maximum likelihood estimation,

- 2 observations: Stineman algorithm,

- 1 observation: modified hot deck imputation with the only observation,

- 0 observation: modified mean imputation by computing higher aggregational key indicators y (see Section 4.3.4) back to the missing lower aggregational key figures x.

The MLSDI's multiple imputation method is determined in the following section, Section 4.3.3.3.

4.3.3.3   Multiple panel data imputation: Amelia II algorithm

Multiple imputation is a simulation technique that treats parameters as random rather than fixed. Thereby, multiple plausible results are rendered possible, and uncertainty of the imputation process is accounted for by adding random noise (Rässler et al., 2013; Schafer & Graham, 2002; Schafer & Olsen, 1998). The imputation is accomplished by random draws from a posterior distribution (Rässler et al., 2013; van Buuren, 2012). The multiple results are combined into one result; usually by the arithmetic mean (Schafer & Graham, 2002). The convergence of the algorithm to the posterior distribution depends on the rate of missing values λ and the *number of imputations* m. Rubin (1987) shows that the *relative efficiency in convergence of an estimate* η equals (Schafer & Graham, 2002; Schafer & Olsen, 1998):

$$\eta = \left(1 + \frac{\lambda}{m}\right)^{-1}.^{31} \tag{4.6}$$

Equalising the number of imputations m to the percentage rate of missing values λ is recommended by van Buuren (2012). Furthermore, multiple imputation methods are well suited for any missing data pattern (Enders, 2010), and differentiations as in single imputation (see Section 4.3.3.2) are not required.

---

[31]Rubin's (1987) original formula in units of standard deviations has been adjusted.

Generally, two modelling types exist in the field of multiple imputation: joint modelling (e.g. Rubin, 1987; Schafer, 1997) and fully conditional specification (e.g. van Buuren, 2007; van Buuren, Brand, Groothuis-Oudshoorn & Rubin, 2006). Joint modelling fills missing data by drawing simultaneously from one joint multivariate distribution. In contrast, fully conditional specification imputes missing values One-at-a-Time (OAT) on a series of univariate distributions that are directly specified by the modeller (Mistler & Enders, 2017; van Buuren, 2012). According to Hughes et al. (2014); Liu, Gelman, Hill, Su and Kropko (2014); and Mistler and Enders (2017), joint modelling and fully conditional specification are equivalent under single level multivariate normal data. In contrast, van Buuren (2012) emphasises better theoretical properties of joint modelling and advises to prefer this modelling type if the data fulfil the modelling assumptions and if flexibility of individual specification is not demanded. In addition to van Buuren's (2012) argument, joint modelling is preferable for the MLSDI because multiple panel data imputation is aimed to be tested against single time series imputation. A joint multivariate distribution is therefore favoured over a series of univariate distributions.

Several software packages for multiple imputation by joint modelling exist, and overviews can be found in, e.g. Mistler and Enders (2017); and Yucel (2011). Amelia II is applied for multiply imputing the MLSDI's missing data (Honaker, King & Blackwell, 2018). It is the most promising software application in multiple imputation for four reasons: First, it is the only application that uses an expectation maximisation with bootstrapping algorithm (see below), second, several prior information can be included, third, simulation studies provide evidence that Amelia II outperforms other programmes such as NORM (Blankers, Koeter & Schippers, 2010; Novo & Schafer, 2015; Schafer, 1997), and fourth, its developers claim it to work well under violation of the normality assumption (Honaker, King & Blackwell, 2011). Non-normal data are likely in index construction, given the numerous key figures x and key indicators y to include for comprehensiveness of the index (see Table 3.1 and Section 4.3.4; e.g. Hacking & Guthrie, 2008). However, the last argument should be carefully considered. Demirtas, Freels and Yucel (2008) show that a violation of normality in multiple imputation produces biased results in their small sample of size 40. The results are only not distorted for their large sample of size 400, even with high rates of missing values λ such as 75%.

Amelia II works in three steps: bootstrapping, expectation maximisation, and imputation. These are repeated m times. Bootstrapping is a random sampling technique that is faster, more flexible, and easier to use than other techniques such as Markov chain Monte Carlo approaches (Blankers et al., 2010; Honaker et al., 2011).[32] An expectation maximisation algorithm is a framework for maximum likelihood estimation and estimates parameters of a predictive distribution function (Han, Kamber & Pei,

---

[32]More information on bootstrapping can be found in, e.g. Davison and Hinkley (1998); Efron and Tibshirani (1993); and G. James et al. (2013).

2012).[33] Last, missing values are imputed by drawing from the bootstrapped parameters. Given the m repetitions, m imputed data sets are at hand and combined into one result (Honaker et al., 2011, 2018).

For the MLSDI, Amelia II's panel data model is applied on the set of key figures c_5. As many key figures x as possible are included in the model: Complete key figures x are generally incorporated, and only highly correlated key figures x are excluded (Honaker et al., 2011; Rässler et al., 2013). The correlation analysis can be based on three different correlation coefficients: Pearson's coefficient, Spearman's rho, or Kendall's tau. Pearson's coefficient assumes normally distributed data, while Spearman's rho and Kendall's tau are non-parametric statistics without distributional assumptions (Field, 2009). Normality of key figures x is tested (see Section 4.3.3.4 and Section 5.2.2) to determine the adequate coefficient. Should the data be normal, Pearson's coefficient is chosen. Otherwise, Kendall's tau is calculated because it features better statistical properties than Spearman's rho despite being less popular. The threshold for being highly correlated is set to 0.8 (Field, 2009), boundaries on estimates are equalised to the observed range of values, time effects are specified to be linear and constant across time series and cross sections, the number of imputations m is levelled to the percentage rate of missing values λ, and last, the arithmetic mean is applied to combine the results (see above; Schafer & Graham, 2002; van Buuren, 2012).

In the following section, Section 4.3.3.4, tests for the underlying assumptions of both single and multiple imputation are outlined.

4.3.3.4   Statistical tests of model assumptions

The first assumption to be tested of both single and multiple imputation is the MAR assumption (see Section 4.3.3.1). However, MCAR is the only testable missing data mechanism as the required information for a MAR or MNAR test is missing (Enders, 2010; van Buuren, 2007). Enders (2010) predicate the impossibility of MAR and MNAR tests to be an important problem in practice. In contrast, Collins, Schafer and Kam (2001); Rässler et al. (2013); and Schafer and Graham (2002) assert minor effects and valid inferences as a result of violating assumptions on missing data mechanisms. Furthermore, Rässler et al. (2013) recommend MAR methods in any case because they facilitate the modelling and analysis process while still reducing biases compared to non-treatment. For the MLSDI, Little's (1988) MCAR test is performed because a confirmation of MCAR implies approving MAR. The MCAR test is a multivariate extension of the t-test, evaluating mean differences across subgroups. Under the null hypothesis, data are MCAR: The missing data patterns share a common mean, and the test statistic is approximately χ^2 distributed (Beaujean, 2015; Enders, 2010). The null hypothesis is desired to be accepted, and large *p-values*, which represent standard

---

[33]More information on expectation maximisation algorithms can be found in, e.g. Han et al. (2012); and McLachlan and Krishnan (1997).

normal probabilities, are demanded. Statistical significance is chosen to occur above p-values of 0.05. However, the test suffers from low power, and its usefulness is therefore limited (Enders, 2010).[34]

Regarding single time series imputation, the three assumptions of the basic structural time series model – normality, stationarity, and i.i.d. – are tested. The Shapiro-Wilk and Kolmogorov-Smirnov tests serve to investigate normality (Conover, 1980; CRAN, 2019; Royston, 1982; Shapiro & Wilk, 1965), stationarity is examined by the augmented Dickey-Fuller test (Dickey & Fuller, 1979, 1981; Trapletti, Hornik & LeBaron, 2018), and the Ljung-Box test is implemented to control for independence of residuals (CRAN, 2019; Ljung & Box, 1978). The Shapiro-Wilk and Kolmogorov–Smirnov tests are non-parametric tests that compare variance scores and distribution functions of the sample to a normal distribution, respectively. Under the null hypothesis, the data are normally distributed. The null hypothesis is desired to be accepted with p-values larger than 0.05. Tests are performed for every time period t because time is an implicit variable. For conciseness, the test results are compiled into one result by the arithmetic mean. In large samples, both tests suffer from type I error (rejection of a true null hypothesis), and thus, visualisation of the data by, for example, histograms should accompany the tests (Field, 2009). The augmented Dickey-Fuller test is a likelihood ratio test, and its null hypothesis states that data are generated by a unit root. That is, data are non-stationary (Dickey & Fuller, 1979, 1981). Consequently, the null hypothesis is desired to be rejected with p-values smaller than 0.05 (Greene, 2003). Last, under the null hypothesis of the Ljung-Box test, residuals are i.i.d. The null hypothesis is desired to be accepted with p-values larger than 0.05 (Brockwell & Davis, 2016; Ljung & Box, 1978). Both the augmented Dickey-Fuller and Ljung-Box tests refer to the temporal dimension, and the tests are carried out once for the total time series; compiling test results is not required.

In the case of the Amelia II algorithm, joint multivariate normality is tested with the multivariate Shapiro-Wilk test (Jarek, 2015). Convergence of the algorithm is investigated with overdispersed start values. Amelia II functions correctly if its convergence is independent of the diverse start values (Honaker et al., 2011).

As missing values are not allowed in the aforementioned tests (CRAN, 2019; Jarek, 2015; Trapletti et al., 2018), they are performed after the imputation process. Circular effects might be present, but these are assumed to be low, such that robust tests results are obtained.

---

[34]Details on shortcomings of this test can be found in Enders (2010).

4.3.4   Standardisation to sustainable development key indicators

Standardisation is the transformation of different scales into one common scale and is generally a univariate problem. It is also referred to as *scaling* or *normalisation* (Pollesch & Dale, 2016). In this fourth calculation step, the key figures x are standardised to the *sustainable development key indicators* y. When regarding this type of transformation, the term "standardisation" is exclusively used.

To implement the multilevel perspective (see Section 2.3.1; Rotmans et al., 2001), only key indicators y that are applicable at micro, meso, and macro levels are admitted to the MLSDI. Object comparability (see Table 3.1; e.g. Hacking & Guthrie, 2008) of micro, meso, and macro objects is ensured by the standardisation. Moreover, key indicators y define "the whole issue" (Moldan, Janoušková & Hák, 2012; Pollesch & Dale, 2016) and critically determine the comprehensiveness (Böhringer & Jochem, 2007; Custance & Hillier, 1998; Zuo et al., 2017) and quality (Amor-Esteban et al., 2018) of an index. Therefore, the key indicators y must be connected to the definition of sustainable development (Böhringer & Jochem, 2007; Pezzey, 1992). Only then, information about sustainable development is captured appropriately, pertinently, and correctly (Amor-Esteban et al., 2018; Janoušková et al., 2018). In conclusion, key indicators are responsible for assuring the assessment principles compliance with a framework (see Table 3.1; e.g. Hacking & Guthrie, 2008; Pintér et al., 2018) and relevance (see Table 3.1; Janoušková et al., 2018).

In Section 2.1, various definitions of sustainable development have been discussed, and in Section 2.2, each contentual domain has been defined. These definitions now serve to define environmental, social, and economic key indicators: *Environmental key indicators* are data that reflect harm induced by mankind or degradation of the natural world, *social key indicators* are defined as data that indicate a just satisfaction of human needs, and last, *economic key indicators* are data that allude to material and financial success required for environmental protection and social development.

At the macro level, 234 SDG indicators (see Section 2.3.3; UN, 2018, 2019b) are relevant, as the UN has released the most elaborated concept of sustainable development (see Section 2.1; Lock & Seele, 2017). At the meso level, the GRI disclosures (see Section 3.3.1; GRI, 2016) are most pertinent because GRI is the most widely used standard for corporate reporting on sustainable development (see Section 3.3.1; KPMG, 2017). The economic domain's disclosures are supported by the International Accounting Standards (IAS) and the International Financial Reporting Standards (IFRS) (IASB, 2018) because the GRI and the SDG frameworks lack several economic disclosures, presumably to avoid repetitions with the IAS and the IFRS. Micro frameworks could not be identified, such that embracement of multiple perspectives is currently limited to the meso and the macro levels. The intersection of the meso GRI and the macro

SDG frameworks determines the ideal *set of sustainable development key indicators* c_4, which is formally represented by:

$$c_4 = c_4(n, y, t, r), \tag{4.7}$$

where $y \epsilon [1, Y]$. The alignment of the frameworks is based on GRI and UNGC (2018a). From the ideal set of key indicators c_4, the ideal set of key figures c_5 is inferred (see Section 4.3.1). By aligning the GRI and the SDG frameworks, the criticism of the GRI framework following the business case of sustainability (see Section 3.3.1; Landrum & Ohsowski, 2018) is implicitly handled because the SDGs follow societal instrumental finality and paradox teleological integration by definition (see Section 2.3.3).

Furthermore, the set of key indicators c_4 is required to fulfil the assessment principle efficiency and effectiveness (see Table 3.1; Figge & Hahn, 2004). Therefore, two types of indicators – efficiency and effectiveness indicators – build the MLSDI. Efficiency indicators were initially developed in the environmental domain (Schaltegger & Sturm, 1989) and termed "eco-efficiency indicators". Maxime, Marcotte and Arcand (2006); and Verfaillie and Bidwell (2000) define an *eco-efficiency indicator* as the ratio of the production value and corresponding environmental influence. The *production value* quantifies the volume of produced products in physical or monetary units.[35] The *environmental influence* measures the effect on the environment arising from the production. Hence, eco-efficiency indicators capture the relationship of economic growth and environmental degradation. Their decoupling is desired, but their causal relationship is ambiguous (see Section 2.2.3). The eco-efficiency concept can be transferred to the social and economic domain, with the general indicator label *efficiency indicator*. Efficiency indicators are also referred to as *productivity indicators* (e.g. Eurostat, 2018; Huppes & Ishikawa, 2005; UN, 2018), whereas their reciprocal yields *intensity indicators* (Huppes & Ishikawa, 2005; Maxime et al., 2006; Verfaillie & Bidwell, 2000).[36]

Efficiency indicators' components – their specific metrics and reporting units – are controversially discussed, and diverse recommendations are given. Examples include standardisation by units of products, production volume in physical units (GRI, 2016; Maxime et al., 2006; Schneider et al., 2011; Verfaillie & Bidwell, 2000), revenues in monetary units, or sales in monetary units (GRI, 2016). Despite a preference for units of products or production volume in physical units in the literature, these standardisations metrics are disadvantageous as they harm comparability. "Apples and oranges" cannot be compared meaningfully neither can one kilogram of "apples" and one kilogram of

---

[35]In a macro-economic context, the production value is the value that quantifies all activities of an establishment. It comprises the production of goods and provision of services to another unit of the same establishment. In contrast, the output only includes production, disregarding internal provisions, and should thus be the generally preferred measure (see Section 4.3.2.1; EC et al., 2009).

[36]Huppes and Ishikawa (2005) further classify measures on environmental improvements such as environmental cost-effectiveness as eco-efficiency measures. However, as they regard effectiveness, they are classified as effectiveness indicators in this work (see below).

"oranges". Cubas-Díaz and Martínez Sedano's (2018) statement that benchmarks are only meaningful across companies of the same industry applies. To enable meaningful multilevel object comparability, the standardising measure should be stated in monetary units. However, revenues and sales as recommended by GRI (2016) are inexpedient. First, costs are not but should be deducted because they include goods and services used up in the production process (see Section 4.3.2.1; EC et al., 2009). Second, revenues and sales are not but should be comparable to the macro level (see Section 4.3.2). GVA overcomes both shortcomings: It does not include intermediate consumption, and it links the meso and the macro levels because it measures an economic object's contribution to GDP (see Section 4.3.2.1; EC et al., 2009). Furthermore, recall that the GDP quantifies the size of an economy in terms of monetary market value (see Section 2.2.3; e.g. van den Bergh, 2009), and therefore, GVA as a standardisation measure exactly meets its purpose. The GVA and, respectively, the GDP approach is also used by, e.g. Eurostat (2018); and UN (2018).

Moreover, reporting units of the environmental domain are controversially discussed. Assessment methods may involve transformation of physical to monetary units (see Section 3.2). However, it was already pointed out in the late 1990s that market prices should not be assigned to ecosystem services. Monetary-based approaches mislead and distort the analysis, irrespective of the assignment mechanism. Several reasons are demonstrated: Biophysical properties are endogenous qualities that are independent of current prices, and thus, prices cannot reflect biophysical scarcity; nature's goods and services are rather complements than substitutes; future biophysical goods and services cannot be discounted as money can; and last, money can grow but nature cannot (Prescott-Allen, 2001; Rees & Wackernagel, 1999; Wackernagel & Rees, 1996). Additionally, empirical studies demonstrate the difficulty in monetisation of environmental impacts: Wide value ranges result, and clear pricing cannot be achieved (e.g. Antheaume, 2004; Epstein et al., 2011). In conclusion, transfers to monetary units should be refrained from, and units ought to be retained according to their domains: physical units in the environmental domain and monetary units in the economic domain. Efficiency indicators may feature mixed units.

Some scholars regard efficiency indicators as valuable tools and improved measures because they link sustainable development influences and economic performances, facilitating management and decision making (e.g. Charmondusit, Phatarachaisakul & Prasertpong, 2014; Gusmão Caiado, de Freitas Dias, Veiga Mattos, Gonçalves Quelhas & Leal Filho, 2017; Maxime et al., 2006; Müller, Holmes, Deurer & Clothier, 2015; Uhlman & Saling, 2010). Spangenberg (2015) even argues that data on sustainable development influences are meaningless if not put in relation to their generating activity.

Nonetheless, efficiency indicators require caution. For instance, eco-efficiency indicators reflect trade-offs between the environmental and the economic domains (Carvalho, Govindan, Azevedo & Cruz-Machado, 2017; Gusmão Caiado et al., 2017). However,

paradox teleological integration is required (see Section 2.3.2), explicitly acknowledging
tensions of oppositional sustainable development elements. Therefore, efficiency indicators need to be coupled with further indicators (Gusmão Caiado et al., 2017; B.
Zhang, Bi, Fan, Yuan & Ge, 2008), contradicting Spangenberg's (2015) autocracy on
efficiency indicators. Figge and Hahn (2004) suggest absolute measures to accompany
relative measures (see Table 3.1). Managing only relative decoupling is not sufficient,
but absolute decoupling should be overseen additionally. The inclusion of absolute
measures would sacrifice comparability across economic objects n. If economic sizes
are unknown, "apples" are compared to "oranges" (see above). Growth rates assist
to circumvent this inherent trade-off between comparability and inclusion of absolute
measures. Growth rates indicate percentage changes to a prior time period and are thus
relative measures that capture effectiveness. As sustainability is a long-term goal (see
Section 2.1; Dragicevic, 2018), long-term growth rates are the *effectiveness indicators*
of the MLSDI.

In conclusion, the MLSDI deploys three approaches to compute the set of key
indicators c_4: First, key figures x are standardised by an economic object's size in
terms of GVA, second, key figures x are standardised by another reference, and third,
key figures x are expressed in growth rates from the first period ($t = 1$) to the last
period ($t = T$) of the time horizon. Clearly, the first type is an intensity indicator
referring to efficiency, while the latter reflects effectiveness. Intensity indicators instead
of productivity indicators are computed, given their popularity (e.g. Eurostat, 2018;
UN, 2018).[37] According to the definition of, e.g. Maxime et al. (2006), the MLSDI's
second type of key indicators y does not depict intensity indicators because the reference
is rather a total of the respective sustainable development influence (e.g. share of
marginally-employed employees; Table 5.6). However, this type of key indicator y may
be regarded as an intensity indicator in a broader sense because the calculation scheme
is identical. The MLSDI adopts the broader view and a *sustainable development ratio
indicator* y_r, referring to efficiency, reads:

$$y_r(n, t, r) = \frac{x(n, t, r)}{x_{std}(n, t, r)}, \tag{4.8}$$

where $y_r \epsilon [1, Y_r]$, $x_{std} \epsilon [1, X]$ portrays a *standardising key figure* with $x_{std} \neq x$. A
sustainable development growth indicator y_g, reflecting effectiveness, is calculated by:

$$y_g(n, r) = \frac{x(n, t = T, r) - x(n, t = 1, r)}{x(n, t = 1, r)}, \tag{4.9}$$

where $y_g \epsilon [1, Y_g]$.

At this point, the *effective direction* ξ of a key indicator y can be positive or

---

[37]However, several indicators will be changed to productivity indicators later on (see Table 5.10).

negative. Key indicators y with a *positive effective direction* ξ^+ increase their sustainable development performance with an increasing score, whereas key indicators y with a *negative effective direction* ξ^- decrease their sustainable development performance with an increasing score (Krajnc & Glavič, 2005). Harmonisation of the key indicators' effective directions ξ is accomplished during the scaling process (see Section 4.3.6). Previous to that, outliers are detected and treated in the next section, Section 4.3.5.

4.3.5   Outlier detection and treatment

An *outlying observation, outlier,* or *anomaly* is defined as a data point that deviates significantly from other members of the sample (Barnett & Lewis, 1994; Grubbs, 1969; Han et al., 2012). Assuming that at least 50% of the data set is homogeneous, outliers represent the minority (Hadi et al., 2009), not fitting the normal pattern (Aggarwal, 2017; Barnett & Lewis, 1994). Outliers need to be detected and treated because statistical analyses customarily assume homogeneous data (Hadi et al., 2009). Otherwise, the assessment principle methodological soundness (credibility, validity, and reliability) would be violated (see Table 3.1; Cash et al., 2003; Janoušková et al., 2018). In index construction, the scaling process especially suffers from outliers (see Section 4.3.6; Nardo et al., 2008) because outliers are extreme values (Barnett & Lewis, 1994), setting a scale's limits. The weighting process is indirectly affected via scales (see Section 4.3.7).

In *outlier detection*, data points with significantly diverging behaviour are identified (Han et al., 2012). The *outlier rate* β is the ratio of outlying to total data and alludes to the severity of the outlier problem. *Outlier treatment* regards the handling process. Criticism on "overidentifying" outliers is expressed by, e.g. McGregor and Pouw (2017). Outlier treatment distorts the true picture of data by ignoring the minority of cases and focusing on average behaviour. Information loss as expressed for aggregation by Zhou et al. (2010) is caused. Therefore, when determining the MLSDI's outlier detection and treatment method, the trade-off between statistical distortion and distortion of the true picture is taken into account to balance statistical bias and information loss. Furthermore, temporal comparability and progress analysis (see Section 4.3.6.1; Nardo et al., 2008) should be enabled. Outlier handling should thus – similar to scales and weights (see Section 4.3.6 and Section 4.3.7) – be time invariant. With respect to geographical regions r, variability is suggested by Nilsson et al. (2016), such that countries can interpret progress in sustainable development according to their national circumstances. This approach disables country comparison and should be abandoned if the goal is to conduct multinational analyses.

In the following, outliers are characterised (see Section 4.3.5.1), and the MLSDI's detection and treatment method is established (see Section 4.3.5.2).

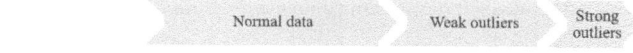

Figure 4.7 Spectrum from normal data to strong outliers (based on Aggarwal, 2017; with friendly permission of © Springer International Publishing AG 2017)

4.3.5.1 Characterisation of outliers

Similar to missing values, outliers can be characterised according to their pattern, degree, and mechanism (see Section 4.3.3.1).[38] Regarding the pattern, an outlier can be, among others, global or local. *Global outliers* deviate significantly from the entire sample, whereas *local outliers* differ from the local area (Han et al., 2012). The degree of outlyingness may be *weak* or *strong*. Borders are fluid, and the spectrum from normal data over weak outliers to strong outliers is illustrated in a simple flow diagram in Figure 4.7. The underlying mechanism that generates outliers can be classified into three types. First, outliers may exist because of a *measurement error* in the data generation process. Second, an error in the data collection might have occurred, also known as an *execution error*. Third, *inherent variability*, which is a natural variation in the population, may cause anomalies in the data (Barnett & Lewis, 1994).

For the MLSDI, outliers are assumed to be present due to inherent variability. In this case, overidentifying outliers and distortion of the true picture (see Section 4.3.5; McGregor & Pouw, 2017) causes information loss. Therefore, only global, strong outliers are aimed to be identified and treated. The following section, Section 4.3.5.2, determines outlier detection and treatment methods that satisfy this setting.

4.3.5.2 Univariate Interquartile Range (IQR) method

Simple univariate outlier detection methods establish outlier thresholds based on a combination of single measures. Examples include the mean and standard deviation, median and median absolute deviation, and skewness and kurtosis. Recommended thresholds for these measures can be found in, e.g. Aggarwal (2017); and Field (2009). Mean and standard deviation are sensitive to outliers. Outliers inflate these measures such that they suffer from masking (Field, 2009). *Masking* occurs when an outlier is not detected as such (Hadi et al., 2009). Skewness and kurtosis also suffer from masking because they are based on the mean and the standard deviation (Field, 2009). The median and the median absolute deviation remain robust measures in simple outlier detection (Leys, Ley, Klein, Bernard & Licata, 2013).

More advanced multivariate outlier detection models include statistical methods, proximity-based methods, or clustering-based methods. In statistical methods, observations that deviate significantly from the assumed distribution are outliers. Proximity-

---

[38]In contrast to the academic literature on missing values (see Section 4.3.3.1; e.g. Little & Rubin, 2002) the literature on outliers (e.g. Aggarwal, 2017) does not explicitly use these terms.

based methods detect outliers based on proximity measures from a data point to its neighbours. Last, clustering-based methods declare data points as outliers that belong to a small or no cluster (Han et al., 2012). Each method has advantages and disadvantages, and details can be found in, e.g. Aggarwal (2017); and Han et al. (2012). Simulation studies suggest preferring proximity-based over clustering-based methods (e.g. Aggarwal & Sathe, 2015, 2017; Goldstein & Uchida, 2016), and generally, simple intuitive models are likely to yield better results than highly complex models (Aggarwal, 2017).

For the MLSDI, outliers are detected by univariate methods because the primary goal of outlier detection is the reduction of scale distortion (see Section 4.3.5), and scaling is a univariate task (see Section 4.3.6.1). Two robust univariate outlier detection methods that are based on the median and the median absolute deviation are present. First, the Interquartile Range (IQR) method classifies an observation as outlying if it surpasses or falls below the *outlier thresholds* θ. These are defined by:

$$\left\{ \begin{array}{l} \theta_{max}(y,r) = Q_3(y,r) + \alpha \cdot q(y,r) \\ \theta_{min}(y,r) = Q_1(y,r) - \alpha \cdot q(y,r) \end{array} \right\}, \tag{4.10}$$

where θ_{max} is the *upper threshold*, θ_{min} represents the *lower threshold*, α portrays the *outlier coefficient*, Q_3 is the *75th percentile*, Q_1 depicts the *25th percentile*, and q measures the IQR. The outlier coefficient α is typically set equal to 1.5. The 75th percentile is also called the *third* or *upper quartile* and cuts off the highest 25% of the data. Accordingly, the 25th percentile is also referred to as the *first* or *lower quartile* and truncates the lowest 25% of the data (Aggarwal, 2017; Han et al., 2012). Last, the IQR q is described by:

$$q(y,r) = Q_3(y,r) - Q_1(y,r). \tag{4.11}$$

The second method that is based on the median and the median absolute deviation is suggested by Leys et al. (2013). The 75th and the 25th percentiles Q_3 and Q_1 of Equation (4.10) are replaced by the median, and the IQR q is substituted by the median absolute deviation. The outlier coefficient α is recommended to be set equal to 2.5. Both methods are essentially the same because they are based on deviations from the median. As the IQR method is more widely spread and used in, for example, boxplots (see Figure 5.7b and Figure 5.8b; e.g. Han et al., 2012), the IQR method is applied in the MLSDI, with the typical coefficient α set equal to 1.5.

After outlier detection, outlier treatment is the next step. It can be conducted in four ways: Outliers may be removed and ignored; data may be transformed, such that outliers do not occur; outliers may be weighted less; or the score of the outlying observation may be changed (Field, 2009). Analogous to addressing missing values, removing and weighting are procedures that yield invalid inferences (see Section 4.3.3; Rässler et al., 2013). Furthermore, transformations are not recommended in index calculation.

First, a transformation is a form of scaling (Pollesch & Dale, 2016), and clarity may be forfeited if it is performed in addition to scaling for indicator comparability (see Section 4.3.6). Second, particularly non-linear transformations are harmful in index calculation because they impact correlations (Oh & Lee, 1994), while the determination of the key indicators' weights is based on correlation analysis (see Section 4.3.7). In conclusion, an *outlying sustainable development key indicator* y_o is treated by changing its score to the thresholds θ:

$$y(n,t,r) = y_o(n,t,r) = \begin{cases} \theta_{max}(y,r), & \text{if } y(n,t,r) > \theta_{max}(y,r) \\ \theta_{min}(y,r), & \text{if } y(n,t,r) < \theta_{min}(y,r) \end{cases}, \qquad (4.12)$$

where $y_o \epsilon [1, Y_o]$.

The MLSDI's outlier detection and treatment cannot be tested because it is an unsupervised problem setting. The true outlyingness is unknown and impossible to learn (Aggarwal, 2017).

4.3.6   Scaling

By definition, a variety of key indicators y are reported in index calculation. These typically feature diverse units (Pollesch & Dale, 2016), such that the required cross indicator comparability (see Table 3.1; e.g. Pintér et al., 2018) and meaningful aggregation (see Section 4.3.8; e.g. Ebert & Welsch, 2004) for methodological soundness in terms of credibility, validity, and reliability (see Table 3.1; e.g. Cash et al., 2003; Janoušková et al., 2018) is not guaranteed. To ensure achievement of these principles, key indicators y are scaled. As stated in Section 4.3.4, scaling is a univariate problem and refers to the transformation of diverse scales into one common scale (Pollesch & Dale, 2016). The denotation "scaling" is exclusively used for the present calculation step of unifying key indicators' scales. Scales are time invariant but may vary over geographical regions (see Section 4.3.5; Nardo et al., 2008; Nilsson et al., 2016).

Non-internal scaling depends on additional exogenous data (Pollesch & Dale, 2016) and should be deployed in sustainable development indices to incorporate targets and boundaries, enabling the assessment principle target and boundary orientedness (see Table 3.1; Sala et al., 2015). Resulting scores from this type of scaling can then be interpreted as distance to target (Moldan et al., 2012; Pollesch & Dale, 2016). The scaling procedure should also minimise information loss (Zhou et al., 2006; Zhou et al., 2010), and resulting scales should be easily understandable to effectively communicate an index's results, attracting a broad audience (see Table 3.1; e.g. Pintér et al., 2018).

In the following, scales are characterised in Section 4.3.6.1, and the MLSDI's scaling procedure is derived and described in Section 4.3.6.2.

4.3.6.1   Characterisation of scales

To fully understand a sustainable development index's scaling problem, several definitions are introduced. Subsequently, scales of a sustainable development index are
characterised. A *scale* is the dimension (e.g. temporal, spatial, or analytical) used
to measure a phenomenon. Its *extent* forms the overall size or magnitude, and its
resolution regards the precision (Gibson et al., 2000; Rotmans, 2002). An *absolute
scale* is objectively calibrated, whereas a *relative scale* is a transformation of the former
to picture relationships of objects to each other (Gibson et al., 2000; Turner, Dale &
Gardner, 1989). A scale's type can be nominal, ordinal, interval, or ratio. A *nominal
scale* assigns labels; an *ordinal scale* results from rank ordering (Pollesch & Dale, 2016;
Stevens, 1946); an *interval scale* preserves constant distances between values, and zero
does not indicate absence of a variable; and last, a *ratio scale* is characterised by a
natural fixed origin, with a vanished variable at zero. The type of scale determines the
form of a variable's comparability. A nominal variable's equality may be ascertained,
an ordinal variable's ordinal position may be determined, an interval variable's absolute
differences may be evaluated, and a relative distance of a ratio variable may be assessed
(Ebert & Welsch, 2004; Pollesch & Dale, 2016; Stevens, 1946).

A sustainable development index's scales correspond to the conceptual framework's
dimensions (see Figure 2.11). Table 4.3 reports the technical dimension, extent, resolution, hierarchy, relation, and type of each conceptual dimension that is captured in
the MLSDI. The temporal horizon contains yearly reported time periods t and is an
absolute interval scale (Gibson et al., 2000; Stevens, 1946). The contentual domain is an
analytical scale (Gibson et al., 2000) and is composed of key indicators y with diverse
units on relative ratio scales (see Section 4.3.4; Pollesch & Dale, 2015). Geographical
regions r are recorded in countries on an absolute nominal scale.[39] The change agent
group business is a quantitative dimension (Gibson et al., 2000) with economic objects
n on an absolute nominal scale. Hierarchical ordering of economic objects n occurs
when incorporating the multilevel perspective (see Section 2.3.1; Rotmans et al., 2001)
and the dimension aggregational size. The aggregational size is a functional dimension
(Rotmans, 2002), which is organised in an inclusive hierarchy (see Section 4.3.1; Gibson et al., 2000) and features a trivariate resolution (micro, meso, and macro). The
decisional tier is also classified as a functional dimension, with the trivariate options
operational, strategic, and normative (see Section 2.3.2; e.g. Baumgartner, 2014). All
scales except the functional scales are captured in the MLSDI's data structure (see
Figure 4.5). The aggregational size is included in the economic objects n, and the
decisional tier is addressed before and after the calculation in conceptualisation and
decision making.

---

[39]Any other resolution for time periods t and geographical regions r is possible but may be limited
by data availability.

Conceptual dimension	Technical dimension	Extent	Resolution	Hierarchy	Relation	Type
Temporal horizon	Temporal	$t\epsilon[1,T]$	Years	None	Absolute	Interval
Contentual domain	Analytical	$y\epsilon[1,Y]$	Diverse	None	Relative	Ratio
Geographical region	Spatial	$r\epsilon[1,R]$	Countries	None	Absolute	Nominal
Change agent group business	Quantitative	$n\epsilon[1,N]$	Objects	None	Absolute	Nominal
Aggregational size	Functional	Micro to macro	Trivariate	Inclusive hierarchy	Absolute	Ordinal
Decisional tier	Functional	Operational to normative	Trivariate	Hierarchy	Absolute	Ordinal

Table 4.3 Scale characterisation of the conceptual dimensions of the Multilevel Sustainable Development Index (MLSDI); n, economic object; N, number of economic objects; r, geographical region; R, number of geographical regions; t, time period; T, number of time periods; y, sustainable development key indicator; Y, number of sustainable development key indicators

The required scaling procedure regards the harmonisation of the different units of the key indicators y and is determined in the next section, Section 4.3.6.2. The temporal dimension's scale is already comparable. In the case of the economic objects n and the geographical regions r, comparability that goes beyond the scope of nominal scales (equality check) has already been reached via the standardisation procedure in Section 4.3.4.

4.3.6.2   Rescaling between ten and 100

Generally, scaling may result in common monetary units, physical units, or unitless performance scores (Prescott-Allen, 2001). In Section 4.3.4, it has been emphasised that physical units should not be transferred to monetary units (e.g. Rees & Wackernagel, 1999) and vice versa. Scaling to unitless performance scores remains to be the only option. Respective methods include, among others, ranking, growth rates, z-scores, logarithmic transformation, ratio scaling, and rescaling. With ranking, key indicators y are scaled by determining an order, growth rates represent percentage changes to a reference, and z-scores feature a sample mean of zero and standard deviation of one, logarithmic transformation applies a logarithmic function, ratio scaling divides the key indicator y by a reference value such as a target, and rescaling assigns new scores on a defined range (Field, 2009; Nardo et al., 2008; Pollesch & Dale, 2016).

In sustainable development index calculation, rankings, growth rates, z-scores, and logarithmic transformations are not suitable. Rankings would reduce the key indicators

y to ordinal scales, leading to information loss. Growth rates would entail information loss of the original scores (Nardo et al., 2008), and growth rates are not able to include targets and boundaries.[40] Z-scores are difficult to interpret because a z-score indicates the distance to the mean measured in standard deviations. Furthermore, z-scores are defined on positive and negative value ranges, limiting the possibilities of aggregation (see Section 4.3.8). However, z-scores are required for multivariate statistical weighting techniques (see Section 4.3.7.2 and Section 4.3.7.3). Last, because logarithmic transformations are non-linear, they are harmful in index calculation and should not be applied. Non-linear transformations affect correlations (see Section 4.3.5.2; Oh & Lee, 1994), which are investigated in the weighting process (see Section 4.3.7). Nardo et al.'s (2008) statement that arithmetic aggregation of logarithmically transformed indicators is equivalent to geometric aggregation of non-transformed indicators only holds true if weights are not derived by statistical procedures. This in turn is not the ideal approach (see Section 4.3.7). Ratio scaling is a candidate for the key indicators' scaling procedure because it does not result in information loss nor in negative values. Moreover, targets and boundaries can be included. However, ratio scaling affects key indicators y differently depending on their effective direction ξ. Rescaling in combination with target setting stands out as a scaling method (Pollesch & Dale, 2016).[41] Targets and boundaries can be included, and mathematical discrepancies between key indicators y of different effective directions ξ are not present (Pollesch & Dale, 2016). Last, resulting scores are straightforward to interpret: The score depicts the performance of an economic object n in time period t in geographical region r relative to the *minimum of the rescaling range* δ_{min} and the *maximum of the rescaling range* δ_{max}. This clear interpretation benefits the assessment principle effective communication (see Table 3.1; e.g. Pintér et al., 2018).

For the MLSDI, key indicators y are rescaled on an identical range from ten to 100. A minimum of zero is avoided because the subsequent geometric aggregation would lead to an overall index score of zero (see Equation (4.25); Saisana & Philippas, 2012). For key indicators y with a positive effective direction ξ^+, a rescaled score of ten represents the *minimum of a sustainable development key indicator in the sample* y_{min}, and a rescaled score of 100 depicts the *maximum of a sustainable development key indicator in the sample* y_{max}. For key indicators y with a negative effective direction ξ^-, minima y_{min} and maxima y_{max} are reverted. Moreover, a score of ten indicates a boundary, whereas a score of 100 denotes a target. If an economic object n exceeds a target, the rescaled score will be higher than 100. However, targets and boundaries have not been finalised at corporate nor at national levels yet (see Section 6.3; e.g. O'Neill et al., 2018;

---

[40]In this context, growth rates would only refer to ratio indicators y_r. Growth indicators y_g (see Section 4.3.4) would not require a further scaling.

[41]Pollesch and Dale (2016) refer to rescaling with target setting as "target normalisation". This term is not adopted because it does not indicate the underlying scaling method and could be mistaken for ratio scaling with target setting.

Whiteman et al., 2013). Therefore, the rescaling range is merely determined by internal data. For positively affecting key indicators y, a rescaled score of 100 represents the sample maximum of the respective key indicator y_{max}. For negatively affecting key indicators y, a rescaled score of 100 represents the sample minimum of the respective key indicator y_{min}. Scores that exceed 100 are not possible with internal scaling. To realise the above described rescaling, a *rescaled sustainable development key indicator* y_s is computed by the following formula (Bravo, 2014; Krajnc & Glavič, 2005; Saisana & Philippas, 2012):

$$y_s(n,t,r) = \begin{cases} (\delta_{max} - \delta_{min}) \frac{y(n,t,r) - y_{min}(r)}{y_{max}(r) - y_{min}(r)} + \delta_{min}, & \text{if } \xi = \xi^+ \\ (\delta_{max} - \delta_{min}) \frac{y_{max}(r) - y(n,t,r)}{y_{max}(r) - y_{min}(r)} + \delta_{min}, & \text{if } \xi = \xi^- \end{cases}, \quad (4.13)$$

where $y_s \epsilon [1, Y_s]$ and $Y_s = Y$. A rescaled key indicator y_s may be a *rescaled sustainable development ratio indicator* $y_{rs} \epsilon [1, Y_{rs}]$ or a *rescaled sustainable development growth indicator* $y_{gs} \epsilon [1, Y_{gs}]$. Because rescaling relies on the extremes (i.e. y_{max} and y_{min}), it is highly sensitive to outliers (Nardo et al., 2008). Hence, outliers have been detected and treated in the previous calculation step (see Section 4.3.5.2).

The rescaled scores are interpreted as follows (Prescott-Allen, 2001):

- $10 \leq y_s < 20$: *bad* performance (unacceptable),
- $20 \leq y_s < 40$: *poor* performance (undesirable),
- $40 \leq y_s < 60$: *medium* performance,
- $60 \leq y_s < 80$: *fair* performance (acceptable),
- $80 \leq y_s \leq 100$: *good* performance (desirable).

The *set of rescaled sustainable development indicators* c_{4s} is formally described by:

$$c_{4s} = c_{4s}(n, y_s, t, r). \quad (4.14)$$

The rescaled key indicators y_s are weighted in the following section, Section 4.3.7.

4.3.7   Weighting

Weighting in index calculation refers to the process of assigning coefficients to the index's underlying variables in order to increase or decrease a variable's importance on the composite measure (Greco et al., 2019; Nardo et al., 2008). In sustainable development index calculation, weighting leads to compliance of the principles synergies and trade-offs as well as relevance: Weighting integrates themes, addresses relationships, determines interconnection of goals, and assesses their unequal contributions to sustainable development (see Table 3.1; e.g. Costanza, Fioramonti & Kubiszewski, 2016; Janoušková et al., 2018). Eventually, weighting closes the knowledge gap (see

Section 2.3.3; e.g. Weitz et al., 2018). Moreover, weighting ideally captures the relative benefit or harmfulness to society (T. Hahn & Figge, 2011) and should be objective (see Table 3.1; Sala et al., 2015).

In the MLSDI's weighting procedure, all contentual domains are addressed simultaneously in a multivariate setting because sustainable development is one integrated crisis and not three separate crises (see Section 2.1; WSSD, 2002). However, to account for the unbalanced number of key indicators y within the three contentual domains (see Section 5.3.1), the initially estimated coefficients are adjusted to sum up to one in each domain. An adjusted coefficient is a *weight*, denoting a key indicator's importance within a domain. An *importance factor* is a modified weight that signals a key indicator's influence on the overall index (Becker et al., 2017). The modification is accomplished by the rule of three: Weights are related to the number of indicators within a domain, and importance factors are related to the total number of indicators included in the MLSDI. Consistent with outlier detection and scales, weights are time invariant but may vary over geographical regions r (see Section 4.3.5 and Section 4.3.6; Nardo et al., 2008; Nilsson et al., 2016).

In the following section, Section 4.3.7.1, an overview on weighting methods is given to determine the MLSDI's approach. The applied methods are introduced in Section 4.3.7.2 to Section 4.3.7.4. Statistical tests are performed in Section 4.3.7.5.

4.3.7.1   Overview of weighting methods

Weighting methods in sustainable development index construction are controversially discussed because a range of possible pathways to sustainability exists (see Section 2.2.4; Leach et al., 2013). These possibilities are coupled with uncertainties in, for example, the environmental domain (see Section 2.2.1; Steffen et al., 2015). Weights of the environmental domain can only be determined properly if the natural scientific relationship is known (see Section 6.3; Ebert & Welsch, 2004). Established targets and boundaries are irrelevant for the weighting method because they are limits expressed in the scales (see Section 4.3.6.2). The possible pathways and uncertainties lead to three different approaches on weighting: expert surveys, equal weighting, and statistical weighting. Expert surveys and inclusion of subjective opinion can be advantageous because, for example, experts are a key source of information in corporate decision making (Escrig-Olmedo, Muñoz-Torres, Fernández-Izquierdo & Rivera-Lirio, 2017). However, subjective methods are severely criticised because subjectivity leads to volatile results, disagreements, and a lack of science (Giannetti, Bonilla, Silva & Villas Bôas de Almeida, 2009; Rogge, 2012). Mixed methods such as multicriteria decision-making methods (e.g. Boggia & Cortina, 2010; Triantaphyllou, 2000) reduce the amount of subjectivity by providing "objective mathematics to process subjective and personal preferences" (Saaty, 2001). One example of such a method is the analytical hierarchy process.

Weights are determined by decomposing the problem into a system of hierarchies and comparing the decomposed elements in a pairwise manner (Saaty, 1980; Triantaphyllou, 2000). Despite being diminished, subjectivity remains a critical issue (Zhou et al., 2006) as decision makers might be tempted to take advantage of their mediating power (see Section 3.2; Jesinghaus, 2018). Second, e.g. Schmidt-Traub et al. (2017b) argue equal weighting should be applied because a consensus on weights in expert surveys could not be established, and equal weights would reflect a policy maker's commitment of equal goal priority. Further arguments for equal weighting include simplicity of construction, a lack of theoretical structure to justify other weighting schemes, and inadequate statistical knowledge (Decancq & Lugo, 2013; Greco et al., 2019; Nardo et al., 2008). Top-down equal weighting is an enhanced version of equal weighting because variables are first equally weighted into categories, then categories are equally weighted into domains, and last, domains are equally weighted into an overall index (e.g. Schmidt-Traub et al., 2017b; Zuo et al., 2017). Nilsson et al. (2016) warn to ignore overlaps of targets and goals: Double counting would occur, resulting in an implicit higher weighting of equally weighted correlated variables (Greco et al., 2019; Nardo et al., 2008). Rogge (2012) also concludes that the simplicity of equal weighting "is often thoroughly misleading". In conclusion, equal weighting is "convenient but [...] universally considered to be wrong" (Chowdhury & Squire, 2006; Decancq & Lugo, 2013; Greco et al., 2019). To tackle synergies and trade-offs as well as relevance, statistical methods must be applied until the natural scientific relationships are known (see above; Ebert & Welsch, 2004) because statistical weighting is least biased and least subjective (Greco et al., 2019; Mayer, 2008; Zhou, Ang & Poh, 2007).

Statistical weighting in index calculation essentially regards data reduction (Mayer, 2008). The sustainable development elements (i.e. the rescaled key indicators y_s) are cleaned with respect to correlations and mutually included information. Multivariate statistical techniques for dimensionality reduction include a variety of methods, and an overview can be found in, e.g. Meng et al. (2016). In the field of sustainable development assessment, data envelopment analysis, factor analysis, and PCA are conducted (e.g. Bolcárová & Kološta, 2015; Shaker, 2018; Tseng et al., 2018; B. Zhang et al., 2008; Zhou et al., 2007). Data envelopment analysis is not suitable as a weighting method for a sustainable development index because it is a technique for measuring efficiencies of decision-making objects, not being concerned with data reduction (Charnes, Cooper & Rhodes, 1978; Ramanathan, 2003; Rogge, 2012). Moreover, efficiencies are obtained by dividing weighted sums of data outputs by weighted sums of data inputs. Weights in turn are determined by an optimisation function defined by the modeller (Greco et al., 2019). This procedure entails three issues. First, weights maximise the composite indicator (Ramanathan, 2003), while sustainable development index construction is not an optimisation problem. Instead, the index is designed to quantify unsupervised sustainable development performances (see Chapter 3 and Chapter 4; e.g. Bell &

Morse, 2008). Data envelopment analysis overemphasises well-performing elements, such that economic objects n may appear as brilliant performers, while they are not (Rogge, 2012). Second, the target function involves a modeller's subjectivity, and third, aggregation by weighted sums does not minimise substitutability as required along with weak sustainability (see Section 2.2.4 and Section 4.3.8). Factor analysis and PCA are dimensionality reduction techniques and generally suitable for weighting. They are closely related to each other but differ in the direction of analysis. Factor analysis is a top-down approach that aims to describe a number of latent factors with a smaller number of observed variables. A model is fitted, and the solution to it is non-unique (Haerdle & Simar, 2012). PCA functions vice versa: PCA is a bottom-up method that reduces observed variables into a smaller number of latent components. Because sustainable development index calculation is an unsupervised modelling task, it is a bottom-up problem setting in which the latent index is driven by the behaviour of the observed variables (Mayer, 2008). Consequently, PCA instead of factor analysis is suitable for weighting. Furthermore, PCA yields one unique solution, such that subjective interpretations are absent (Haerdle & Simar, 2012). However, factor analysis is a useful tool in problem settings such as studied by Tseng et al. (2018). An explanatory factor analysis is applied to derive latent constructs by underlying, observed attributes of corporate sustainability such as stakeholder management and corporate culture.

The next section, Section 4.3.7.2, describes the PCA as the first method to derive a *weight of a sustainable development key indicator* ω and an *importance factor of a sustainable development key indicator* ψ. Two further methods follow in Section 4.3.7.3 and Section 4.3.7.4.

4.3.7.2   Multivariate statistical analysis: Principal Component Analysis (PCA)

PCA (Pearson, 1901) is a linear, static technique to reduce a data set's dimensionality by only incorporating data that are responsible for a certain variation (Haerdle & Simar, 2012; G. James et al., 2013; Jolliffe, 2002). This technique can be used for determining key indicators' weights ω because rescaled key indicators y_s that are responsible for more variation in the data set contain more information and should thus receive a higher weight. Because PCA focuses on variances (G. James et al., 2013; Jolliffe, 2002), data must be free of outliers and z-score scaled (see Section 4.3.5.2 and Section 4.3.6.2; Field, 2009). Otherwise, weights of high variance variables would be overestimated (G. James et al., 2013). PCA does not impose a distributional assumption (Jolliffe, 2002), but as linear correlations are investigated, it is assumed that variables are linearly related.

To achieve the dimensionality reduction, data are transformed to a number of latent, uncorrelated *Principal Components (PCs)*, which are sorted in a descending order according to their variation along with the original data set (G. James et al., 2013;

Jolliffe, 2002). A system of linear equations is set up and solved subject to several constraints. The linear equations contain original variables and associated coefficients, also referred to as *loadings*. The first PC is found by maximising the PC's variance subject to the loadings having a unit length of one. This is obtained by equalising the sum of squared elements of the vector of loadings to one. The second PC is derived by maximising the variance and appending the constraint of being orthogonal to the first PC; the product of the first and the second PCs' loadings is equalised to zero. The following PCs are found in a similar fashion. After solving the system for each equation, each PC's loading and eigenvalue are specified (Jolliffe, 2002). Definitions of *eigenvalues* are typically complex, mathematical definitions (Field, 2009) and can be found in, e.g. Haerdle and Simar (2012). In PCA, eigenvalues refer to the variance-covariance matrix and reveal the evenness of distribution of variances throughout the data set (Field, 2009). Loadings are stored in a matrix with variables in the rows and PCs in the columns (Jolliffe, 2002). Squaring each element of this matrix yields the substantive importance of a variable to a PC (Field, 2009). To receive the weights, this matrix is multiplied with a vector of variances of the PCs. However, not all PCs are included, but only a few are chosen that adequately account for a certain variation in the data set. Rules for inclusion involve thresholds on eigenvalues and the explained cumulative variance. These thresholds are critically discussed in the literature. Kaiser (1960) suggests including PCs with eigenvalues larger than one as these explain at least one variable. Jolliffe (2002) argues that Kaiser's (1960) criterion is too strict and recommends a threshold of 0.7. There is evidence that Kaiser's (1960) criterion is accurate if the chosen PCs explain a cumulative variance greater or equal than 70% with a sample size smaller than 30 or 60% with a sample size greater than 250 (Field, 2009).

For the MLSDI, the sample size equals 62 (see Section 5.1), and thus, PCs with eigenvalues larger than one or to reach a cumulative variance of 70% are included. The PCA is performed (CRAN, 2019) for each time period t, and a *weight of a sustainable development key indicator derived by the PCA* ω^{PCA} is obtained by applying the arithmetic mean over the time periods t:

$$\omega^{PCA}(y_s, r) = \frac{1}{T} \sum_{t=1}^{T} \omega_t^{PCA}(y_s, t, r), \tag{4.15}$$

where ω_t^{PCA} represents a *weight of a sustainable development key indicator derived by the PCA in a time period t*. The corresponding *importance factor of a sustainable development key indicator derived by the PCA* ψ^{PCA} is formally represented by:

$$\psi^{PCA} = \psi^{PCA}(y_s, r). \tag{4.16}$$

A PC is the weighted sum of the loadings and *z-score scaled key indicators* y_z, where

$y_z \epsilon [1, Y_z]$ and $Y_z = Y$. It corresponds to a *sustainable development key component* p, and its set – the *set of sustainable development key components* c_3 – is formally represented by:

$$c_3 = c_3(n, p, t, r), \tag{4.17}$$

where $p\epsilon[1, P]$. However, as the weighted sum is not deployed for aggregation (see Section 4.3.8), key components p and their set c_3 are obsolete.

Disadvantages of the PCA are incorrect assessment of the temporal dimension and limitation to linearity (see above). In the following section, Section 4.3.7.3, the PCA is extended to the Partial Triadic Analysis (PTA) to overcome the first shortcoming of the incorrect temporal assessment.

4.3.7.3   Multivariate statistical analysis: Partial Triadic Analysis (PTA)

The PTA expands the PCA by incorporating time. Three-dimensional panel data are interpreted as a sequence of two-dimensional tables.[42] In doing so, a multivariate time series structure is captured in three steps. The first step is called *interstructure* and aims to derive the importance of each time period. A matrix of scalar products between two-dimensional tables is computed to derive temporal weights. In a second step, the weighted sum of the original time series of tables is computed, yielding the so-called *compromise matrix*. This matrix captures the common structure of the two-dimensional tables. As a last step, rows and columns of all original tables of the time series are projected onto a PCA of the compromise. Thus, this step is called *trajectory*. The trajectories summarise the variability of the time series around the compromise (Gallego-Álvarez, Galindo-Villardón & Rodríguez-Rosa, 2015; Thioulouse et al., 2004).

The application utilised in the MLSDI is based on Dray, Dufour and Thioulouse (2018). A *weight of a time period derived by the PTA* Ω^{PTA} is formally denoted by:

$$\Omega^{PTA} = \Omega^{PTA}(t, r). \tag{4.18}$$

A *weight of a sustainable development key indicator derived by the PTA* ω^{PTA} is determined similarly to the PCA (see Section 4.3.7.2), but the temporal dimension is implicitly accounted for (see above), such that the arithmetic mean is not required:

$$\omega^{PTA} = \omega^{PTA}(y_s, r). \tag{4.19}$$

The corresponding *importance factor of a sustainable development key indicator*

---

[42]Several authors controversially discuss the originality and mathematical details of this approach (e.g. Kroonenberg, 1983; Thioulouse, Simier & Chessel, 2004). According to the research of this work, first versions of temporal extensions date back to Tucker (1964), who extended factor analysis to three-dimensional matrices. Levin (1965); and Tucker (1966) followed this approach and referred to it as "three-mode factor analysis". Kroonenberg (1983) applied the idea to PCA and named it "Partial Triadic Analysis (PTA)". Thioulouse and Chessel (1987) first applied it to ecology.

derived by the PTA ψ^{PTA} is represented by:

$$\psi^{PTA} = \psi^{PTA}(y_s, r). \tag{4.20}$$

Discussion on the number of PCs to retain could not be identified in the literature. Transferring Kaiser's (1960) criterion to the PTA and its implicit inclusion of time, PCs with eigenvalues exceeding the number of time periods T are retained. Given the cumulative variance's relative character, its threshold value remains at 70%. Key components p would be determined analogously to their derivation in the PCA but are also redundant (see Section 4.3.7.2).

The following section, Section 4.3.7.4, deals with the Maximum Relevance Minimum Redundancy Backward (MRMRB) algorithm. It is an information-theoretic application that overcomes the shortcoming of the PCA and the PTA of being limited to linearity (see Section 4.3.7.2). Hereafter, the term "PC family" is used when referring to both PCA and PTA. Their weights and importance factors are summarised in the symbols ω^{PC} and ψ^{PC}, respectively.

4.3.7.4   Information theory: Maximum Relevance Minimum Redundancy Backward (MRMRB) algorithm

Information theory has its origins in communication theory (Shannon, 1948) but relates to many disciplines nowadays. Of interest for this work are its relations to statistics and computer science (Cover & Thomas, 1991). How can key indicators' weights ω be derived by statistical approaches of information theory, and what are efficient algorithms in application? Motivation for information-theoretic applications are non-linearity as well as its known efficiency and effectiveness (P. E. Meyer, 2008; P. E. Meyer, Lafitte & Bontempi, 2008; Peng, Long & Ding, 2005; Yu & Liu, 2004). Similar to the PC family, information theory is a bottom-up approach, in which the underlying variables drive the index's behaviour (see Section 4.3.7.1; Mayer, 2008).

Information-theoretic index construction may be based on the Fisher information or entropy. *Fisher information* measures the amount of information that a variable contains about a parameter and is defined in the context of a family of parametric distributions. Similar to the Fisher information is *entropy*, which also measures the amount of information a variable contains. It is a function of an underlying process's probability distribution and "is a measure of the average uncertainty in the random variable". In contrast to the Fisher information, entropy is non-parametric and defined for all distributions (Cover & Thomas, 1991). Because an index is based on a variety of variables that originate in diverse distributions, entropy is the preferred measure. *Mutual information* is closely related to entropy and is the reduction of uncertainty in a random variable due to another random variable. It measures the dependency between two random variables but can be extended to be multivariate (Cover & Thomas, 1991).

Moreover, it is also referred to as *total correlation* and is a natural measure of relevance (Jakulin & Bratko, 2004; P. E. Meyer, 2008; Watanabe, 1960). A variable is *relevant* if it reduces uncertainty (Kojadinovic, 2005) and if its removal alters the overall or a subset's conditional probability distribution (Kohavi & John, 1997; P. E. Meyer, 2008). In contrast, a variable is *redundant* if and only if it is not relevant (Yu & Liu, 2004). To yield inference about the variables' relationships, multivariate data are understood as a network, and three steps are carried out. First, data are discretised, second, a matrix containing mutual information is calculated, and third, an inference algorithm is performed. Discretisation is the partitioning of an interval into subintervals. It suffers from information loss because differentiation between values of one interval is not possible (Schäfer & Strimmer, 2005; Yang & Webb, 2009). Nonetheless, estimators are constructed for discrete variables (P. E. Meyer, 2008) because simulation studies provide evidence that discretisation yields better results than basing the analysis on distributional assumptions (Dougherty, Kohavi & Sahami, 1995; Yang & Webb, 2009).

Several algorithms were developed to assess gene networks in the field of bioinformatics (e.g. P. E. Meyer et al., 2008). These types of algorithms are of interest in sustainable development index calculation because the individual sustainable development elements also represent a network of mutually correlated nodes that go beyond linear correlations. In this work, the MRMRB algorithm is deployed (P. E. Meyer et al., 2008, 2019) because experiments deliver evidence of superior performance relative to several other algorithms (Bourdakou, Athanasiadis & Spyrou, 2016; P. E. Meyer, Marbach, Roy & Kellis, 2010). The MRMRB algorithm first determines the difference of mutual information between two random variables (i.e. relevance) and the average mutual information along the selected variables (i.e. redundancy). Subsequently, the algorithm ranks these differences, with direct interactions being ranked before indirect interactions. As a third step, backward elimination is performed: Variables with the lowest mutual information are first eliminated from the network (P. E. Meyer et al., 2010). With the MRMRB algorithm, four estimators can be implemented: empirical estimator, Miller-Madow corrected estimator, Shrink entropy estimator, and Schurmann-Grassberger estimator (P. E. Meyer et al., 2008). In calculating the MLSDI, the Miller-Madow corrected estimator is chosen as it corrects the asymptotic bias of the empirical estimator. The Shrink entropy estimator is less general and only suitable for small sample sizes (P. E. Meyer et al., 2008; Schäfer & Strimmer, 2005). The Schurmann-Grassberger estimator is parametric and makes distributional assumptions (P. E. Meyer et al., 2008). Key indicators y are discretised by equal frequency discretisation. In this discretisation method, the partitioned interval may be of different sizes, but the frequency of occurrence within an interval is identical in each interval (P. E. Meyer, 2008; Yang & Webb, 2009). Especially when combined with the Miller-Madow corrected estimator, this discretisation method is more efficient than methods such as equal width (P. E. Meyer, 2008; Yang & Webb, 2003). The number of intervals controls the variance-bias trade-off in estimation: Too many intervals result in too few data points and an increased variance, whereas too few intervals lead to information loss and an increased bias (see above; Cover & Thomas, 1991; P. E. Meyer, 2008; Yang & Webb, 2009). Recommendation by P. E. Meyer et al. (2008); and Yang and Webb (2003) on the bin size of the interval is followed: The *bin size of equal frequency discretisation* χ_s, which depicts the number of economic objects N in one bin, is set equal to the square root of the sample size:

$$\chi_s = \sqrt{N}. \tag{4.21}$$

Given the square root, the *number of bins of equal frequency discretisation* χ_n is equivalent to the bin size χ_s:

$$\chi_n = \frac{N}{\chi_s} = \frac{N}{\sqrt{N}} = \sqrt{N} = \chi_s. \tag{4.22}$$

A *weight of a sustainable development key indicator derived by the MRMRB algorithm* ω^{MRMRB} is formally denoted as follows:

$$\omega^{MRMRB} = \omega^{MRMRB}(y_s, r). \tag{4.23}$$

The corresponding *importance factor of a sustainable development key indicator derived by the MRMRB* ψ^{MRMRB} is formally described by:

$$\psi^{MRMRB} = \psi^{MRMRB}(y_s, r). \tag{4.24}$$

Because the MRMRB algorithm is capable of detecting higher order correlations, it is expected to yield superior results compared to the PC family.

The next section, Section 4.3.7.5, deals with statistical tests of the PC family (see Section 4.3.7.2 and Section 4.3.7.3). The MRMRB algorithm does not require statistical tests because it does not make distributional assumptions (see above), and the total correlation is simply zero in the absence of correlations (Cover & Thomas, 1991).

4.3.7.5   Statistical tests of model assumptions

The PC family is tested with the Kaiser-Meyer-Olkin (KMO) measure of sampling adequacy (Kaiser, 1970) and Bartlett's test of sphericity (Bartlett, 1950, 1951).[43] The KMO measure is the ratio of squared correlations between variables to the squared partial correlation between variables. It indicates the degree of diffusion in the pattern of correlations: A value close to zero indicates a relatively small numerator and diffusion in the pattern of correlations, whereas a value close to one indicates a relatively large

---

[43]These tests were initially developed for factor analysis but can also be applied to PCA (Field, 2009; Jolliffe, 2002).

numerator and a compact pattern of correlations. In the latter case, the sample is adequate for performing the PC family (Field, 2009; Kaiser, 1970). Values of the KMO measure and resulting factorial simplicity are interpreted as follows (Kaiser, 1974):

- $KMO < 0.5$: *unacceptable*,

- $0.5 \leq KMO < 0.6$: *miserable*,

- $0.6 \leq KMO < 0.7$: *mediocre*,

- $0.7 \leq KMO < 0.8$: *middling*,

- $0.8 \leq KMO < 0.9$: *meritorious*,

- $0.9 \leq KMO \leq 1.0$: *marvellous*.

To evaluate whether the KMO measure should be based on Pearson's coefficient or Kendall's tau (see Section 4.3.3.3; Field, 2009), normality of the z-score scaled key indicators y_z is tested. Similar to the key figures x, the univariate Shapiro-Wilk and Kolmogorov-Smirnov tests are performed (see Section 4.3.3.4; e.g. CRAN, 2019). For consistency to the PC family's calculation procedure, tests are performed for each year and averaged subsequently.

Bartlett's test of sphericity examines whether there are PCs to determine. Under the null hypothesis, the correlation matrix is proportional to the identity matrix: Group variances are the same or similar to each other, and covariances are equal or close to zero. In this case, variables are not correlated, and PCs do not exist. The null hypothesis is desired to be rejected with p-values smaller than 0.05 (Field, 2009). The same correlation coefficient (Pearson vs. Kendall) as for the KMO test is chosen.

Multicollinearity is not an issue for the PC family (Field, 2009) and thus not tested.

4.3.8   Aggregation

Aggregation theory is an area of mathematics that investigates aggregation functions (Pollesch & Dale, 2015). An index or composite measure is an *aggregate*, which is a single value that represents "an arbitrary long set of related values" (Pollesch & Dale, 2015). An *aggregation function* performs the mathematical operation of mapping diverse variables into one aggregate (Grabisch et al., 2009; Pollesch & Dale, 2015). This mathematical operation is called *aggregation*. Aggregation is considered as the major step in index construction (Zhou et al., 2010) because it moderates the degree of substitutability (Grabisch et al., 2009). To map weak sustainability with minimised substitutability (see Section 2.2.4), a *compensatory* aggregation function ought to be applied because high input components may be offset by low input components and vice versa. In contrast, setoffs are not possible in *non-compensatory* aggregation functions (Pollesch & Dale, 2015). These hence map strong sustainability. For methodologically sound aggregation in terms of credibility, validity, and reliability (see Table 3.1; Cash et

	Non-comparability	Comparability
Interval scale	Dictatorial ordering	Arithmetic mean, weighted sum
Ratio scale	Geometric mean, weighted product	Any homothetic function

Table 4.4 Aggregation rules (Böhringer & Jochem, 2007; Ebert & Welsch, 2004; Pollesch & Dale, 2015)

al., 2003; Janoušková et al., 2018), aggregation rules must be obeyed. Ebert and Welsch (2004) show that meaningful aggregation of diverse variables into an aggregate depends on the variables' scales. Their aggregation rules regard the type of scale (interval vs. ratio) as well as non-comparability and comparability of scales. *Non-comparable* or *independent* scales are present when all input and output variables are measured on the same scale but do not share the same unit. *Comparable* or *single* scales are present when input and output variables share the exact same scale and unit of measurement. In this context, input and output variables refer to the index: Inputs are the unscaled key indicators y and outputs are the resulting composite measures. The aggregation rules' matrix is shown in Table 4.4. Dictatorial ordering is an aggregation function in which one input variable is responsible for the output and is thus non-compensatory (Ebert & Welsch, 2004; Pollesch & Dale, 2015). The geometric mean is equivalent to the weighted product with equal weights (Zhou et al., 2006) and is hence a special case of the weighted product. The same applies to the arithmetic mean and weighted sum. The aggregation rules by Ebert and Welsch (2004) can therefore be extended to the weighted product and weighted sum (see Table 4.4). Geometric aggregation (geometric mean or weighted product) and arithmetic aggregation (arithmetic mean or weighted sum) are both compensatory aggregation functions (Pollesch & Dale, 2015).

As probably most other sustainable development indices, the MLSDI comprises ratio-scaled, non-comparable key indicators y (see Table 4.3). Therefore, only geometric aggregation is meaningful. Moreover, geometric aggregation implicates two advantages. First, it maps weak sustainability with minimised substitutability because it is a compensatory aggregation function that penalises poor performances and rewards good performances (Yoon & Hwang, 1995; Zhou et al., 2006). Balanced performances yield better aggregated scores than unbalanced performances. The lower an indicator's score, the lower the rate of compensation is. If only one indicator equals zero, the composite measure vanishes. To avoid this non-compensatory case, the geometric aggregation is combined with rescaled key indicators y_s between ten — instead of zero — and 100 (see Section 4.3.6.2; Saisana & Philippas, 2012). Second, the weighted product performs best in respect of information loss: The system of information before aggregation is closest to the system of information after aggregation (Zelený, 1982; Zhou et al., 2006).

The weighted product (Pollesch & Dale, 2015) is applied to aggregate the rescaled key indicators y_s of a contentual domain, accounting for synergies and trade-offs (see Table 3.1; e.g. Costanza, Fioramonti & Kubiszewski, 2016) and yielding a *subindex of a contentual domain* d:

$$d(n,t,r) = \prod_{y_s=1}^{Y_s} y_s(n,t,r)^{\omega(y_s,r)}, \qquad (4.25)$$

where $d \epsilon [1, D]$. The *set of sustainable development subindices* c_2 then reads:

$$c_2 = c_2(n,d,t,r). \qquad (4.26)$$

To yield the *overall MLSDI* c_1, the geometric mean is deployed on the subindices d:

$$c_1(n,t,r) = \prod_{d=1}^{D} d(n,t,r)^{\frac{1}{D}}. \qquad (4.27)$$

Statistical weighting of the contentual domains is not feasible because methods approximately reflect the contentual domains' number of key indicators Y. Scores of the four composite measures – the subindices of each contentual domains d and the overall MLSDI c_1 – are interpreted in the same fashion as the rescaled key indicators' scores (see Section 4.3.6.2).

In the final step of the MLSDI, sensitivities are investigated. The following section, Section 4.3.9, outlines the methodology of this investigation.

4.3.9   Sensitivity analyses

Sensitivity analysis is the study of appointing individual sources of uncertainty in the model input to variances of the model output (Saisana, Saltelli & Tarantola, 2005; Saltelli et al., 2008; Saltelli, Tarantola, Campolongo & Ratto, 2004). In index construction, sensitivities of each calculation step should be analysed to ensure methodological soundness in terms of credibility, validity, and reliability as well as robustness and transparency (see Table 3.1; Cash et al., 2003; Janoušková et al., 2018; Pintér et al., 2018; Saisana et al., 2005; Sala et al., 2015).

Sophisticated methods for sensitivity analyses include, for instance, elementary effects methods, variance-based methods, factor mapping, and meta-modelling (Saltelli et al., 2008). However, for the MLSDI, profound theoretical and methodological research has been carried out (see Chapter 2 to Section 4.3.8), such that a simple OAT sampling for non-unique calculation steps is sufficient. In an OAT sampling, one parameter is varied at a time (Saltelli et al., 2008). Non-unique calculation steps that involve alternatives are missing value imputation (see Section 4.3.3), outlier detection (see Section 4.3.5), and weighting (see Section 4.3.7). For missing value imputation and weighting, sensitivities of the different presented methods are investigated. Regarding outlier detection, the outlier coefficient α is varied, and three cases are investigated:

the outlier coefficient α equals 1.5, 3.0, and infinity. The first case is the base case (see Section 4.3.5.2; e.g. Aggarwal, 2017) and depicts the *inner fence*, the second case is laxer and constitutes the *outer fence* (Tukey, 1977), and the last case corresponds to a non-treatment case (see Section 4.3.9). The latter is of importance as distortion of the true picture is a general concern in outlier treatment (see Section 4.3.5; McGregor & Pouw, 2017). Sensitivities are examined by economic objects' average rank shift in the four composite measures and changes in their performance scores (Greco et al., 2019).

4.4   Summary and interim conclusion

Thus far, a conceptual framework of sustainable development has been derived, and in doing so, the first four related research gaps – the perspective, operational-to-normative, knowledge, and the sustainability gaps – have been identified and partially addressed. By including the multilevel perspective and the St. Gallen management model in the conceptual framework, the perspective and the operational-to-normative gaps are theoretically closed. Comprehensive and comparable measurement of sustainable development performances by multilevel objects are inevitable for the sustainability transition because sustainable development is a society-level concept and can only be achieved if micro and meso objects contribute. Sustainable development assessment principles that account for the first four related gaps assist to determine the most useful analytical tool for a comprehensive and comparable measurement. Indicator sets that include a composite measure stand out as such tools. Indicators are able to map all six dimensions of the conceptual framework, including the aggregational size for multilevel measurement, and are capable of obeying the conceptual as well as the assessment principles. They continue closing the perspective and the operational-to-normative gaps. Sustainable development indices address the knowledge gap by exploring synergies and trade-offs of individual sustainable development elements. However, multilevel sustainable development indices could not be identified in the academic literature, and previous single level indices lack compliance of the assessment principles and exhibit methodological shortcomings. The lack of methodological soundness constitutes the fifth and last research gap. Hence, the MLSDI's main contributions are multilevel applicability and methodological strength.

To quantify meso-level corporate contributions to the macro concept sustainable development, the MLSDI is derived in nine well-researched steps: collection of key figures, preparation of key figures, imputation of missing values, standardisation to key indicators, outlier detection and treatment, scaling, weighting, aggregation, and sensitivity analyses. The data collection of key figures relies on official, open source statistics to address the sustainability gap and ensure the assessment principle transparency. Two methods for missing value imputation are tested: single time series imputation and multiple panel data imputation. The key indicators are determined by aligning the meso GRI and the macro SDG frameworks. Multilevel comparability is established by standardisation to the GVA and further metrics. Macro-level GVA instead of, for example, meso-level profits is chosen because comparable measurement of meso contributions to the macro SDGs is aimed at. Outliers are detected and treated by the IQR method, and key indicators are rescaled between ten and 100. Three weighting methods are examined: the PCA, PTA, and the MRMRB algorithm. The latter is theoretically superior and thus expected to yield more accurate results. Geometric aggregation is implemented to project weak sustainability with minimised substitutability. Sensitivities of the four composite measures – the three subindices and the overall MLSDI – are tested for missing value imputation, outlier detection, and weighting. In conclusion, the MLSDI overcomes previous indices' methodological shortcomings in several aspects:

1. The MLSDI cleans data objectively and credibly. In contrast, only one of the reviewed indices reduces the statistical bias of missing values objectively, and none treats outliers credibly.

2. The MLSDI weights individual sustainable development elements by sophisticated multivariate statistical techniques and an information-theoretic algorithm. On the other hand, less than half of the reviewed indices investigate the interconnections and relevance of indicators, and only one of these does so in an objective and credible manner.

3. The MLSDI obeys mathematical aggregation rules, whereas only one third of the reviewed indices perform objective and credible aggregation.

4. The MLSDI performs sensitivity analyses for three calculation steps. On the contrary, only one third of the reviewed indices investigate sensitivities, and only one of these does so for more than one calculation step.

A summary of the methodological approaches and assessment principle compliance by each calculation step of previous sustainable development indices and the MLSDI is displayed in Table 4.5.

In the following chapter, Chapter 5, the MLSDI is applied to a sample region. The application crafts reliable empirical knowledge about sustainable development performances of this region and empirically tackles the knowledge gap. By broadly disclosing the calculation results, the sustainability gap is further approached.

Calculation step, assessment principle	DJSI	ICSD	FEEM SI	HSDI	MISD	SDGI	SDI	SSI	WI	MLSDI
1. Collection	Company data	Company data	IGO data	IGO data	U	IGO data	Official data	IGO and further data	IGO and further data	Official data
Transparency	N	Y	Y	Y	N	Y	Y	Y	Y	Y
2. Preparation	U	N	N	N	Transformation to normality	N	N	N	N	Y
Multilevel comparability	N	N	N	N	N	N	N	N	N	Y
Methodological soundness	U	U	U	U	Y	U	U	U	U	Y
3. Imputation	U	N	N	N	Multiple	P	Mean	Expert judgement	P	Single, multiple
Methodological soundness	U	P	N	N	Y	N	P	N	N	Y
4. Standardisation	U; 81 indicators	Y, e.g. per production unit; 38 GRI indicators	Y, e.g. per GDP; 19 indicators	Y, e.g. p.c.; 4 indicators	U; 31 indices	Y, e.g. p.c.; 77 SDG indicators	Y, e.g. per GDP; 12 indicators	Y, e.g. p.c.; 21 indicators	Y, e.g. per GDP; 86 indicators	Y, e.g. per GVA: 44 GRI and SDG indicators[1]
Comprehensiveness	Y	P	Y	N	U	Y	Y	Y	Y	Y
Multilevel comparability	N	N	N	N	N	N	N	N	N	Y
Methodological soundness	U	N	Y	Y	U	Y	Y	Y	Y	Y
Efficiency and effectiveness	Y	Y	Y	Y	U	Y	Y	Y	Y	Y
5. Outlier	U	N	Lower weights on outliers	N	N	Truncation of the bottom below the 2.5 percentile	N	Thresholds on skewness and kurtosis; non-linear transformation	Truncation of the top above the 90% base-best	IQR method
Methodological soundness	U	P	P	P	N	P	N	N	P	Y
6. Scaling	U	Continuous ratio scaling	Discrete rescaling	Continuous rescaling	Continuous rescaling	Continuous rescaling	Continuous z-scores	Continuous rescaling	Continuous rescaling	Continuous rescaling
Indicator comparability	U	Y	Y	Y	Y	Y	Y	Y	Y	Y
Methodological soundness	U	N	N	P	P	Y	P	Y	Y	Y

continued

Calculation step. assessment principle	DJSI	ICSD	FEEM SI	HSDI	MISD	SDGI	SDI	SSI	WI	MLSDI
Target orientedness	N	Y	Y	Y	U	Y	N	Y	Y	Y
Effective communication	N	N	Y	Y	Y	Y	N	Y	Y	Y
7. Weighting	U; floating, industry-specific weights	Analytical hierarchy process	Experts' elicitation	Equal weighting	Factor analysis	Top-down equal weighting	PCA	Top-down equal weighting	Arbitrary weighting	PCA, PTA, MRMRB
Synergies and trade-offs	U	Y	Y	N	Y	N	Y	N	U	Y
Methodological soundness	N	N	N	N	P	N	Y	N	N	Y
8. Aggregation	U	Arithmetic aggregation	Choquet integral	Geometric aggregation	Geometric aggregation	Arithmetic aggregation	Arithmetic aggregation	Geometric aggregation	Arithmetic aggregation	Geometric aggregation
Minimised substitutability, methodological soundness	U	N	N	Y	Y	N	N	Y	N	Y
9. Sensitivity analyses	U	N	Weighting	N	N	Outliers, aggregation	N	Weighting	N	Imputation, outliers, weighting
Methodological soundness, transparency	N	N	Y	N	N	Y	N	Y	N	Y

Table 4.5 Summary of methodological approaches and assessment principle compliance of previous sustainable development indices and the MLSDI: Y, yes; P, partially; N, no; U, unknown; †, see Section 5.3.1: DJSI, Dow Jones Sustainability Indices; FEEM SI, FEEM Sustainability Index; GDP, Gross Domestic Product; GRI, Global Reporting Initiative; GVA, Gross Value Added; HSDI, Human Sustainable Development Index; ICSD, Composite Sustainable Development Index; IGO, Intergovernmental Organisation; IQR, Interquartile Range; MISD, Mega Index of Sustainable Development; MRMRB, Maximum Relevance Minimum Redundancy Backward algorithm; p.c., per capita; PCA, Principal Component Analysis; PTA, Partial Triadic Analysis; SDG, Sustainable Development Goal; SDGI, Sustainable Development Goal Index; SDI, Sustainable Development Index; SSI, Sustainable Society Index; WI, Wellbeing Index

Chapter 5

Empirical findings

In this chapter, the previously developed methodology of the MLSDI (see Chapter 4) is computed for a sample region, and the empirical findings are presented and discussed. Thereby, the knowledge (see Section 2.3.3; e.g. Weitz et al., 2018) and the sustainability gap (see Section 2.3.4; e.g. Hall et al., 2017) are tackled.

This chapter is structured as follows. First, the sample (except the key figures x and the key indicators y) is introduced in Section 5.1. Hereafter, results of the sustainable development key figures are exhibited in Section 5.2: Section 5.2.1 presents results of the data collection and preparation process, and Section 5.2.2 fills the incomplete sample's data gaps. Section 5.3 deals with the multilevel key indicators y. First, they are derived from the meso GRI and the macro SDG frameworks in Section 5.3.1, and second, their empirical findings are analysed. To this end, summary statistics of the unscaled growth indicators y_g are investigated in Section 5.3.2, whereas an analysis of the unscaled ratio indicators y_r is refrained from, given their non-comparability. The key indicators' outlier detection and treatment are outlined in Section 5.3.3, and the empirical findings of the cleaned and rescaled key indicators y_s are examined in Section 5.3.4. The main contribution to the knowledge gap's missing understanding of the dynamic interactions of the individual sustainable development elements makes Section 5.4. A comparative analysis of weights ω and importance factors ψ by the three applied weighting methods – PCA, PTA, and MRMRB algorithm – is carried out in Section 5.4.3. Section 5.4.1 and Section 5.4.4 deal with the PC family's statistics, and Section 5.4.2 outlines the MRMRB algorithm's diagnostics. Section 5.5 analyses the four composite sustainable development measures' summary statistics (see Section 5.5.1) and results for the selected branches (see Section 5.5.2). Last, sensitivities of the applied methods are tested in Section 5.6.

© The Author(s) 2021
C. Lemke, *Accounting and Statistical Analyses for Sustainable Development*, Sustainable Management, Wertschöpfung und Effizienz, https://doi.org/10.1007/978-3-658-33246-4_5

5.1   Data base, objects of investigation, and time periods

Because the MLSDI's calculation mechanisms are driven by macro-economic objects n (see Section 4.3.1), macro-economic data from official statistics comprise the data base. These statistics deliver best benchmarks (Carraro et al., 2013) for methodological soundness (see Section 3.1; e.g. Cash et al., 2003) and are open access. Therefore, they are easily acquired (Zuo et al., 2017), and transparency is provided (see Section 3.1; e.g. Pintér et al., 2018). As it has been anticipated in Section 4.3.2, the sample's geographical region r is Germany, and thus, data are collected from the following three official institutions: Destatis, Eurostat, and the Federal Employment Agency (BA). Destatis and Eurostat mainly cover key figures x of the environmental and the economic domain, whereas social key figures x are primarily acquired from the BA. More information on the collected key figures x will follow in Section 5.2.1. The time horizon reaches from 2008 ($t = 1$) to 2016 ($T = 9$). Data before 2008 are not comparable as they are released in a predecessor classification of the currently valid NACE Rev. 2 standard (Eurostat, 2008b). 2016 is the most recent year of major statistics by economic objects n at the time of research (e.g. Destatis, 2018h). The macro-economic objects n are industries or branches in NACE (see Section 4.3.2.2) that are organised in an inclusive hierarchy (see Section 4.3.1; Gibson et al., 2000). NACE's granularity varies according to four levels: classes, groups, divisions, and sections. 385 *classes* nest in 177 groups, 177 *groups* add up to 64 divisions, and 64 *divisions* condense into 20 *sections* (Eurostat, 2008b). Owing to their identifying NACE code, economic objects n at these levels are also said to be classified at *one-digit, two-digit, three-digit*, or *four-digit* level, respectively. For the MLSDI, computation at all levels is desired to support the collective responsibility for sustainable development (see Section 2.1; WSSD, 2002). As many stakeholders as possible should be informed, and a broad audience should be attracted with effective communication (see Section 3.1; e.g. Pintér et al., 2018). However, data for groups and classes are rarely available (i.e. unit non-response occurs), and the MLSDI's determinative economic objects n are divisions at two-digit level. The 64 divisions as well as their superordinate sections are listed in Table A.1 in the Appendix A.1. The last two divisions – 97-98 Activities of households as employers; undifferentiated goods- and services-producing activities of households for own use and 99 Activities of extraterritorial organisations and bodies – are omitted due to their frequent zero output (e.g. Destatis, 2018h). Therefore, the sample's number of economic objects N equals 62. In parts of the analysis, not all but selected economic objects n are focused. These *selected branches* involve the health economy, agricultural sector, manufacturing sector, chemical industry, car industry, service sector, Information Technology (IT) industry, financial industry, real estate industry, and the overall German economy. *Sectors* correspond to sections at one-digit level, and *industries* are divisions

Section code	Division code	Abbreviated denotation
n/a	n/a	Health economy
A-S	01-96	Overall German economy
A	01-03	Agricultural sector
C	10-33	Manufacturing sector
	20	Chemical industry
	29-30	Car industry
G-S	45-96	Service sector
	62-63	IT industry
	64	Financial industry
L	68	Real estate industry

Table 5.1 Selected branches of the sample (Eurostat, 2008b); IT, Information Technology; n/a, not applicable

at two-digit level. These abbreviated denotations and the associated NACE codes (except for the health economy; see below) are enumerated in Table 5.1.

The health economy is a cross-sectional industry, and its definition is based on product delimitation performed by the economic research institute WifOR and the Federal Ministry for Economic Affairs and Energy (BMWi) (Gerlach et al., 2018). For consistency to the MLSDI's determinative economic objects n, the health economy is defined at NACE two-digit level in this work. The health economy's stakes in two-digit divisions are attached to the Appendix A.2, Table A.2. The health economy is of interest because it contributes most to the German GDP and labour market among the divisions, with GVA and working population shares of 12.1% and 17.0% in 2018, respectively (BMWi, 2019). Furthermore, corporate responsibility[44] reporting in the worldwide health economy features a considerably increasing trend: Its reporting rate grew from 68% in 2015 to 76% in 2017 (KPMG, 2017).[45] The overall German economy and aggregated sectors (agricultural, manufacturing, and service sectors) are selected to attract a broad audience (see above). The chemical industry is worthwhile to be examined because of its negative impact on the environment and efforts in industry self-regulation (e.g. Johnson, 2012; King & Lenox, 2000). Large corporations such as BASF engage in environmental sustainable development (e.g. Saling et al., 2002; Uhlman & Saling, 2010), voluntary initiatives such as the Responsible Care Program (CEFIC, 2019) are found, and an industry-specific sustainable development index has

---

[44]Generally, the present work is concerned with corporate sustainability and not corporate responsibility (see Section 2.3.2; e.g. Bansal & Song, 2017). However, a distinction of these terms is not made in the cited reference (KPMG, 2017), and the original wording is adopted.

[45]Sample: 4,900 top 100 companies in terms of revenues in 49 countries, thereof corporations allocated to healthcare.

been developed (AIChE & IfS, 2019). Similar to the health economy, the chemical industry's corporate responsibility reporting rate experienced a substantial increase from 75% in 2015 to 81% in 2017 (KPMG, 2017).[46] In contrast, the German car industry, which is the largest industry in the manufacturing sector in terms of GVA (share of 22.6% in 2016; Destatis, 2018h), rather attracts attention with embroilment in fraud scandals on cars' true Carbon Dioxide (CO_2) emission factors. A timeline of the fraud scandal can be found in, e.g. Clean Energy Wire (2019). However, the car industry earns the fourth place in global corporate responsibility reporting, with a rate of 79% in 2017 (KPMG, 2017).[47] The IT industry is examined due to digitalisation being a global megatrend, requiring enhanced computer programming as well as data and information services across industries and business functions (Alcácer & Cruz-Machado, 2019). Its importance for society is also reflected by the fact that IT skills are addressed in the SDGs (SDG 4.4.1; UN, 2018). The finance industry pursues sustainable development by, for example, the implementation of a sustainable development index (i.e. the DJSI; see Section 3.3.2 and Section 4.2; e.g. RobecoSAM, 2018a) or innovative sustainable products and services (de Bettignies & Lépineux, 2009; Wiek & Weber, 2014). However, sustainable development performances of the financial industry's activities as a whole might be questionable (Wiek & Weber, 2014). In terms of corporate responsibility reporting, the financial industry decreased its rate from 75% in 2015 to 71% in 2017 (KPMG, 2017).[48] Last, the real estate industry is a selected branch because housing prices constantly rise since 2015 (Eurostat, 2019b), causing debates on inequalities and social justice (Dustmann, Fitzenberger & Zimmermann, 2018). Moreover, it is the biggest two-digit level industry in the service sector in terms of GVA, with a share of 15.9% in 2016 (Destatis, 2018h).

The sample does not include meso-economic objects n yet, but especially corporations are strongly encouraged to quantify their sustainable development performances as advised in this work. Corporations should benchmark their results to the results of macro-economic objects n of this sample in order to derive coordinated actions for improved sustainable development.

The next section, Section 5.2, deals with the sample's key figures x.

5.2 Sustainable development key figures

This section presents the empirical findings of the calculation steps one to three (see Section 4.3.1 to Section 4.3.3) and is structured accordingly. First, the MLSDI's key

---

[46]Sample: 4,900 top 100 companies in terms of revenues in 49 countries, thereof corporations allocated to chemicals.

[47]Sample: 4,900 top 100 companies in terms of revenues in 49 countries, thereof corporations allocated to automotive.

[48]Sample: 4,900 top 100 companies in terms of revenues in 49 countries, thereof corporations allocated to financial services.

figures x are collected, defined, and prepared in Section 5.2.1. Because the key figures x are inferred from the key indicators y (see Section 4.3.1 and Section 4.3.4), derivation of the key figures' significance in relation to sustainable development is postponed to Section 5.3.1. Second, results of the missing value imputation are exhibited and discussed in Section 5.2.2.

5.2.1 Collection and preparation of sustainable development key figures

The MLSDI's ideal set of key indicators c_4 is the intersection of the GRI and the SDG frameworks (see Section 4.3.4 and Section 5.3.1). From this intersection, the ideal set of key figures c_5 is inferred (see Section 4.3.1). The actual sets are reduced versions of the ideal sets because of macro-data restrictions by official statistics. Severe item non-response entails too high uncertainties in the imputation process, and the item is excluded from the calculation. Three different forms of severe item non-response are present: A key figure x may be totally unavailable, only available at one-digit level, or only available for several divisions with incomplete sections. The present sample comprises six environmental, 16 social, and 14 economic key figures x, with the total number of key figures X amounting to 36. The unbalanced number of available key figures x across the contentual domains might demonstrate a focus on social and economic issues. However, indicators of the environmental domain are less similar to each other (e.g. the social domain contains four tax indicators; see Table 5.3) and the main topics and impacts are covered by the relatively small number of indicators. Table 5.2 to Table 5.4 list and characterise the MLSDI's environmental, social, and economic key figures x by their statistical classifications and reporting units. Data sources are provided in the last columns of the tables.

Definitions of the key figures x are provided in the following, and if not indicated otherwise, they are compiled by definitions of their data sources and Eurostat (2019c). The environmental domain reports *air emissions* (see Table 5.2), which are the amount of pollution of a plant or a product released into the air and include GHG emissions according to the Kyoto protocol (UNFCCC, 1998). The value of taxes levied on physical units that negatively impact the environment is called *environmental tax* and involves energy taxes and transport taxes. Energy taxes are composed of the energy tax, electricity tax, emission rights, fee for the Compulsory Oil Storage Association, and the nuclear fuel tax. Transport taxes consist of the motor vehicle tax and the air traffic tax. *Hazardous waste* regards the amount of hazardous substances generated by primary producers that require records according to the European regulation of waste (BMJV, 2019b). *Primary energy consumption* is the amount of energy used in the first place, irrespective of its purpose (energy or non-energy purpose) and conversation losses or other leakages. *Waste water* is used water that does not fulfil the quality criteria of

Environmental key figure x	Classification	Unit	Data source
Air emissions	CPA	Kilogram CO_{2e}	Destatis, 2018f
Environmental tax	NACE	Euro	Destatis, 2019e
Hazardous waste	NACE	Kilogram	Destatis, 2011b, 2012b, 2013c, 2014d, 2016f, 2016g, 2017d, 2019d
Primary energy consumption	CPA	Joule	Destatis, 2018e
Waste water	NACE	Litre	Destatis, 2018g
Water use	NACE	Litre	Destatis, 2018g

Table 5.2 List of the environmental key figures; CO_{2e}, Carbon Dioxide Equivalents; CPA, Classification of Products by Activity; NACE, Statistical Classification of Economic Activities in the European Community

its initial purpose. The amount of water used by end users is termed *water use*.

The social domain's key figures x encompass the following (see Table 5.3). *Apprentices* are the number of employees in vocational training. The value of tax levied on taxable incomes of the economic objects n is referred to as the *Corporate Income Tax (CIT)*. The *compensation of employees* represents the value of remuneration by employers to employees in return for work. It includes gross wages and salaries as well as social insurance contributions by both employers and employees. German compulsory social insurances involve the accident, health, nursing care, and the unemployment insurances. The key figure *employees* comprises the number of people contracted to carry out work for an employer in return for remuneration. The *female labour force* is constituted by the number of economically active females and includes female employees, self-employed, and unemployed women.[49] The number of female employees with a compensation below 450 Euro per month or a short-term contract below approximately three months of duration are termed *female marginally-employed employees*. Marginal employment is not subject to participation in the compulsory social insurances. In contrast, the *female socially-insured employees* are the number of female employees contributing to and benefiting from compulsory social insurances. The gender-unspecific counterparts *labour force*, *marginally-employed employees*, and *socially-insured employees* are defined correspondingly. After defining the last type of employment in the economic domain (see below), relations of the different employment types are established. The allocation of employment key figures to the social as well as the economic domain is based on the key indicators' assignment (see Section 5.3.1.2 and Section 5.3.1.3) and demonstrates the employment's dual purpose: It is a source of income but goes beyond

---

[49] As unemployed people cannot be assigned to an industry, the (female) labour force is only available for the overall German economy. Industry-specific data are not required as the labour forces only serve the computation of the key indicators y on gender differences, further elaborated in Section 5.3.1.2.

Social key figure x	Classification	Unit	Data source
Apprentices	NACE	aHC	BA, 2019
CIT	NACE	Euro	Destatis, 2012a, 2013a, 2014a, 2015b, 2016b, 2018b, 2018h, 2019b
Compensation of employees	NACE	Euro	Destatis, 2018h
Employees	NACE	aHC	Destatis, 2018h
Female labour force	n/a	aHC	Destatis, 2009, 2010b, 2011a, 2014c, 2015d, 2015e, 2015f, 2016e, 2017a
Female marginally-employed employees	NACE	aHC	BA, 2019
Female socially-insured employees	NACE	aHC	BA, 2019
Labour force	n/a	aHC	Destatis, 2009, 2010b, 2011a, 2014c, 2015d, 2015e, 2015f, 2016e, 2017a
Local business tax	NACE	Euro	Destatis, 2015a, 2016a, 2017b, 2017c, 2018a, 2018h
Marginally-employed employees	NACE	aHC	BA, 2019
Net taxes on products	CPA	Euro	Destatis, 2012c, 2013d, 2015g, 2016h, 2016i, 2017e, 2018i, 2019f
Severely-disabled employees	NACE	aHC	BA, 2011, 2012, 2013, 2014a, 2014b, 2016a, 2016b, 2017, 2018
Socially-insured employees	NACE	aHC	BA, 2019
VAT	NACE	Euro	Destatis, 2013b, 2014b, 2015c, 2016c, 2016d, 2018c, 2018d
Working hours of employees	NACE	Hour	Destatis, 2018h
Workplaces for severely-disabled employees	NACE	aHC	BA, 2011, 2012, 2013, 2014a, 2014b, 2016a, 2016b, 2017, 2018

Table 5.3 List of the social key figures; aHC, average Headcount; CIT, Corporate Income Tax; CPA, Classification of Products by Activity; n/a, not applicable; NACE, Statistical Classification of Economic Activities in the European Community; VAT, Value Added Tax

its economic purpose by being key to any successful transition (Harangozo et al., 2018). The *local business tax* is a local government charge and encompasses the value of tax levied on trade income of business enterprises. By computing the difference of the value of taxes levied on products and subsidies granted for products, the *net taxes on products* are obtained. Products may be produced or traded goods and services. The number of employees with disability status according to BMJV (2019a) build the key figure *severely-disabled employees*. The *Value Added Tax (VAT)* is the value of taxes

Economic key figure x	Classification	Unit	Data source
Consumption of fixed capital	NACE	Euro	Destatis, 2018h
Export	CPA	Euro	Destatis, 2018h
Gross fixed assets	NACE	Euro	Destatis, 2018h
Gross fixed capital formation	NACE	Euro	Destatis, 2018h
GVA	NACE	Euro	Destatis, 2018h
Import	CPA	Euro	Destatis, 2018h
Imported input	CPA	Euro	Destatis, 2012c, 2013d, 2015g, 2016h, 2016i, 2017e, 2018i, 2019f
Input	NACE	Euro	Destatis, 2018h
Internal R&D expenditures	NACE	Euro	Eurostat, 2019a
Net fixed assets	NACE	Euro	Destatis, 2018h
Output	NACE	Euro	Destatis, 2018h
R&D employees	NACE	aHC	Eurostat, 2019d
Working hours of working population	NACE	Hour	Destatis, 2018h
Working population	NACE	aHC	Destatis, 2018h

Table 5.4 List of the economic key figures; aHC, average Headcount; CPA, Classification of Products by Activity; GVA, Gross Value Added; NACE, Statistical Classification of Economic Activities in the European Community; R&D, Research and Development

levied on the value added of goods and services, and is computed by the difference of total VAT and deductible VAT on inputs. The number of hours actually worked by employees (excluding, e.g. holidays and sick days) composes the *working hours of employees*. *Workplaces for severely-disabled employees* are the number of mandatory workplaces for severely-disabled employees, set by an employer's type and size.

Last, the economic domain's key figures x (see Table 5.4) are defined. *Consumption of fixed capital* is the value of impairment of fixed assets (see below). The value of goods and services that change ownerships from residents to non-residents is termed *export*. *Gross fixed assets* represent the reinstatement value of stock of fixed assets that are used in production for more than one year. Fixed assets include machinery, equipment, buildings, and other structures. The *gross fixed capital formation* refers to the value of acquisitions of fixed assets, excluding fixed asset disposals, and is therefore also termed "investment". Definitions of GVA, output, and input can be found in Section 4.3.2.1. The key figure *import* regards the value of goods and services that change ownerships from non-residents to residents; the *imported input* is defined correspondingly. The value of expenditures within a statistical unit on creative work conducted by own employees to increase the stock and use of knowledge is reported in the *internal Research and Development (R&D) expenditures*. *Net fixed assets* regard the current value of stock of fixed assets, which is equivalent to gross fixed assets less the accumulated consumption of fixed capital. The number of employees in the field of R&D depicts the key figure *R&D employees*. *Working hours of working population* is the working population's equivalent of working hours of employees, where the *working population* represents the number of people that perform a production activity. The relations of apprentices, employees, labour force, marginally-employed employees, socially-insured employees, and working population are as follows. The labour force is the broadest key figure x as it comprises employees, self-employed, and unemployed people. The working population is obtained by disregarding unemployed people. Self-employed people are not further distinguished but employees are. These include apprentices, marginally-employed employees, socially-insured employees, and further employment types such as civil servants. However, data of these key figures x are not comparable as they are retrieved from different data bases.

Key figures x are generally defined on a positive value range. Exceptions are the VAT and the net taxes on products. Positive values indicate monetary outflows from the object of investigation, and negative values denote monetary inflows to the object of investigation.

Preparation of key figures x cover macro-level transformations from NACE to CPA. These yield standard results and are thus not disclosed. Data sources for the transformation include Destatis' supply tables retrieved from the national accounts (Destatis, 2012c, 2013d, 2015g, 2016h, 2016i, 2017e, 2018i, 2019f).

The following section, Section 5.2.2, turns the incomplete sample into a complete one by missing value imputation.

5.2.2 Imputation of missing values

The collected sample (see Section 5.2.1) contains item non-responses and features a general missing data pattern. Sustainable development data remain to be scarce despite the digital era of big data that is deemed to generate richness of data and information (Esty, 2018). 17 of 36 key figures x require missing value imputation and the average rate of missing values λ amounts to 22.63%, with a minimum of 14.87% in 2013 and a maximum of 32.19% in 2008. The missing data patterns of these years are illustrated in Figure 5.1 and Figure 5.2. The x-axis contains the key figures x, while the y-axis comprises the economic objects n. Light patches signal missing data. More than twice as many values are missing in the service sector ($\lambda = 28.13\%$) compared to the manufacturing sector ($\lambda = 13.29\%$). In Figure 5.1 and Figure 5.2, approximately the upper half represents the manufacturing sector, and approximately the lower half depicts the service sector (see Table A.1).

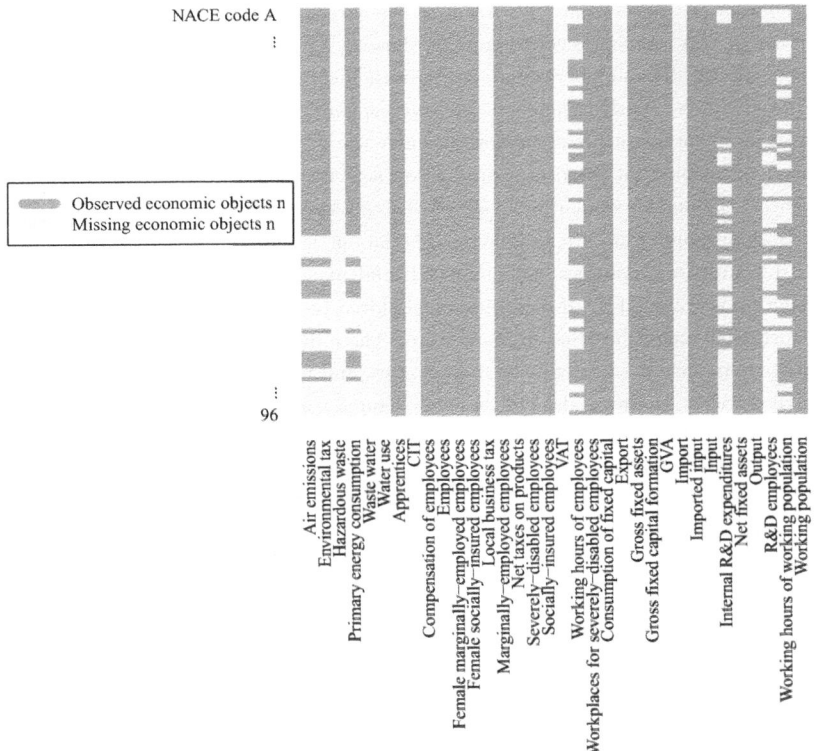

Figure 5.1 Missing data pattern in the German economy in 2008; CIT, Corporate Income
Tax; GVA, Gross Value Added; NACE, Statistical Classification of Economic
Activities in the European Community; R&D, Research and Development; VAT,
Value Added Tax

The first application to gain upon the data shortage is single time series imputation
(see Section 4.3.3.2). The imputation generally yields stable results, and exemplary
results of the key figure import for the selected branches are displayed in Figure 5.3. The
import's missing data pattern is monotone in the temporal dimension and thus easily
visualised with solid lines for observed data and dashed lines for imputed data. The
Kalman smoothing and maximum likelihood estimation (see Section 4.3.3.2; e.g. Harvey,
1989) are applied on the agricultural sector and industries in the manufacturing sector
in 2008 and 2009. Industries in the service sector require modified mean imputation
as their total time series are unobserved. Because single imputation produces stable
results as expected, estimates are considered to be valid. Test results on the model

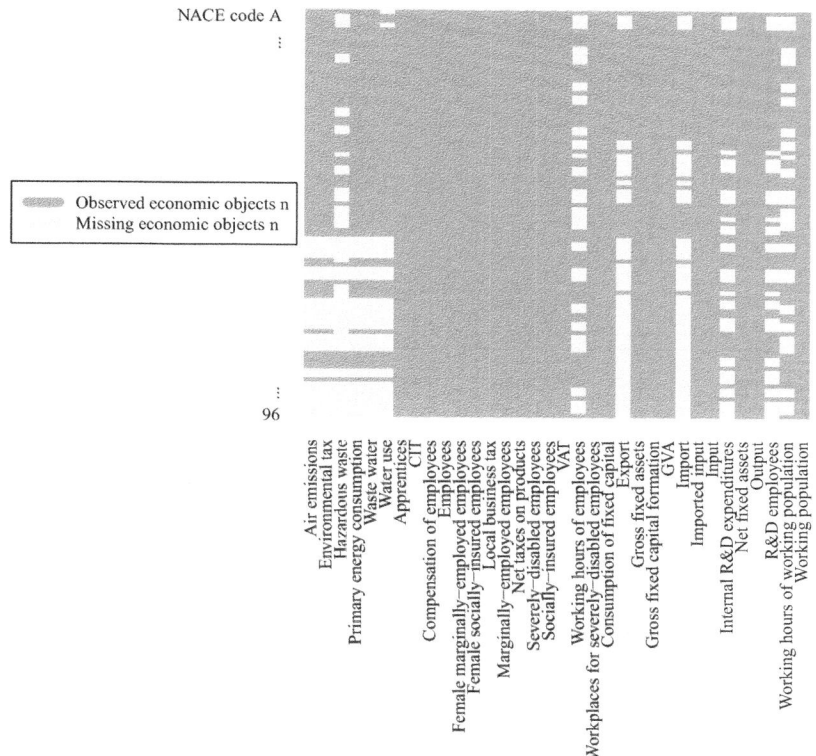

Figure 5.2 Missing data pattern in the German economy in 2013; CIT, Corporate Income Tax; GVA, Gross Value Added; NACE, Statistical Classification of Economic Activities in the European Community; R&D, Research and Development; VAT, Value Added Tax

assumptions follow below.

With regard to Amelia II (see Section 4.3.3.3; e.g. Honaker et al., 2011), dropped, highly correlated key figures x that are free from missing values encompass the compensation of employees, employees, female marginally-employed employees, socially-insured employees, workplaces for severely-disabled employees, consumption of fixed capital, gross fixed assets, net fixed assets, and the output. Kendall's tau is the used correlation coefficient because the key figures x are non-normal (see below). The compensation of employees and the output correlate with the GVA and the input; female marginally-employed employees are associated with marginally-employed employees; female socially-insured employees, socially-insured employees, and employees depend on the working

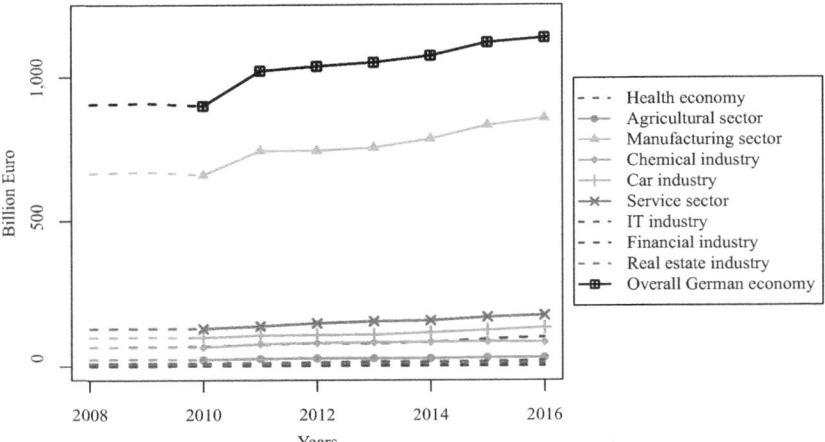

Figure 5.3 Single time series imputation on import in billion Euro for the selected branches
in the German economy from 2008 to 2016; solid line, observed data; dashed line,
imputed data; IT, Information Technology

population; workplaces for severely-disabled employees vary along with severely-disabled
employees; and the key figures on capital and assets are associated with the gross fixed
capital formation. The Amelia II algorithm performs $m = 23$ imputations, which
corresponds to a relative efficiency η of 99.03% (see Equation (4.6)). Amelia II's result
of the exemplary key figure import is shown in Figure 5.4. Despite the restricting
bounds to the observed range of values, missing values are heavily overestimated for
industries in the service sector and moderately overestimated for several industries in
the manufacturing sector. Not setting bounds would lead to even higher variances in
estimates. The difference in severity of misspecification across the manufacturing and
the service sectors may originate in their different rates of missing values λ (see above).

To verify the assumptions of the imputation models, statistical tests are performed
(see Section 4.3.3.4). First, Little's MCAR test is intended to be executed but fails
because the sample involves key figures x that are missing for an entire time period t.
The key figure import in 2008 is such an example (see Figure 5.1). Whether the MAR
assumption is valid remains unknown, but minor effects are expected from its violation
(see Section 4.3.3.4; e.g. Rässler et al., 2013).

For single time series imputation, the Shapiro-Wilk, Kolmogorov-Smirnov, augmented Dickey-Fuller, and the Ljung-Box tests are performed to investigate normality,
stationarity, and i.i.d. of the key figures x and residuals, respectively. Results can be
found in Table A.3 to Table A.5 in the Appendix A.3. The Shapiro-Wilk test statistics
range from 0.1728 for waste water and 0.8082 for output. P-values are less or equal than
0.0001. The test statistics of the Kolmogorov-Smirnov test vary on an interval between

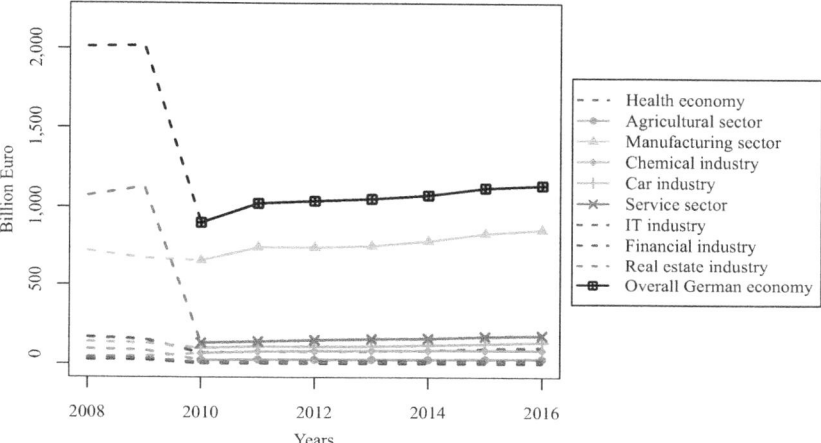

Figure 5.4 Multiple imputation on import in billion Euro for the selected branches in the German economy from 2008 to 2016; solid line, observed data; dashed line, imputed data; IT, Information Technology

0.5 for the CIT and local business tax and one for several variables, with p-values less or equal than 0.0001. Both tests yield the same result: The null hypotheses are rejected with p-values less or equal than 0.0001. The data are non-normal. Non-normality of key figures x is confirmed by examination of histograms, such that type I errors are not expected. Exemplary histograms of import and air emissions in 2016 are displayed in Figure 5.5, visualising the key figures' typical right skewness. The augmented Dickey-Fuller test statistics range from -11.17 for the net taxes on products to -3.88 for the imported input. P-values remain below 0.01, except the imported input's p-value yields 0.0152. However, it is still below the decisional threshold of 0.05. The null hypotheses of the augmented Dickey-Fuller tests are rejected, and stationarity of the data are confirmed. The Ljung-Box test statistics' minimum of 0.0001 is obtained for the input, and the maximum of 0.5481 is achieved for the net taxes on products. All p-values exceed the threshold value 0.05, concluding that the error terms of the residuals are i.i.d. These p-values are listed in the last columns of Table A.3 to Table A.5.

Concerning multiple imputation, the multivariate Shapiro-Wilk test yields a test statistic of 0.0327 with a p-value less or equal than 0.0001. The null hypothesis is rejected, and the data are multivariate non-normal. Overdispersed start values indicate that the Amelia II algorithm functions well. Figure 5.6 illustrates the convergence of the largest PC after two imputations. The largest PC is utilised to summarise the data.

In conclusion, data are neither univariate nor multivariate normal. Single time series imputation does not appear to be distorted by the normality violation, and the Kalman filter proves to be an optimal estimator under violation of the normality assumption

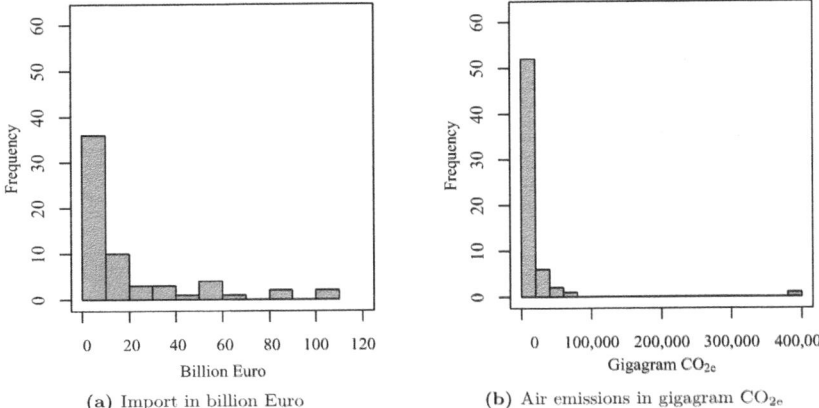

Figure 5.5 Frequency distribution of import and air emissions in the German economy in
2016; CO_{2e}, Carbon Dioxide Equivalents

(see Section 4.3.3.2; Harvey, 1989). The inclusive hierarchy leads to relatively low
uncertainty in the imputation process, and the assumption of the temporal dimension
being a reliable predictor seems to be valid. In contrast, the Amelia II algorithm yields
implausible results, endorsing Demirtas et al. (2008) evidence of Amelia II producing
biases under non-normal, small samples. The implausible results may further confirm
the supposition of cross sections to be unreliable predictors in sustainable development
assessment: Economic objects n feature unique characteristics with regard to the
sustainable development key figures x. Both conclusions on Amelia II's implementation
are supported by the diagnostics of algorithm convergence: The algorithm is not the
origin of misspecification, but the input data are.

   In the following, Amelia II's results are disregarded, and the subsequent calculation
is based on the singly imputed set of key figures c_5. The next section, Section 5.3,
addresses the sustainable development key indicators y.

5.3   Sustainable development key indicators

This section addresses results of the calculation steps four to six (see Section 4.3.4 to
Section 4.3.6) and is organised correspondingly. First, the key indicators y are derived
in Section 5.3.1, and results of the growth indicators y_g are outlined in Section 5.3.2.
Empirical findings of the ratio indicators y_r are not presented because they are reported
in diverse units (see Table 5.2 to Table 5.4), such that results are not comparable before
scaling (see Section 4.3.6). Outlying key indicators y_o are removed in Section 5.3.3, and
last, cleaned and rescaled key indicators' summary statistics as well as data results of
the selected branches are exhibited and analysed in Section 5.3.4.

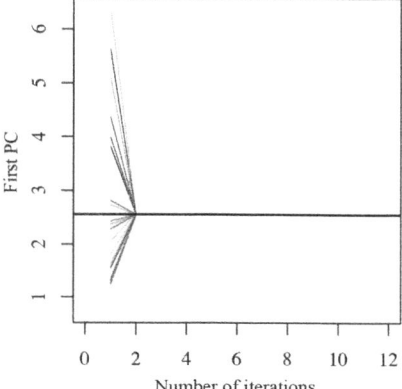

Figure 5.6 Convergence of the Amelia II algorithm with overdispersed start values for the largest Principal Component (PC)

5.3.1 Alignment of the Global Reporting Initiative (GRI) and the Sustainable Development Goal (SDG) disclosures

Based on GRI and UNGC (2018a), this section aligns the meso GRI disclosures with the macro SDG indicators and targets and adjusts the alignment to the MLSDI's key figures x and the key indicators y. Detailed information about the GRI disclosures and the SDG indicators and targets are retrieved from GRI (2016); and UN (2018). The economic domain is further supported by IASB (2018). Hereafter, when referring to both a SDG indicator and a SDG target, the term "SDG disclosure" is used. Because of methodological shortcomings or data restrictions by official statistics (see Section 5.2.1), the alignment is bounded, and adjustments are made. For example, GVA instead of revenue is used as a standardising key figure x_{std}, or data of a similar variable are acquired. The following sections, Section 5.3.1.1 to Section 5.3.1.3, address the resulting key indicators y by the contentual domains.

5.3.1.1 Environmental sustainable development key indicators

The environmental domain's GRI and SDG disclosures are mainly concerned with the reduction of absolute negative environmental impacts (i.e. increase of effectiveness) and the reduction of environmental intensities (i.e. increase of efficiency). The latter is achieved by relative decoupling of economic activity and environmental degradation. Environmental key indicators y generally affect sustainable development performances negatively. One exception is indicated below. Table 5.5 shows the MLSDI's environmental key indicators y, their effective directions ξ, and reporting units. Ratio indicators' calculation schemes are indicated, whereas the growth indicators' formula

Environmental key indicator y	Calculation scheme	Effective direction ξ	Unit
Growth of air emissions		-1	Percentage
Air emissions intensity	$\dfrac{Air\ emissions}{GVA}$	-1	Gram CO_{2e} per Euro
Growth of primary energy consumption		-1	Percentage
Energy intensity	$\dfrac{Primary\ energy\ consumption}{GVA}$	-1	Mega joule per Euro
Growth of water use		-1	Percentage
Water intensity	$\dfrac{Water\ use}{GVA}$	-1	Litre per Euro
Growth of waste water		-1	Percentage
Waste water intensity	$\dfrac{Waste\ water}{GVA}$	-1	Litre per Euro
Growth of hazardous waste		-1	Percentage
Hazardous waste intensity	$\dfrac{Hazardous\ waste}{GVA}$	-1	Gram per Euro
Environmental tax intensity	$\dfrac{Environmental\ tax}{GVA}$	$+1$	Percentage

Table 5.5 Environmental key indicators and their characterisation; CO_{2e}, Carbon Dioxide Equivalents; GVA, Gross Value Added

can be found in Equation (4.9).

As a first topic, air pollution is covered, which is addressed in several GRI and SDG disclosures. Air pollution leads to climate change (Rockström et al., 2009b), a planetary boundary that has been transgressed (see Section 2.2.1; e.g. Steffen et al., 2015). Therefore, there is an urgent need to measure and manage air pollution. Substances into the air should be reduced (SDG 12.4), impacts of ocean acidification ought to be minimised (SDG 14.3), and forests are required to be managed sustainably (SDG 15.2). From a societal perspective, reduction of deaths and illnesses from air pollution should be aimed at (SDG 3.9), and resilience to climate related hazards is required to be strengthened (SDG 13.1). Contributing to the management of these targets, the MLSDI collects data of the key figure air emissions (GRI 305-1) and computes the key indicators *growth of air emissions* (GRI 305-5)[50] and *air emissions intensity* (GRI 305-4; SDG 8.4; SDG 9.4.1). The latter is obtained by the ratio of air emissions and GVA (see Table 5.5), specifying the amount of emissions in gram Carbon Dioxide Equivalents (CO_{2e}) released into the air per Euro of generated GVA. A reduction of this

---

[50]The GRI disclosure 305-5 comprises reduction of air emissions. However, as data of the key figure air emissions are collected, its growth rate is computed, and its effective direction ξ is accounted for in the scaling procedure (see Section 4.3.6.2 and Section 5.3.4). This case occurs for further key indicators y but is not pointed out repetitively.

ratio indicator y_r implies a successful relative decoupling of environmental degradation in terms of air emissions and economic activity measured by GVA. All ratio indicators y_r that are labelled with "intensity" operate in this fashion. Data on GVA are collected in the economic domain (see below).

A major cause of air emissions is energy consumption as its supply mainly relies on air-polluting technologies (Destatis, 2018f; EEA, 2018). To further support the SDG targets 8.4 and 13.1, natural resources for energy consumption should be managed sustainably and efficiently (SDG 12.2). For this purpose, data on primary energy consumption are acquired, and the key indicators *growth of primary energy consumption* (GRI 302-4) and *energy intensity* (GRI 302-3; SDG 7.3.1; SDG 8.4) are encompassed in the MLSDI.

A further natural resource to be managed sustainably and efficiently (SDG 12.2) is water. The planetary boundary freshwater use is currently in the safe zone and has not been crossed (see Section 2.2.1; e.g. Steffen et al., 2015). For prevalence of this status, economic objects n should contribute to the improvement of water quality (SDG 6.3), protection of water-related ecosystems (SDG 6.6), and reduction of water pollution (SDG 12.4; SDG 14.1). Moreover, similar to air pollution, deaths and illnesses from water contamination ought to be minimised (SDG 3.9). Both key figures water use and waste water add to the meso-to-macro comparable measurement of these targets with their growth indicators *growth of water use* (GRI 303-1) and *growth of waste water* (GRI 306-1) as well as their ratio indicators *water intensity* (SDG 6.4.1; SDG 8.4) and *waste water intensity* (SDG 8.4).

Waste is another source of pollution, and especially hazardous waste should be assessed and managed (SDG 12.4). The key figure hazardous waste (GRI 306-2) results in the key indicators *growth of hazardous waste* (SDG 12.5) and *hazardous waste intensity* (SDG 8.4; SDG 12.4.2).

The last included topic of the environmental domain are taxation matters. Generally, fiscal policies should be adopted for greater equality (SDG 10.4), and in particular, environmental harmful subsidies should be phrased out (SDG 12.c.1). The polluter pays principle should be implemented, which was already a subject in the 1970s (UNCHE, 1972; WCED, 1987). Data on environmental tax are collected to compute the key indicator *environmental tax intensity* (SDG 12.c.1). This key indicator y features the exceptional positive effective direction as paying up environmental damages positively impacts environmental protection. The relation to GVA is not optimal but standardising by the environmental damage in physical units would be. Necessary to this end would be an aggregation of the diverse physical units arising from the multiple tax bases (see Section 5.2.1). The aggregation in turn would require a scaling procedure such as the scaling of the key indicators y (see Section 4.3.6). For rectilinearity, GVA is chosen as the standardising key figure x_{std}, implying that high value-generating economic objects n should channel financial resources for environmental protection. Furthermore, growth of environmental tax is not computed because it would not indicate the effectiveness of the taxation system but an increase in the tax bases and environmentally-damaging consumption. Evaluation of a taxation system's effectiveness is complex and typically investigated with computable general equilibrium models (e.g. Bergman, 2005). Research on environmental tax's effectiveness and relation to sustainable development can be found in, e.g. Bosquet (2000); R. E. López and Figueroa (2016); and Morley (2012).

The social key indicators y are determined in the following section, Section 5.3.1.2.

5.3.1.2   Social sustainable development key indicators

Main topics of the social domain's intersection of the meso GRI and the macro SDG disclosures are income and employment. Employment is more than a source of income (see Section 5.2.1; Harangozo et al., 2018), and both income and employment are key for life above the social boundaries (see Section 2.2.2; e.g. Raworth, 2012). However, social boundaries are not as well developed as the planetary boundaries are. The current framework is not universal but rather applicable to the developing than the developed world (see Section 2.2.2; Raworth, 2017). As the investigated geographical region is Germany, one of the seven major economies of the world (UN, 2019c), the social boundaries are disregarded, and only the GRI and the SDG disclosures are relied on. Social key indicators y generally feature a positive effective direction ξ^+ (see Table 5.6), and negatively affecting key indicators y are explicitly emphasised.

The first target to be covered by meso-economic and macro-economic objects n is poverty reduction (SDG 1.2), entailing the target full employment and decent work for all (SDG 8.5). Assessing contributions to these targets, the key figures compensation of employees (SDG 10.1) and employees (GRI 102-8) are acquired for computing the following growth indicators y_g and ratio indicators y_r: the *growth of compensation of employees* (SDG 10.1.1), *growth of employees, average compensation of employees p.c.*, *average compensation of employees per hour (p.h.)* (SDG 8.5.1), and the *labour share* (SDG 10.4.1). The average compensations of employees are obtained by standardising the compensations of employees to the employees and, their working hours, respectively (see Table 5.6), alluding to an employee's average purchasing power. Employees are measured in headcount, including both part-time as well as full-time employees. This imprecision causes a distortion but cannot be avoided because data on employees in full-time equivalents are unavailable at two-digit level. The labour share provides information on the proportion of GVA granted to employees (see Table 5.6). Growth of working hours of employees is not computed. It is an accumulated measure that does not unfold information on the number of hours worked per employee per day or per week. Hours per employee per day or per week is a meso sustainable development disclosure (GRI 102-17), but macro data are not available.

In further achieving poverty reduction (SDG 1.2), social protection systems should

Social key indicator y	Calculation scheme	Effective direction ξ	Unit
Growth of compensation of employees		+1	Percentage
Growth of employees		+1	Percentage
Average compensation of employees p.c.	$\dfrac{Compensation\ of\ employees}{Employees}$	+1	Euro per headcount
Average compensation of employees p.h.	$\dfrac{Compensation\ of\ employees}{Working\ hours\ of\ employees}$	+1	Euro p.h.
Labour share	$\dfrac{Compensation\ of\ employees}{GVA}$	+1	Percentage
Growth of socially-insured employees		+1	Percentage
Growth of marginally-employed employees		−1	Percentage
Share of marginally-employed employees	$\dfrac{Marginally\text{-}employed\ employees}{Socially\text{-}insured\ employees}$	−1	Percentage
Growth of female socially-insured employees		+1	Percentage
Quota of gender difference	$\left\lvert \dfrac{Female\ socially\text{-}insured\ employees}{Socially\text{-}insured\ employees} - \dfrac{female\ labour\ force}{labour\ force} \right\rvert$	−1	Percentage point
Growth of female marginally-employed employees		−1	Percentage
Quota of gender difference of marginally-employed employees	$\left\lvert \dfrac{Female\ marginally\text{-}employed\ employees}{Marginally\text{-}employed\ employees} - \dfrac{female\ socially\text{-}insured\ employees}{socially\text{-}insured\ employees} \right\rvert$	−1	Percentage point
Growth of severely-disabled employees		+1	Percentage
Quota of severely-disabled employees	$\dfrac{Severely\text{-}disabled\ employees}{Wp\ for\ severely\text{-}disabled\ employees}$	+1	Percentage
Growth of apprentices		+1	Percentage
Share of apprentices	$\dfrac{Apprentices}{Socially\text{-}insured\ employees}$	+1	Percentage
VAT intensity	$\dfrac{VAT}{GVA}$	+1	Percentage
Intensity of net taxes on products	$\dfrac{Net\ taxes\ on\ products}{GVA}$	+1	Percentage

continued

Social key indicator y	Calculation scheme	Effective direction ξ	Unit
CIT intensity	$\dfrac{CIT}{GVA}$	+1	Percentage
Local business tax intensity	$\dfrac{Local\ business\ tax}{GVA}$	+1	Percentage

Table 5.6 Social key indicators and their characterisation; CIT, Corporate Income Tax; GVA, Gross Value Added; p.c., per capita; p.h., per hour; VAT, Value Added Tax; Wp, Workplaces

be in force (SDG 1.3). Hence, the key figures socially-insured employees and marginally-employed employees are gathered. Their growth indicators y_g comprise the *growth of socially-insured employees* and the *growth of marginally-employed employees*, with the resulting ratio indicator *share of marginally-employed employees* (SDG 1.3.1). The effective directions ξ of the growth and the share of marginally-employed employees are negative: Marginally-employed employees are not covered by social security systems (see Section 5.2.1; BA, 2019), and thus, employees should be prevented from this type of employment.

Supporting SDG 10.2 and SDG 10.3 on inclusion and equal opportunities, discrimination against all women and girls should be ended (SDG 5.1). Assessing meso-economic and macro-economic objects' contributions to these targets, data on female socially-insured employees, (female) labour force, and female marginally-employed employees are collected. Growth indicators y_g encompass the *growth of female socially-insured employees* and the *growth of female marginally-employed employees*. Because the (female) labour force is composed of the working population and unemployed people, its growth rate is only meaningful for overall economies and hence not implied in the MLSDI. Ratio indicators y_r are the *quota of gender difference* (SDG 16.7.1) and the *quota of gender difference of marginally-employed employees* (SDG 1.3.1). Calculation schemes of the quotas of gender differences are displayed in Table 5.6. The first parts of the differences represent the status of employment by gender in percentage. The second parts of the differences indicate possibilities of employment by gender with regard to the first parts of the equations: The share of female labour force represents the population of the share of female socially-insured employees, and the share of socially-insured employees constitute the population of the share of female marginally-employed employees. Because equality is aimed at (SDG 10.2; SDG 10.3), neither men nor women should be privileged, and absolute values are taken. Moreover, striving for equality, an increase of the quotas of gender differences degrade social development, such that their effective directions ξ are negative.

Continuing to operationalise empowerment and equal opportunities for all (SDG

10.2; SDG 10.3), the key figures severely-disabled employees and workplaces for severely-disabled employees are gathered. The *growth of severely-disabled employees* and the *quota of severely-disabled employees* (SDG 16.7.1) are computed to measure meso-economic and macro-economic objects' contributions to these targets. Growth of workplaces for severely-disabled employees is not calculated because these workplaces depend on the type and the size of an employer (see Section 5.2.1; BA, 2018). This fixed calculation scheme prevents individual performances, and the key figure workplaces for severely-disabled employees only serves standardisation.

Equal access to vocational education (SDG 4.3) and the increase in number of youths and adults who possess vocational skills (SDG 4.4) should be endeavoured. The key figure apprentices is gathered, and its key indicators *growth of apprentices* and *share of apprentices* are computed to assess meso and macro contributions to the aforementioned targets. The share of apprentices is the proportion of apprentices in socially-insured employees (see Table 5.6).

Fiscal instruments are demanded for reaching social development (SDG 10.4). The data collection for this target results in the key figures VAT (GRI 201-1), net taxes on products (GRI 201-1), CIT (GRI 201-1), and local business tax (GRI 201-1). Their ratio indicators y_r are intensities (see Table 5.6) that state the share of GVA passed to the government. These taxes' growth indicators y_g are excluded from the MLSDI because, similar to the environmental tax, their growth would not reveal effectiveness of the taxation system but an increase in the tax bases and economic activity, which is not part of sustainable development (see Section 2.2.3; e.g. Jackson, 2009).

The next section, Section 5.3.1.3, derives the MLSDI's economic key indicators y.

5.3.1.3   Economic sustainable development key indicators

The economic domain's alignment of GRI and SDG disclosures results in key indicators y that mainly strive for economic productivity. Enhancements of economic key indicators y imply improved sustainable development performances. Their effective directions ξ are positive. Because economic growth is only required to eliminate poverty (see Section 2.2.3; e.g. WCED, 1987), and Germany is one of the seven major economies of the world (see Section 5.3.1.2; UN, 2019c), economic growth indicators y_g are disregarded for the present sample. One exemption is made: The *growth of working population* is investigated as it contributes – jointly with the key indicators y on employment of the social domain – to the achievement of full and productive employment as well as decent work for all (SDG 8.5; see Section 5.3.1.2).

To increase economic productivities, technological upgrading should be accomplished (SDG 8.2). To this end, the key figures gross fixed assets (IAS 16.73d), net fixed assets (IAS 1.54), consumption of fixed capital (IAS 1.102; IAS 1.103; IAS 1.104), and gross fixed capital formation (IAS 7.21) are collected. The MLSDI's resulting ratio indicators

Economic key indicator y	Calculation scheme	Effective direction ξ	Unit
Gross capital productivity	$\dfrac{GVA}{Gross\ fixed\ assets}$	+1	Percentage
Net capital productivity	$\dfrac{GVA}{Net\ fixed\ assets}$	+1	Percentage
Degree of modernity	$\dfrac{Net\ fixed\ assets}{Gross\ fixed\ assets}$	+1	Percentage
Consumed capital productivity	$\dfrac{GVA}{Consumption\ of\ fixed\ capital}$	+1	Percentage
Investment intensity	$\dfrac{Gross\ fixed\ capital\ formation}{GVA}$	+1	Percentage
Internal R&D intensity	$\dfrac{Internal\ R\&D\ expenditures}{GVA}$	+1	Percentage
Share of R&D employees	$\dfrac{R\&D\ employees}{Employees}$	+1	Percentage
GVA rate	$\dfrac{GVA}{Output}$	+1	Percentage
Growth of working population		+1	Percentage
Labour productivity p.c.	$\dfrac{GVA}{Working\ population}$	+1	Euro per headcount
Labour productivity p.h.	$\dfrac{GVA}{Working\ hours\ of\ WP}$	+1	Euro per hour
Net import intensity	$\dfrac{Import - export}{GVA}$	+1	Percentage
Share of imported input	$\dfrac{Imported\ input}{Input}$	+1	Percentage

Table 5.7 Economic key indicators and their characterisation; GVA, Gross Value Added; p.c., per capita; p.h., per hour; R&D, Research and Development; WP, Working Population

y_r read: *gross capital productivity, net capital productivity, degree of modernity, consumed capital productivity*, and *investment intensity*. The gross capital productivity indicates the value of the factor input gross fixed assets to realise GVA (see Table 5.7). The other productivity indicators of the economic domain function analogically. The gross fixed capital formation's ratio indicator y_r is an intensity. The degree of modernity is the ratio of net and gross fixed assets, shedding light on the process of ageing as it represents the share of fixed assets that has not been consumed (Schmalwasser & Weber, 2012).

Targeting productivity through innovation (SDG 8.2), data on internal R&D expenditures (IAS 38.126; IAS 38.127) and R&D employees are collected. Technological knowledge may result in future economic benefits (IASB, 2018). The computed ratio indicators y_r are *internal R&D intensity* (SDG 9.5.1) and *share of R&D employees* (SDG 9.5.2). Because R&D is an investment (Schmalwasser & Weber, 2012), its intensity instead of productivity is computed.

Additionally, SDG 8.2 suggests emphasising high value-added sectors. The key figure output is gathered for the computation of the *GVA rate*, which states the proportion of GVA in the output.

Labour-intensive sectors should be focused to achieve higher levels of economic productivity (SDG 8.2). The key figures working population and working hours of working population are collected to compute the key indicators *growth of working population* (SDG 8.5; see Section 5.3.1.2), *labour productivity p.c.* (SDG 8.2.1), and *labour productivity p.h.*

As a last topic of the economic domain, international trade is considered. To strengthen developing countries, reduction of poverty (SDG 1.2; see Section 5.3.1.2) and enablement of decent work (SDG 8.5; see Section 5.3.1.2) should be targeted by significantly increasing exports of these countries (SDG 17.11). From Germany's point of view, imports from developing countries should be augmented because Germany is one of the major seven world economies (see Section 5.3.1.2; UN, 2019c). The key figures import, export, and imported input are collected to calculate the following ratio indicators y_r: *net import intensity* and *share of imported input*. Their calculation schemes are indicated in Table 5.7.

To sum up, the MLSDI comprises several ratio indicators y_r and several growth indicators y_g to map efficiency and effectiveness. From the 36 acquired key figures x, 30 ratio indicators y_r are computed of which six belong to the environmental, 12 to the social, and another 12 to the economic domain. The total number of growth indicators Y_g amounts to 14, with five environmental, eight social, and one economic growth indicator y_g. The number of ratio indicators Y_r and growth indicators Y_g as well as the number of key indicators Y across the contentual domains are unbalanced. The environmental domain contains 11, the social domain is built by 20, and the economic domain consists of 13 key indicators y. The total number of key indicators Y amounts to 44. Due to limitations on data availabilities for economic objects n at two-digit level, several topics could not be included in the MLSDI.

Concluding on Section 5.3.1.1 to Section 5.3.1.3, several SDG targets are repetitively stated and measured by more than one key indicator y. Moreover, SDG targets do not always follow their goals' assignment to the contentual domains (e.g. Folke et al., 2016). For instance, a target that belongs to a social goal might be assigned to the environmental domain. Especially the environmental domain connects all three domains: Environmental efficiency regards the environmental and the economic domains, and health-related issues caused by environmental degradation concern the environmental

and the social domains. Other examples have been provided in Section 2.2.4. These findings verify the interconnectedness of the goals and strengthen the assessment principle
synergies and trade-offs (see Section 3.1; e.g. Costanza, Fioramonti & Kubiszewski, 2016)
to be tackled by the MLSDI's weighting procedure (see Section 4.3.7 and Section 5.4).

The following section, Section 5.3.2, describes and analyses the summary statistics
of the growth indicators y_g.

5.3.2   Summary statistics of the sustainable development growth indicators

At this stage of the calculation, the key indicators y are unscaled and not comparable to
each other. However, growth indicators y_g are uniformly reported in percentages, and
their empirical results reveal greater insights when unscaled: Their signs indicate the
direction of change. The direction of change is desired to be in line with the effective
direction ξ. For example, positively affecting key indicators y are desired to exhibit
positive growth rates. Rescaled growth indicators y_{gs} trade this straightforwardness
for comparability to rescaled ratio indicators y_{rs} (see Section 4.3.6.2) and subsequent
aggregation (see Section 4.3.8). Therefore, summary statistics of the unscaled growth
indicators y_g are analysed in this section before the scaling procedure. Outlying key
indicators y_o are untreated, but conclusions of this analysis remain valid as growth
indicators y_g are characterised by a relatively low outlier rate β (see Section 5.3.3). Full
summary statistics of both the unscaled growth indicators y_g and the unscaled ratio
indicators y_r are provided in the Appendix A.4, Table A.6 to Table A.8.

Summary statistics classify a distribution according to its *centre, spread* or *dispersion,*
and *frequency.* Central measures to be analysed are the mean and median. High central
measures are endeavoured for key indicators y that feature a positive effective direction
ξ^+. Common measures of dispersion are the standard deviation, median absolute
deviation, minimum, maximum, and the 25th and the 75th percentiles. Neither the
standard deviation nor the median absolute deviation are included in the analysis
because deviations from central measures are not crucial in sustainable development
assessment, but deviations from targets should be quantified (see Section 3.1; e.g. Sala
et al., 2015). Owing to lacks in data, targets could not be included but are replaced by
distributional minima and maxima (see Section 4.3.6.2). Changes in the extremes signal
alteration in the performance of the worst and the best economic object n, respectively.
If a key indicator's effective direction ξ is positive, an increase in the extremes is desired.
The 25th and the 75th percentiles are of interest in order to localise the interior 50%
of the distribution. Analysed frequency measures are skewness and kurtosis. The
relation of the mean and the median raise expectations about the skewness. If the mean
exceeds the median, frequent values occur at the bottom, such that the distribution
is positively (right) skewed. Vice versa, if the median surpasses the mean, frequent

Environmental growth indicator y_g							
Year	Mean	Median	Min	Max	Q_1	Q_3	Skewness Kurtosis
Growth of air emissions							
2008-2016	-0.0197	-0.0560	-0.5725	0.8553	-0.1543	0.1370	0.6864 1.0852
Growth of primary energy consumption							
2008-2016	-0.0158	-0.0479	-0.4671	0.5762	-0.1336	0.0803	0.5046 0.5235
Growth of water use							
2008-2016	-0.0096	-0.0049	-0.6255	0.6064	-0.1261	0.1022	0.0996 1.0119
Growth of waste water							
2008-2016	-0.0304	-0.0098	-1.0000	0.6045	-0.1407	0.0870	-0.6825 2.6684
Growth of hazardous waste							
2008-2016	-0.0607	-0.0969	-0.6637	1.4894	-0.2958	0.1581	1.2043 2.6282

Table 5.8 Summary statistics of the environmental growth indicators in the German economy from 2008 to 2016; Max, Maximum; Min, Minimum; Q_1, 25th percentile; Q_3, 75th percentile

scores are located at the top, entailing negative (left) skewness. These rules on resulting skewness hold true in most but not all cases (von Hippel, 2005). A distribution is fairly symmetrical if absolute skewness remains below 0.5. Moderate skewness ranges between absolute values of 0.5 to 1.0, and distributions with absolute skewness higher than 1.0 are highly skewed (Bulmer, 1979). Negatively skewed distributions are favourable for sustainable development. In this case, light tails (negative kurtosis) are desired because the tail refers to the bottom of the distribution. The opposite is preferred for positively skewed distributions, such that the kurtosis is ambiguous for sustainable development. A distribution is platykurtic (light tails) for kurtosis values below -2.0, mesokurtic (normal) for scores between -2.0 and 2.0, and leptokurtic (heavy tails) for values above 2.0 (George & Mallery, 2005). If sustainability is reached, the distribution of key indicators y will be non-normal (Schmidt-Traub et al., 2017b). All statements can be reverted for key indicators y that have a negative effect on sustainable development.

Summary statistics of the growth indicators y_g are provided in Table 5.8 for the environmental domain and in Table 5.9 for the social and the economic domains. Central measures of the environmental domain's growth indicators y_g are negative (see Table 5.8). Given their negative effective direction ξ^-, this finding is desirable with regard to improved environmental effectiveness, supporting a variety of SDGs (see Section 5.3.1.1). The lowest negative growth rate is obtained for the median growth of hazardous waste. Median hazardous waste reduced by -9.69% from 2008 to 2016. Its mean amounts to -6.07%. Moreover, growth of hazardous waste are highly positively skewed (skewness of 1.20) and leptokurtic (kurtosis of 2.63). Asymmetry is directed towards the bottom (in favour of environmental protection), but frequent observations occur in the tails, which approach the top of the distribution. The other key indicators'

Social or economic growth indicator y_g								
Year	Mean	Median	Min	Max	Q_1	Q_3	Skewness	Kurtosis
Growth of compensation of employees								
2008-2016	0.2581	0.2504	-0.2456	0.7671	0.1438	0.3701	0.0959	0.4252
Growth of employees								
2008-2016	0.0426	0.0358	-0.3789	0.4471	-0.0471	0.1495	-0.1090	0.4946
Growth of socially-insured employees								
2008-2016	0.0928	0.0735	-0.3922	0.4890	-0.0249	0.1863	0.0227	-0.1974
Growth of marginally-employed employees								
2008-2016	-0.1113	-0.1125	-0.4362	0.3536	-0.2603	-0.0006	0.4193	-0.4219
Growth of female socially-insured employees								
2008-2016	0.1036	0.1061	-0.4750	0.4394	-0.0154	0.2130	-0.3150	0.5848
Growth of female marginally-employed employees								
2008-2016	-0.2078	-0.2056	-0.4707	0.2130	-0.3575	-0.1061	0.4022	-0.7059
Growth of severely-disabled employees								
2008-2016	0.2331	0.1962	-0.8048	1.0693	0.0816	0.3610	0.1145	2.3748
Growth of apprentices								
2008-2016	-0.0950	-0.0889	-0.6537	0.7309	-0.2206	0.0351	0.4514	2.1157
Growth of working population								
2008-2016	0.0254	0.0205	-0.3763	0.3393	-0.0512	0.1129	-0.2320	0.3135

Table 5.9 Summary statistics of the social and economic growth indicators in the German economy from 2008 to 2016; Max, Maximum; Min, Minimum; Q_1, 25th percentile; Q_3, 75th percentile

growth rates feature moderate positive skewnesses and are mesokurtic. Growth of waste water is an exception as it is moderately skewed to the left and leptokurtic (undesired).

Results of the central measures of the growth indicators y_g of the social and the economic domains follow their effective directions ξ (see Table 5.9), contributing to effective achievement of the respective SDGs (see Section 5.3.1.2 and Section 5.3.1.3). Only the growth of apprentices is not in line with this finding, and its mean and median are negative with values amounting to -9.50% and -8.89%, respectively. The SDG target to increase the number of people with vocational skills (SDG 4.4) is missed, exacerbating the shortage of future skilled workers, which are already missing today (e.g. Bonin, 2019). The growth of severely-disabled employees experiences the lowest minimum (-80.48%) and highest maximum (106.93%). Skewnesses and kurtoses of the social growth indicators y_g are mostly negligible and close to be normal. Growth of severely-disabled employees and apprentices are exceptions with leptokurtic distributions; their kurtoses amount to 2.37 and 2.12, respectively. Because skewness is negligible, frequent values occur at both the bottom and the top. Bottom results are desired to be shifted towards the top.

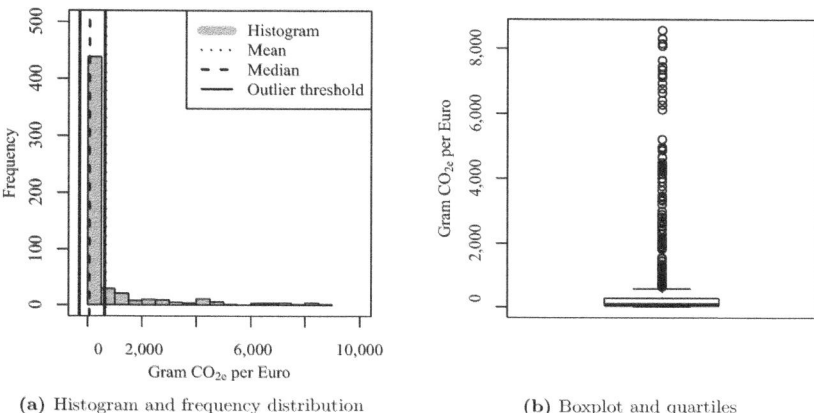

(a) Histogram and frequency distribution   (b) Boxplot and quartiles

Figure 5.7 Outliers of the air emissions intensity in gram Carbon Dioxide Equivalents (CO_{2e}) in the German economy from 2008 to 2016

The following section, Section 5.3.3, detects and removes outlying key indicators y_o.

5.3.3 Outlier detection and treatment

Outlier rates β and degrees of outlyingness are diverse across the three contentual domains and across ratio indicators y_r and growth indicators y_g. The environmental domain suffers most from outlyingness, with an outlier rate β of 10.77% and very strong outlying key indicators y_o especially for ratio indicators y_r. The economic domain exhibits an outlier rate β of 8.66% and diverse degrees of outlyingness, ranging from none (e.g. GVA rate), weak (e.g. share of imported input), moderate (e.g. investment intensity), to strong (e.g. labour productivity p.h.). The social domain's outlier rate β is the lowest (3.09%), and outlyingness is weak. The outlier rate β of ratio indicators y_r is more than twice as high as the growth indicators' outlier rate β: 8.06% vs. 3.34%.

Outlier illustration in histograms as displayed earlier in Figure 5.5 may assist outliers' visual analysis. However, boxplots are more valuable in this context because they picture the IQR method. Boxes indicate the IQR q, whiskers denote the product of the outlier coefficient α and the IQR q, and outliers are expressed by circles. An exemplary histogram and boxplot of the key indicator air emissions intensity are shown in Figure 5.7a and Figure 5.7b, respectively. The key indicator air emissions intensity is chosen due to its exemplariness of the environmental domain. The distribution of the air emissions intensity is positively skewed (average skewness of 3.16; see Table A.6), and numerous outlying key indicators y_o exist at the top of the distribution. The mean equals 665.35 g_{CO2e} per Euro, while the median only reaches 65.94 g_{CO2e} per Euro from 2008 to 2016 (see Table A.6). This finding demonstrates the effect of masking

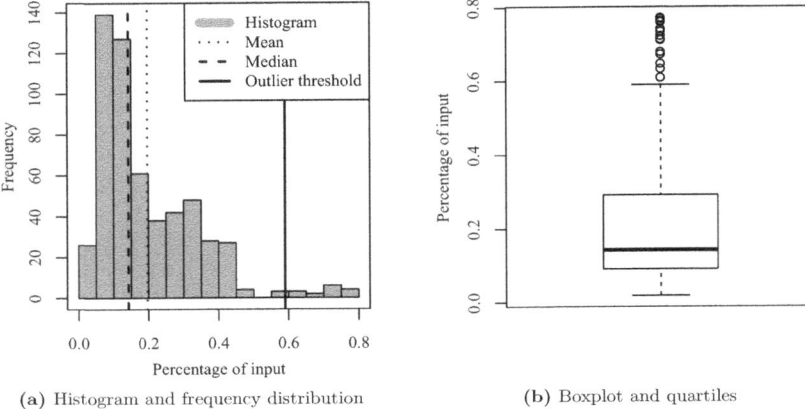

(a) Histogram and frequency distribution   **(b)** Boxplot and quartiles

Figure 5.8 Outliers of the share of imported input in percentage of input in the German
economy from 2008 to 2016

and inappropriateness of the mean and measures based on it for outlier detection (see
Section 4.3.5.2; Field, 2009): The vast number of outlying key indicators y_o at the top
influence the mean to a degree that it exceeds the upper outlier threshold θ_{max} equal to
619.63 g_{CO2e} per Euro (see Table A.9). Outlier thresholds of each key indicator y can
be found in Table A.9 to Table A.11 in the Appendix A.5.

As a further example, the share of imported input and its weak outlyingness are
chosen (see Figure 5.8). Because outlying key indicators y_o are weaker and fewer in
number compared to the air emissions intensity, the box of the boxplot is larger, and
whiskers are longer (see Figure 5.8b). Given the weakness of outlyingness, the mean is
close to the median, not approaching the outlier thresholds θ (see Figure 5.8a).

In both examples, outlying key indicators y_o occur at the top of the distribution.
However, outlying key indicators y_o at the bottom occur for the key indicators share of
apprentices, VAT intensity, intensity of net taxes on products and net import intensity.
Therefore, a two-sided outlier treatment is required.

After replacing outlying key indicators y_o with the respective thresholds θ (see
Table A.9 to Table A.11), key indicators y are rescaled and described along with their
empirical findings in the following section, Section 5.3.4.

5.3.4 Empirical findings of the cleaned and rescaled sustainable development key indicators

The rescaled key indicators y_s feature positive effective directions ξ^+ (see Section 4.3.6.2)
and are free from missing values and outliers (see Figure 4.1). Key indicators y with a
positive effective direction ξ^+ retain their labels after scaling, while negatively affecting

Key indicator y	Rescaled key indicator y_s
Growth of air emissions	Reduction of air emissions
Air emissions intensity	Air emissions efficiency
Growth of primary energy consumption	Reduction of primary energy consumption
Energy intensity	Energy efficiency
Growth of water use	Reduction of water use
Water intensity	Water efficiency
Growth of waste water	Reduction of waste water
Waste water intensity	Waste water efficiency
Growth of hazardous waste	Reduction of hazardous waste
Hazardous waste intensity	Hazardous waste efficiency
Growth of marginally-employed employees	Reduction of marginally-employed employees
Share of marginally-employed employees	Share of non-marginally-employed employees
Quota of gender difference	Quota of gender equality
Growth of female marginally-employed employees	Reduction of female marginally-employed employees
Quota of gender difference of marginally-employed employees	Quota of gender equality of marginally-employed employees

Table 5.10 Denotation of negatively affecting key indicators before and after scaling

key indicators' notations change. Negatively affecting growth indicators y_g alter their denotation from "growth" to "reduction", environmental ratio indicators y_r except the environmental tax intensity are now reported as efficiencies, the share of marginally-employed employees is interpreted as non-marginally-employed employees, and gender differences are translated into gender equalities. The labels are compared in Table 5.10.

The empirical findings of the cleaned and rescaled key indicators y_s are analysed in two manners: Summary statistics are investigated in Section 5.3.4.1, and the selected branches (see Table 5.1) are analysed in Section 5.3.4.2. The evaluation of the performance scores follows Prescott-Allen (2001; see Section 4.3.6.2). Scores should be at least fair to be acceptable. Bad results require actions for improvements.

5.3.4.1 Summary statistics

Interpretations of the summary statistics towards sustainable development (see Section 5.3.2) remain valid for rescaled performance scores with one additional aspect: If a key indicator's score of the 25th or the 75th percentile is higher than 25.00 (poor performance) or 75.00 (fair performance), respectively, it approximately contributes more to sustainable development than a normally-distributed key indicator y would.[51] Therefore, scores exceeding 25.00 and 75.00, respectively, are strived for.

Results of the rescaled growth indicators y_{gs} of the environmental domain (see Table 5.11) are in line with their unscaled counterparts analysed in Section 5.3.2. Distributional properties among the rescaled environmental growth indicators y_{gs} are relatively homogeneous. The economic objects n exhibit a medium central (mean and median) performance of environmental effectiveness. Only the median reduction of air emissions and both mean and median reduction of hazardous waste score fair results. The outstanding median reduction of hazardous waste of -9.69% (see Section 5.3.2) is converted into a score of 67.04, a fair and acceptable performance. Rescaled environmental ratio indicators y_{rs} yield fair mean performances and good median performances (see Table 5.11). Central measures generally show stable, increasing trends. This is a positive finding for environmental efficiency as relative decoupling of environmental degradation and economic activity (SDG 8.4) is centrally achieved. The biggest increase in central environmental efficiency occurs for the hazardous waste efficiency's mean: It increased from 72.60 in 2008 to 77.67 in 2016, which corresponds to a growth rate of 6.98%. Because the median only increased by 2.40%, it is supposed that the mean's increase is caused by few economic objects n. Enhancements by further economic objects n are desirable. The improvement of the hazardous waste efficiency is followed by the waste water efficiency's mean, which grew by 6.57% from 2008 to 2016. Concerning the 25th and the 75th percentiles, 50% of the distribution is shifted upward by one bracket: Instead of the normal poor to fair performances, at least medium to good performances are reached by 50% of the distribution, respectively. As a result, the distributions are mostly highly negatively skewed. Kurtoses are mostly negative but relatively small and negligible. Not in favour of environmental protection are the extremes as they are nearly invariant over time without improvements. Constant extremes appear due to outlier treatment. The environmental tax intensity is an exception to these findings. Its central outcomes are poor to medium, the 25th and the 75th percentiles are below those of a normal distribution, and the data are highly positively skewed. Improvements over time are reported but insignificant.

Rescaled key indicators y_s of the social domain are more diverse than those of the environmental domain (see Table 5.12). Central measures feature wider ranges (poor to good), their trends are increasing as well as decreasing, and skewnesses and kurtoses are both positive and negative. The rescaled growth indicators y_{gs} of the compensation of employees and employees achieve medium results with a rather normal shape. Average compensations of employees (p.c. and p.h.) exhibit central performances at the lower end of being medium. However, the average compensations of employees' minima

---

[51] The contribution is only "approximately" higher because key indicators y are not rescaled on an interval from zero to 100 but ten to 100.

Rescaled environmental key indicator y_s								
Year	Mean	Median	Min	Max	Q_1	Q_3	Skewness	Kurtosis
Reduction of air emissions								
2008-2016	58.22	63.85	10.00	100.00	44.49	72.06	-0.3345	-0.4290
Air emissions efficiency								
2008	70.89	89.35	10.00	99.88	60.46	93.54	-1.0737	-0.6268
2009	70.85	90.46	10.00	99.95	56.69	94.19	-1.0485	-0.6845
2010	70.87	90.43	10.00	99.95	59.28	93.89	-1.0516	-0.6745
2011	71.78	91.44	10.00	100.00	62.00	94.78	-1.0974	-0.5997
2012	72.15	91.44	10.00	99.98	62.46	94.76	-1.1186	-0.5604
2013	72.02	91.83	10.00	99.99	63.08	94.74	-1.1107	-0.5659
2014	72.71	92.33	10.00	99.98	62.19	94.68	-1.1202	-0.5494
2015	72.83	92.14	10.00	99.93	62.67	94.93	-1.1307	-0.5177
2016	73.08	92.01	10.00	99.90	59.82	94.98	-1.1149	-0.5618
Reduction of primary energy consumption								
2008-2016	52.44	56.09	10.00	100.00	37.24	66.25	-0.0612	-0.4713
Energy efficiency								
2008	69.71	87.81	10.00	99.88	57.25	90.93	-1.0431	-0.5586
2009	69.34	89.00	10.00	99.93	52.79	91.96	-1.0083	-0.6775
2010	69.36	87.87	10.00	99.89	57.34	91.00	-1.0208	-0.6160
2011	70.85	89.63	10.00	100.00	62.50	92.40	-1.0941	-0.4749
2012	71.51	89.44	10.00	99.93	64.31	92.99	-1.1516	-0.3423
2013	71.21	89.40	10.00	99.97	60.13	92.70	-1.1109	-0.4305
2014	72.29	90.09	10.00	99.99	62.33	93.38	-1.1503	-0.3136
2015	72.13	90.42	10.00	99.91	64.57	93.26	-1.1553	-0.3463
2016	72.53	91.14	10.00	99.92	66.13	93.55	-1.1788	-0.2861
Reduction of water use								
2008-2016	51.13	52.51	10.00	100.00	35.85	65.80	-0.0164	-0.5466
Water efficiency								
2008	72.43	91.57	10.00	100.00	56.70	97.26	-1.0635	-0.5928
2009	71.66	90.25	10.00	99.99	54.04	97.44	-1.0257	-0.6702
2010	72.41	91.25	10.00	99.99	54.54	97.20	-1.0657	-0.6007
2011	73.30	92.03	10.00	100.00	62.02	97.10	-1.1311	-0.4504
2012	73.70	91.46	10.00	99.99	65.29	96.98	-1.1675	-0.3766
2013	74.40	91.21	10.00	99.99	67.93	97.12	-1.2155	-0.2894
2014	74.58	91.80	10.00	99.99	67.96	97.40	-1.2268	-0.2490
2015	75.04	92.05	10.00	100.00	70.46	97.54	-1.2513	-0.2143
2016	75.28	92.54	10.00	100.00	72.20	97.54	-1.2709	-0.1668
Reduction of waste water								
2008-2016	51.68	52.18	10.00	100.00	38.61	64.72	0.0602	-0.5638
Waste water efficiency								
2008	69.56	85.49	10.00	100.00	58.57	95.47	-0.9662	-0.6636
2009	68.59	84.46	10.00	100.00	48.54	95.15	-0.8927	-0.8238
2010	69.62	84.23	10.00	100.00	56.87	95.51	-0.9752	-0.6576
2011	70.79	85.59	10.00	100.00	61.70	95.73	-1.0432	-0.4924
2012	71.38	85.15	10.00	100.00	62.68	95.80	-1.0941	-0.3422

continued

| Rescaled environmental key indicator y_s | | | | | | | | |
Year	Mean	Median	Min	Max	Q_1	Q_3	Skewness	Kurtosis
2013	72.42	85.62	10.00	100.00	69.38	95.94	-1.1863	-0.1574
2014	72.93	86.82	10.00	100.00	70.92	96.18	-1.1977	-0.1111
2015	73.55	87.59	10.00	100.00	72.72	96.27	-1.2260	-0.0713
2016	74.12	88.44	10.00	100.00	72.22	96.29	-1.2688	0.0538
Reduction of hazardous waste								
2008-2016	64.17	67.04	10.00	100.00	49.62	77.97	-0.5339	-0.3767
Hazardous waste efficiency								
2008	72.60	88.03	10.00	99.74	60.64	93.38	-1.1313	-0.2924
2009	71.56	87.34	10.00	99.82	53.03	92.09	-1.0496	-0.4506
2010	75.44	89.30	10.00	99.84	62.92	97.22	-1.2557	0.0822
2011	77.09	92.59	10.00	99.38	65.07	96.84	-1.3958	0.5447
2012	75.76	90.75	10.00	99.56	60.93	96.27	-1.3301	0.3780
2013	76.76	90.84	10.00	100.00	59.54	98.24	-1.3202	0.3681
2014	76.38	91.10	10.00	99.95	59.20	98.28	-1.3308	0.2999
2015	77.35	91.73	10.00	99.50	63.35	97.00	-1.4417	0.7013
2016	77.67	90.14	10.00	99.77	64.50	96.75	-1.4614	0.7529
Environmental tax intensity								
2008	40.15	30.91	10.05	100.00	20.35	48.00	1.1634	0.2100
2009	42.47	32.19	10.00	100.00	20.52	61.00	0.9366	-0.3914
2010	40.30	30.48	10.12	100.00	20.13	46.42	1.1231	-0.0222
2011	42.89	32.37	10.36	100.00	21.39	54.16	1.0237	-0.2513
2012	41.36	29.91	10.33	100.00	19.85	51.35	1.1073	-0.0556
2013	41.43	31.37	10.15	100.00	19.87	52.72	1.0841	-0.0692
2014	41.10	31.49	10.12	100.00	18.84	52.16	1.1156	0.0475
2015	40.59	29.68	10.13	100.00	19.05	50.98	1.1563	0.2018
2016	40.76	30.59	10.17	100.00	18.80	49.47	1.1308	0.1639

Table 5.11 Summary statistics of the rescaled environmental key indicators in the German economy from 2008 to 2016; Max, Maximum; Min, Minimum; Q_1, 25th percentile; Q_3, 75th percentile

| Rescaled social key indicator y_s | | | | | | | | |
Year	Mean	Median	Min	Max	Q_1	Q_3	Skewness	Kurtosis
Growth of compensation of employees								
2008-2016	55.10	54.35	10.00	100.00	43.96	65.94	0.0939	0.0603
Growth of employees								
2008-2016	54.09	53.24	10.00	100.00	44.13	65.89	-0.0425	0.2290
Average compensation of employees p.c.								
2008	40.96	39.15	10.00	80.45	28.48	56.10	0.1618	-1.0535
2009	41.51	38.40	10.35	84.16	28.55	58.63	0.2776	-0.9296
2010	42.82	40.35	10.85	82.01	28.85	59.86	0.2001	-1.0649
2011	44.74	41.87	11.36	87.96	29.84	60.93	0.2900	-0.9443
2012	45.70	42.88	11.77	97.06	30.40	61.16	0.3135	-0.8280
2013	46.75	43.79	11.94	90.55	31.41	62.40	0.2494	-1.0653
2014	48.25	45.04	12.78	90.94	32.21	64.56	0.2231	-1.1074
2015	50.14	46.08	13.98	100.00	34.46	66.48	0.2900	-1.0037
2016	51.40	47.93	14.71	96.96	36.63	68.18	0.2942	-0.9838
Average compensation of employees p.h.								
2008	39.33	35.10	10.00	73.28	27.60	54.20	0.3180	-1.0283
2009	42.43	37.41	10.86	90.76	29.62	58.64	0.4109	-0.8332
2010	43.00	37.44	11.18	86.30	30.29	60.64	0.3181	-0.9929
2011	44.73	38.30	13.03	88.76	31.42	61.13	0.3625	-0.9759
2012	46.87	40.52	13.62	98.81	33.74	63.29	0.3956	-0.8187
2013	48.20	40.66	15.13	91.62	35.01	65.22	0.3986	-0.9901
2014	49.68	41.67	15.98	96.57	36.03	67.58	0.4191	-0.9604
2015	51.49	43.40	16.49	100.00	37.13	69.66	0.4234	-0.9610
2016	53.33	46.25	18.40	96.70	39.47	73.24	0.4256	-0.9522
Labour share								
2008	58.82	61.95	10.02	96.06	44.82	72.46	-0.3736	-0.4180
2009	62.17	67.43	10.04	97.90	46.00	77.95	-0.5212	-0.4225
2010	59.95	63.67	10.07	97.28	45.18	72.32	-0.4230	-0.3094
2011	59.94	64.24	10.00	96.02	43.20	71.04	-0.3408	-0.3462
2012	60.37	63.73	10.19	94.97	44.67	72.08	-0.4006	-0.3166
2013	60.38	64.15	10.01	95.52	43.65	73.54	-0.5000	-0.3311
2014	60.46	63.79	10.16	95.11	44.57	72.88	-0.4271	-0.3507
2015	59.79	63.64	10.20	97.36	45.58	71.62	-0.3987	-0.2410
2016	60.07	61.75	10.35	100.00	47.11	72.32	-0.2688	-0.2626
Growth of socially-insured employees								
2008-2016	57.16	54.98	10.00	100.00	44.55	67.13	0.0932	-0.4334
Reduction of marginally-employed employees								
2008-2016	65.70	67.10	10.00	100.00	52.45	85.03	-0.4750	-0.6180
Share of non-marginally-employed employees								
2008	70.67	80.26	10.00	99.59	58.61	93.43	-1.0404	-0.1308
2009	70.75	80.45	10.00	99.73	59.39	93.64	-1.0340	-0.1559
2010	71.17	80.85	10.00	99.65	59.18	93.64	-1.0569	-0.1071
2011	71.70	81.53	10.00	99.79	59.40	94.08	-1.0819	-0.0465
2012	72.21	82.14	10.00	99.83	60.32	94.24	-1.1094	0.0189

continued

| Rescaled social key indicator y_s | | | | | | | | |
Year	Mean	Median	Min	Max	Q_1	Q_3	Skewness	Kurtosis
2013	72.41	82.23	10.00	99.81	60.62	94.12	-1.1304	0.0585
2014	72.86	82.41	10.00	99.87	61.00	93.85	-1.1447	0.1019
2015	74.19	83.16	10.00	99.98	62.59	93.78	-1.2147	0.3628
2016	74.93	83.89	10.00	100.00	63.68	93.47	-1.2612	0.5464
Growth of female socially-insured employees								
2008-2016	62.31	62.38	10.00	100.00	48.82	74.43	-0.0535	-0.3389
Quota of gender equality								
2008	54.94	54.69	10.00	97.40	34.36	74.31	0.0409	-1.1385
2009	55.00	53.83	10.53	98.94	34.44	75.11	0.0487	-1.1417
2010	54.89	54.57	11.09	99.01	34.77	75.48	0.0669	-1.1529
2011	54.56	54.59	10.92	98.77	33.95	73.97	0.1088	-1.1442
2012	54.79	54.46	12.07	99.06	34.49	73.34	0.1108	-1.1364
2013	54.86	54.13	12.40	98.55	34.18	73.47	0.0958	-1.1526
2014	54.95	54.64	13.30	99.50	34.02	73.55	0.0886	-1.1746
2015	55.09	55.29	13.90	99.65	33.64	73.89	0.0872	-1.1878
2016	55.42	56.30	13.99	99.96	33.58	74.05	0.0956	-1.1772
Reduction of female marginally-employed employees								
2008-2016	65.39	65.11	10.00	100.00	52.39	85.07	-0.3935	-0.7714
Quota of gender equality of marginally-employed employees								
2008	62.42	60.80	10.00	98.23	48.47	78.87	0.0031	-0.4813
2009	63.30	61.69	10.00	98.56	50.17	80.27	-0.0981	-0.4790
2010	64.27	62.71	11.94	98.88	50.74	81.11	-0.0994	-0.5372
2011	65.58	63.97	16.71	99.27	51.91	80.51	-0.0937	-0.5829
2012	66.91	65.05	24.59	99.95	52.71	81.57	-0.0350	-0.8109
2013	68.32	66.65	28.05	98.27	54.81	82.73	-0.0376	-0.8852
2014	69.72	68.35	32.45	99.41	56.58	83.32	-0.0544	-0.9419
2015	72.06	72.00	38.38	99.55	58.56	84.97	0.0667	-1.0547
2016	73.26	72.37	39.89	100.00	59.68	85.40	0.0788	-1.0101
Growth of severely-disabled employees								
2008-2016	55.80	52.98	10.00	100.00	43.82	65.80	0.4418	0.0470
Quota of severely-disabled employees								
2008	51.64	52.78	10.00	92.93	40.25	61.82	0.1020	0.0099
2009	54.12	54.61	15.66	97.60	42.52	64.08	0.2105	0.0382
2010	55.45	56.06	13.82	100.00	42.87	65.19	0.2147	-0.0128
2011	55.45	56.09	15.39	100.00	43.50	64.93	0.0945	-0.0054
2012	56.81	57.29	19.28	100.00	44.99	66.31	0.1780	-0.1356
2013	57.61	58.92	20.43	100.00	45.64	66.62	0.0944	-0.2096
2014	57.77	58.84	20.37	100.00	45.49	67.20	0.2036	-0.2337
2015	58.26	60.35	20.35	100.00	44.55	67.51	0.1971	-0.4598
2016	57.64	59.44	20.49	98.37	44.49	67.80	0.1085	-0.5001
Growth of apprentices								
2008-2016	55.59	55.76	10.00	100.00	44.15	66.35	0.0705	0.0546

continued

| Rescaled social key indicator y_s | | | | | | | | |
Year	Mean	Median	Min	Max	Q_1	Q_3	Skewness	Kurtosis
Share of apprentices								
2008	58.05	51.74	12.46	100.00	44.04	75.60	0.3571	-0.6579
2009	58.47	52.61	12.38	100.00	45.05	73.13	0.3183	-0.6347
2010	56.49	52.03	11.71	100.00	44.16	70.84	0.3364	-0.4958
2011	53.35	47.78	11.15	100.00	41.39	67.10	0.4233	-0.2972
2012	52.99	48.43	11.43	100.00	42.44	65.03	0.4083	-0.1035
2013	52.13	48.03	11.47	100.00	40.68	63.67	0.4235	0.0097
2014	51.11	47.69	11.01	100.00	39.55	62.68	0.4370	0.2129
2015	49.83	47.81	10.27	100.00	39.01	58.72	0.5270	0.4848
2016	49.02	47.56	10.00	100.00	38.78	56.73	0.6208	0.7671
VAT intensity								
2008	55.24	55.23	19.45	100.00	44.10	63.59	0.2960	0.5069
2009	56.31	55.62	17.76	100.00	43.99	67.11	0.1450	0.2017
2010	55.57	54.59	20.98	100.00	43.84	66.96	0.2585	0.0195
2011	55.26	53.93	17.42	100.00	43.63	66.49	0.1767	-0.0038
2012	55.17	53.93	10.00	100.00	43.97	65.59	-0.1045	0.4064
2013	55.32	53.55	15.92	100.00	43.94	65.14	0.2124	0.2400
2014	55.33	53.41	17.35	100.00	44.22	65.64	0.2962	0.3298
2015	55.24	53.04	17.73	100.00	43.46	65.85	0.3263	0.4051
2016	55.09	52.63	18.62	100.00	43.67	65.09	0.3192	0.3857
Intensity of net taxes on products								
2008	56.63	52.75	10.00	100.00	45.37	67.64	0.2344	0.2854
2009	55.84	51.53	10.00	100.00	44.84	66.45	0.2919	0.1559
2010	52.87	48.31	10.00	100.00	40.84	62.48	0.3356	-0.0150
2011	54.78	49.13	10.00	100.00	42.79	66.91	0.2172	-0.1624
2012	56.07	49.11	10.00	100.00	44.13	68.55	0.3430	-0.1786
2013	54.76	49.01	10.00	100.00	43.19	66.45	0.3252	0.0223
2014	55.18	49.88	10.00	100.00	44.19	66.07	0.2739	0.1280
2015	54.15	49.91	10.00	100.00	44.17	64.40	0.2693	0.3485
2016	53.78	49.83	10.00	100.00	44.26	64.58	0.3268	0.3124
CIT intensity								
2008	30.86	25.44	10.00	100.00	18.71	34.62	2.0185	3.9838
2009	31.74	26.76	10.00	100.00	17.76	38.01	1.8150	3.2957
2010	39.91	34.91	10.00	100.00	22.85	49.58	1.1350	0.6548
2011	46.68	41.68	10.00	100.00	28.89	60.80	0.7437	-0.3645
2012	46.55	41.81	10.00	100.00	24.40	58.85	0.7490	-0.3689
2013	49.41	46.35	10.00	100.00	26.00	65.76	0.5418	-0.7899
2014	49.50	47.11	10.00	100.00	26.18	72.07	0.5063	-0.9185
2015	48.46	44.49	10.00	100.00	26.52	59.78	0.6123	-0.7019
2016	48.89	44.74	10.00	100.00	26.77	65.96	0.5428	-0.8404
Local business tax intensity								
2008	42.40	38.89	10.00	100.00	27.05	53.64	0.7753	0.3818
2009	45.37	42.82	10.00	100.00	27.35	62.80	0.4247	-0.5243
2010	41.98	40.77	10.00	100.00	26.52	52.41	0.8393	0.4811

continued

| Rescaled social key indicator y_s | | | | | | | |
Year	Mean	Median	Min	Max	Q_1	Q_3	Skewness	Kurtosis
2011	46.01	44.98	10.00	100.00	30.17	59.59	0.5739	-0.1319
2012	46.57	45.57	10.00	100.00	28.03	57.67	0.5841	-0.3130
2013	45.13	44.71	10.00	100.00	27.22	55.40	0.4980	-0.1700
2014	45.80	46.26	10.00	100.00	27.47	56.07	0.5600	-0.2632
2015	45.12	45.58	10.00	100.00	27.90	54.34	0.6508	0.0884
2016	44.96	45.62	10.00	100.00	28.15	55.86	0.6750	0.1738

Table 5.12 Summary statistics of the rescaled social key indicators in the German economy from 2008 to 2016; CIT, Corporate Income Tax; Max, Maximum; Min, Minimum; p.c., per capita; p.h., per hour; Q_1, 25th percentile; Q_3, 75th percentile; VAT, Value Added Tax

experienced increases of 47.13% and 83.98%, respectively, and the 25th percentiles advanced by 28.62% and 43.00%, respectively, from 2008 to 2016. Contributions to the SDG target of sustaining income growth of the bottom 40% are made (SDG 10.1). The labour share yields higher performances with mostly fair central measures. The IQR is reduced over time, and the GVA distributed to employees becomes more homogeneous across economic objects n. Central reduction of marginally-employed employees as well as the mean share of non-marginally-employed employees achieve fair results. Additionally, the latter rescaled key indicator y_s steadily increases its performance, and its medians are appraised with good. The 25th and the 75th percentiles exceed those of a normal distribution, and 75% of the economic objects n perform at least medium (58.61 in 2008). This leads to a highly negatively skewed distribution with skewness amounting to -1.26 in 2016. This is favourable for implementation of social protection systems (SDG 1.3). Economic objects n perform fair in central rescaled growth indicators y_{gs} on female employees and the quota of gender equality of marginally-employed employees. In contrast, medium results are reported for the quota of gender equality. The quota of gender equality should be enhanced. However, marginal employment is more critical in view of social development as social protection is not provided (see Section 5.3.2; BA, 2019). Furthermore, the improvement of the minima of the quota of gender equality of marginally-employed employees is remarkable: It enhanced from 10.00 in 2008 to 39.89 in 2016. This improvement is attributable to the divisions 17 Manufacture of paper and paper products and 93 Sports activities and amusement and recreation activities (see Table A.1). Such results are also desirable for the quota of gender equality. The growth rate and the quota of severely-disabled employees report medium central performances, with the quota experiencing a positive evolution over time. Their 25th percentiles exceed scores of 25.00, but the 75th percentiles remain below 75.00. Improvements in inclusion and equal opportunities for all are demanded (SDG 10.2). Unscaled growth rates of apprentices are negative (see Table 5.9) and are translated into a mean and median score of 55.59 and 55.76, respectively. Both results are classified as medium performances, requiring improvements. Apprentices' ratio indicator, share of apprentices, exhibits a negative trend (mean reduction of -15.56% from 2008 to 2016), and the 75th percentiles remain below the normal 75.00 after the first year of reporting. The aggravation of skilled workers' shortage revealed by the growth of apprentices (see Section 5.3.2) is confirmed with the ratio indicator share of apprentices. Rescaled social ratio indicators y_{rs} on taxes score poor to medium central results. Owing to outlier treatment, the minima and the maxima are mostly constant. The VAT intensity varies over time, but the trend is not steady. The 75th percentiles of the tax intensities remain below 75.00, and the distributions are positively skewed. Concluding, contributions to fiscal policies for greater equality (SDG 10.4) should be upgraded.

Summary statistics of the economic domain's rescaled key indicators y_s are shown in Table 5.13. Similar to the social domain, distributional properties of rescaled economic key indicators y_s diverge. The capital productivities and the investment intensity yield poor to medium central measures, ranging between 28.28 (median gross capital productivity in 2009) and 43.15 (mean net capital productivity in 2016). The extremes neither experience significant evolution at the bottom nor at the top. The 25th and the 75th percentiles are mostly located below normal percentiles, and the distributions are moderately to highly skewed to the right. The degree of modernity performs better and mostly achieves fair central scores. However, its trend is decreasing with a mean reduction of -5.49% from 2008 to 2016. A decreasing trend is also observed in its maxima. These diminished from 100.00 in 2010 to 88.81 in 2016. During the same period, the minima advanced from 10.00 to 20.78 (107.76%), entering the bracket of poor performance. Enhancement of economic productivity through technology (SDG 8.2) is realised only by bottom performers for the degree of modernity. In respect of innovation triggered by R&D activities, economic productivity is neither tackled. Performances of the internal R&D intensity and the share of R&D employees are bad (median) to poor (mean). The 75th percentiles remain below 50.00 (medium instead of normal fair performance), and the distributions are highly skewed to the right, which is unfavourable for economic sustainable development. GVA rates achieve medium central results and a positive incline of 82.70% in its minima from 2008 to 2016. However, the worst performer's growth is accompanied by a reduction of the best performer (-10.89%). Labour productivities yield poor to medium central scores and feature increasing trends in the minima. However, in this case, the advancement of the minima is not associated with a deterioration of the best performer. Undesired positive skewness is present, signalling frequent values at the bottom. Performances supporting economic productivity through GVA-intensive and labour-productive activities (SDG 8.2) should be improved. Rescaled ratio indicators y_{rs} on trade yield poor (central share of imported input) to fair (median net import intensity) scores. The 25th and the 75th percentiles

| Rescaled economic key indicator y_s | | | | | | | | |
Year	Mean	Median	Min	Max	Q_1	Q_3	Skewness	Kurtosis
Gross capital productivity								
2008	42.36	30.00	10.44	100.00	21.22	52.74	0.9228	-0.6244
2009	40.61	28.28	10.31	100.00	21.59	55.56	0.9698	-0.4878
2010	41.42	30.14	10.25	100.00	21.05	51.19	0.9377	-0.4885
2011	41.89	31.98	10.27	100.00	20.81	51.57	0.9142	-0.5609
2012	41.89	32.27	10.12	100.00	20.52	48.17	0.9339	-0.5331
2013	41.88	32.24	10.11	100.00	20.85	49.07	0.9473	-0.5063
2014	42.19	33.35	10.05	100.00	20.62	49.80	0.9284	-0.5299
2015	42.77	34.17	10.04	100.00	21.16	51.19	0.9106	-0.5110
2016	43.05	34.40	10.00	100.00	21.55	52.32	0.8892	-0.4931
Net capital productivity								
2008	42.08	33.85	10.25	99.79	21.19	53.75	0.8458	-0.6573
2009	40.35	32.01	10.16	100.00	20.93	54.38	0.9119	-0.5025
2010	41.26	33.49	10.13	100.00	21.45	51.46	0.8580	-0.5198
2011	41.72	34.52	10.16	100.00	21.44	54.45	0.8375	-0.5619
2012	41.75	35.10	10.05	100.00	21.48	51.03	0.8537	-0.5540
2013	41.81	34.37	10.06	100.00	21.74	51.18	0.8585	-0.5593
2014	42.20	34.65	10.01	100.00	21.61	52.44	0.8376	-0.5912
2015	42.86	35.51	10.02	100.00	21.76	52.43	0.8222	-0.5577
2016	43.15	36.18	10.00	100.00	22.17	54.21	0.8055	-0.5224
Degree of modernity								
2008	61.40	62.03	10.00	99.13	48.49	78.51	-0.2833	-0.5965
2009	60.48	62.29	10.00	95.87	48.13	75.46	-0.2817	-0.5359
2010	60.09	62.51	10.00	100.00	47.25	74.58	-0.2457	-0.4480
2011	59.97	62.83	11.33	96.16	47.23	73.01	-0.2775	-0.4788
2012	59.42	62.31	14.14	90.76	47.71	73.04	-0.3439	-0.4840
2013	58.75	60.59	16.82	90.86	47.61	72.93	-0.3664	-0.5066
2014	58.41	59.07	20.79	89.63	47.53	72.14	-0.3690	-0.5220
2015	58.13	60.27	21.40	89.06	48.39	70.84	-0.3972	-0.4005
2016	58.03	60.42	20.78	88.81	49.18	69.29	-0.3761	-0.2630
Consumed capital productivity								
2008	41.56	31.33	10.63	100.00	20.94	55.35	1.0285	-0.2310
2009	39.59	28.78	10.26	100.00	20.04	57.60	1.0355	-0.1924
2010	40.07	29.68	10.23	100.00	20.71	51.78	1.0562	-0.1022
2011	40.38	31.19	10.21	100.00	19.98	52.22	1.0131	-0.1438
2012	40.22	30.68	10.00	100.00	19.89	50.74	1.0521	-0.0550
2013	40.33	31.04	10.01	100.00	20.51	49.82	1.0895	0.0304
2014	40.57	31.49	10.26	100.00	20.06	49.73	1.0592	-0.0254
2015	41.06	33.10	10.41	100.00	20.34	50.84	1.0524	-0.0098
2016	41.40	34.10	10.29	100.00	21.08	51.69	1.0801	0.1030
Investment intensity								
2008	42.87	35.84	10.00	100.00	22.86	54.45	0.9193	-0.1735
2009	42.15	33.13	10.32	100.00	22.17	58.52	0.9417	-0.2366
2010	41.12	32.64	11.00	100.00	24.74	47.93	1.1283	0.3028
2011	41.47	32.87	11.80	100.00	24.72	53.51	1.0900	0.2291

continued

Rescaled economic key indicator y_s

Year	Mean	Median	Min	Max	Q_1	Q_3	Skewness	Kurtosis
2012	40.62	33.17	10.38	100.00	25.03	47.30	1.1431	0.5340
2013	39.60	32.26	10.42	100.00	24.80	50.09	1.1050	0.5500
2014	41.08	33.16	10.48	100.00	23.83	58.58	1.0488	0.2564
2015	40.77	31.73	10.13	100.00	23.49	53.20	1.1724	0.5127
2016	40.69	33.49	10.22	100.00	24.38	54.65	1.2021	0.5609

Internal R&D intensity

Year	Mean	Median	Min	Max	Q_1	Q_3	Skewness	Kurtosis
2008	31.41	16.18	10.00	100.00	10.91	37.66	1.3422	0.3404
2009	33.69	15.61	10.00	100.00	10.88	44.75	1.1327	-0.1918
2010	32.94	14.97	10.00	100.00	10.94	44.73	1.2048	0.0343
2011	33.18	15.55	10.00	100.00	10.93	46.45	1.1719	-0.1042
2012	33.02	14.73	10.00	100.00	10.80	46.75	1.1889	-0.0541
2013	32.90	15.34	10.00	100.00	10.86	43.33	1.2248	0.0110
2014	32.97	15.24	10.00	100.00	10.77	41.99	1.2033	-0.0557
2015	34.34	14.73	10.00	100.00	10.63	52.64	1.1349	-0.3245
2016	33.94	14.69	10.00	100.00	10.63	49.97	1.1364	-0.3025

Share of R&D employees

Year	Mean	Median	Min	Max	Q_1	Q_3	Skewness	Kurtosis
2008	31.23	15.70	10.00	100.00	10.72	38.84	1.3938	0.5500
2009	32.95	17.43	10.00	100.00	10.77	47.82	1.2204	0.0005
2010	33.49	17.48	10.00	100.00	10.79	46.46	1.2016	-0.0632
2011	33.72	16.75	10.00	100.00	10.89	49.54	1.1756	-0.1709
2012	33.75	16.89	10.00	100.00	10.97	48.48	1.1646	-0.2069
2013	32.65	17.30	10.00	100.00	10.77	46.39	1.2758	0.1630
2014	33.00	17.12	10.00	100.00	10.79	44.81	1.2534	0.0486
2015	33.67	16.36	10.00	100.00	10.87	48.43	1.1955	-0.1563
2016	33.50	15.33	10.00	100.00	10.80	49.82	1.1964	-0.1575

GVA rate

Year	Mean	Median	Min	Max	Q_1	Q_3	Skewness	Kurtosis
2008	56.42	55.30	10.00	100.00	43.98	68.10	0.0287	-0.3635
2009	56.34	55.67	13.00	97.43	44.60	66.91	0.1001	-0.4297
2010	55.89	53.34	14.53	88.82	44.69	65.87	-0.0012	-0.6227
2011	55.21	53.09	10.01	88.71	43.32	66.38	-0.0726	-0.5455
2012	55.97	54.93	10.36	89.09	43.76	68.71	-0.1211	-0.5502
2013	56.39	54.32	11.57	90.29	45.59	68.58	-0.0405	-0.5332
2014	56.50	55.69	10.69	92.46	44.92	68.12	-0.0636	-0.5291
2015	56.91	54.55	16.08	95.10	44.40	69.13	0.0890	-0.6474
2016	57.00	55.57	18.27	89.11	45.13	68.46	0.0173	-0.7312

Working population growth

Year	Mean	Median	Min	Max	Q_1	Q_3	Skewness	Kurtosis
2008-2016	55.40	55.63	10.00	100.00	43.16	69.48	-0.0750	-0.3053

Labour productivity p.c.

Year	Mean	Median	Min	Max	Q_1	Q_3	Skewness	Kurtosis
2008	41.06	33.21	10.66	100.00	24.28	51.32	1.2254	0.5718
2009	39.35	30.50	10.00	100.00	22.71	46.89	1.3106	0.6708
2010	41.50	32.24	10.48	100.00	24.38	55.45	1.1102	0.1707
2011	42.75	33.90	11.04	100.00	25.31	55.86	1.0488	0.0621
2012	43.00	34.04	11.47	100.00	25.61	55.43	1.0308	-0.0042

continued

| Rescaled economic key indicator y_s | | | | | | | | |
Year	Mean	Median	Min	Max	Q_1	Q_3	Skewness	Kurtosis
2013	43.52	34.97	11.09	100.00	25.81	55.18	1.0563	0.0962
2014	44.67	35.95	11.67	100.00	27.31	57.81	0.9862	-0.0592
2015	46.63	37.58	12.57	100.00	28.92	62.84	0.8237	-0.5247
2016	47.58	39.13	12.83	100.00	28.80	62.76	0.7862	-0.6243
Labour productivity p.h.								
2008	41.83	33.73	10.53	100.00	28.13	49.98	1.2922	1.1815
2009	40.96	33.67	10.00	100.00	27.85	54.82	1.3147	1.2922
2010	43.28	34.96	10.72	100.00	27.86	57.25	1.0695	0.3496
2011	44.45	34.97	11.78	100.00	28.04	54.88	1.0495	0.1819
2012	45.40	36.14	12.80	100.00	29.01	59.44	0.9821	0.0693
2013	46.41	38.31	12.77	100.00	31.08	60.12	1.0464	0.2055
2014	47.69	38.49	13.87	100.00	33.11	60.75	1.0312	0.0522
2015	49.00	39.99	15.05	100.00	33.86	61.79	0.9078	-0.2007
2016	50.44	40.83	15.67	100.00	33.89	63.33	0.8672	-0.3456
Net import intensity								
2008	56.30	64.19	10.00	100.00	46.69	65.91	-0.3258	-0.8759
2009	56.77	65.04	10.00	100.00	48.76	66.45	-0.3748	-0.8862
2010	56.22	64.44	10.00	100.00	46.85	67.30	-0.3340	-0.8976
2011	58.06	64.89	10.00	100.00	53.62	69.09	-0.4384	-0.6789
2012	56.87	66.25	10.00	100.00	47.04	66.25	-0.3690	-0.7118
2013	55.75	63.76	10.00	100.00	36.23	74.75	-0.2481	-0.8921
2014	54.20	61.67	10.00	100.00	33.27	63.07	-0.1502	-0.8442
2015	53.86	61.67	10.00	100.00	26.10	61.67	-0.1184	-0.9193
2016	55.19	61.19	10.00	100.00	49.86	61.19	-0.2208	-0.7384
Share of imported input								
2008	35.61	28.01	10.50	100.00	20.51	46.34	1.1876	0.7299
2009	34.38	27.35	10.37	100.00	19.58	44.90	1.3586	1.5468
2010	37.32	30.30	10.27	100.00	20.41	52.24	1.0514	0.5389
2011	37.71	29.62	10.00	100.00	20.91	52.58	1.0248	0.4422
2012	38.64	31.06	10.02	100.00	21.96	51.58	1.0007	0.3388
2013	38.65	29.78	12.70	100.00	22.16	53.06	1.0452	0.5051
2014	38.25	29.94	12.22	100.00	21.82	53.12	1.0649	0.5651
2015	39.06	29.49	12.20	100.00	22.21	55.41	0.9321	0.0487
2016	38.89	29.79	11.71	100.00	22.09	55.14	1.0423	0.3256

Table 5.13 Summary statistics of the rescaled economic key indicators in the German economy from 2008 to 2016; GVA, Gross Value Added; Max, Maximum; Min, Minimum; p.c., per capita; p.h., per hour; Q_1, 25th percentile; Q_3, 75th percentile; R&D, Research and Development

of the share of imported input are located below normal percentiles, such that the distribution is heavily skewed to the right. Contributions to international trade (SDG 17.11) should be advanced.

Concluding, efficiency and effectiveness gains are present in the environmental domain. Rescaled ratio indicators y_{rs}, which map efficiencies, reach fair to good central scores, but effectiveness gains should be enhanced from medium to at least fair performances. Moreover, environmental fiscal policies could be tightened as deficiency payments for environmental damages only yield medium central performances. In the social domain, the sample exhibits mostly medium performances for both efficiency and effectiveness. Improvements are desired with the exception of rescaled key indicators y_s that depict social security protection. These yield fair performances for both efficiency and effectiveness. Rescaled economic key indicators y_s paint a bleak picture, with desired upgrading in economic productivity. Note that key indicators y of the economic domain focus on productivities and investments, which are part of sustainable development. Economic growth is not represented in the economic domain because it is not key to sustainable development (see Section 2.2.3; e.g. Vermeulen, 2018).

After analysing the summary statistics of the rescaled key indicators y_s, the next section, Section 5.3.4.2, deals with the rescaled key indicators' results of the selected branches (see Table 5.1).

5.3.4.2 Comparative analysis of the selected branches

The comparative analysis of the selected branches (see Table 5.1) conducted in this section is structured according to the three contentual domains. Efficiency and effectiveness of sustainable development contributions by the selected branches are first evaluated for the environmental domain, followed by the social and the economic domains. Rescaled ratio indicators' results refer to the last year of observation (i.e. 2016), whereas rescaled growth indicators y_{gs} refer to changes from 2008 to 2016. Because the ratio indicators' trends are stable over time (see Table 5.11 to Table 5.13), results from 2016 are representative for the entire time horizon.

The fair to good central scores and the high negative skewnesses of the rescaled environmental ratio indicators' distributions (see Section 5.3.4.1) are generally reflected by the selected branches (see Figure 5.9): Most selected branches are clustered at the outskirts of the radar chart and yield good performances. Only few economic objects n are located at the interior, scoring bad to poor performances. Industries in the service sector are environmentally efficient, thus obtaining low scores in the environmental tax intensity. The agricultural sector reports poor performances in three environmental efficiency indicators while achieving a fair performance in the waste water efficiency and good performances in the hazardous waste efficiency and the environmental tax intensity. Its environmental tax intensity transcends the chemical industry's tax intensity due to its lower economic productivity and resulting lower GVA generation (see below). In each other environmental efficiency indicator, the chemical industry is a bad performer. The health economy, which is a cross-sectional economy of both the manufacturing and

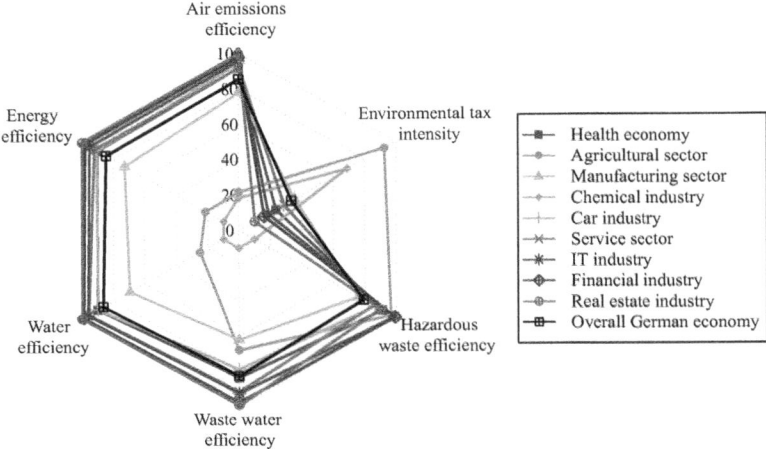

Figure 5.9 Environmental ratio indicators in rescaled performance scores for the selected branches in the German economy in 2016; IT, Information Technology

the service sectors, is clustered along with the service sector's selected branches. Its stakes in the manufacturing sector are not concentrated on environmentally polluting industries. For example, only 5.23% of the chemical industry is attributable to the health economy in 2016 (see Appendix A.2).

The environmental growth indicators' distributions are clustered approximately between medium and fair performance scores (see Figure 5.10). Best displayed performers are the financial industry in the reduction of air emissions (63.94 in 2016) and primary energy consumption (67.60 in 2016) as well as the car industry in the reduction of water use (65.83 in 2016) and waste water (65.06 in 2016). The IT industry scores best among the selected branches in the reduction of hazardous waste (77.05 in 2016). However, the IT industry's further outcomes are sparse. The chemical industry neither scores with environmental efficiency (see Figure 5.9) nor with environmental effectiveness: Its reduction rates are among the lowest, and only yield medium for the reduction of air emissions (44.26 in 2016) and hazardous waste (42.51 in 2016). The agricultural industry obtains consistent medium scores, with the exceptions of a fair performance in the reduction of air emissions and a bad performance in the reduction of hazardous waste. However, it achieves a good performance in the ratio indicator hazardous waste efficiency (see Figure 5.9), and it may be concluded that a lack in the reduction of hazardous waste is less harming.

Rescaled ratio indicators y_{rs} of the social domain are rather distributed across the scale, and performances of the selected branches range from bad to good (see Figure 5.11). In contrast to the environmental domain, a segmentation of industries in

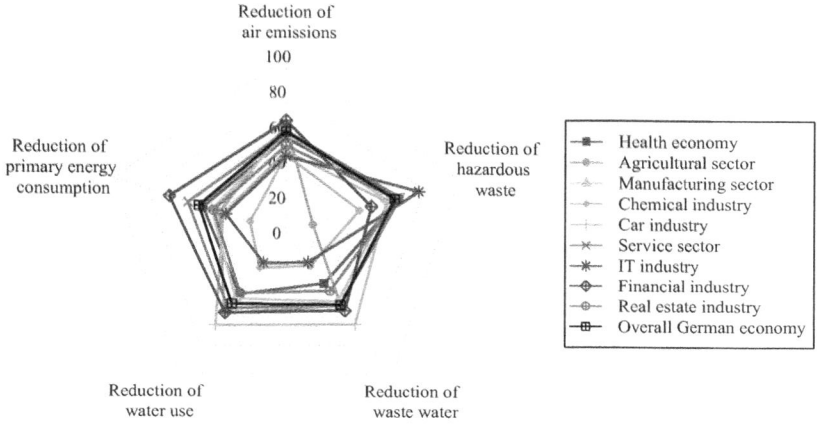

Figure 5.10 Environmental growth indicators in rescaled performance scores for the selected branches in the German economy; IT, Information Technology

the manufacturing and the service sectors is not observed. Positively outstanding is the financial industry with regard to three tax indicators, average compensations of employees, labour share, and the share of non-marginally-employed employees, contributing to approaching decent work for all (SDG 8.5). A further leading industry is the car industry with highest results among the selected branches for the average compensations of employees, share of non-marginally-employed employees, and the quota of severely-disabled employees. Despite the high values in the average compensations of employees, the car industry only performs medium in the labour share and could distribute more income to its employees. Weaknesses of this industry are the quota of gender equality and the VAT intensity. Contributions to inclusion and equal opportunities (SDG 10.2; SDG 10.3; SDG 10.4) should be improved. The real estate industry's performances are diverse. It yields good performances in the gender equalities but bad performances in the labour share and the share of non-marginally-employed employees, harming decent work for all (SDG 8.5). The IT industry is a mid-ranging industry, which is neither among the best nor among the worst performers. The health economy operates well in the quota of gender equality of marginally-employed employees; fairly in the labour share, share of non-marginally-employed employees and the quota of severely-disabled employees; but it features medium performances in the average compensation of employees p.h., the quota of gender equality, and the share of apprentices. Its average compensation of employees p.c. is only poor. Targets on social protection are managed (SDG 1.3), but targets on decent work (SDG 8.5) are not succeeded in. The overall German economy, which is typically located between the manufacturing and the service

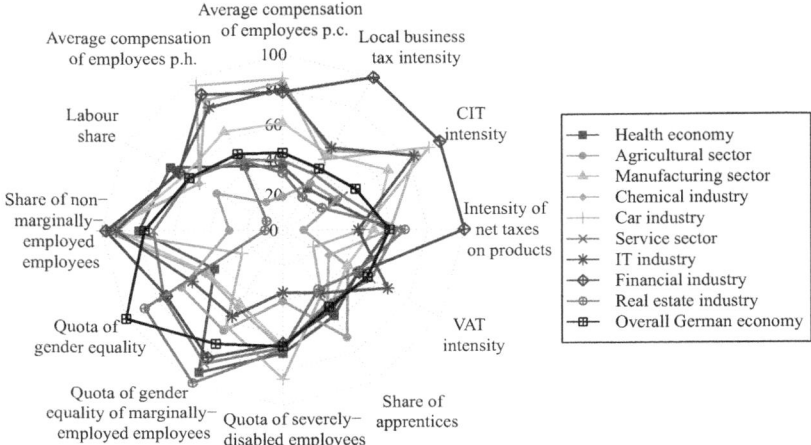

Figure 5.11 Social ratio indicators in rescaled performance scores for the selected branches in the German economy in 2016; CIT, Corporate Income Tax; IT, Information Technology; p.c., per capita; p.h., per hour; VAT, Value Added Tax

sectors, experiences an exceptional peak in the quota of gender equality. The share of female socially-insured employees and the share of female labour force, an indicator that always refers to the overall German economy, are nearly equivalent. A difference of 0.0004 percentage points is reported for the unscaled quota of gender difference in 2016. This is the sample's minimum and translated into a rescaled performance score of 100.00. The agricultural industry is a poor performer and only scores fairly with the quotas of gender equalities and share of apprentices. The other industries are mid-ranging without extraordinary incidents.

Rescaled growth indicators y_{gs} of the social domain are relatively homogeneous among the selected branches (see Figure 5.12). The IT industry scores best. An exception is the reduction of female marginally-employed employees as the financial industry takes over the first place. A further star of the financial industry is the reduction of marginally-employed employees, which is in line with the corresponding efficiency indicator (see above). However, the financial industry exhibits poor to medium performances in the remaining social rescaled growth indicators y_{gs}. Improvements are required to approach targets on, for example, decent work (SDG 8.5). The chemical industry stands out with good performances in the reduction of marginally-employed employees (85.55 from 2008 to 2016) and the reduction of female marginally-employed employees (84.14 from 2008 to 2016). It further operates fairly in the growth of apprentices. Its positive unscaled growth rate of 10.19% from 2008 to 2016 is transformed into a performance score of 72.13, positively contributing to Germany's shortage of skilled workers (see Section 5.3.2; e.g. Bonin, 2019) and the SDG 4.3 on vocational education. The agricultural and the

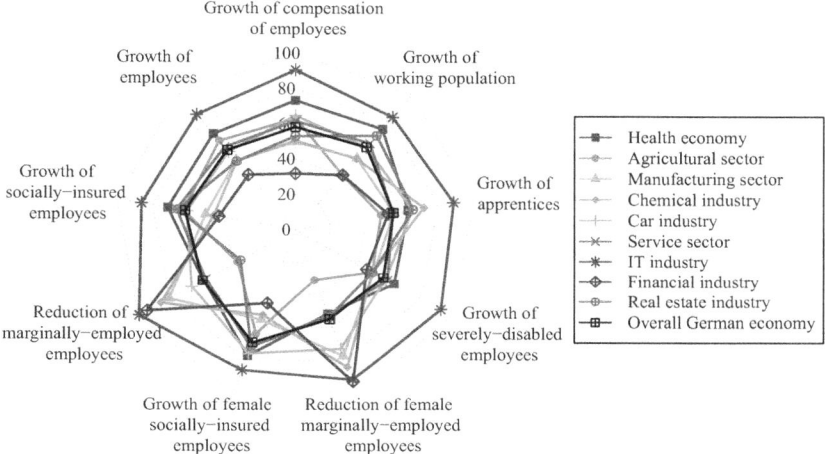

Figure 5.12 Social and economic growth indicators in rescaled performance scores for the selected branches in the German economy; IT, Information Technology

real estate industries are not able to strike with efficiencies but achieve mid-ranging results in effectiveness.

Economic performances of the selected branches in the rescaled ratio indicators y_{rs} are displayed in Figure 5.13. In accordance with impressions from the summary statistics (see Section 5.3.4.1), performances of the selected branches are skewed towards the interior of the radar chart. However, the real estate industry stands out in five economic rescaled ratio indicators y_{rs} as the best performer among the selected branches. It achieves good results in the degree of modernity, investment intensity, GVA rate, and the labour productivities (p.c. and p.h.). It further stands out as the worst performer among the selected branches in six economic rescaled ratio indicators y_{rs}: the gross capital productivity, net capital productivity, consumed capital productivity, internal R&D intensity, share of R&D employees, and the share of imported input. Economic productivity ought to be improved (SDG 8.2). The IT industry performs best in the gross and the net capital productivity with further medium to good performances in several economic rescaled ratio indicators y_{rs}. The chemical and the car industries yield similar performances with fair results in the rescaled ratio indicators y_{rs} on R&D and labour productivities. The agricultural sector's economic performance remains bad to medium, except for fair performances in the net import intensity. Economic productivity (SDG 8.2) is not provided, but contributions to international trade (SDG 17.11) are realised. The manufacturing sector generally overshoots the service sector, with the health and the overall German economies in its midst.

The economic domain's only growth indicator – growth of working population – is

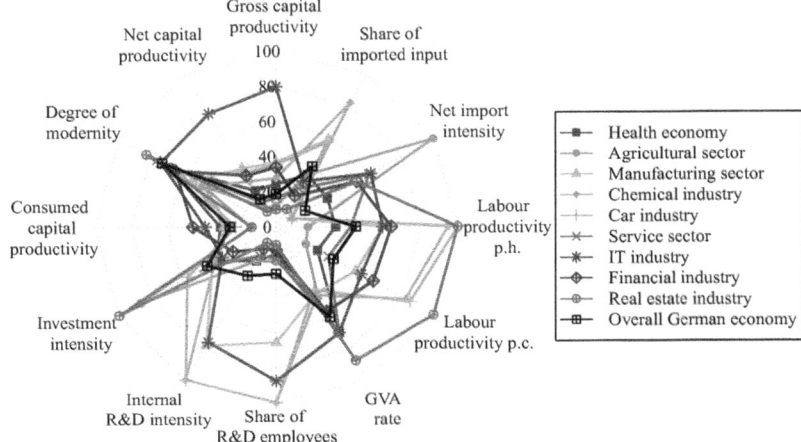

Figure 5.13 Economic ratio indicators in rescaled performance scores for the selected branches in the German economy in 2016; GVA, Gross Value Added; IT, Information Technology; p.c., per capita; p.h., per hour; R&D, Research and Development

reported along with the social domain (see Figure 5.12) and yields similar results to the social domain's growth indicators y_{gs}.

After scaling, weights ω are derived, and the diverse weighting methods' results are presented in the next section, Section 5.4.

5.4   Weighting

Three methods are applied to determine the MLSDI's weights ω and importance factors ψ: the PCA (see Section 4.3.7.2), PTA (see Section 4.3.7.3), and the MRMRB algorithm (see Section 4.3.7.4). The PC family requires a priori analyses of eigenvalues and explained cumulative variances to determine the included PCs. This is accomplished in the first subsection of this section, Section 5.4.1. Section 5.4.2 outlines the MRMRB algorithm's diagnostics, and Section 5.4.3 compares and discusses the empirical findings of the three weighting methods. The PC family further demands posteriori evaluations of statistical test results, conducted in Section 5.4.4.

5.4.1   The Principal Component (PC) family's eigenvalues and explained cumulative variances

In the case of the PCA, PCs with eigenvalues larger than one are included (Kaiser's criterion), and at least 70% of the cumulative variance must be explained (see Section 4.3.7.2; e.g. Field, 2009). The modified Kaiser's criterion for the PTA requests

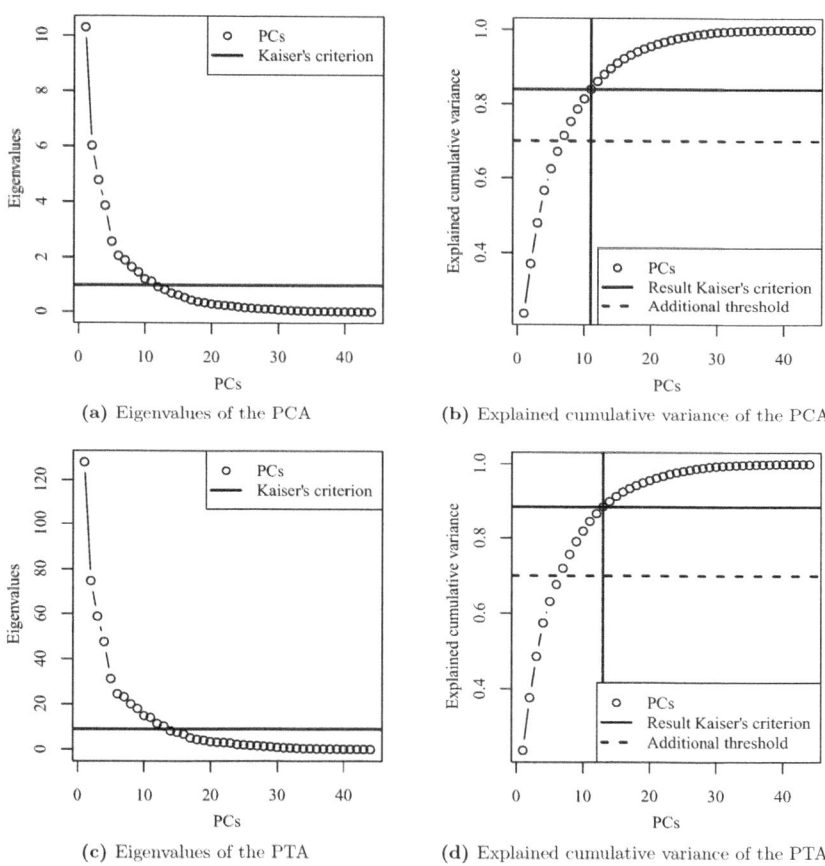

(a) Eigenvalues of the PCA

(b) Explained cumulative variance of the PCA

(c) Eigenvalues of the PTA

(d) Explained cumulative variance of the PTA

Figure 5.14 Eigenvalues and explained cumulative variances of the Principal Component Analysis (PCA) and the Partial Triadic Analysis (PTA); PCs, Principal Components

to retain PCs with eigenvalues larger than the number of time periods T (see Section 4.3.7.3), which is equivalent to nine (see Section 5.1). The additional threshold on the explained cumulative variance remains unchanged.

The PC family's eigenvalues and explained cumulative variances are shown in Figure 5.14. The application of the Kaiser's criterion results in inclusion of the first 11 PCs for the PCA (see Figure 5.14a). The first PC yields an eigenvalue of 10.30, while the 11th PC's eigenvalue amounts to 1.14. The additional threshold on the explained cumulative variance is not required as 83.95% of the sample's variance is explained by including the first 11 PCs: The additional threshold's dashed line crosses the solid line of the Kaiser's criterion on the right and below the circled curve of the

PCs (see Figure 5.14b). Compared to the PCA, the PTA's eigenvalues and number of included PCs are higher because time periods t are implicit variables. The first PC reaches a score of 127.97, and the last PC to involve in the further analysis is the 13th PC (see Figure 5.14c) with an eigenvalue score of 10.22. The resulting explained cumulative variance amounts to 88.39%, and the additional threshold is not required (see Figure 5.14d).

Diagnostics of the MRMRB algorithm follow in the next section, Section 5.4.2.

5.4.2 The Maximum Relevance Minimum Redundancy Backward (MRMRB) algorithm's discretisation and backward elimination

The discretisation method applied in the MRMRB algorithm is equal frequency discretisation (see Section 4.3.7.4; Yang & Webb, 2009). The bin size χ_s and the number of bins χ_n equal 7.87. The backward elimination process of the MRMRB algorithm starts with rescaled key indicators y_s that contain the lowest mutual information. The rescaled key indicators' ranking, with an ascending mutual information, can be found in Table 5.14. The quota of gender equality features the lowest mutual information and is hence eliminated first. The last eliminated rescaled key indicator y_s is the energy efficiency. The backward elimination ranking diverges from the reverse ranking of importance factors (see Figure 5.15) because it refers to the integrated assessment before coefficients are adjusted to sum up to one in each contentual domain (see Section 4.3.7). The mutual information matrix is not attached, given its size of YxY, which is equivalent to 44x44.

In the following section, Section 5.4.3, the PC family's weights ω^{PC} resulting from the first 11 and 13 included PCs are analysed and compared to weights derived by the MRMRB algorithm ω^{MRMRB}.

5.4.3 Comparative analysis of weights

Before analysing and comparing weights derived by the PC family ω^{PC} and MRMRB algorithm ω^{MRMRB}, the PTA's results of temporal assessment are examined. The PTA's weights of time periods Ω^{PTA} range from 11.03% in 2008 to 11.16% in 2012, 2013, and 2014. These weights Ω^{PTA} nearly correspond to equal weights (11.11%). In conclusion, the PTA provides evidence that the temporal dimension is irrelevant, and structures remain constant over time periods t. This finding approves equal temporal weighting of the PCA and the MRMRB algorithm.

Weights to be applied on the rescaled key indicators y_s derived by the PC family ω^{PC} and the MRMRB algorithm ω^{MRMRB} are contrasted in Table 5.15 to Table 5.17. Weights derived by the PC family ω^{PC} are generally similar to each other. Moreover, the

Rank	Rescaled key indicator y_s	Rank	Rescaled key indicator y_s
1	Quota of gender equality	23	Local business tax intensity
2	Share of apprentices	24	Environmental tax intensity
3	Intensity of net taxes on products	25	Reduction of marginally-employed employees
4	Quota of gender equality of marginally-employed employees	26	Growth of female socially-insured employees
5	Quota of severely-disabled employees	27	Hazardous waste efficiency
6	GVA rate	28	Labour productivity p.h.
7	Labour share	29	Consumed capital productivity
8	Degree of modernity	30	Growth of compensation of employees
9	Growth of apprentices	31	Investment intensity
10	VAT intensity	32	Air emissions efficiency
11	Share of non-marginally-employed employees	33	Net import intensity
12	Reduction of air emissions	34	Average compensation of employees p.h.
13	Reduction of primary energy consumption	35	Working population growth
14	Reduction of hazardous waste	36	Net capital productivity
15	Share of imported input	37	Water efficiency
16	Growth of severely-disabled employees	38	Waste water efficiency
17	Reduction of waste water	39	Internal R&D intensity
18	CIT intensity	40	Growth of employees
19	Reduction of female marginally-employed employees	41	Gross capital productivity
20	Labour productivity p.c.	42	Share of R&D employees
21	Reduction of water use	43	Growth of socially-insured employees
22	Average compensation of employees p.c.	44	Energy efficiency

Table 5.14 Rescaled key indicators' ranking according to the backward elimination of the Maximum Relevance Minimum Redundancy Backward (MRMRB) algorithm; CIT, Corporate Income Tax; GVA, Gross Value Added; p.c., per capita; p.h., per hour; R&D, Research and Development; VAT, Value Added Tax

PC family's weights ω^{PC} remain close to equal weights. Equal weights would correspond to values of 9.09% in the environmental domain, 5.00% in the social domain, and 7.69% in the economic domain. Weights derived by the MRMRB algorithm ω^{MRMRB} feature higher variations.

Environmental key indicator y	Weight ω^{PCA}	Weight ω^{PTA}	Weight ω^{MRMRB}
Equal weights	0.0909	0.0909	0.0909
Reduction of air emissions	0.0942	0.0940	0.0692
Air emissions efficiency	0.0990	0.0965	0.1036
Reduction of primary energy consumption	0.0956	0.0962	0.0700
Energy efficiency	0.0998	0.0964	0.1307
Reduction of water use	0.0909	0.0947	0.0805
Water efficiency	0.0917	0.0884	0.1114
Reduction of waste water	0.0865	0.0946	0.0760
Waste water efficiency	0.0888	0.0850	0.1115
Reduction of hazardous waste	0.0842	0.0895	0.0705
Hazardous waste efficiency	0.0885	0.0863	0.0904
Environmental tax intensity	0.0809	0.0782	0.0863

Table 5.15 Environmental key indicators' weights derived by the Principal Component Analysis (PCA), Partial Triadic Analysis (PTA), and the Maximum Relevance Minimum Redundancy Backward (MRMRB) algorithm

Weights ω applied on the rescaled environmental key indicators y_s are shown in Table 5.15. Environmental rescaled ratio indicators y_{rs} are generally weighted more heavily than their corresponding rescaled growth indicators y_{gs}, with exceptions in the case of the PTA. Despite the exceptions, it may be concluded that focus should be directed towards environmental efficiency. Highest weight ω in the environmental domain receives the topic climate change, with its rescaled key indicators y_s on air emissions and energy consumption. The climate change topic is also emphasised in the GRI and the SDG disclosures (see Section 5.3.1.1). In the case of the MRMRB algorithm, energy efficiency obtains the highest weight ω^{MRMRB}, with a value equivalent to 13.07%, exceeding the weight ω^{MRMRB} of the closely related air emissions efficiency (10.36%). From a natural science perspective, rescaled key indicators y_s on air emissions are contentually richer. However, from an anthropocentric point of view, sources of air emissions – among others primary energy consumption – ought to be managed (see Section 5.3.1.1). Thus, the MRMRB algorithm upgrades the energy efficiency and assigns the highest weight ω^{MRMRB} to this rescaled key indicator y_s. In contrast, the PC family does not distinguish between energy efficiency and air emissions efficiency but assigns similar weights ω^{PC} to both (e.g. PTA: 9.64% and 9.65%, respectively). Rescaled growth indicators y_{gs} on energy and air emissions are ascribed slightly lower weights ω, with higher variances in the case of the MRMRB algorithm. The second most important environmental topic identified by the MRMRB algorithm is efficiency of water use and waste water. The rescaled ratio indicators y_{rs} on water obtain similar weights by the MRMRB algorithm ω^{MRMRB} (11.14% and 11.15%, respectively), but the PC family allocates a higher weight ω^{PC} to the water efficiency compared to the waste water efficiency (e.g. PCA: 9.17% vs. 8.88%, respectively). These weights ω^{PC} are in line with the MRMRB algorithm's result on rescaled ratio indicators y_{rs} on climate change: Rescaled key indicators y_s that point towards the source of pollution receive a higher weight ω. Relatively low weights ω are allocated to the hazardous waste efficiency (e.g. MRMRB algorithm: 9.04%), despite the fact that it achieves best central results among the rescaled key indicators y_s of the environmental domain (see Section 5.3.4.1). This finding demonstrates that weights' magnitudes do not depend on the empirical results of the rescaled key indicators y_s but their interconnectedness, reflecting synergies and trade-offs as desired (see Section 3.1; e.g. Costanza, Fioramonti & Kubiszewski, 2016).

Regarding the social domain, rescaled growth indicators y_{gs} receive higher weights ω than their rescaled ratio indicators' counterparts (see Table 5.16). Most important in the social domain across the three weighting methods are the growth of socially-insured employees and the growth of employees (e.g. MRMRB algorithm: 7.85% and 7.38%, respectively). This finding is reasonable in two aspects: First, employment possesses a dual purpose (source of income and key to transition; see Section 5.2.1; Harangozo et al., 2018), and second, the key figure socially-insured employees is contentually richer than the key figure employees because employees include decent as well as precarious employment (see Section 5.2.1). A further interesting finding rests in the weighting of the rescaled key indicators y_s on compensations of employees. The average compensation of employees p.h. receives a higher weight by the MRMRB algorithm ω^{MRMRB} (6.89%) than the average compensation of employees p.c. (5.36%). This is reasonable because the latter rescaled key indicator y_s is less precise, given its standardising key figure's mixture of full-time and part-time employees (see Section 5.2.1). Moreover, the labour share receives the lowest weight ω^{MRMRB} (4.02%) among the rescaled key indicators y_s on compensations of employees. From an employee's perspective this finding is reasonable: Not the proportion of the GVA distributed is of interest but the monetary value received in relation to the work done. The PTA follows the MRMRB algorithm's relation, but the magnitude is nearly insignificant. In opposition, the PCA does not pursue this relation but weights the labour share more heavily than the average compensation of employees p.c. A further reasonable finding is the MRMRB algorithm's higher (though, nearly insignificant) weight ω^{MRMRB} of the quota of gender equality of marginally-employed employees and the quota of gender equality (3.51% and 3.17%, respectively). At least two SDG targets are addressed with the first mentioned rescaled key indicator y_s – SDG 1.3 (social protection) and SDG 5.1 (end discrimination against women and girls) – while the latter rescaled key indicator y_s only addresses the SDG 1.3. The PCA

Social key indicator y	Weight ω^{PCA}	Weight ω^{PTA}	Weight ω^{MRMRB}
Equal weights	0.0500	0.0500	0.0500
Growth of compensation of employees	0.0531	0.0515	0.0656
Growth of employees	0.0552	0.0538	0.0738
Average compensation of employees p.c.	0.0532	0.0515	0.0536
Average compensation of employees p.h.	0.0543	0.0524	0.0689
Labour share	0.0537	0.0512	0.0402
Growth of socially-insured employees	0.0559	0.0559	0.0785
Reduction of marginally-employed employees	0.0492	0.0514	0.0568
Share of non-marginally-employed employees	0.0472	0.0511	0.0446
Growth of female socially-insured employees	0.0542	0.0526	0.0583
Quota of gender equality	0.0514	0.0536	0.0317
Reduction of female marginally-employed employees	0.0528	0.0523	0.0516
Quota of gender equality of marginally-employed employees	0.0397	0.0385	0.0351
Growth of severely-disabled employees	0.0491	0.0527	0.0470
Quota of severely-disabled employees	0.0494	0.0476	0.0353
Growth of apprentices	0.0531	0.0526	0.0425
Share of apprentices	0.0358	0.0516	0.0333
VAT intensity	0.0418	0.0423	0.0434
Intensity of net taxes on products	0.0447	0.0429	0.0334
CIT intensity	0.0532	0.0451	0.0507
Local business tax intensity	0.0531	0.0494	0.0558

Table 5.16 Social key indicators' weights derived by the Principal Component Analysis
(PCA), Partial Triadic Analysis (PTA), and the Maximum Relevance Minimum
Redundancy Backward (MRMRB) algorithm; CIT, Corporate Income Tax; p.c.,
per capita; p.h., per hour; VAT, Value Added Tax

reverses this relation and assigns a higher weight ω^{PCA} to the quota of gender equality.
With regard to apprentices, only the PTA reflects the problematic shortage of skilled
labour (see Section 5.3.2; e.g. Bonin, 2019) and allocates a relatively high weight ω^{PTA}
of 5.16% to the share of apprentices.

Table 5.17 displays weights ω of the economic rescaled key indicators y_s. Among

Economic key indicator y	Weight ω^{PCA}	Weight ω^{PTA}	Weight ω^{MRMRB}
Equal weights	0.0769	0.0769	0.0769
Gross capital productivity	0.0862	0.0844	0.0940
Net capital productivity	0.0858	0.0843	0.0891
Degree of modernity	0.0692	0.0686	0.0518
Consumed capital productivity	0.0824	0.0825	0.0797
Investment intensity	0.0784	0.0763	0.0815
Internal R&D intensity	0.0840	0.0815	0.0907
Share of R&D employees	0.0820	0.0788	0.0961
GVA rate	0.0650	0.0650	0.0492
Working population growth	0.0776	0.0764	0.0885
Labour productivity p.c.	0.0852	0.0821	0.0646
Labour productivity p.h.	0.0785	0.0808	0.0729
Net import intensity	0.0596	0.0740	0.0842
Share of imported input	0.0661	0.0652	0.0578

Table 5.17 Economic key indicators' weights derived by the Principal Component Analysis (PCA), Partial Triadic Analysis (PTA), and the Maximum Relevance Minimum Redundancy Backward (MRMRB) algorithm; GVA, Gross Value Added; p.c., per capita; p.h., per hour; R&D, Research and Development

the rescaled ratio indicators y_{rs} on capital, the gross capital productivity receives the highest weight ω by all three weighting methods. This finding may be justified by the fact that the gross capital productivity contains most information: It includes the current value of assets as well as the depreciated value in relation to the generated GVA (see Section 5.2.1; Section 5.3.1.3). The degree of modernity receives the lowest weight ω among the capital indicators because it disregards the GVA, which is essential in assessing economic productivity enhancements as of SDG 8.2. The GVA rate receives a relatively low weight by the MRMRB algorithm ω^{MRMRB} (4.92%). It does not indicate productivity but merely value generation in proportion of the output (see Section 5.3.1.3). The PC family does not recognise the GVA rate's low explanatory power regarding productivity and assigns weights ω^{PC} of 6.50%. Similar to the average compensations of employees, the labour productivities are weighted in an economically reasonable way by the MRMRB algorithm: The rescaled key indicator p.h. receives a higher weight ω^{MRMRB} than its p.c. counterpart (7.29% vs. 6.46%, respectively). In contrast, the PC family neglects this aspect and valorises the rescaled key indicator p.c. Last, the MRMRB algorithm weights the net import intensity more heavily than the share of imported input (8.42% vs. 5.78%, respectively). The net import intensity includes both imports of input and imports for final consumption and is thus informationally richer. The PTA follows this relation (however with a lower spread), but the PCA does not.

Weights ω indicate importances within a contentual domain but not towards the overall MLSDI c_1. The key indicators' importance factors ψ towards the overall MLSDI c_1 are computed by adjusting weights ω with the rule of three (see Section 4.3.7). Figure 5.15 portrays the importance factors ψ in a decreasing order according to the MRMRB algorithm. Equal importance factors would correspond to values of 2.27%. In view of the MRMRB algorithm, most important towards the overall MLSDI c_1 are the growth of socially-insured employees, growth of employees, and the energy efficiency. Least important are the quota of gender equality, GVA rate, and the share of apprentices. Ordering of the importance factors derived by the PC family ψ^{PC} differs from the MRMRB algorithm's ordering: Highest importance factors ψ^{PC} are assigned to the gross capital productivity, growth of socially-insured employees, and the net capital productivity. Because employment serves a dual mission (see Section 5.2.1; Harangozo et al., 2018) and climate change is the main topic of the environmental domain (see Section 5.3.1.1), the MRMRB algorithm's ordering of importance factors ψ^{MRMRB} is more plausible.

To sum up, the PC family does not clearly differentiate between diverse rescaled key indicators y_s, but weights ω^{PC} are sticky around equal weights. The main aspects of sustainable development are not captured. In contrast, the MRMRB algorithm assigns higher weights ω^{MRMRB} to informationally richer rescaled key indicators y_s by detecting higher order correlations. As a result, importance factors ψ^{MRMRB} towards the overall MLSDI c_1 correctly reflect most important topics of sustainable development. In conclusion, the MRMRB algorithm outperforms the PC family, and the theoretical superiority of the MRMRB algorithm (see Section 4.3.7.4) is supported by empirical evidence. The MRMRB algorithm is the preferred and applied weighting method in the further analysis. For the German sample, the MRMRB algorithm asserts to focus efficiency in the environmental domain and effectiveness in the social domain.

Before applying weights derived by the MRMRB algorithm ω^{MRMRB} on the rescaled key indicators y_s, statistical tests of the PC family are examined in the following section, Section 5.4.4.

5.4.4   Statistical tests of the Principal Component (PC) family

Statistical tests of the PC family are conducted and analysed to verify the statistical validity of the PC family's results. Performed statistical tests include the KMO test for sampling adequacy and the Bartlett's test of sphericity (see Section 4.3.7.5; e.g. Bartlett, 1950; Kaiser, 1970). To evaluate whether the tests should be based on Pearson's correlation coefficient for normal data or Kendall's tau for non-normal data, normality of z-score scaled key indicators y_z are tested in the fashion of the key figures' normality tests

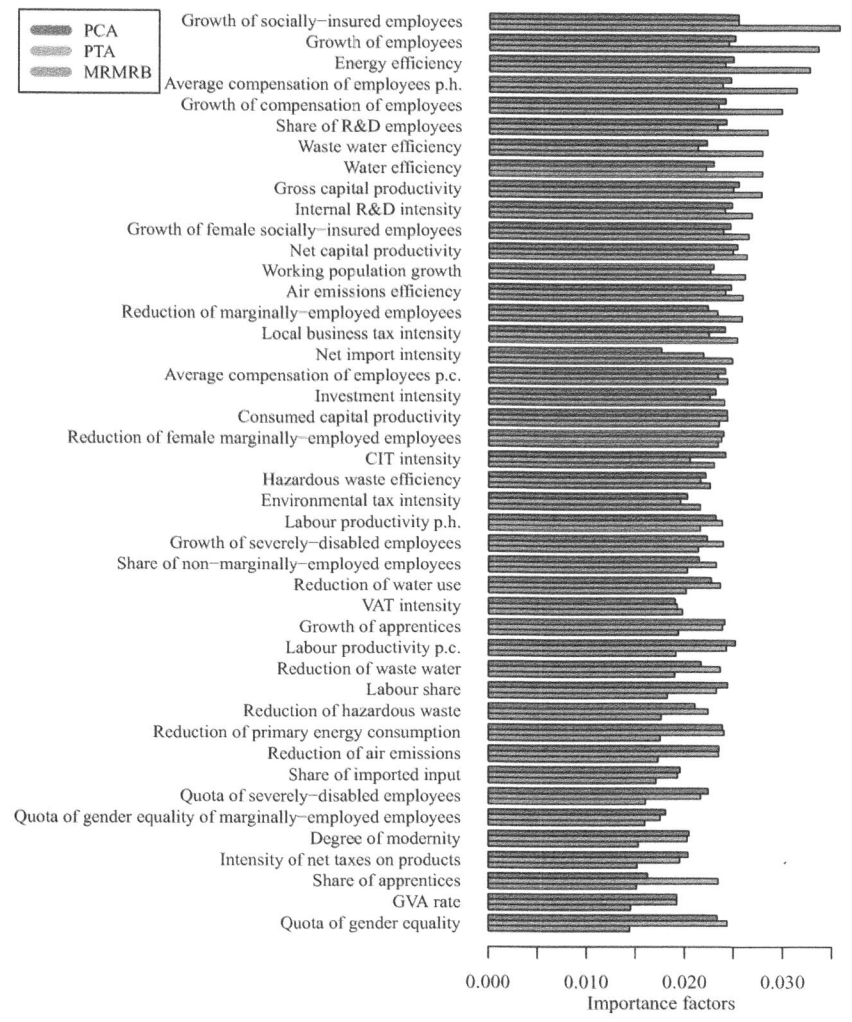

Figure 5.15 Importance factors of the Principal Component Analysis (PCA), Partial Triadic Analysis (PTA), and the Maximum Relevance Minimum Redundancy Backward (MRMRB) algorithm; CIT, Corporate Income Tax; GVA, Gross Value Added; p.c., per capita; p.h., per hour; R&D, Research and Development; VAT, Value Added Tax

(see Section 4.3.3.4 and Section 5.2.2). The Shapiro-Wilk and the Kolmogorov-Smirnov tests both conclude that 20 z-score scaled key indicators y_z are normally distributed and 14 z-score scaled key indicators y_z are non-normal. Ambiguous results are obtained for the remaining ten z-score scaled key indicators y_z, with the following pattern: Data are non-normal under the Shapiro-Wilk test but normal under the Kolmogorov-Smirnov test. Therefore, histograms are consulted, but a clear decision cannot be made. The test statistics and p-values are disclosed in Table A.12 to Table A.14, and two example histograms of z-score scaled key indicators y_z with ambiguous test results are provided in Figure A.1 in the Appendix A.6. The average compensation of employees p.c. and the consumed capital productivity experience the weakest and the strongest rejections of the null hypotheses by the Shapiro-Wilk tests, respectively, with p-values of 0.04 and 0.0000, respectively. According to the multivariate Shapiro-Wilk test, the data are multivariate non-normal, with a test statistic of 0.7483 and a p-value less or equal than 0.0001 (rejection of the null hypothesis). Given the ambiguities, the non-parametric Kendall's tau is preferred over the parametric Pearson's coefficient for the KMO test of sampling adequacy.

The KMO measure reveals the meritorious sampling adequacy of both the PCA and the PTA with values amounting to 0.8370 (average from 2008 to 2016) and 0.8391, respectively. The null hypotheses of the Bartlett's tests are rejected in both cases with p-values less or equal than 0.0001. The data are suitable for applying the PC family. In conclusion, results of the PC family as of Section 5.4.3 remain valid.

The following section, Section 5.5, analyses the resulting subindices d and the overall MLSDI c_1 based on the MRMRB algorithm's weights ω^{MRMRB}.

5.5 Empirical findings of the four composite sustainable development measures

The rescaled key indicators y_s are weighted and geometrically aggregated to obtain the subindices of each contentual domain d (see Section 4.3.8). The subindices d are then aggregated into the overall MLSDI c_1 via the geometric mean. Summary statistics of the four composite measures are analysed in Section 5.5.1, and results of the selected branches are evaluated in Section 5.5.2.

5.5.1 Summary statistics

The summary statistics of the subindices d mirror the impressions gained in the detailed descriptions and analyses of the rescaled key indicators y_s (see Section 5.3.4.1). Highest scores in terms of the mean, median, maximum, and the 75th percentile are reached by the environmental subindex (see Table 5.18). Its lead is followed by the social domain, whereas the economic domain scores lowest.

The environmental subindex yields medium to fair central performances. Progress over time is insignificant, but the distributional shape is in favour of environmental

Composite measure Year	Mean	Median	Min	Max	Q_1	Q_3	Skewness	Kurtosis
Environmental subindex								
2008	55.19	61.04	12.61	82.86	41.91	69.80	-0.6895	-0.6591
2009	54.86	60.85	12.61	83.00	41.87	69.93	-0.6379	-0.7408
2010	55.22	61.31	12.61	82.65	42.12	69.87	-0.6775	-0.7207
2011	56.32	62.27	12.61	83.29	42.92	70.49	-0.7388	-0.6524
2012	56.27	61.99	12.61	82.93	42.70	70.08	-0.7648	-0.6346
2013	56.55	62.03	12.61	83.66	42.52	70.60	-0.7506	-0.6500
2014	56.83	63.01	12.61	83.87	42.64	70.51	-0.7727	-0.6090
2015	56.95	62.91	12.61	84.34	42.76	70.72	-0.7606	-0.6632
2016	57.16	63.33	12.61	84.40	42.90	70.78	-0.7604	-0.6782
Social subindex								
2008	49.19	49.60	31.42	70.42	43.66	54.19	0.2653	-0.1445
2009	49.97	49.46	31.25	71.84	44.39	55.12	0.2807	-0.0123
2010	50.29	49.93	31.59	72.36	44.73	55.74	0.3624	0.0664
2011	51.19	50.52	34.80	72.76	45.74	55.88	0.3944	0.0219
2012	51.66	51.24	33.86	73.42	46.12	56.76	0.4416	0.1150
2013	51.98	51.63	33.77	73.88	45.99	57.40	0.3840	0.0409
2014	52.31	51.55	33.98	73.93	46.48	57.19	0.3986	0.0367
2015	52.48	52.19	34.54	74.16	46.82	57.49	0.4811	0.2606
2016	52.74	52.29	35.16	74.65	46.86	57.65	0.5000	0.2418
Economic subindex								
2008	35.98	34.23	23.90	60.29	28.83	42.10	0.8642	-0.2037
2009	35.56	33.83	23.86	59.75	28.16	40.45	0.8844	-0.0433
2010	36.19	34.01	23.24	59.75	28.51	42.23	0.8258	-0.3054
2011	36.68	34.86	22.70	61.04	28.99	43.63	0.7793	-0.3650
2012	36.73	34.71	22.29	60.95	29.03	43.34	0.7658	-0.3882
2013	36.66	34.62	22.15	62.97	29.37	42.93	0.8159	-0.1276
2014	36.85	35.06	21.96	61.42	29.59	43.19	0.7642	-0.2943
2015	37.33	34.82	22.05	62.46	29.77	43.73	0.8390	-0.2724
2016	37.65	34.76	21.16	61.31	30.06	45.03	0.7827	-0.4680
Overall MLSDI c_1								
2008	45.16	45.71	30.78	62.33	39.70	50.48	-0.1574	-0.8220
2009	45.10	46.11	30.71	62.21	39.48	50.48	-0.1775	-0.7813
2010	45.58	46.88	30.97	62.86	39.68	51.41	-0.1570	-0.8301
2011	46.38	47.49	31.97	63.96	40.93	51.87	-0.1372	-0.8286
2012	46.50	47.63	31.68	64.34	41.09	51.98	-0.1618	-0.7792
2013	46.69	47.54	31.84	63.97	40.98	52.04	-0.1279	-0.8010
2014	46.96	47.73	32.37	64.03	42.27	52.12	-0.1343	-0.8289
2015	47.22	48.18	32.00	65.18	42.15	52.61	-0.1477	-0.8216
2016	47.49	48.54	31.60	65.20	42.44	53.10	-0.1301	-0.8264

Table 5.18 Summary statistics of the subindices and the overall Multilevel Sustainable Development Index (MLSDI) in the German economy from 2008 to 2016; Max, Maximum; Min, Minimum; Q_1, 25th percentile; Q_3, 75th percentile

protection: The medians exceed the means, the 25th percentiles are located above a score of 25.00, resulting in moderate negative skewnesses. Bottom performers should be focused to enhance their performances, lifting the central measures to be at least fair.

Compared to the environmental subindex, the social subindex's central performances are weaker. A higher effort is required to yield fair performances. The social subindex's minima are the highest among the four composite measures' minima. However, the 75th percentiles do not reach the fair bracket the normal score of 75.00 is located in. Not the bottom but the centre of the distribution should be focused to improve social development.

Among the three subindices d, the economic subindex performs worst. Its central scores are rated as poor performances, and enhancements over time of the central measures, maxima, and the percentiles are insignificant. Additionally, minima deteriorate in the course of time. The 25th percentiles just surpass the normal score of 25.00, and the 75th percentiles just reach the bracket of medium performances, remaining far from the normal fair performances at scores of 75.00. Moderate positive skewnesses result, which are undesirable distributional properties for economic prosperity. Major improvements are required across the whole distribution.

The overall MLSDI's distributional properties result from the subindices' properties. Central measures are located between the medium to fair performances of the environmental subindex and the poor performances of the economic subindex. However, the effect of the geometric aggregation comes to light. The overall MLSDI c_1 is inclined towards the poor economic performances: Its central measures only yield medium performances at the lower end of the bracket, and the 75th percentiles do not yield the normal 75.00.

The sample's results of the four composite measures are illustrated in Figure 5.16 and Figure 5.17. Figure 5.16 contains the four composite measures' performance scores of the 62 economic objects n in the German economy from 2008 to 2016. The environmental subindex features the highest spread, with relatively few economic objects n at the bottom and relatively many economic objects n at the top of the distribution. Compared, the social subindex's spread is smaller, and especially the bottom of the distribution is enhanced. The economic subindex features relatively many outcomes at the bottom, and the overall MLSDI c_1 overlaps the subindices d. Progress over time has been made but should be enhanced for higher significance.

Figure 5.17 plots the four composite measures' frequency distributions and densities, strengthening the empirical findings of the previous analysis. The environmental domain exhibits economic objects n with bad performances. These should be focused for improvements. The social domain is not but should be represented at the top of the distribution. Last, economic performances should be enhanced in their entirety.

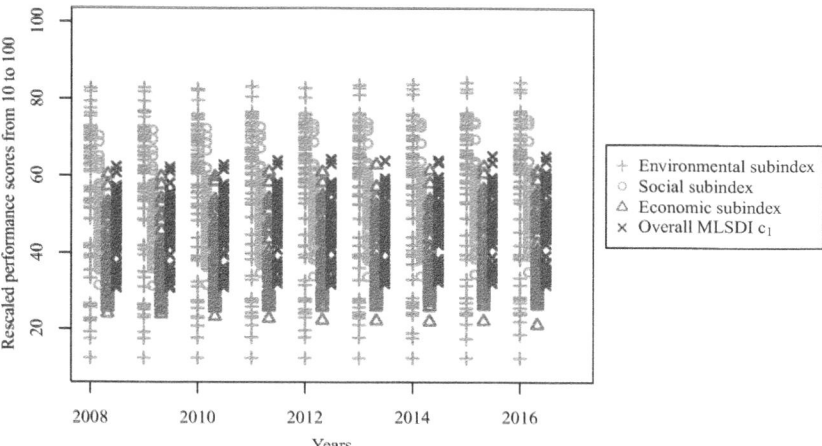

Figure 5.16 The four composite measures in rescaled performance scores in the German economy from 2008 to 2016; MLSDI, Multilevel Sustainable Development Index

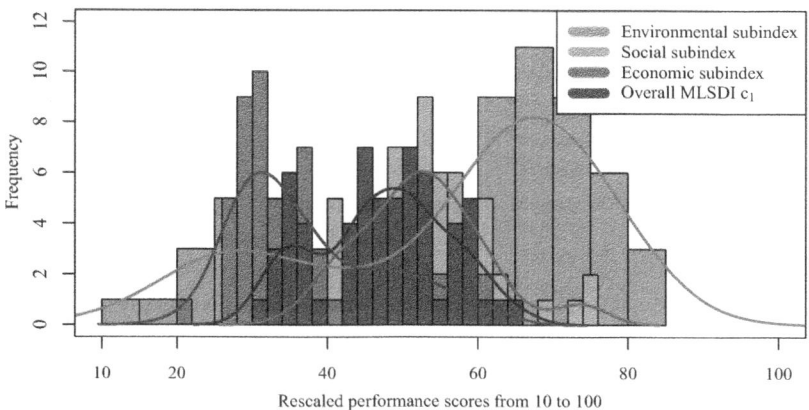

Figure 5.17 Frequency distribution and density of the four composite measures in the German economy in 2016; MLSDI, Multilevel Sustainable Development Index

5.5.2 Comparative analysis of the selected branches

The environmental subindices for the selected branches are displayed in Figure 5.18. Results are relatively stable over time except for volatilities in the agricultural sector and the car industry at the beginning of the time horizon. Given the financial industry's fair performances in the environmental ratio indicators y_r and the environmental growth indicators y_g (see Section 5.3.4.2), its environmental subindex ranks first. The car industry belongs to the top performers owing to its fair environmental effectiveness. The

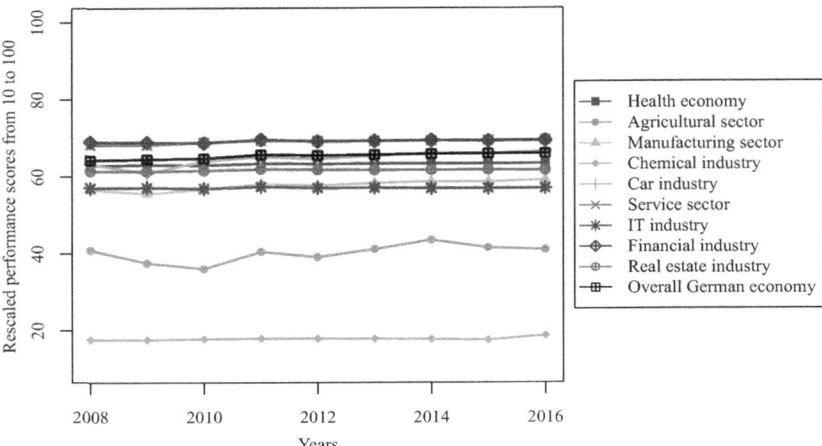

Figure 5.18 Environmental subindex in rescaled performance scores for the selected branches
in the German economy from 2008 to 2016; IT, Information Technology

health and the overall German economies are located between the manufacturing and
the service sectors. The IT industry features good environmental efficiency performances
but is downgraded, given its sparse performances in environmental effectiveness. In
contrast to the chemical industry, the agricultural sector offsets its bad performances in
the air, energy, and the water efficiency by fair performances in the further rescaled
environmental ratio indicators y_{rs} and environmental effectiveness. Resulting is an
environmental subindex around 40.00 (medium). At the bottom of the distribution,
the following branches should be focused for improvements in environmental protection
along with the chemical industry: 19 Manufacture of coke and refined petroleum
products; 23 Manufacture of other non-metallic mineral products; 24 Manufacture of
basic metals; D Electricity, gas, steam, and air conditioning supply; and 17 Manufacture
of paper and paper products (see Section 5.5.1 and Table A.1).

The social subindices of the selected branches feature slight increasing trends (see
Figure 5.19). The financial and the car industries feature unbalanced performances
(bad to poor and fair to good performances) in the rescaled social key indicators y_s
(see Section 5.3.4.2). Their social subindices are downgraded because the weighted
product punishes bad performances. These cannot be offset easily, and balanced
performances yield better aggregated scores. The IT industry is the leader among the
selected branches with respect to the social subindex, given its balanced medium to
fair performances. The chemical industry and the aggregated branches are mid-ranging.
The real estate industry also suffers from the geometric aggregation: Its several bad
to medium performances annihilate its other fair to good performances in the social

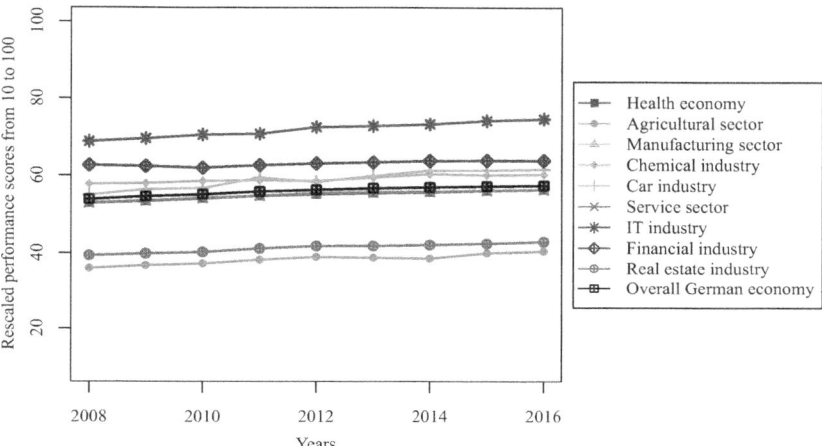

Figure 5.19 Social subindex in rescaled performance scores for the selected branches in the German economy from 2008 to 2016; IT, Information Technology

domain. The agricultural sector performs worst.

The economic subindex is slightly volatile, and increasing trends are visible for some industries towards the end of the time horizon (see Figure 5.20). Similar to the social subindex, the IT industry ranks first owing to its regular fair to good performances. Mid-ranging are the car and the chemical industries, which feature several fair and several poor performances. As the real estate industry is heavily unbalanced and stands out in both good and bad performances (see Section 5.3.4.2), its geometrically aggregated score is relatively low, just entering the bracket of medium. The financial industry yields a slightly better economic subindex with stable poor to medium performances. Once more, the agricultural sector is the worst performer, with poor performance scores. This sector is important for sustainable development and therefore explicitly addressed in the SDGs. For instance, targets on agricultural productivity are established (SDG 2.3; SDG 2.4). The data analysis of this work highlights that the agricultural sector requires assistance in contributing to sustainable development.

Last, Figure 5.21 portrays the overall MLSDI c_1 for the selected branches. Due to constant medium to good performances in the subindices d, the IT industry comes first with regard to overall sustainable development. The second rank is taken by the car industry. The car and the chemical industries perform similarly in the social and the economic domains. However, the environmental domain sorts the wheat from the chaff: The chemical industry does not recover from its poor environmental performances because the geometric mean exacerbates substitutability of the domains. The criterion to implement weak sustainability with minimised substitutability (see Table 4.1) is

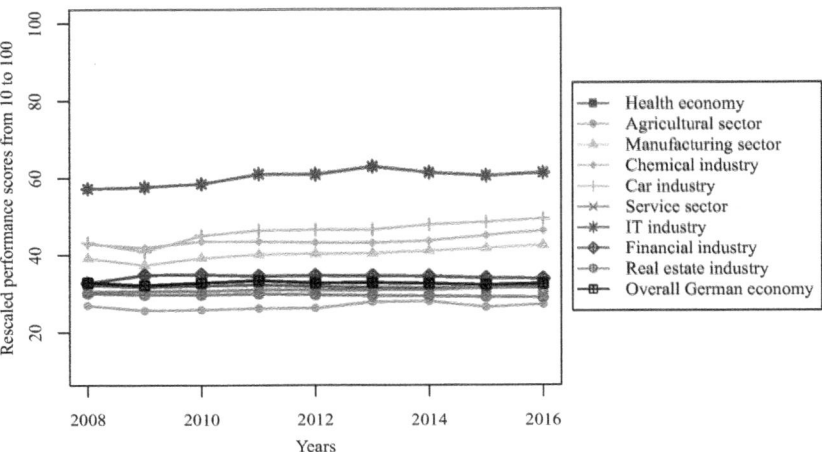

Figure 5.20 Economic subindex in rescaled performance scores for the selected branches in
the German economy from 2008 to 2016; IT, Information Technology

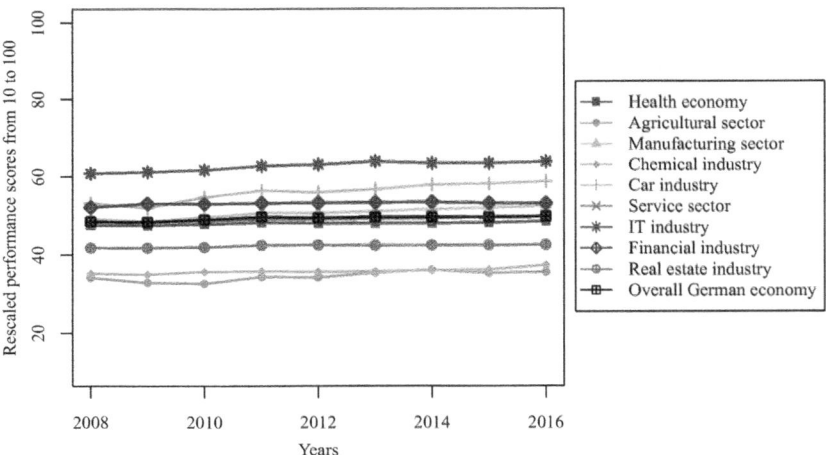

Figure 5.21 Overall Multilevel Sustainable Development Index (MLSDI) in rescaled performance scores for the selected branches in the German economy from 2008 to
2016; IT, Information Technology

realised and comes into effect in aggregating the rescaled key indicators y_s into the
subindices d (see above) and in aggregating the subindices d into the overall MLSDI c_1.

The next section, Section 5.6, analyses the MLSDI's sensitivities.

	$\alpha = 1.5$ vs. $\alpha = 3$	$\alpha = 1.5$ vs. $\alpha = \infty$	$\alpha = 3.0$ vs. $\alpha = \infty$	PCA vs. PTA	PCA vs. MRMRB	PTA vs. MRMRB
Environmental subindex	2.9412	11.2647	9.6765	0.3824	1.7353	1.9706
Social subindex	2.5294	3.7941	1.8529	0.9118	1.9118	1.8529
Economic subindex	2.5000	8.5588	7.4706	0.7353	1.7059	1.3824
Overall MLSDI c_1	3.0882	9.4706	8.7059	0.9706	1.8824	2.0882

Table 5.19 Average rank shifts of economic objects by the four composite measures and the three outlier and weighting methods in 2016; α, outlier coefficient; MLSDI, Multilevel Sustainable Development Index; MRMRB, Maximum Relevance Minimum Redundancy Backward algorithm; PCA, Principal Component Analysis; PTA, Partial Triadic Analysis

5.6   Sensitivity analyses

Sensitivity analyses should be carried out for calculation steps with alternative approaches (see Section 4.3.9). These include missing value imputation (see Section 4.3.3 and Section 5.2.2), outlier detection (see Section 4.3.5 and Section 5.3.3), and weighting (see Section 4.3.7 and Section 5.4). However, because Amelia II yields implausible results (see Section 5.2.2), options for missing value imputation vanish. Hence, only sensitivities of outlier detection and weighting are tested and analysed.

Average shifts in economic objects' ranks by the four composite measures and the three outlier detection methods are displayed in the first three columns of Table 5.19. Full disclosure of the economic objects' ranks by outlier coefficient α can be found in Table A.15 in the Appendix A.7. As a result of a change of the outlier coefficient α from 1.5 to 3.0, economic objects n alter their ordinal rank position in the environmental subindex on average by 2.94. With regard to the social and the economic subindices, average rank shifts are slightly lower with values approximately equal to 2.50. Lower outlier rates β in these two domains are responsible for this result. The average rank shifts of the social and the economic subindices are approximately equal despite the fact that the economic domain's outlier rate β exceeds the social domain's outlier rate β (8.66% vs. 3.09%; see Section 5.3.3). This finding is explained by the differences in the degree of outlyingness: The social domain involves strong outlying key indicators y_o (e.g. key indicators y on taxes; see Section 5.3.3) that are treated in both outlier treatment cases ($\alpha = 1.5$ and $\alpha = 3.0$), whereas the economic domain features mixed outlying key indicators y_o (weak to strong; see Section 5.3.3) that are only treated partially in the laxer case. The highest average rank shift is reported for the overall MLSDI c_1 (3.09) because average rank shifts of the contentual domains enforce each other. When

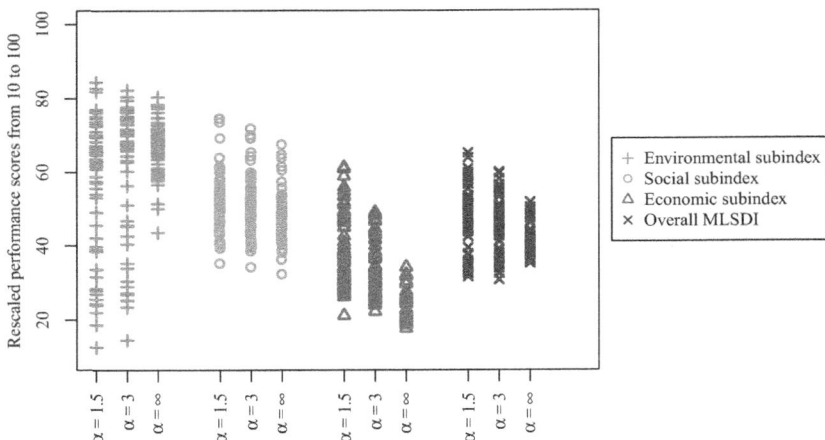

Figure 5.22 The four composite measures by the three outlier detection methods in rescaled performance scores in the German economy in 2016; MLSDI, Multilevel Sustainable Development Index

comparing both outlier detection cases to the non-treatment case, average rank shifts increase. The increases in rank shifts are in line with the outlier rates β because in the non-treatment case, outlying key indicators y_o are not treated at all irrespective of the degree of outlyingness. The maximum average rank shift is reported by the environmental subindex and detection at the inner fence vs. the non-treatment case. Generally, average rank shifts of this case exceed average rank shifts of the detection at the outer fence vs. the non-treatment case because detection at the outer fence is laxer, such that fewer key indicators y are classified as outlying key indicators y_o.

Figure 5.22 displays the sample's four composite measures by the three outlier detection methods. First, distributional differences are remarkable for the subindices d that feature relatively high outlier rates β. These are the environmental and economic subindices. In the non-treatment case, the economic objects n are closely clustered, and the distributions feature low spreads. In the environmental domain, the distribution is clustered at the top because strong outlying key indicators y_o exist at the bottom (see e.g. Figure 5.7b[52]). As a result of removing these, scales of the key indicators y are shortened, such that more economic objects n feature bad or poor performances in the key indicators y. As a result, these economic objects' environmental subindices are downgraded towards the lower end of the distribution. In the economic domain, the opposite occurs: In the wake of outlier treatment, the distribution spreads towards the top because outlying

---

[52]Because of the air emissions intensity's negative effective direction ξ^-, the portrayed outlying key indicators y_o at the top constitute outlying key indicators y_o at the bottom in view of the composite measures.

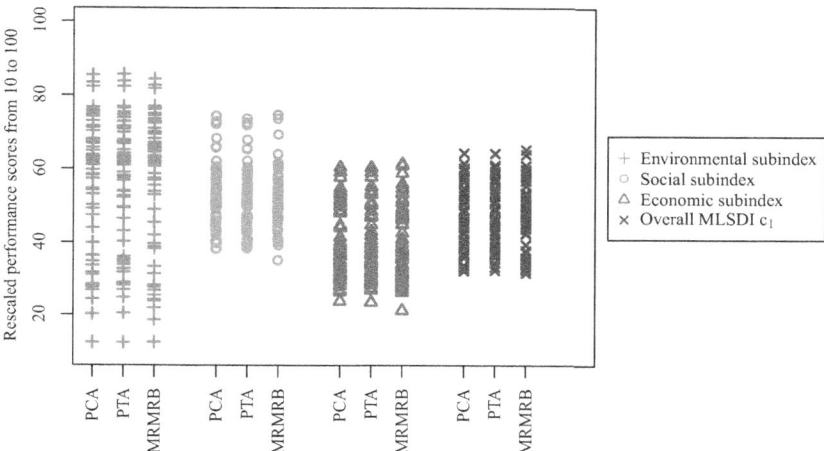

Figure 5.23 The four composite measures by the three weighting methods in rescaled performance scores in the German economy in 2016; MLSDI, Multilevel Sustainable
Development Index; MRMRB, Maximum Relevance Minimum Redundancy
Backward algorithm; PCA, Principal Component Analysis; PTA, Partial Triadic Analysis

key indicators y_o rather exist at the top (see e.g. Figure 5.8b). Second, variations in
the outlier coefficient α only result in significant changes in the economic domain. This
domain is the only domain with numerous weak to moderate outlying key indicators y_o.
These are not detected in the laxer detection case. Sensitivities of the outlier detection
method of the sample's full frequency distributions can be found in Figure A.2 in the
Appendix A.7.

Average rank shifts as a result of a change in the weighting method range from
0.3824 to 2.09 (see Table 5.19). The four composite measures are relatively robust
against changes in the weighting method. Average rank shifts of the PC family remain
below 1.00: On average, economic objects n change their ranks of the four composite
measures below one position. This finding is in line with the PC family's similar weights
ω^{PC} (see Section 5.4.3). Changing the weighting method from the PC family to the
MRMRB algorithm yields slightly higher average rank shifts. A complete report of
the economic objects' ranks by the four composite measures and the three weighting
methods is provided in Table A.16 in the Appendix A.7.

Figure 5.23 illustrates the sample's distributional changes as a result of the different
weighting methods, endorsing the average rank shifts' finding: The four composite
measures' distributions are relatively stable and robust to alterations in the weighting
method. Full frequency distributions of the sample by the four composite measures and
the three weighting methods can be found in Figure A.3 in the Appendix A.7.

In conclusion, economic objects' rankings and performance scores are sensitive to outlier detection but not to weighting. Outlier treatment distorts the true picture (see Section 4.3.5.1; McGregor & Pouw, 2017) but is desired to remove statistical biases. Outlier treatment should be accomplished in order to shorten scales and dissolve the closely clustered economic objects n. Differentiation between economic objects n is enabled, which is required to direct actions for improvement in sustainable development. Especially the environmental domain profits from distortion of the true picture because observations are lowered towards the bottom. Economic objects n at the bottom should be focused for improved environmental protection. The strictness of the outlier detection method only has an impact if weak to moderate outlying key indicators y_o are present. This is especially the case in the economic domain. To also reduce statistical bias in this domain, the stricter base case ($\alpha = 1.5$) is preferred. Furthermore, the superior MRMRB algorithm remains to be recommended for weighting.

5.7   Summary

In this chapter, the novel methodology of the MLSDI has been deployed to the sample region Germany. 62 branches of the German economy as well as five aggregated branches, including the cross-sectional health economy, constitute the objects of investigation. The time horizon reaches from 2008 to 2016. Sustainable development key figures are collected from statistical authorities, and missing values are imputed by single time series imputation. The sophisticated multiple panel data imputation algorithm Amelia II fails because the normality assumption is violated. Missing values are filled by single time series imputation. 44 sustainable development key indicators are derived by aligning the meso GRI and the macro SDG frameworks, establishing multilevel comparability of the MLSDI and finally addressing the perspective gap empirically. Outliers are treated by the IQR method and are especially strong in the environmental domain. Weights are derived by the PCA, PTA, and the MRMRB algorithm. The theoretical advantage of the MRMRB algorithm to capture higher order correlations is confirmed by the empirical findings: The MRMRB algorithm weights informationally richer indicators more heavily, while the PC family does not establish this clear pattern. Environmental efficiency indicators on climate change and social effectiveness indicators on employment receive highest weights and should be focused for improvements in sustainable development performances. The application of the geometric aggregation achieves the desired effect of weak sustainability with minimised substitutability: Bad performances are punished and cannot be easily compensated. In conclusion, industries with unbalanced performances lag industries with rather balanced results. The comparative analysis of the selected branches demonstrates their contributions to sustainable development. The IT industry contributes most, while improvements in the chemical industry's environmental performance and the agricultural industry's performance with respect to all domains are required. The agricultural industry's importance for sustainable development is highlighted in the SDGs and thus, actions and aid are urgently needed. Generally, the environmental domain yields the highest central outcomes, while the economic domain yields the lowest results. The environmental domain requires improvements in its bottom performers, whereas the economic domain demands enhancements across the whole distribution. The sensitivity analyses on outlier detection and weighting confirm the previously derived results.

Chapter 6

Discussion and conclusion

This chapter discusses and reflects on the accomplished theoretical (see Chapter 2 and Chapter 3), methodological (see Chapter 4), and the empirical research (see Chapter 5). The present work is part of Phase C of the transdisciplinary research agenda in sustainability science (see Section 2.3.4; e.g. Lang et al., 2012). It draws on previous studies and problem framings from research and practice (Phase A), makes use of prior disclosures from the scientific and the practitioner community (Phase B), and finally provides new results that are relevant for both research and practice (Phase C). Implications of the results for research, which bear on the descriptive-analytical mode of sustainable development, are discussed in Section 6.1. Section 6.2 provides implications for practice, which relate to the transformational mode outside the science community (see Section 2.1; Wiek et al., 2012). Section 6.3 discusses limitations of the present study, unfolding opportunities for future research. This dissertation ends with an overall summary and conclusion in Section 6.4.

6.1 Implications for research

This work contributes to the debate on measurement and assessment of sustainable development performances. In particular, it contributes a novel sustainable development indicator set that includes a composite measure. Five related research gaps have been identified: the perspective, operational-to-normative, knowledge, and the sustainability gaps as well as methodological deficiencies of existing sustainable development indices. On the one hand, sustainable development demands multiple perspectives (see Section 2.3.1; e.g. Lock & Seele, 2017) because the macro SDGs can only be achieved if micro and meso objects contribute (see Section 2.3.1 and Section 2.3.2; e.g. Dahl, 2012; Griggs et al., 2014; T. Hahn et al., 2015). However, multiple perspectives are frequently disregarded outside the sustainability transitions literature, constituting the perspective gap. This work is the first to include the multilevel perspective in a conceptual framework of sustainable development (see Section 2.3.1; Rotmans et al.,

© The Author(s) 2021
C. Lemke, *Accounting and Statistical Analyses for Sustainable Development*, Sustainable Management, Wertschöpfung und Effizienz, https://doi.org/10.1007/978-3-658-33246-4_6

2001) and thereby updates existing frameworks (see Chapter 2; e.g. Chofreh & Goni, 2017). The perspective gap has been closed theoretically, and further contributions result. First, this work is the first to review sustainable development assessment methods by a method's level of applicability (i.e. by the aggregational size of an object of investigation; see Figure 3.1). This organisation is advantageous in further aspects that are outlined in Section 6.2. Second, resulting from this review and based on the sustainable development assessment principles, this work is the first to identify the most suitable multilevel assessment method for comprehensive sustainable development measurement. Indicator sets that include a composite measure have been revealed as such a method. Third, this work contributes an advanced multilevel indicator set that includes a composite measure and can be applied to meso and macro objects for comparative analyses and benchmarking. The intersection of the meso GRI and the macro SDG frameworks at target level as outlined in GRI and UNGC (2018a) has been refined to indicator level and adjusted to current data availabilities for the German economy by official statistics. On the other hand, decisions for sustainable development should be made at operational, strategic, and normative tiers (see Section 2.3.2; e.g. Ulrich, 2001). An operational-to-normative gap is present because decision makers mostly address the operational tier only (see Section 2.3.2; e.g. Baumgartner & Rauter, 2017). Including the St. Gallen management model in the conceptual framework also points towards indicator sets that include a composite measure as the most successful tool in comprehensive multilevel measurement of sustainable development performances: Indicators and indices address the operational and the strategic tiers (see Section 3.2; e.g. Baumgartner, 2014) while being inherently normative (see Section 3.2; e.g. Waas et al., 2014).

The third identified research gap is the knowledge gap (see Section 2.3.3; e.g. Weitz et al., 2018). By tackling this gap, this work contributes insights about the interconnections of individual sustainable development elements. In doing so, this work is the first to apply an entropy-based information-theoretic algorithm to compute a sustainable development index. Indices in the field of environmental sustainable development that apply methods of information theory include, e.g. Fath and Cabezas (2004); P. E. Meyer, Kontos, Lafitte and Bontempi (2007); and Pawlowski, Fath, Mayer and Cabezas (2005). These are based on the parametric Fisher information, but the non-parametric entropy should be preferred (see Section 4.3.7.4). Entropy-based index approaches include, e.g. Rajsekhar, Singh and Mishra (2015); Ulanowicz, Goerner, Lietaer and Gomez (2009); and Y. Zhang, Yang and Li (2006). Furthermore, Nie, Lv and Gao (2017) apply information-theoretic entropy and the multilevel perspective on technological change (see Section 2.3.1; Geels, 2002) to develop an index for power system transitions. An example of an entropy-based application in a broader context of sustainable development includes Wang et al. (2015), who assess sustainable development capacities with an entropy-based weighting coefficient. However, to the best of the author's knowledge, aggregated sustainable development performances have not been estimated by means of information-theoretic entropy. The application of an information-theoretic algorithm to tackle synergies and trade-offs of individual sustainable development elements constitutes the major methodological contribution of this work. Moreover, this study is the first to compare two multivariate statistical techniques – the PCA and the PTA – to an information-theoretic approach. It is also the first to estimate the three weighting methods' sensitivities on four composite measures of sustainable development.

The fourth identified research gap – the sustainability gap – regards the bottleneck of the science-practice linkage (see Section 2.3.4; e.g. Hall et al., 2017). The present work contributes to this bottleneck by providing detailed information about its methodological approach and data sources, such that the MLSDI can be re-built by interested change agents. Furthermore, this work is the first to publish data on 44 sustainable development key indicators, three subindices, and an overall sustainable development index for 62 two-digit industries as well as five aggregated branches, including the cross-sectional health economy, in the German economy from 2008 to 2016. Providing detailed information about the methodological approach, data sources, and objective, macro-economic benchmarks entails two advantages: First, it enhances decision usefulness across the decisional tiers by identifying and improving relevant sustainable development key indicators; and second, it encourages corporations and further objects of investigation to compare their performances to the provided macro-economic benchmarks, preventing greenwashing.

Fifth and last, previous sustainable development indices do not only lack compliance with the conceptual framework (see Section 3.3 and above), but especially the assessment principle methodological soundness is violated (see Section 4.2). Insufficient data cleaning, weighting, aggregation, and a lack of sensitivity analyses are frequent shortcomings. This work has overcome these deficits and contributes a methodologically sound sustainable development index: The MLSDI imputes missing values and treats outliers, establishing credibility, validity, and reliability of measurement; it applies a sophisticated information-theoretic algorithm to objectively determine relevances and interconnections of individual sustainable development elements; it obeys mathematical aggregation rules for credibility, validity, and reliability; and it conducts sensitivity analyses, proving the measurement's robustness and confirming its previously claimed credibility, validity, and reliability.

Compared to the reviewed sustainable development indices, the MLSDI is the only index that can be deployed at multiple levels (see Table 4.5). Hence, it features a wider scope than the previous indices. Because the reviewed indices are distinct in their indicator bases and regional scopes, data results are not comparable, and the MLSDI is only related to the previous indices in respect of its methodology. The MLSDI may serve management decisions, national industry policy, and international affairs, whereas single level indices only address one level of decision making. For example, the DJSI support corporate decision making, and the SSI assists international policy making by comparing country performances. In comparison with indices of single domains (e.g. the EPI; Esty & Emerson, 2018), the MLSDI supports decision making with regard to all three contentual domains of sustainable development. The MLSDI is based on 44 key indicators and exceeds the number of indicators of five of the nine reviewed indices. Previous indices with a narrower indicator base include the ICSD (Krajnc & Glavič, 2005), FEEM SI (e.g. Pinar et al., 2014), HSDI (e.g. Bravo, 2018), SDI (Bolcárová & Kološta, 2015), and the SSI (e.g. van de Kerk et al., 2014). Their number of indicators range from four to 38 (HSDI vs. ICSD, respectively). In conclusion, the MLSDI assists a broader range of essential topics in sustainable development performance measurement. Moreover, decision making based on the MLSDI will be more accurate in general because of its overall methodological soundness. Only one of the nine reviewed indices – the MISD (e.g. Shaker, 2018) – eliminates statistical biases by sound missing value imputation. Statistical biases that originate in outlying observations remain for all nine previous indices. With regard to scaling, three of the nine reviewed indices – the SDGI (e.g. Schmidt-Traub et al., 2017a), SSI, and the WI (Prescott-Allen, 2001) – apply a scaling method that correctly interplays with the deployed aggregation method. However, of these three indices, the SSI is the only index that implements geometric aggregation, which is essential to map the desired weak sustainability with minimised substitutability (see Section 2.2.4 and Table 4.1). Only one of the reviewed indices – the SDI – deploys the required bottom-up statistical weighting. The SDI determines weights by a PCA, a powerful tool that is used in further sustainable development indices (e.g. Barrios & Komoto, 2006; T. Li, Zhang, Yuan, Liu & Fan, 2012) and adjacent fields of quantitative investigations of sustainable development (e.g. Fernandez-Feijoo, Romero & Ruiz, 2014; Hansmann, Mieg & Frischknecht, 2012; Wallis, 2006). Nonetheless, the methodological and empirical analyses have shown that the information-theoretic algorithm outperforms this multivariate statistical technique because both linear and higher order correlations are detected. Among the reviewed indices, the MLSDI is the only index that implements an information-theoretic algorithm (see above) and hence contributes a major methodological advancement to the index literature in general. Last, only three of the reviewed indices – the FEEM SI, SDGI, and the SSI – investigate sensitivities. The MLSDI improves their sensitivity analyses by intending to investigate three calculation steps instead of one or two steps only. However, testing sensitivities of missing value imputation becomes superfluous, given the Amelia II's failure (see Section 5.2.2).

6.2   Implications for practice

The present work provides several implications for corporate and political practices on sustainable development. This work encourages practitioners to always view sustainable development as one integrated crisis of environmental protection, social development, and economic prosperity (see Section 2.2.4; WSSD, 2002). The economic domain is hallmarked by the misconception that economic growth or profits are part of sustainable development. This work reminds practitioners to eliminate this misconception (see Section 2.2.3; e.g. Jackson, 2009; Vermeulen, 2018). The present study advises corporate practitioners to follow societal instrumental finality (see Section 2.3.2; e.g. T. Hahn & Figge, 2011) because not the long-term survival of the company (i.e. profits) is part of corporate sustainability, but corporations should contribute to the society level concept of sustainable development. In fact, their contributions are inevitable for achieving the SDGs (see Section 2.3.1; e.g. Dahl, 2012; Griggs et al., 2014). Furthermore, this work recommends politicians to abandon GDP (i.e. economic growth) as a measure of societal wellbeing (see Section 3.3.3; Costanza, Fioramonti & Kubiszewski, 2016) and replace it by the MLSDI, which alludes to progress comprehensively and soundly. However, political will might be lacking to let up on GDP (Jesinghaus, 2018).

This work further provides practitioners with an updated compilation of sustainable development assessment principles, which should be considered in any sustainable development assessment. The present study also delivers an updated overview of sustainable development methods. For practitioners, the provided overview by aggregational size might be easier to follow than, for example, overviews that are structured by the methodological approach (see Section 3.2; e.g. Sala et al., 2015). Practitioners might be unaware of the methods required for their problem setting, but they most likely know if they want to appraise, among others, a product, corporation, or a policy. The evaluation of sustainable development assessment methods by means of the assessment principles (see Section 3.2) entails two implications for practice. First, this work delivers an understanding of each method, and second, the present study encourages practitioners to implement sustainable development indicator sets that include a composite measure if they aim to comprehensively measure sustainable development performances by multilevel objects. Moreover, the evaluations of assessment principle compliances (see Section 3.3) and methodological approaches (see Section 4.2) of previous sustainable development indices result in two implications for practice. First, this work informs practitioners about existing alternatives of sustainable development indices. Second, the present study serves practitioners information about "do's" and "don'ts" in sustainable development index construction with regard to both the conceptual and the methodological phase. Concerning the methodology, this work discloses profound knowledge, such that the MLSDI can be re-built (see Section 6.1). The probably most important methodological aspect for corporations provided in this work might be the utilisation of GVA instead of revenues, sales, or profits (see Section 4.3.4). By means of the derived effectiveness and efficiency indicators, the present study supports practitioners to manage absolute and relative decoupling of sustainable development influences and economic activity, respectively. This is a major challenge for decision makers (see Section 3.2; Holden et al.,

2014). Furthermore, this work promotes the implementation of paradox teleological
integration to practitioners. All indicators should be followed at the same time, even
if they are conflicting (see Section 2.3.2; e.g. T. Hahn & Figge, 2011). Moreover, this
study delivers an advanced alignment of the GRI and the SDG frameworks at indicator
level for the geographical region Germany. The indicator base is expected to be valid in
further European countries. It further invites corporations that seek to report their performances on the macro SDGs to rely on this alignment. The provided alignment might
be especially useful for corporations that are not able to allocate sufficient resources to
report on the comprehensive option of the GRI framework but are not satisfied with
the sparse core option. This study suggests collecting 36 key figures, a number that
balances comprehensiveness and resources in practice. Further, this work encourages
practitioners who are interested in data beyond the selected branches or Germany to
take advantage of the benchmarking opportunities the MLSDI provides by enclosing
detailed empirical analyses and data sources to re-produce the sample. Last, this work
may support the action plan for financing green growth in the EU. First, the present
study contributes to Action 1 of this plan, which encompasses the establishment of a
unified classification system for sustainable activities, also termed "EU taxonomy" (EC,
2018). On the one hand, the derived conceptual framework (see Figure 2.11) may guide
the establishment of the "shared understanding of what 'sustainable' means" (EC, 2018).
On the other hand, the elaborated indicator set that is applicable to both the meso and
the macro levels may support determining the environmental and the social objectives
investors should aim for. Second and foremost, this work contributes to Action 5:
developing sustainability benchmarks. More transparent and sounder methodologies
of sustainable development indices are demanded in order to halt greenwashing (EC,
2018). The MLSDI and its well-researched and transparently exposed methodology (see
Chapter 4) is capable to serve exactly this purpose.

6.3   Limitations and future outlook

Several limitations remain and may be investigated in future research. The social domain
requires further conceptual development. The leading framework of the social boundaries
(see Section 2.2.2; e.g. Raworth, 2017) mostly applies to needs of the developing, not the
developed world. Because Maslow's hierarchy of needs (e.g. Maslow, 1987) covers needs
of both developing and developed countries, an alignment of the social boundaries and
Maslow's hierarchy of needs might be expedient (see Section 2.2.2). Further research
on the concept of needs and possible harmonisations should be carried out. Similar to
the concept of the planetary boundaries (see Section 2.2.1; e.g. Steffen et al., 2015), the
finalised framework of social boundaries should be able to verify an indicator's relevance
towards sustainable development (see Section 5.3.1.1 and Section 5.3.1.2).

The consideration of multiple levels sacrifices detailed analysis within one level.

In contrast to footprints, indicator sets typically report sustainable development performances of one object of investigation while disregarding upstream or downstream sustainable development performances. To deliver a holistic picture of the supply chain, the MLSDI should be combined with footprint analyses: A multilevel sustainable development footprint should be derived in future research. A combination of the multilevel index with single level life cycle assessment, a powerful tool to quantify a product's sustainable development performance, for example, from "cradle to grave" (see Section 3.2; Finnveden et al., 2009), might also spread interesting insights but could be methodologically challenging. Topics such as economic proximity (e.g. Torre & Zuindeau, 2009) are only reflected in the performance scores, and benefits that economic objects may experience through proximity cannot be analysed in detail. The literature review is limited by the definition of sustainable development indices, but indices that are not included in the review might provide valuable methodological insights. Further indices that apply information-theoretic weighting have been outlined in Section 6.1.

Moreover, the MLSDI's methodology is subject to several limitations. Adjustments of current prices of key figures reported in monetary units would increase methodological soundness (see Section 4.3.1) because nine years of calculation are covered, and efficiency indicators rely on both monetary and non-monetary units. An iterative algorithm on the single missing value imputation that matches the aggregated branches would refine the imputation results (see Section 4.3.3.2) and also enhance methodological soundness. The multiple missing value imputation by the Amelia II algorithm might not only fail because of the violation of the normality assumption, but because outliers are still present (see Section 4.3.3.3 and Section 5.2.2). An iterative algorithm over the calculation steps missing value imputation and outlier treatment could be tested. Only one micro index – the BLI (see Section 3.3.3; OECD, 2017) – has been identified in the literature, and the MLSDI's key indicator base is currently limited to the alignment of the meso GRI and the macro SDG frameworks (see Section 4.3.4). Further micro indices and a micro framework should be developed. Literature to verify the GRI and the SDG frameworks might unfold gaps and weaknesses in these reporting schemes. Conflicts might be present (Spaiser et al., 2017), and the frameworks' reflections of the planetary and the social boundaries (i.e. the safe and just operating space) could be investigated. Despite theoretical justifications, more sophisticated outlier detection and treatment methods could be explored in future studies because the conducted sensitivity analyses have revealed the importance of this calculation step. As the information-theoretic algorithm outperformed established multivariate statistical methods for weighting, information-theoretic outlier detection and treatment might be of interest. Further information can be found in, e.g. Aggarwal (2017).

Probably the major limitation of the MLSDI is the applied internal scaling (see Section 4.3.6.2). Targets and boundaries are excluded due to unavailable data. Results depend on the distribution, and their significance is reduced. For example, there will still be well performing economic objects, if all objects feature a bad performance (Dahl, 2018). Therefore, the safe and just operating space must be converted into lower aggregational levels of corporations, industries, and nations expressed in terms of the SDGs (Dahl, 2018; Schmidt-Traub et al., 2017a; Steffen et al., 2015). Research on this breakdown only emerged recently and especially lacks the connection of the safe and just operating space and the SDGs. The probably most relevant study is released by O'Neill et al. (2018), who split up the planetary and the social boundaries into 150 nations. Linkage of the planetary boundaries and the SDGs is not available as a peer-reviewed contribution yet (Randers, Rockström & Stoknes, 2019), and literature regarding the nexus of the social boundaries and the SDGs could not be identified. Other adjacent studies, for example, design a framework for translating the planetary boundaries into fair shares at national levels (Häyhä, Lucas, van Vuuren, Cornell & Hoff, 2016), develop a methodology to assess a country's contribution to transgressing the planetary boundary phosphorus (M. Li, Wiedmann & Hadjikakou, 2019), or investigate whether growth has occurred within the planetary boundaries (i.e. *genuine green growth*) (Stoknes & Rockström, 2018). Studies that deal with linking corporate sustainability and the planetary boundaries include, e.g. Antonini and Larrinaga (2017); Dahlmann, Stubbs, Griggs and Morrell (2019); Haffar and Searcy (2018); and Whiteman et al. (2013). Nonetheless, to the best of the author's knowledge, the safe and just operating space has neither been disassembled to corporate nor to industry level yet. Consequently, targets and boundaries could not be included in the German sample (nor in any other geographical region). Methods and precise data generation at corporate, industry, and national levels of the planetary and the social boundaries constitute a major future field of research. The MLSDI connects to this new stream: Once the boundaries are broken down, these data can be fed in the MLSDI to precisely quantify a meso object's contribution to the macro SDGs. Moreover, the boundaries' scientific relationship must be known and hence explored in future research for accurate weighting (see Section 4.3.7; e.g. Ebert & Welsch, 2004; Steffen et al., 2015), making statistical weighting obsolete.

Furthermore, the three applied weighting methods (see Section 4.3.7) will never assign zero weights because indicators that are not perfectly correlated always add variation to the data set. The indicator selection and derivation process (see Section 4.3.4) cannot be reverted. Weighting across the contentual domains currently fails, and the sum of weights of one domain reflects the number of included key indicators. Subsequent adjustment is accomplished (see Section 4.3.7), but the MLSDI remains biased towards efficiency. More ratio than growth indicators are comprised without subsequent adjustments. Further research is required to develop methods that implicitly account for unbalanced numbers of indicators. The equal temporal weighting of the MRMRB algorithm is justified by the PTA's temporal weights (see Section 4.3.7.4 and Section 5.4.3). This procedure might be inaccurate as the PC family is generally outperformed. Structures of the temporal dimension could be investigated by information-theoretic applications in future studies.

To strengthen the MRMRB algorithm's empirical results, sensitivities of discretisation methods could be tested. Despite successful punishment of bad performances by the geometric aggregation, the MLSDI is not capable of indicating urgency. This judgement remains with decision makers and is hence subjective. Sensitivity analyses could be advanced as OAT is generally criticised in the literature. More sophisticated methods are available (Saltelli & Annoni, 2010; Saltelli et al., 2008).

The current sample is limited to meso-level and macro-level applications because micro-level frameworks are not available. For a complete micro-to-macro connection, micro frameworks must be developed, and macro boundaries must be downscaled to lower aggregational levels (see above). To demonstrate the MLSDI's capability of implementing the multilevel perspective and highlighting the benchmarking opportunities across aggregational levels, an empirical application to meso objects (i.e. corporations) should be prospectively performed. Data sources are attached in the supplementary material to facilitate future applications. Generally, the change agent group society is underrepresented in the present sample. Business is involved by constituting the objects of investigation, policy is reflected by the SDG framework, and science is included by the investigation itself. Incorporating micro objects of investigation (i.e. individuals) would solve these two limitations simultaneously. Moreover, the present indicator selection exhibits several limitations. First, the inclusion of more indicators in the MLSDI is desirable to cover all multilevel aspects of the SDGs, but further data are missing for the German sample. Second, interpretability of existing indicators may be limited. For example, the environmental tax intensity, which is the ratio of environmental taxes and the GVA, rises if more environmental taxes are paid. On the one hand, the increase affects sustainable development positively because pollution is paid up for. On the other hand, more taxes are paid because more pollution is generated, harming sustainable development. Effectiveness as well as efficiency of a taxation system remains subject to further investigations (see Section 5.3.1.1). Regarding the social domain, the VAT's effective direction may also be questionable as the VAT is a non-progressive tax on an economic object's created value added. Financially well-placed economic objects are equally burdened in nominal terms as economic objects in weaker financial positions. The latter might suffer from financing social development. The key indicators on apprentices might be limited in their explanatory power. The number of university students may complete the picture on education, and data on labour market demands by educational level is required to draw reliable conclusions on the effective directions key indicators on education should carry. Indicators on trade also feature ambiguities. First, trade's effect on sustainable development may be ambiguous in general. Further information on the contribution of trade to the SDGs can be found in, e.g. WTO (2018). Second, Germany's net import intensity might not indicate support for developing countries. Products are mainly imported from the People's Republic of China, the Netherlands, France, United States of America, and Italy (descending order; Destatis,

2019a). Only China is an economy in transition, while the other countries of origin are developed countries (UN, 2019c). The poor to medium performances of the capital indicators entail uncertain interpretations. Classically, a decrease in capital indicators is interpreted negatively. However, in the digital era of big data and digitalisation, economic prosperity might be possible to be achieved despite decapitalisation and deinvestments – the IT industry stands out as the best performer (see Section 5.5.2).

Forward-looking scenarios as approached by, e.g. Carraro et al. (2013; see Section 3.3.3) should be explored to develop future pathways for comprehensive multilevel solutions by means of the MLSDI (see Section 2.2.4 and Section 2.3.4; e.g. Lang et al., 2012; Leach et al., 2013). A forecast of six SDG indicators can be found in Joshi, Hughes and Sisk (2015), and a review that provides assistance for national SDG scenario modelling can be found in Allen, Metternicht and Wiedmann (2017). More research is required in this field. The MLSDI's current selection of key indicators focuses on developed countries such as Germany. For instance, growth indicators of the economic domain are disregarded because Germany is one of the major economies of the world (see Section 5.3.1.3; UN, 2019c). However, the SDGs are universally applicable to all countries (see Section 2.3.3; e.g. Glaser, 2012), inviting multinational applications and country comparisons. In such applications, outlier thresholds, scales, and weights must be homogeneous. To evaluate the usefulness of national vs. multinational calculations, the MLSDI's sample should be enlarged to explore both scopes.

Effectiveness of performance measurement by the MLSDI is not investigated in the present work. Testa et al. (2018) find that greenwashing does not pay off (see Chapter 3). However, more case studies on the use of sustainable development indicators are required (Bell & Morse, 2018) to further evaluate the influence of sustainable development indicator sets that include a composite measure on sustainable development performance. Do such indicator systems only entail a bureaucratic burden, or do they trigger improved sustainable development performances? Research on the nexus of sustainable development indicators and sustainable development performances include, e.g. Bond and Morrison-Saunders (2013); Bond et al. (2015); and Ramos and Caeiro (2010), but further studies are needed. Additionally, future research should investigate whether indicators or other tools should be mandatory and rather standardised in view of effectiveness of measurement, supporting political decisions on reporting regulations. Last, the usefulness of comprehensive, multilevel indicators and indices for managerial and political decision making might be explored in future studies.

6.4   Summary and conclusion

In this dissertation, a methodological sound sustainable development index that is applicable to the micro, meso, and the macro levels has been developed. Multilevel assessment is crucial because the society level concept sustainable development can only be achieved if micro and meso objects contribute. Moreover, methodological soundness is a prerequisite for serving as a credible, valid, and reliable basis for decision making.

First, this work has elaborated a conceptual framework and assessment principles of sustainable development. Based on these, indicator sets that include a composite measure have been proven to be most successful in comprehensively quantifying multilevel sustainable development performances. A new index – the MLSDI – has been derived by linking the conceptual framework and the assessment principles to each index calculation step. The empirical analysis has confirmed the accuracy and robustness of the MLSDI's methodology. For improved sustainable development, environmental efficiency indicators on climate change and social effectiveness indicators on employment as well as the chemical industry's environmental performances and the agricultural industry's performances in all three contentual domains should be focused.

Manifold implications for research and practice follow from the conducted research. This work is the first to contribute a methodologically sound multilevel indicator set and a multilevel index (perspective gap) that address operational, strategic, and normative tiers (operational-to-normative gap). It is also the first to deploy an entropy-based, information-theoretic algorithm to examine interactions of individual sustainable development elements (knowledge gap). This work provides unrestricted transparency for replicability (sustainability gap), and the MLSDI serves a wide scope of managerial and political decision-making purposes. An alignment of the meso GRI and the macro SDG frameworks at indicator level is delivered for corporate practice, and politicians are encouraged to replace GDP as a measure of wellbeing with the MLSDI.

In conclusion, the usefulness of the suggested approach for informed managerial and political decision making is expected to be high from both theoretical and methodological viewpoints but remains subject to further investigations at the micro, meso, and the macro levels to succeed in the long-term goal and vision of sustainability.

Appendix

A.1 Statistical classification scheme of economic activities in the European Union (EU)

Section code	Division code	Denotation
n/a	n/a	Health economy
A-U	01-99	Total German economy
A	01-03	Agriculture, forestry, and fishing
	01	Crop and animal production, hunting and related service activities
	02	Forestry and logging
	03	Fishing and aquaculture
B	05-09	Mining and quarrying
C	10-33	Manufacturing
	10-12	Manufacture of food products; manufacture of beverages; manufacture of tobacco products
	13-15	Manufacture of textiles; manufacture of wearing apparel; manufacture of leather and related products
	16	Manufacture of wood and of products of wood and cork, except furniture; manufacture of articles of straw and plaiting materials
	17	Manufacture of paper and paper products
	18	Printing and reproduction of recorded media
	19	Manufacture of coke and refined petroleum products
	20	Manufacture of chemicals and chemical products
	21	Manufacture of basic pharmaceutical products and pharmaceutical preparations
	22	Manufacture of rubber and plastic products
	23	Manufacture of other non-metallic mineral products
	24	Manufacture of basic metals

C. Lemke, *Accounting and Statistical Analyses for Sustainable Development*, Sustainable Management, Wertschöpfung und Effizienz, https://doi.org/10.1007/978-3-658-33246-4

continued

Section code	Division code	Denotation
	25	Manufacture of fabricated metal products, except machinery and equipment
	26	Manufacture of computer, electronic, and optical products
	27	Manufacture of electrical equipment
	28	Manufacture of machinery and equipment not elsewhere classified
	29	Manufacture of motor vehicles, trailers, and semi-trailers
	30	Manufacture of other transport equipment
	31-32	Manufacture of furniture; other manufacturing
	33	Repair and installation of machinery and equipment
D	35	Electricity, gas, steam, and air conditioning supply
E	36-39	Water supply; sewerage, waste management, and remediation activities
	36	Water collection, treatment, and supply
	37-39	Sewerage; waste collection, treatment, and disposal activities; materials recovery; remediation activities and other waste management services
F	41-43	Construction
G-S	45-96	Services
G	45-47	Wholesale and retail trade; repair of motor vehicles and motorcycles
	45	Wholesale and retail trade, and repair of motor vehicles and motorcycles
	46	Wholesale trade, except of motor vehicles and motorcycles
	47	Retail trade, except of motor vehicles and motorcycles
H	49-53	Transportation and storage
	49	Land transport and transport via pipelines
	50	Water transport
	51	Air transport
	52	Warehousing and support activities for transportation
	53	Postal and courier activities
I	55-56	Accommodation and food service activities
J	58-63	Information and communication
	58	Publishing activities
	59-60	Motion picture, video, and television programme production, sound recording and music publishing activities; programming and broadcasting activities
	61	Telecommunications

continued

Section code	Division code	Denotation
	62-63	Computer programming, consultancy, and related activities; information service activities
K	64-66	Financial and insurance activities
	64	Financial service activities, except insurance and pension funding
	65	Insurance, reinsurance, and pension funding, except compulsory social security
	66	Activities auxiliary to financial services and insurance activities
L	68	Real estate activities
M	69-75	Professional, scientific, and technical activities
	69-70	Legal and accounting activities; activities of head offices; management consultancy activities
	71	Architectural and engineering activities; technical testing and analysis
	72	Scientific research and development
	73	Advertising and market research
	74-75	Other professional, scientific, and technical activities; veterinary activities
N	77-82	Administrative and support service activities
	77	Rental and leasing activities
	78	Employment activities
	79	Travel agency, tour operator reservation service, and related activities
	80-82	Security and investigation activities; services to buildings and landscape activities; office administrative, office support, and other business support activities
O	84	Public administration and defence; compulsory social security
P	85	Education
Q	86-88	Human health and social work activities
	86	Human health activities
	87-88	Residential care activities; social work activities without accommodation
R	90-93	Arts, entertainment, and recreation
	90-92	Creative, arts, and entertainment activities; libraries, archives, museums, and other cultural activities; gambling and betting activities
	93	Sports activities and amusement and recreation activities
S	94-96	Other service activities
	94	Activities of membership organisations
	95	Repair of computers and personal and household goods

continued

Section code	Division code	Denotation
	96	Other personal service activities
T[†]	97-98[†]	Activities of households as employers of domestic personnel; undifferentiated goods- and services-producing activities of households for own use[†]
U[†]	99[†]	Activities of extraterritorial organisations and bodies[†]

Table A.1 Sections and divisions in the German economy according to the Statistical Classification of Economic Activities in the European Community (NACE) (Eurostat, 2008b); [†], omitted in the present calculation; n/a, not applicable

A.2 German health economy's statistical delimitation

Division code	2008	2009	2010	2011	2012	2013	2014	2015	2016
01	0.1071	0.1118	0.1147	0.1118	0.1230	0.1138	0.1193	0.1248	0.1285
02	0.0000	0.0000	0.0000	0.0000	0.0000	0.0000	0.0000	0.0000	0.0000
03	0.0250	0.0258	0.0274	0.0301	0.0311	0.0300	0.0314	0.0319	0.0328
B	0.0003	0.0003	0.0002	0.0001	0.0002	0.0002	0.0002	0.0002	0.0002
10-12	0.0521	0.0558	0.0568	0.0561	0.0565	0.0526	0.0547	0.0588	0.0593
13-15	0.0463	0.0477	0.0475	0.0490	0.0547	0.0577	0.0594	0.0641	0.0651
16	0.0001	0.0001	0.0001	0.0001	0.0000	0.0000	0.0000	0.0000	0.0000
17	0.1040	0.1036	0.1027	0.0976	0.0984	0.0993	0.0911	0.0929	0.0955
18	0.0878	0.0907	0.0939	0.0951	0.0921	0.0978	0.1005	0.1000	0.0955
19	0.0000	0.0000	0.0000	0.0000	0.0000	0.0000	0.0000	0.0000	0.0000
20	0.0380	0.0412	0.0439	0.0450	0.0509	0.0500	0.0488	0.0510	0.0523
21	0.8618	0.8693	0.8780	0.8800	0.8664	0.8626	0.8674	0.8771	0.8816
22	0.0150	0.0154	0.0141	0.0114	0.0138	0.0139	0.0140	0.0141	0.0140
23	0.0187	0.0181	0.0184	0.0167	0.0165	0.0175	0.0176	0.0178	0.0179
24	0.0008	0.0006	0.0007	0.0004	0.0007	0.0007	0.0007	0.0008	0.0008
25	0.0758	0.0763	0.0772	0.0704	0.0738	0.0745	0.0744	0.0747	0.0749
26	0.0793	0.0781	0.0812	0.0846	0.0847	0.0875	0.0886	0.0887	0.0899
27	0.0130	0.0121	0.0142	0.0100	0.0079	0.0083	0.0086	0.0085	0.0086
28	0.0005	0.0005	0.0005	0.0004	0.0005	0.0005	0.0005	0.0005	0.0006

continued

Division code	2008	2009	2010	2011	2012	2013	2014	2015	2016
29	0.0000	0.0000	0.0000	0.0000	0.0000	0.0000	0.0000	0.0000	0.0000
30	0.0140	0.0145	0.0139	0.0149	0.0094	0.0103	0.0110	0.0124	0.0124
31-32	0.4077	0.4040	0.4084	0.4310	0.4221	0.4295	0.4317	0.4321	0.4328
33	0.0085	0.0078	0.0078	0.0079	0.0077	0.0078	0.0077	0.0081	0.0080
D	0.0004	0.0004	0.0004	0.0004	0.0003	0.0003	0.0003	0.0003	0.0003
36	0.0000	0.0000	0.0000	0.0000	0.0003	0.0003	0.0003	0.0003	0.0003
37-39	0.0001	0.0001	0.0001	0.0001	0.0001	0.0001	0.0001	0.0001	0.0001
F	0.0493	0.0513	0.0497	0.0461	0.0468	0.0466	0.0471	0.0474	0.0471
45	0.0000	0.0000	0.0000	0.0000	0.0000	0.0000	0.0000	0.0000	0.0000
46	0.1036	0.1052	0.1045	0.1061	0.1094	0.1102	0.1094	0.1113	0.1122
47	0.1445	0.1494	0.1493	0.1385	0.1443	0.1447	0.1470	0.1495	0.1511
49	0.0027	0.0029	0.0027	0.0029	0.0037	0.0039	0.0038	0.0040	0.0041
50	0.0000	0.0000	0.0000	0.0000	0.0000	0.0000	0.0000	0.0000	0.0000
51	0.0001	0.0001	0.0001	0.0000	0.0000	0.0000	0.0000	0.0000	0.0000
52	0.0000	0.0000	0.0000	0.0000	0.0000	0.0000	0.0000	0.0000	0.0000
53	0.0000	0.0000	0.0000	0.0000	0.0000	0.0000	0.0000	0.0000	0.0000
I	0.1089	0.1084	0.1061	0.1001	0.0999	0.0975	0.0958	0.0938	0.0936
58	0.1322	0.1362	0.1365	0.1240	0.1360	0.1462	0.1514	0.1517	0.1489
59-60	0.0003	0.0004	0.0004	0.0003	0.0003	0.0002	0.0002	0.0003	0.0003
61	0.0181	0.0188	0.0189	0.0193	0.0164	0.0175	0.0176	0.0178	0.0178
62-63	0.0329	0.0350	0.0336	0.0304	0.0332	0.0338	0.0332	0.0332	0.0334
64	0.0000	0.0000	0.0000	0.0000	0.0000	0.0000	0.0000	0.0000	0.0000
65	0.1351	0.1255	0.1407	0.1328	0.1285	0.1331	0.1193	0.1392	0.1248
66	0.0000	0.0000	0.0000	0.0000	0.0000	0.0000	0.0000	0.0000	0.0000
L	0.0097	0.0105	0.0102	0.0106	0.0097	0.0104	0.0106	0.0105	0.0106
69-70	0.0140	0.0143	0.0140	0.0129	0.0126	0.0139	0.0135	0.0139	0.0136
71	0.0230	0.0241	0.0232	0.0202	0.0196	0.0204	0.0206	0.0203	0.0201
72	0.1230	0.1215	0.1169	0.1243	0.1441	0.1494	0.1482	0.1431	0.1508
73	0.0532	0.0491	0.0448	0.0452	0.0464	0.0497	0.0470	0.0475	0.0456
74-75	0.0000	0.0000	0.0000	0.0000	0.0000	0.0000	0.0000	0.0000	0.0000
77	0.0197	0.0205	0.0198	0.0196	0.0255	0.0224	0.0224	0.0224	0.0224
78	0.0245	0.0244	0.0237	0.0272	0.0248	0.0272	0.0263	0.0263	0.0260

continued

Division code	2008	2009	2010	2011	2012	2013	2014	2015	2016
79	0.0354	0.0356	0.0351	0.0325	0.0312	0.0348	0.0340	0.0322	0.0323
80-82	0.0200	0.0211	0.0205	0.0209	0.0238	0.0253	0.0251	0.0249	0.0249
O	0.0593	0.0596	0.0609	0.0586	0.0589	0.0584	0.0579	0.0582	0.0596
P	0.0722	0.0654	0.0641	0.0636	0.0680	0.0658	0.0666	0.0672	0.0662
86	0.9990	0.9991	0.9990	0.9988	0.9988	0.9989	0.9987	0.9986	0.9987
87-88	0.6493	0.6521	0.6525	0.6393	0.6319	0.6427	0.6320	0.6398	0.6458
90-92	0.0000	0.0000	0.0000	0.0000	0.0000	0.0000	0.0000	0.0000	0.0000
93	0.5792	0.5775	0.5752	0.5799	0.5804	0.5841	0.5815	0.5807	0.5816
94	0.0191	0.0203	0.0200	0.0203	0.0253	0.0240	0.0241	0.0242	0.0239
95	0.0539	0.0564	0.0571	0.0570	0.0604	0.0675	0.0691	0.0671	0.0652
96	0.0119	0.0128	0.0127	0.0128	0.0142	0.0147	0.0151	0.0143	0.0150

Table A.2 German health economy's stakes in divisions at two-digit level in percentage from 2008 to 2016; see Table A.1 for denotation of section codes

A.3 Statistical tests of sustainable development key figures

Environmental key figure x	SW statistic[****]	KS statistic[****]	aDF statistic[**]	LB statistic	LB p-values
Air emissions	0.2453	1.0000	-7.0959	0.0022	0.9624
Environmental tax	0.6172	1.0000	-7.9234	0.0014	0.9700
Hazardous waste	0.4722	0.9442	-8.0509	0.0012	0.9725
Primary energy consumption	0.3594	1.0000	-6.1263	0.0035	0.9528
Waste water	0.1728	0.8420	-8.5787	0.3866	0.5341
Water use	0.2258	0.8884	-8.3291	0.4063	0.5239

Table A.3 Environmental key figures' test statistics and p-values of the Shapiro-Wilk (SW), Kolmogorov-Smirnov (KS), augmented Dickey-Fuller (aDF), and the Ljung-Box (LB) tests; [**], p-values ≤ 0.01; [****], p-values ≤ 0.0001

Social key figure x	SW statistic[****]	KS statistic[****]	aDF statistic[**]	LB statistic	LB p-values
Apprentices	0.6837	1.0000	-9.0546	0.0061	0.9377
CIT	0.5082	0.5000	-8.5699	0.0003	0.9853
Compensation of employees	0.7636	0.8981	-8.5447	0.0001	0.9918
Employees	0.7473	0.9987	-8.4599	0.0003	0.9852
Female marginally-employed employees	0.5427	1.0000	-6.8606	0.1399	0.7084
Female socially-insured employees	0.5749	1.0000	-8.5962	0.0003	0.9871
Local business tax	0.6772	0.5000	-8.1844	0.0005	0.9818
Marginally-employed employees	0.5994	1.0000	-6.4522	0.1828	0.6690
Net taxes on products	0.6405	0.8835	-11.1679	0.5481	0.4591
Severely-disabled employees	0.4205	1.0000	-7.2963	0.0009	0.9763
Socially-insured employees	0.7668	1.0000	-9.2555	0.0003	0.9870
VAT	0.7808	0.8351	-8.2260	0.0010	0.9752
Working hours of employees	0.7507	1.0000	-8.3081	0.0003	0.9855
Workplaces for severely-disabled employees	0.5614	1.0000	-7.3779	0.0011	0.9735

Table A.4 Social key figures' test statistics and p-values of the Shapiro-Wilk (SW), Kolmogorov-Smirnov (KS), augmented Dickey-Fuller (aDF), and the Ljung-Box (LB) tests; [**], p-values ≤ 0.01; [****], p-values ≤ 0.0001; CIT, Corporate Income Tax; VAT, Value Added Tax

Economic key figure x	SW statistic[****]	KS statistic[****]	aDF statistic[**]	LB statistic	LB p-values
Consumption of fixed capital	0.3806	0.7074	-8.9499	0.0004	0.9835
Export	0.5526	0.7726	-5.6363	0.0132	0.9085
Gross fixed assets	0.2117	0.9651	-9.2947	0.0004	0.9835
Gross fixed capital formation	0.3447	0.6847	-8.5214	0.0015	0.9690
GVA	0.7037	0.9616	-9.4581	0.0002	0.9900
Import	0.6851	0.7572	-5.2980	0.0002	0.9895
Imported input	0.6601	1.0000	-3.8761[*]	0.0014	0.9700
Input	0.7859	0.9575	-5.8920	0.0001	0.9925
Internal R&D expenditures	0.3853	0.8138	-6.1364	0.0002	0.9882
Net fixed assets	0.2000	0.9191	-9.1827	0.0004	0.9834
Output	0.8082	0.9692	-9.0331	0.0001	0.9920
R&D employees	0.4832	0.9839	-6.7173	0.0009	0.9760

continued

Economic key figure x	SW statistic[****]	KS statistic[****]	aDF statistic[**]	LB statistic	LB p-values
Working hours of working population	0.7568	1.0000	-7.4592	0.0006	0.9800
Working population	0.7523	1.0000	-7.9765	0.0004	0.9840

Table A.5 Economic key figures' test statistics and p-values of the Shapiro-Wilk (SW), Kolmogorov-Smirnov (KS), augmented Dickey-Fuller (aDF), and the Ljung-Box (LB) tests; [*], p-values ≤ 0.05; [**], p-values ≤ 0.01; [****], p-values ≤ 0.0001; GVA, Gross Value Added; R&D, Research and Development

A.4 Summary statistics of the sustainable development key indicators

Environmental key indicator y Year	Mean	Median	Min	Max	Q_1	Q_3	Skewness	Kurtosis
Growth of air emissions								
2008-2016	-0.0197	-0.0560	-0.5725	0.8553	-0.1543	0.1370	0.6864	1.0852
Air emissions intensity								
2008	740.0618	76.5767	4.5252	7,633.74	47.9451	274.3351	2.9616	8.2157
2009	702.1362	68.9819	4.0484	6,938.17	43.4678	300.0807	2.8036	7.3242
2010	650.8067	69.2182	4.0557	7,198.94	45.5473	282.4208	2.7945	7.8123
2011	693.1062	62.3071	3.7265	8,305.25	39.4546	263.7724	3.1604	10.1605
2012	657.2317	62.2896	3.8583	7,342.85	39.5712	260.6077	2.9123	7.9614
2013	625.6249	59.6361	3.8028	8,073.17	39.7349	256.3883	3.2539	11.3931
2014	664.4906	56.2030	3.8716	8,313.35	40.1189	262.4902	3.1647	10.0471
2015	621.3121	57.4957	4.2395	8,560.17	38.4426	259.1875	3.4037	12.7795
2016	633.3430	58.4076	4.4250	8,151.27	38.0750	278.6782	3.2551	10.8856
2008-2016	665.3459	65.9377	3.7265	8,560.17	41.6562	272.8455	3.1634	10.0871
Growth of primary energy consumption								
2008-2016	-0.0158	-0.0479	-0.4671	0.5762	-0.1336	0.0803	0.5046	0.5235
Energy intensity								
2008	9.2799	1.5279	0.1338	121.7181	1.1676	5.0548	3.6302	13.7945
2009	8.6230	1.3904	0.1280	102.0254	1.0484	5.5702	3.3188	11.9052
2010	8.0307	1.5207	0.1325	70.7095	1.1586	5.0453	2.6260	6.2292
2011	8.4961	1.3170	0.1202	109.2000	0.9972	4.4493	3.4865	13.2817
2012	8.0524	1.3397	0.1284	94.8419	0.9289	4.2402	3.2299	10.7227
2013	7.8677	1.3444	0.1235	87.1698	0.9633	4.7223	3.0704	9.5571
2014	8.3229	1.2642	0.1210	106.3678	0.8848	4.4682	3.3892	12.1084
2015	7.4378	1.2266	0.1301	79.1303	0.8978	4.2100	2.9808	8.8616
2016	7.5598	1.1435	0.1289	75.9435	0.8649	4.0302	2.9719	8.3767
2008-2016	8.1856	1.4090	0.1202	121.7181	0.9687	4.7851	3.4236	12.7592

continued

Environmental key indicator y								
Year	Mean	Median	Min	Max	Q_1	Q_3	Skewness	Kurtosis
Growth of water use								
2008-2016	-0.0096	-0.0049	-0.6255	0.6064	-0.1261	0.1022	0.0996	1.0119
Water intensity								
2008	25.2698	0.5808	0.0093	398.5435	0.1953	2.9462	3.5481	12.2671
2009	27.7041	0.6703	0.0095	384.1619	0.1830	3.1265	3.3905	10.8404
2010	25.8273	0.6028	0.0095	375.2354	0.1988	3.0925	3.5223	11.8754
2011	24.9958	0.5496	0.0093	382.8308	0.2060	2.5853	3.5830	12.5445
2012	22.7153	0.5887	0.0098	311.2781	0.2142	2.3637	3.3038	10.2336
2013	22.0370	0.6051	0.0097	332.6692	0.2042	2.1844	3.4091	11.1674
2014	21.7927	0.5653	0.0096	322.5074	0.1856	2.1823	3.4109	11.2472
2015	21.0388	0.5483	0.0093	310.5653	0.1760	2.0128	3.4553	11.5052
2016	20.2084	0.5155	0.0091	310.1846	0.1761	1.8949	3.5167	12.0757
2008-2016	23.5099	0.5885	0.0091	398.5435	0.1814	2.5543	3.6177	12.8055
Growth of waste water								
2008-2016	-0.0304	-0.0098	-1.0000	0.6045	-0.1407	0.0870	-0.6825	2.6684
Waste water intensity								
2008	15.1231	0.4646	0.0000	380.3413	0.1451	1.3264	4.9920	24.7270
2009	16.4905	0.4976	0.0000	366.6164	0.1552	1.6474	4.8457	22.7362
2010	15.7122	0.5047	0.0000	358.0976	0.1437	1.3807	4.8961	23.1271
2011	15.5349	0.4613	0.0000	367.9070	0.1368	1.2261	4.9055	23.3314
2012	13.4333	0.4755	0.0000	299.8621	0.1346	1.1947	4.8083	22.4942
2013	13.0867	0.4604	0.0000	320.7330	0.1299	0.9801	4.9417	24.0018
2014	13.2695	0.4219	0.0000	311.2860	0.1223	0.9308	4.8628	23.1090
2015	12.7358	0.3973	0.0000	300.2054	0.1193	0.8735	4.9070	23.2931
2016	12.3534	0.3700	0.0000	300.4149	0.1187	0.8893	4.9367	23.7086
2008-2016	14.1933	0.4517	0.0000	380.3413	0.1346	1.2333	5.0949	25.3993
Growth of hazardous waste								
2008-2016	-0.0607	-0.0969	-0.6637	1.4894	-0.2958	0.1581	1.2043	2.6282
Hazardous waste intensity								
2008	12.7503	2.1804	0.1070	195.0220	1.2337	7.0249	4.3639	19.0733
2009	13.7338	2.3026	0.0940	201.8064	1.4607	8.3719	4.1945	17.7138
2010	12.1120	1.9556	0.0907	197.9858	0.5538	6.6220	4.4817	19.9947
2011	10.8786	1.3732	0.1714	179.8533	0.6202	6.2422	4.5241	20.3257
2012	11.4148	1.6980	0.1405	176.5302	0.7214	6.9751	4.3659	19.1437
2013	11.1520	1.6831	0.0619	171.8367	0.3739	7.2200	4.2847	18.4622
2014	11.2985	1.6358	0.0702	168.5726	0.3664	7.2813	4.1763	17.6493
2015	10.5369	1.5248	0.1505	158.3226	0.5929	6.5457	4.2126	17.8944
2016	10.8324	1.8063	0.1026	160.8691	0.6365	6.3423	4.0731	16.5535
2008-2016	11.6344	1.9324	0.0619	201.8064	0.5948	6.7510	4.4526	19.9410
Environmental tax intensity								
2008	0.0137	0.0072	0.0004	0.1181	0.0037	0.0127	3.3405	11.8295
2009	0.0152	0.0076	0.0003	0.1221	0.0038	0.0170	3.1639	10.3301
2010	0.0130	0.0070	0.0004	0.0797	0.0036	0.0122	2.5053	5.9596

continued

Environmental key indicator y								
Year	Mean	Median	Min	Max	Q_1	Q_3	Skewness	Kurtosis
2011	0.0146	0.0076	0.0005	0.1143	0.0041	0.0148	2.9625	10.2733
2012	0.0137	0.0068	0.0004	0.0918	0.0036	0.0138	2.5122	6.3285
2013	0.0130	0.0073	0.0004	0.0813	0.0036	0.0143	2.3581	5.6803
2014	0.0134	0.0074	0.0004	0.1074	0.0032	0.0141	3.0517	11.1017
2015	0.0131	0.0068	0.0004	0.0839	0.0033	0.0137	2.5776	6.6493
2016	0.0129	0.0071	0.0004	0.0789	0.0032	0.0132	2.5305	6.3997
2008-2016	0.0136	0.0071	0.0003	0.1221	0.0036	0.0140	3.0300	10.4539

Table A.6 Summary statistics of the environmental key indicators in the German economy from 2008 to 2016; Max, Maximum; Min, Minimum; Q_1, 25th percentile; Q_3, 75th percentile

Social key indicator y								
Year	Mean	Median	Min	Max	Q_1	Q_3	Skewness	Kurtosis
Growth of compensation of employees								
2008-2016	0.2581	0.2504	-0.2456	0.7671	0.1438	0.3701	0.0959	0.4252
Growth of employees								
2008-2016	0.0426	0.0358	-0.3789	0.4471	-0.0471	0.1495	-0.1090	0.4946
Average compensation of employees p.c.								
2008	39,140	37,779	15,906	68,771	29,775	50,500	0.1618	-1.0535
2009	39,553	37,218	16,167	71,556	29,825	52,398	0.2776	-0.9296
2010	40,533	38,680	16,542	69,941	30,050	53,325	0.2001	-1.0649
2011	41,975	39,824	16,923	74,412	30,798	54,126	0.2900	-0.9443
2012	42,697	40,583	17,230	81,235	31,214	54,300	0.3135	-0.8280
2013	43,481	41,264	17,361	76,353	31,971	55,225	0.2494	-1.0653
2014	44,608	42,200	17,994	76,647	32,576	56,847	0.2231	-1.1074
2015	46,031	42,983	18,891	83,444	34,258	58,288	0.2900	-1.0037
2016	46,970	44,372	19,442	81,167	35,892	59,567	0.2942	-0.9838
2008-2016	42,777	40,024	15,906	83,444	31,2401	55,044	0.3134	-0.8171
Average compensation of employees p.h.								
2008	26.7077	24.8291	13.6836	41.7808	21.4982	33.3102	0.3180	-1.0283
2009	28.0832	25.8533	14.0651	49.5385	22.3940	35.2803	0.4109	-0.8332
2010	28.3333	25.8683	14.2075	47.5600	22.6929	36.1663	0.3181	-0.9929
2011	29.1049	26.2493	15.0295	48.6538	23.1930	36.3840	0.3625	-0.9759
2012	30.0553	27.2340	15.2905	53.1154	24.2228	37.3440	0.3956	-0.8187
2013	30.6458	27.2981	15.9596	49.9231	24.7878	38.1990	0.3986	-0.9901
2014	31.3015	27.7433	16.3370	52.1200	25.2414	39.2481	0.4191	-0.9604
2015	32.1061	28.5139	16.5668	53.6429	25.7308	40.1712	0.4234	-0.9610
2016	32.9225	29.7780	17.4123	52.1786	26.7676	41.7613	0.4256	-0.9522
2008-2016	29.9178	27.2487	13.6836	53.6429	23.4066	37.0156	0.4282	-0.7378
Labour share								
2008	0.5525	0.5853	0.0402	0.9433	0.4056	0.6957	-0.3736	-0.4180

continued

| Social key indicator y | | | | | | | |
Year	Mean	Median	Min	Max	Q_1	Q_3	Skewness	Kurtosis
2009	0.5876	0.6429	0.0404	0.9627	0.4179	0.7532	-0.5212	-0.4225
2010	0.5643	0.6034	0.0408	0.9562	0.4093	0.6942	-0.4230	-0.3094
2011	0.5643	0.6094	0.0400	0.9429	0.3885	0.6808	-0.3408	-0.3462
2012	0.5688	0.6041	0.0420	0.9319	0.4039	0.6917	-0.4006	-0.3166
2013	0.5689	0.6084	0.0401	0.9378	0.3933	0.7070	-0.5000	-0.3311
2014	0.5697	0.6046	0.0417	0.9334	0.4029	0.7001	-0.4271	-0.3507
2015	0.5627	0.6031	0.0421	0.9570	0.4135	0.6869	-0.3987	-0.2410
2016	0.5656	0.5833	0.0437	0.9847	0.4296	0.6942	-0.2688	-0.2626
2008-2016	0.5671	0.6043	0.0400	0.9847	0.4045	0.7022	-0.4135	-0.2629

Growth of socially-insured employees

2008-2016	0.0928	0.0735	-0.3922	0.4890	-0.0249	0.1863	0.0227	-0.1974

Growth of marginally-employed employees

2008-2016	-0.1113	-0.1125	-0.4362	0.3536	-0.2603	-0.0006	0.4193	-0.4219

Share of marginally-employed employees

2008	0.2054	0.1264	0.0079	1.0400	0.0457	0.2590	1.7554	2.7447
2009	0.2045	0.1252	0.0071	1.0051	0.0444	0.2542	1.6712	2.2778
2010	0.2010	0.1227	0.0076	0.9634	0.0444	0.2555	1.6545	2.1345
2011	0.1956	0.1186	0.0068	0.9500	0.0417	0.2541	1.6428	2.1164
2012	0.1890	0.1149	0.0065	0.9110	0.0407	0.2485	1.5855	1.9066
2013	0.1860	0.1143	0.0066	0.9000	0.0415	0.2467	1.5815	1.9230
2014	0.1820	0.1132	0.0063	0.8824	0.0431	0.2444	1.5834	1.9593
2015	0.1693	0.1086	0.0056	0.8144	0.0436	0.2346	1.5656	1.9926
2016	0.1637	0.1042	0.0055	0.7947	0.0455	0.2279	1.5891	2.1315
2008-2016	0.1885	0.1172	0.0055	1.0400	0.0420	0.2479	1.7159	2.5955

Growth of female socially-insured employees

2008-2016	0.1036	0.1061	-0.4750	0.4394	-0.0154	0.2130	-0.3150	0.5848

Quota of gender difference

2008	0.1814	0.1824	0.0109	0.3618	0.1036	0.2640	-0.0409	-1.1385
2009	0.1811	0.1858	0.0047	0.3597	0.1004	0.2637	-0.0487	-1.1417
2010	0.1816	0.1828	0.0044	0.3575	0.0989	0.2624	-0.0669	-1.1529
2011	0.1829	0.1828	0.0054	0.3581	0.1049	0.2657	-0.1088	-1.1442
2012	0.1820	0.1833	0.0042	0.3535	0.1075	0.2635	-0.1108	-1.1364
2013	0.1817	0.1846	0.0063	0.3522	0.1069	0.2648	-0.0958	-1.1526
2014	0.1813	0.1826	0.0024	0.3486	0.1066	0.2654	-0.0886	-1.1746
2015	0.1808	0.1800	0.0018	0.3462	0.1053	0.2669	-0.0872	-1.1878
2016	0.1794	0.1759	0.0006	0.3458	0.1046	0.2671	-0.0956	-1.1772
2008-2016	0.1814	0.1823	0.0006	0.3618	0.1043	0.2655	-0.0851	-1.1016

Growth of female marginally-employed employees

2008-2016	-0.2078	-0.2056	-0.4707	0.2130	-0.3575	-0.1061	0.4022	-0.7059

Quota of gender difference of marginally-employed employees

2008	0.2109	0.2333	0.0083	0.4495	0.1073	0.3077	-0.2190	-1.1136
2009	0.2047	0.2204	0.0001	0.4485	0.0995	0.2926	-0.1152	-1.1013

continued

| Social key indicator y | | | | | | | | |
Year	Mean	Median	Min	Max	Q_1	Q_3	Skewness	Kurtosis
2010	0.1996	0.2101	0.0012	0.4355	0.0902	0.2939	-0.1039	-1.1649
2011	0.1940	0.2043	0.0048	0.4411	0.1042	0.2866	-0.0890	-1.1043
2012	0.1895	0.1959	0.0007	0.4316	0.1004	0.2830	-0.0738	-1.0674
2013	0.1826	0.1795	0.0090	0.4077	0.0947	0.2689	-0.0305	-1.1088
2014	0.1755	0.1713	0.0040	0.4062	0.0986	0.2626	0.0265	-1.0756
2015	0.1649	0.1679	0.0031	0.3742	0.0876	0.2393	-0.0093	-1.0740
2016	0.1587	0.1609	0.0007	0.3651	0.0820	0.2346	-0.0023	-1.0263
2008-2016	0.1867	0.1952	0.0001	0.4495	0.0923	0.2740	-0.0125	-1.0052
Growth of severely-disabled employees								
2008-2016	0.2331	0.1962	-0.8048	1.0693	0.0816	0.3610	0.1145	2.3748
Quota of severely-disabled employees								
2008	0.7820	0.7965	0.2447	1.3053	0.6378	0.9112	0.0906	0.0308
2009	0.8136	0.8198	0.3263	1.3645	0.6667	0.9398	0.2105	0.0382
2010	0.8312	0.8381	0.3030	1.4397	0.6711	0.9538	0.2613	0.0953
2011	0.8307	0.8386	0.3229	1.4091	0.6790	0.9505	0.1115	0.0332
2012	0.8492	0.8537	0.3722	1.4935	0.6979	0.9680	0.2958	0.1697
2013	0.8590	0.8744	0.3867	1.4674	0.7061	0.9720	0.1699	-0.0416
2014	0.8604	0.8734	0.3859	1.4350	0.7042	0.9793	0.2424	-0.1462
2015	0.8697	0.8925	0.3857	1.6183	0.6924	0.9833	0.4229	0.1620
2016	0.8581	0.8809	0.3875	1.3743	0.6916	0.9869	0.1085	-0.5001
2008-2016	0.8393	0.8440	0.2447	1.6183	0.6822	0.9673	0.2407	0.1195
Growth of apprentices								
2008-2016	-0.0950	-0.0889	-0.6537	0.7309	-0.2206	0.0351	0.4514	2.1157
Share of apprentices								
2008	0.0562	0.0473	0.0065	0.1407	0.0393	0.0722	0.9402	0.5276
2009	0.0558	0.0482	0.0064	0.1381	0.0404	0.0696	0.8101	0.4919
2010	0.0532	0.0476	0.0057	0.1310	0.0395	0.0672	0.7368	0.5472
2011	0.0495	0.0432	0.0051	0.1258	0.0366	0.0633	0.7707	0.7991
2012	0.0491	0.0439	0.0054	0.1262	0.0377	0.0612	0.8356	1.3821
2013	0.0482	0.0435	0.0054	0.1272	0.0358	0.0598	0.9129	1.8421
2014	0.0471	0.0431	0.0050	0.1249	0.0347	0.0587	0.9218	2.0376
2015	0.0457	0.0433	0.0042	0.1219	0.0341	0.0546	0.9579	2.1107
2016	0.0449	0.0430	0.0039	0.1215	0.0338	0.0525	1.0445	2.3917
2008-2016	0.0500	0.0441	0.0039	0.1407	0.0375	0.0615	0.9963	1.5627
VAT intensity								
2008	0.0924	0.0637	-0.1069	2.0527	0.0106	0.1035	6.8608	48.8492
2009	0.0961	0.0656	-0.1149	1.9647	0.0101	0.1203	6.7125	47.4342
2010	0.0823	0.0607	-0.0996	1.3269	0.0094	0.1196	5.7892	38.7353
2011	0.0904	0.0575	-0.1166	1.9224	0.0084	0.1174	6.5571	45.9287
2012	0.0834	0.0575	-0.3102	1.6769	0.0100	0.1131	5.8098	39.6847
2013	0.0821	0.0557	-0.1237	1.3911	0.0099	0.1110	5.7205	38.1117
2014	0.0898	0.0550	-0.1169	1.8645	0.0112	0.1133	6.4297	44.6718
2015	0.0788	0.0532	-0.1151	1.1808	0.0076	0.1144	5.1695	32.9538

continued

Social key indicator y								
Year	Mean	Median	Min	Max	Q_1	Q_3	Skewness	Kurtosis
2016	0.0767	0.0513	-0.1108	1.0816	0.0086	0.1107	4.7974	29.6315
2008-2016	0.0858	0.0583	-0.3102	2.0527	0.0090	0.1162	6.7882	52.5273
Intensity of net taxes on products								
2008	0.0153	0.0173	-0.3144	0.1610	0.0086	0.0347	-3.2862	15.2532
2009	0.0132	0.0158	-0.2929	0.1037	0.0080	0.0333	-3.8463	17.0385
2010	0.0097	0.0121	-0.3278	0.1217	0.0033	0.0287	-3.3638	14.9952
2011	0.0129	0.0130	-0.2791	0.1107	0.0056	0.0338	-3.0039	12.5115
2012	0.0159	0.0130	-0.2567	0.1043	0.0072	0.0358	-3.0055	13.3004
2013	0.0146	0.0129	-0.2122	0.0995	0.0061	0.0333	-2.6728	10.7209
2014	0.0156	0.0139	-0.2460	0.1263	0.0073	0.0329	-2.8453	12.8765
2015	0.0146	0.0139	-0.2412	0.1284	0.0072	0.0309	-2.6529	11.9293
2016	0.0145	0.0139	-0.2507	0.1302	0.0073	0.0311	-2.6640	12.7958
2008-2016	0.0140	0.0140	-0.3278	0.1610	0.0067	0.0331	-3.2438	15.2486
CIT intensity								
2008	0.0043	0.0028	0.0000	0.0321	0.0016	0.0045	3.2890	11.5411
2009	0.0044	0.0030	0.0000	0.0327	0.0014	0.0051	3.3081	12.2824
2010	0.0064	0.0045	0.0000	0.0485	0.0023	0.0072	3.3515	12.7592
2011	0.0083	0.0057	0.0000	0.0578	0.0034	0.0092	3.1430	11.1754
2012	0.0086	0.0058	0.0000	0.0601	0.0026	0.0088	3.0365	10.2052
2013	0.0090	0.0066	0.0000	0.0630	0.0029	0.0101	3.2415	12.0399
2014	0.0087	0.0067	0.0000	0.0605	0.0029	0.0112	3.2465	12.4870
2015	0.0086	0.0062	0.0000	0.0649	0.0030	0.0090	3.4070	13.8647
2016	0.0087	0.0063	0.0000	0.0683	0.0030	0.0101	3.4635	14.5648
2008-2016	0.0074	0.0050	0.0000	0.0683	0.0025	0.0080	3.5376	15.1636
Local business tax intensity								
2008	0.0172	0.0144	0.0000	0.0771	0.0085	0.0218	2.2310	6.8476
2009	0.0187	0.0164	0.0000	0.0910	0.0087	0.0263	2.1599	7.5294
2010	0.0170	0.0154	0.0000	0.0901	0.0082	0.0212	2.5591	9.5505
2011	0.0194	0.0175	0.0000	0.0962	0.0101	0.0247	2.4412	8.3855
2012	0.0198	0.0178	0.0000	0.0994	0.0090	0.0238	2.3458	7.5485
2013	0.0189	0.0173	0.0000	0.0934	0.0086	0.0227	2.5317	8.9029
2014	0.0189	0.0181	0.0000	0.0812	0.0087	0.0230	1.9393	5.4216
2015	0.0188	0.0178	0.0000	0.0803	0.0089	0.0221	2.0268	5.5312
2016	0.0188	0.0178	0.0000	0.0800	0.0091	0.0229	2.0530	5.3517
2008-2016	0.0186	0.0166	0.0000	0.0994	0.0087	0.0232	2.3247	7.6911

Table A.7 Summary statistics of the social key indicators in the German economy from 2008 to 2016; CIT, Corporate Income Tax; Max, Maximum; Min, Minimum; p.c., per capita; p.h., per hour; Q_1, 25th percentile; Q_3, 75th percentile; VAT, Value Added Tax

Economic key indicator y								
Year	Mean	Median	Min	Max	Q_1	Q_3	Skewness	Kurtosis
Gross capital productivity								
2008	0.8185	0.3238	0.0409	10.2611	0.1969	0.6527	4.5418	20.7242
2009	0.7150	0.2989	0.0391	8.1873	0.2022	0.6935	4.4190	19.8595
2010	0.7520	0.3259	0.0382	9.6093	0.1944	0.6302	4.5956	21.6902
2011	0.7540	0.3525	0.0385	9.8559	0.1909	0.6358	4.6739	22.6935
2012	0.7339	0.3567	0.0364	9.3491	0.1868	0.5866	4.6423	22.7405
2013	0.7412	0.3563	0.0362	9.7401	0.1915	0.5997	4.7230	23.8312
2014	0.7434	0.3723	0.0353	9.6715	0.1882	0.6102	4.7076	23.5246
2015	0.7459	0.3841	0.0352	9.5349	0.1960	0.6303	4.7149	23.7958
2016	0.7303	0.3874	0.0346	8.4730	0.2017	0.6466	4.4713	21.3951
2008-2016	0.7482	0.3577	0.0346	10.2611	0.1905	0.6488	4.7617	23.5961
Net capital productivity								
2008	1.5360	0.7208	0.0651	19.5957	0.3692	1.2737	4.5891	21.2061
2009	1.3412	0.6696	0.0628	15.3358	0.3619	1.2914	4.4387	20.0417
2010	1.4012	0.7110	0.0618	16.7112	0.3763	1.2103	4.5124	20.7685
2011	1.3871	0.7394	0.0627	16.1049	0.3761	1.2932	4.4752	20.6132
2012	1.3549	0.7558	0.0597	15.4591	0.3771	1.1981	4.4391	20.6293
2013	1.3698	0.7353	0.0598	16.2299	0.3843	1.2024	4.5107	21.6411
2014	1.3806	0.7431	0.0586	16.3239	0.3807	1.2374	4.5241	21.6233
2015	1.3989	0.7669	0.0589	16.5517	0.3851	1.2372	4.5664	22.1342
2016	1.3795	0.7856	0.0582	15.1008	0.3963	1.2867	4.3948	20.4261
2008-2016	1.3944	0.7378	0.0582	19.5957	0.3754	1.2488	4.6758	22.7766
Degree of modernity								
2008	0.5265	0.5287	0.3522	0.6462	0.4858	0.5809	-0.3294	-0.4590
2009	0.5236	0.5295	0.3549	0.6359	0.4846	0.5712	-0.3188	-0.4255
2010	0.5225	0.5302	0.3596	0.6490	0.4818	0.5684	-0.2637	-0.3971
2011	0.5222	0.5312	0.3680	0.6368	0.4818	0.5635	-0.2775	-0.4788
2012	0.5204	0.5296	0.3769	0.6197	0.4833	0.5636	-0.3439	-0.4840
2013	0.5183	0.5241	0.3854	0.6200	0.4830	0.5632	-0.3664	-0.5066
2014	0.5172	0.5193	0.3980	0.6161	0.4827	0.5607	-0.3690	-0.5220
2015	0.5163	0.5231	0.3999	0.6143	0.4854	0.5566	-0.3972	-0.4005
2016	0.5160	0.5236	0.3980	0.6135	0.4879	0.5517	-0.3761	-0.2630
2008-2016	0.5203	0.5246	0.3522	0.6490	0.4839	0.5640	-0.3048	-0.2896
Consumed capital productivity								
2008	11.5439	6.6066	1.1992	115.1420	3.8919	12.8816	4.4002	22.8315
2009	10.3365	5.9400	1.1023	93.2455	3.6583	13.4676	4.0937	20.5200
2010	10.8589	6.1751	1.0956	116.7000	3.8318	11.9480	4.9387	28.9186
2011	10.9139	6.5692	1.0897	119.8667	3.6428	12.0642	5.1386	31.0443
2012	10.5720	6.4374	1.0348	107.2395	3.6173	11.6762	4.8873	28.8094
2013	10.6097	6.5304	1.0376	108.7338	3.7812	11.4374	4.9492	29.4587
2014	10.6087	6.6479	1.1023	104.4061	3.6628	11.4133	4.7826	27.8628
2015	10.6090	7.0677	1.1415	98.7944	3.7356	11.7030	4.6440	26.6881
2016	10.4520	7.3297	1.1113	87.5120	3.9282	11.9263	4.2165	22.8075
2008-2016	10.7227	6.5277	1.0348	119.8667	3.6716	12.0207	4.8856	28.9152

continued

Economic key indicator y								
Year	Mean	Median	Min	Max	Q_1	Q_3	Skewness	Kurtosis
Investment intensity								
2008	0.2230	0.1609	0.0106	1.3844	0.0854	0.2691	2.8814	10.8944
2009	0.2069	0.1451	0.0125	1.0741	0.0814	0.2927	2.0997	6.3816
2010	0.2138	0.1423	0.0164	1.2707	0.0963	0.2311	2.8986	9.8799
2011	0.2085	0.1436	0.0211	1.1928	0.0962	0.2636	2.6027	9.1867
2012	0.2007	0.1453	0.0128	1.1314	0.0980	0.2275	2.6478	9.6735
2013	0.1944	0.1401	0.0131	1.1713	0.0967	0.2437	2.9895	12.6593
2014	0.2061	0.1453	0.0134	1.1869	0.0910	0.2931	2.6470	9.6084
2015	0.2032	0.1370	0.0114	1.2072	0.0891	0.2618	2.7664	10.4820
2016	0.2060	0.1472	0.0119	1.0959	0.0942	0.2702	2.4988	7.2726
2008-2016	0.2070	0.1454	0.0106	1.3844	0.0919	0.2687	2.7955	10.4642
Internal R&D intensity								
2008	0.0232	0.0039	0.0000	0.2121	0.0006	0.0173	2.8046	7.0817
2009	0.0264	0.0035	0.0000	0.2369	0.0006	0.0217	2.7841	7.0106
2010	0.0241	0.0031	0.0000	0.2073	0.0006	0.0217	2.7121	6.5450
2011	0.0243	0.0035	0.0000	0.2094	0.0006	0.0227	2.7120	6.5834
2012	0.0247	0.0029	0.0000	0.2299	0.0005	0.0229	2.7919	7.1342
2013	0.0235	0.0033	0.0000	0.2235	0.0005	0.0208	2.7610	7.1791
2014	0.0231	0.0033	0.0000	0.2178	0.0005	0.0200	2.7340	7.1053
2015	0.0237	0.0030	0.0000	0.1936	0.0004	0.0266	2.4587	5.5275
2016	0.0231	0.0029	0.0000	0.1841	0.0004	0.0249	2.4470	5.4164
2008-2016	0.0240	0.0032	0.0000	0.2369	0.0005	0.0227	2.7927	7.2378
Share of R&D employees								
2008	0.0191	0.0029	0.0000	0.1862	0.0004	0.0144	2.8258	7.3473
2009	0.0197	0.0037	0.0000	0.1786	0.0004	0.0189	2.7292	6.8741
2010	0.0206	0.0037	0.0000	0.1918	0.0004	0.0183	2.7397	6.9838
2011	0.0214	0.0034	0.0000	0.1933	0.0004	0.0198	2.7196	6.7023
2012	0.0213	0.0034	0.0000	0.2002	0.0005	0.0193	2.7525	7.0105
2013	0.0192	0.0037	0.0000	0.1892	0.0004	0.0182	2.8037	7.5690
2014	0.0195	0.0036	0.0000	0.1917	0.0004	0.0174	2.7795	7.4378
2015	0.0203	0.0032	0.0000	0.1930	0.0004	0.0192	2.6343	6.4761
2016	0.0202	0.0027	0.0000	0.1899	0.0004	0.0199	2.6447	6.4926
2008-2016	0.0201	0.0034	0.0000	0.2002	0.0004	0.0183	2.8049	7.3411
GVA rate								
2008	0.4792	0.4688	0.0458	0.8860	0.3631	0.5882	0.0287	-0.3635
2009	0.4784	0.4722	0.0739	0.8620	0.3688	0.5771	0.1001	-0.4297
2010	0.4742	0.4504	0.0882	0.7817	0.3697	0.5674	-0.0012	-0.6227
2011	0.4679	0.4481	0.0459	0.7807	0.3569	0.5721	-0.0726	-0.5455
2012	0.4750	0.4653	0.0492	0.7841	0.3610	0.5939	-0.1211	-0.5502
2013	0.4789	0.4596	0.0605	0.7954	0.3781	0.5927	-0.0405	-0.5332
2014	0.4799	0.4723	0.0523	0.8157	0.3718	0.5884	-0.0636	-0.5291
2015	0.4838	0.4617	0.1026	0.8403	0.3670	0.5978	0.0890	-0.6474
2016	0.4846	0.4713	0.1230	0.7844	0.3738	0.5916	0.0173	-0.7312
2008-2016	0.4780	0.4631	0.0458	0.8860	0.3670	0.5866	-0.0073	-0.4579

continued

| Economic key indicator y | | | | | | | | |
Year	Mean	Median	Min	Max	Q_1	Q_3	Skewness	Kurtosis
Growth of working population								
2008-2016	0.0254	0.0205	-0.3763	0.3393	-0.0512	0.1129	-0.2320	0.3135
Labour productivity p.c.								
2008	83,714	58,713	20,113	568,205	43,433	89,709	3.5559	15.4814
2009	80,662	54,075	18,989	573,754	40,740	82,131	3.6039	15.9809
2010	86,576	57,059	19,804	577,276	43,595	96,779	3.2723	12.9202
2011	86,779	59,897	20,773	608,305	45,196	97,475	3.7824	18.0996
2012	87,675	60,133	21,499	596,640	45,705	96,739	3.5958	16.5577
2013	89,753	61,721	20,852	630,222	46,046	96,315	3.7517	17.6535
2014	90,118	63,410	21,846	633,637	48,607	100,820	4.0163	20.4509
2015	96,000	66,191	23,383	644,676	51,370	109,415	3.5961	16.3852
2016	97,914	68,836	23,837	660,073	51,159	109,285	3.6413	16.5231
2008-2016	88,799	59,897	18,989	66,0073	45,991	96,803	3.7307	17.3894
Labour productivity p.h.								
2008	51.6057	36.3282	14.3602	463.3060	31.0183	51.7074	5.6110	35.6733
2009	51.3303	36.2651	13.8568	470.3569	30.7558	56.2915	5.4967	34.3859
2010	54.8477	37.4930	14.5352	469.7346	30.7674	58.5954	4.8999	27.8048
2011	54.8121	37.5007	15.5386	504.7401	30.9396	56.3481	5.7151	36.9783
2012	56.3741	38.6033	16.5086	499.3387	31.8539	60.6704	5.4545	34.2123
2013	58.1160	40.6606	16.4775	538.8513	33.8150	61.3120	5.6866	36.3289
2014	58.7549	40.8332	17.5250	538.3009	35.7346	61.9106	5.8460	38.2331
2015	60.9196	42.2494	18.6414	545.7635	36.4462	62.8906	5.5248	34.6680
2016	63.1494	43.0463	19.2219	559.4446	36.4785	64.3460	5.4108	33.4357
2008-2016	56.6567	39.6446	13.8568	559.4446	33.9144	59.9764	5.6701	36.4428
Net import intensity								
2008	0.1783	-0.0069	-1.8850	10.0502	-0.0428	-0.0034	5.1643	30.3137
2009	0.2097	-0.0052	-1.9642	11.9215	-0.0386	-0.0023	5.4430	33.8348
2010	0.1985	-0.0064	-2.0627	12.2980	-0.0425	-0.0006	6.0411	40.4506
2011	0.2881	-0.0055	-2.3804	15.3353	-0.0286	0.0031	5.7782	36.4375
2012	0.2413	-0.0027	-2.5228	15.4300	-0.0421	-0.0027	6.0742	40.4449
2013	0.2591	-0.0078	-2.1258	16.8597	-0.0643	0.0147	6.3208	42.7579
2014	0.2344	-0.0121	-2.4746	15.6015	-0.0703	-0.0092	5.9848	39.1775
2015	0.1652	-0.0121	-2.6442	12.4731	-0.0850	-0.0121	5.7149	37.7941
2016	0.1267	-0.0131	-3.3450	11.2043	-0.0363	-0.0131	5.2493	34.6466
2008-2016	0.2112	-0.0121	-3.3450	16.8597	-0.0488	-0.0027	6.2108	43.7853
Share of imported input								
2008	0.1834	0.1330	0.0218	0.7231	0.0854	0.2495	1.4618	2.1279
2009	0.1773	0.1288	0.0210	0.7415	0.0795	0.2403	1.8248	3.9068
2010	0.1956	0.1476	0.0203	0.7140	0.0848	0.2869	1.4522	2.3560
2011	0.1974	0.1432	0.0186	0.7641	0.0879	0.2890	1.4350	2.5109
2012	0.2042	0.1524	0.0188	0.7725	0.0946	0.2827	1.4617	2.5433
2013	0.2043	0.1442	0.0358	0.7610	0.0959	0.2921	1.5133	2.7375
2014	0.2007	0.1453	0.0328	0.7356	0.0937	0.2925	1.4219	2.2985
2015	0.2052	0.1424	0.0326	0.7119	0.0962	0.3071	1.2011	1.3309

continued

| Economic key indicator y | | | | | | | | |
Year	Mean	Median	Min	Max	Q_1	Q_3	Skewness	Kurtosis
2016	0.2074	0.1444	0.0295	0.7695	0.0955	0.3053	1.6098	2.9522
2008-2016	0.1973	0.1424	0.0186	0.7725	0.0905	0.2904	1.5176	2.6939

Table A.8 Summary statistics of the economic key indicators in the German economy from 2008 to 2016; GVA, Gross Value Added; Max, Maximum; Min, Minimum; p.c., per capita; p.h., per hour; Q_1, 25th percentile; Q_3, 75th percentile; R&D, Research and Development

A.5 Outlier thresholds of the sustainable development key indicators

Environmental key indicator y	Lower threshold θ_{min}	Upper threshold θ_{max}
Growth of air emissions	-0.5912	0.5740
Air emissions intensity	-305.1278[†]	619.6294
Growth of primary energy consumption	-0.4546	0.4012
Energy intensity	-4.7559[†]	10.5097
Growth of water use	-0.4870	0.4754
Water intensity	-3.3779[†]	6.1136
Growth of waste water	-0.4823	0.4286
Waste water intensity	-1.5134[†]	2.8812
Growth of hazardous waste	-0.9767	0.8390
Hazardous waste intensity	-8.6396[†]	15.9854
Environmental tax intensity	-0.0121[†]	0.0297

Table A.9 Environmental key indicators' upper and lower outlier thresholds; [†], theoretical threshold (domain ≥ 0)

Social key indicator y	Lower threshold θ_{min}	Upper threshold θ_{max}
Growth of compensation of employees	-0.1957	0.7095
Growth of employees	-0.3420	0.4444
Average compensation of employees p.c.	-4,463.27[†]	90,748.08
Average compensation of employees p.h.	2.9932	57.4291
Labour share	-0.0420[†]	1.1488

| | continued | |
Social key indicator y	Lower threshold θ_{min}	Upper threshold θ_{max}
Growth of socially-insured employees	-0.3416	0.5031
Growth of marginally-employed employees	-0.6498	0.3889
Share of marginally-employed employees	-0.2668†	0.5567
Growth of female socially-insured employees	-0.3579	0.5555
Quota of gender difference	-0.1376	0.5073
Growth of female marginally-employed employees	-0.7346	0.2710
Quota of gender difference of marginally-employed employees	-0.1802	0.5465
Growth of severely-disabled employees	-0.3376	0.7802
Quota of severely-disabled employees	0.2546	1.3949
Growth of apprentices	-0.6041	0.4186
Share of apprentices	0.0014	0.0976
VAT intensity	-0.1519	0.2771
Intensity of net taxes on products	-0.0328	0.0726
CIT intensity	-0.0058†	0.0163
Local business tax intensity	-0.0130†	0.0449

Table A.10 Social key indicators' upper and lower outlier thresholds; †, theoretical threshold (domain ≥ 0); CIT, Corporate Income Tax; p.c., per capita; p.h., per hour; VAT, Value Added Tax

Economic key indicator y	Lower threshold θ_{min}	Upper threshold θ_{max}
Gross capital productivity	-0.4969†	1.3362
Net capital productivity	-0.9346†	2.5589
Degree of modernity	0.3638	0.6841
Consumed capital productivity	-8.8522†	24.5445
Investment intensity	-0.1733†	0.5340
Internal R&D intensity	-0.0329†	0.0561
Share of R&D employees	-0.0264†	0.0451
GVA rate	0.0376	0.9160
Growth of working population	-0.2974	0.3591

		continued
Economic key indicator y	Lower threshold θ_{min}	Upper threshold θ_{max}
Labour productivity p.c.	-30,228.50[†]	17,3022.17
Labour productivity p.h.	-5.1786[†]	99.0694
Net import intensity	-0.1180	0.0665
Share of imported input	-0.2093	0.5902

Table A.11 Economic key indicators' upper and lower outlier thresholds; [†], theoretical threshold (domain ≥ 0); GVA, Gross Value Added; p.c., per capita; p.h., per hour; R&D, Research and Development

A.6   Normality tests of z-score scaled sustainable development key indicators

Z-score scaled environmental key indicator y_z	SW statistic	SW p-values	KS statistic	KS p-values
Reduction of air emissions	0.9666	0.0891	0.1242	0.2944
Air emissions efficiency	0.6910	0.0000	0.2928	0.0001
Reduction of primary energy consumption	0.9694	0.1235	0.0900	0.6973
Energy efficiency	0.7343	0.0000	0.2504	0.0009
Reduction of water use	0.9876	0.7890	0.0485	0.9986
Water efficiency	0.6909	0.0000	0.2875	0.0002
Reduction of waste water	0.9828	0.5331	0.0614	0.9734
Waste water efficiency	0.7558	0.0000	0.2234	0.0077
Reduction of hazardous waste	0.9618	0.0512	0.0886	0.7148
Hazardous waste efficiency	0.7350	0.0000	0.2759	0.0004
Environmental tax intensity	0.8254	0.0000	0.1747	0.0471

Table A.12 Z-score scaled environmental key indicators' average test statistics and p-values of the Shapiro-Wilk (SW) and the Kolmogorov-Smirnov (KS) tests from 2008 to 2016

Z-score scaled social key indicator y_z	SW statistic	SW p-values	KS statistic	KS p-values
Growth of compensation of employees	0.9815	0.4721	0.0788	0.8357
Growth of employees	0.9887	0.8408	0.0808	0.8131

continued

Z-score scaled social key indicator y_z	SW statistic	SW p-values	KS statistic	KS p-values
Average compensation of employees p.c.	0.9589	0.0400	0.0984	0.5538
Average compensation of employees p.h.	0.9380	0.0045	0.1638	0.0921
Labour share	0.9749	0.2863	0.0996	0.5502
Growth of socially-insured employees	0.9838	0.5887	0.0727	0.8744
Reduction of marginally-employed employees	0.9576	0.0313	0.0831	0.7536
Share of non-marginally-employed employees	0.8293	0.0000	0.1805	0.0390
Growth of female socially-insured employees	0.9864	0.7251	0.0587	0.9747
Quota of gender equality	0.9615	0.0519	0.0822	0.7611
Reduction of female marginally-employed employees	0.9565	0.0277	0.1082	0.4322
Quota of gender equality of marginally-employed employees	0.9707	0.1556	0.0845	0.7348
Growth of severely-disabled employees	0.9632	0.0604	0.1022	0.5367
Quota of severely-disabled employees	0.9866	0.7263	0.0641	0.9284
Growth of apprentices	0.9896	0.8793	0.0577	0.9784
Share of apprentices	0.9627	0.0838	0.1245	0.2901
VAT intensity	0.9829	0.5564	0.0744	0.8541
Intensity of net taxes on products	0.9319	0.0022	0.1439	0.1597
CIT intensity	0.8830	0.0004	0.1381	0.2397
Local business tax intensity	0.9501	0.0273	0.0996	0.5967

Table A.13 Z-score scaled social key indicators' average test statistics and p-values of the Shapiro-Wilk (SW) and the Kolmogorov-Smirnov (KS) tests from 2008 to 2016; CIT, Corporate Income Tax; p.c., per capita; p.h., per hour; VAT, Value Added Tax

Z-score scaled economic key indicator y_z	SW statistic	SW p-values	KS statistic	KS p-values
Gross capital productivity	0.8404	0.0000	0.1853	0.0303
Net capital productivity	0.8740	0.0000	0.1601	0.0815
Degree of modernity	0.9810	0.4672	0.0761	0.8321
Consumed capital productivity	0.8496	0.0000	0.1786	0.0500
Investment intensity	0.8706	0.0000	0.1830	0.0348

continued

Z-score scaled economic key indicator y_z	SW statistic	SW p-values	KS statistic	KS p-values
Internal R&D intensity	0.7304	0.0000	0.2659	0.0004
Share of R&D employees	0.7197	0.0000	0.2820	0.0001
GVA rate	0.9864	0.7148	0.0700	0.8931
Working population growth	0.9895	0.8773	0.0545	0.9929
Labour productivity p.c.	0.8548	0.0000	0.1831	0.0382
Labour productivity p.h.	0.8568	0.0000	0.2421	0.0021
Net import intensity	0.8666	0.0000	0.2030	0.0203
Share of imported input	0.8839	0.0000	0.1737	0.0502

Table A.14 Z-score scaled economic key indicators' average test statistics and p-values of the Shapiro-Wilk (SW) and the Kolmogorov-Smirnov (KS) tests from 2008 to 2016; GVA, Gross Value Added; p.c., per capita; p.h., per hour; R&D, Research and Development

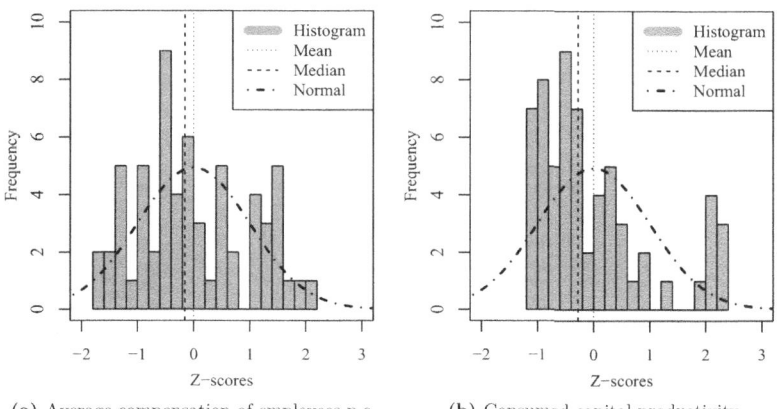

(a) Average compensation of employees p.c.   (b) Consumed capital productivity

Figure A.1 Frequency distribution of z-score scaled average compensation of employees per capita (p.c.) and consumed capital productivity in the German economy in 2016

A.7 Sensitivities by the four composite sustainable development measures

Rank	Environmental subindex			Social subindex			Economic subindex			Overall MLSDI c_1		
	$\alpha = 1.5$	$\alpha = 3$	$\alpha = \infty$	$\alpha = 1.5$	$\alpha = 3$	$\alpha = \infty$	$\alpha = 1.5$	$\alpha = 3$	$\alpha = \infty$	$\alpha = 1.5$	$\alpha = 3$	$\alpha = \infty$
1	95	95	95	62-63	66	66	62-63	74-75	21	69-70	62-63	21
2	61	96	96	66	69-70	69-70	71	62-63	26	62-63	69-70	66
3	96	61	61	69-70	62-63	62-63	74-75	71	72	33	66	29
4	18	33	33	21	21	64	26	26	29	66	29-30	29-30
5	27	18	13-15	65	64	21	33	72	29-30	27	29	69-70
6	33	52	18	64	65	65	19	19	78	28	26	30
7	58	27	49	29-30	29-30	30	72	33	30	29-30	21	26
8	94	94	52	29	29	29-30	69-70	73	20	29	33	62-63
9	77	58	94	71	30	29	73	21	62-63	26	30	20
10	28	77	27	31-32	31-32	31-32	29	29	71	30	71	28
11	79	28	A-S	30	20	20	29-30	29-30	74-75	31-32	27	33
12	69-70	90-92	58	20	71	71	21	30	66	71	28	27
13	73	47	28	28	28	28	30	69-70	19	21	73	C
14	90-92	46	17	D	27	93	27	20	33	73	31-32	22
15	47	79	I	27	59-60	59-60	28	66	C	59-60	64	19
16	46	49	77	59-60	D	27	20	27	27	22	59-60	A-S
17	59-60	69-70	90-92	46	26	A-S	24	28	28	64	58	64
18	66	93	69-70	22	A-S	26	31-32	24	L	58	72	31-32

continued

Rank	Environmental subindex			Social subindex			Economic subindex			Overall MLSDI c_1		
	$\alpha=1.5$	$\alpha=3$	$\alpha=\infty$	$\alpha=1.5$	$\alpha=3$	$\alpha=\infty$	$\alpha=1.5$	$\alpha=3$	$\alpha=\infty$	$\alpha=1.5$	$\alpha=3$	$\alpha=\infty$
19	93	73	73	A-S	46	G-S	22	31-32	73	46	74-75	71
20	G-S	G-S	47	C	C	C	C	78	69-70	C	22	73
21	64	13-15	79	52	22	D	66	C	22	79	46	59-60
22	52	59-60	22	37-39	G-S	he	F	22	31-32	95	C	72
23	31-32	66	G-S	he	he	46	80-82	F	24	25	79	25
24	30	64	O	G-S	52	22	58	80-82	A-S	25	65	13-15
25	29-30	31-32	93	25	37-39	52	59-60	58	77	65	13-15	52
26	29	30	C	26	25	37-39	78	59-60	80-82	96	95	G-S
27	A-S	O	25	47	47	25	13-15	79	25	13-15	F	65
28	86	29-30	30	80-82	93	47	25	23	59-60	74-75	A-S	58
29	65	29	46	10-12	80-82	19	79	13-15	D	G-S	47	he
30	25	A-S	66	33	58	80-82	23	45	F	A-S	52	95
31	P	I	59-60	74-75	10-12	86	45	96	he	F	25	46
32	O	86	64	45	13-15	58	46	25	23	45	80-82	L
33	13-15	25	29-30	17	79	79	96	46	79	52	G-S	79
34	49	65	01	F	45	33	95	D	45	90-92	96	93
35	he	53	A	90-92	33	10-12	64	95	G-S	he	45	17
36	26	P	10-12	49	17	45	53	A-S	58	80-82	he	47
37	I	22	29	13-15	90-92	90-92	47	53	96	72	49	77

continued

Rank	Environmental subindex			Social subindex			Economic subindex			Overall MLSDI c_1		
	$\alpha = 1.5$	$\alpha = 3$	$\alpha = \infty$	$\alpha = 1.5$	$\alpha = 3$	$\alpha = \infty$	$\alpha = 1.5$	$\alpha = 3$	$\alpha = \infty$	$\alpha = 1.5$	$\alpha = 3$	$\alpha = \infty$
38	02	he	23	79	86	13-15	D	64	53	49	90-92	90-92
39	45	45	P	86	74-75	74-75	A-S	47	13-15	86	53	49
40	L	26	31-32	19	F	17	I	L	36	94	77	24
41	22	F	20	58	19	F	he	he	46	77	86	96
42	87-88	02	26	93	49	49	16	I	95	93	93	23
43	C	L	21	23	36	72	65	65	17	53	78	F
44	53	87-88	86	36	73	O	49	G-S	37-39	18	94	78
45	F	62-63	53	24	23	73	G-S	49	I	I	L	86
46	62-63	78	24	87-88	72	36	17	77	52	61	18	10-12
47	78	C	65	16	24	23	02	16	B	P	I	45
48	21	80-82	he	95	16	87-88	94	52	51	78	O	80-82
49	80-82	21	19	72	87-88	51	52	02	64	O	87-88	O
50	71	71	36	O	O	24	86	94	90-92	87-88	P	I
51	50	72	02	51	53	53	61	36	86	L	02	36
52	72	A	45	53	51	16	90-92	86	47	02	61	53
53	A	74-75	F	03	95	95	10-12	18	87-88	16	16	37-39
54	74-75	03	L	77	L	L	36	90-92	10-12	10-12	20	94
55	16	50	87-88	73	77	77	B	B	50	24	03	87-88
56	03	16	16	P	03	P	P	17	P	20	10-12	74-75

continued

Rank	Environmental subindex			Social subindex			Economic subindex			Overall MLSDI c_1		
	$\alpha=1.5$	$\alpha=3$	$\alpha=\infty$	$\alpha=1.5$	$\alpha=3$	$\alpha=\infty$	$\alpha=1.5$	$\alpha=3$	$\alpha=\infty$	$\alpha=1.5$	$\alpha=3$	$\alpha=\infty$
57	10-12	01	51	96	I	I	L	P	94	03	A	P
58	01	10-12	62-63	I	P	03	03	37-39	65	D	37-39	18
59	37-39	37-39	B	94	96	94	18	03	03	A	36	51
60	51	36	78	L	94	96	77	61	49	37-39	D	D
61	36	51	37-39	50	18	B	37-39	10-12	01	17	23	16
62	B	17	03	78	B	01	87-88	87-88	A	36	24	01
63	17	23	80-82	18	50	A	51	O	93	23	01	A
64	D	B	50	A	A	50	A	A	18	50	50	B
65	24	20	71	01	01	18	O	01	O	51	17	03
66	23	D	72	B	02	02	01	51	02	19	51	02
67	20	24	D	02	78	78	93	93	16	01	19	61
68	19	19	74-75	61	61	61	50	50	61	B	B	50

Table A.15 Ranking of the economic objects in Statistical Classification of Economic Activities in the European Community (NACE) codes by the four composite measures and the three outlier detection methods in the German economy in 2016; see Table A.1 for denotation of section codes; α, outlier coefficient; MLSDI, Multilevel Sustainable Development Index

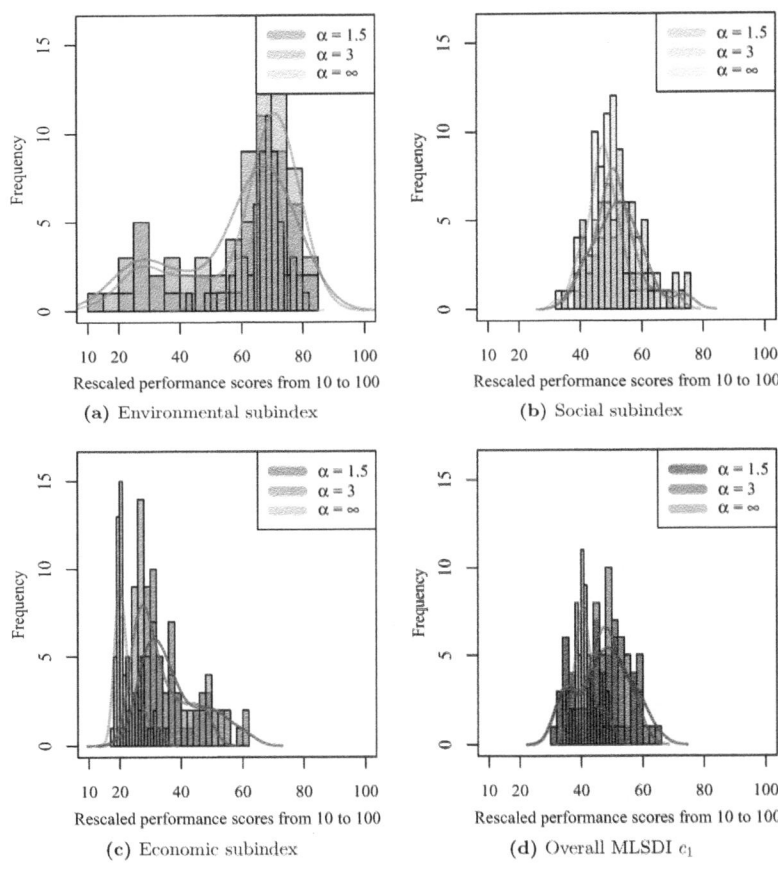

Figure A.2 Frequency distribution by the four composite measures and the three outlier detection methods in rescaled performance scores in the German economy in 2016; α, outlier coefficient; MLSDI, Multilevel Sustainable Development Index

Rank	Environmental subindex			Social subindex			Economic subindex			Overall MLSDI c_1		
	PCA	PTA	MRMRB	PCA	PTA	MRMRB	PCA	PTA	MRMRB	PCA	PTA	MRMRB
1	95	95	95	66	66	62-63	62-63	62-63	62-63	69-70	69-70	69-70
2	61	61	61	69-70	69-70	66	71	71	71	62-63	62-63	62-63
3	96	96	96	62-63	62-63	69-70	74-75	74-75	74-75	33	33	33
4	18	18	18	21	21	21	26	26	26	27	27	66
5	33	33	27	65	65	65	33	33	33	66	66	27
6	58	58	33	64	64	64	72	72	19	28	28	28
7	27	27	58	31-32	31-32	29-30	19	19	72	29-30	29-30	29-30
8	94	94	94	20	20	29	29	69-70	69-70	29	29	29
9	77	28	77	29	29-30	71	21	73	73	21	26	26
10	28	77	28	29-30	29	31-32	29-30	29	29	26	21	30
11	69-70	69-70	79	71	71	30	69-70	21	29-30	30	30	31-32
12	73	73	69-70	28	28	20	73	29-30	21	31-32	31-32	71
13	79	79	73	46	27	28	30	30	30	73	73	21
14	90-92	90-92	90-92	27	46	D	27	27	27	71	58	73
15	47	47	47	30	A-S	27	20	20	28	22	64	59-60
16	59-60	59-60	46	D	30	59-60	28	28	20	64	59-60	22
17	66	66	59-60	A-S	D	46	31-32	31-32	24	58	22	64
18	93	93	66	22	22	22	24	24	31-32	59-60	71	58
19	46	13-15	93	C	C	A-S	22	22	22	95	95	46
20	64	64	G-S	59-60	59-60	C	C	C	C	C	46	C

continued

Rank	Environmental subindex			Social subindex			Economic subindex			Overall MLSDI c_1		
	PCA	PTA	MRMRB	PCA	PTA	MRMRB	PCA	PTA	MRMRB	PCA	PTA	MRMRB
21	G-S	46	64	52	52	52	66	66	66	46	C	79
22	13-15	G-S	52	G-S	G-S	37-39	F	F	F	25	79	95
23	52	52	31-32	he	he	he	59-60	58	80-82	65	25	25
24	31-32	31-32	30	26	25	G-S	58	59-60	58	79	13-15	47
25	A-S	25	29-30	37-39	37-39	25	25	80-82	59-60	13-15	65	65
26	25	A-S	29	25	26	26	80-82	78	78	96	96	96
27	29-30	30	A-S	10-12	10-12	47	78	25	13-15	47	47	13-15
28	P	29-30	86	13-15	47	80-82	23	13-15	25	A-S	A-S	74-75
29	30	I	65	80-82	17	10-12	13-15	45	79	G-S	G-S	G-S
30	29	P	25	47	45	33	45	79	23	90-92	45	A-S
31	86	29	P	17	13-15	74-75	79	23	45	45	52	F
32	I	86	O	45	80-82	45	46	46	46	52	90-92	45
33	O	O	13-15	90-92	33	17	96	96	96	he	F	52
34	65	65	49	33	74-75	F	64	64	95	F	he	90-92
35	49	49	he	74-75	90-92	90-92	95	95	64	74-75	61	he
36	26	26	26	58	F	49	D	D	53	49	94	80-82
37	22	22	I	F	36	13-15	53	53	47	94	77	72
38	he	he	02	36	79	79	A-S	47	D	80-82	49	49
39	45	45	45	49	58	86	47	A-S	A-S	61	86	86

continued

Rank	Environmental subindex			Social subindex			Economic subindex			Overall MLSDI c_1		
	PCA	PTA	MRMRB	PCA	PTA	MRMRB	PCA	PTA	MRMRB	PCA	PTA	MRMRB
40	L	L	L	79	93	19	65	65	I	77	74-75	94
41	02	02	22	93	86	58	he	he	he	86	80-82	77
42	C	C	87-88	23	49	93	17	G-S	16	18	18	93
43	87-88	87-88	C	86	19	23	G-S	16	65	93	93	53
44	53	53	53	19	23	36	16	17	49	72	O	18
45	21	21	F	95	95	24	I	49	G-S	53	72	I
46	F	F	62-63	16	O	87-88	49	I	17	O	I	61
47	62-63	62-63	78	24	16	16	61	61	02	I	P	P
48	78	50	21	O	87-88	95	36	94	94	P	53	78
49	50	78	80-82	87-88	24	72	94	36	52	87-88	87-88	O
50	80-82	80-82	71	53	72	O	52	52	86	L	L	87-88
51	71	71	50	72	03	51	90-92	90-92	61	78	78	L
52	A	A	72	51	53	53	86	86	90-92	02	02	02
53	16	16	A	03	51	03	L	L	10-12	16	16	16
54	03	03	74-75	73	77	77	10-12	02	36	24	24	10-12
55	72	72	16	77	73	73	02	77	B	20	10-12	24
56	10-12	10-12	03	P	P	P	77	B	P	10-12	D	20
57	01	01	10-12	96	96	96	18	P	L	D	20	03
58	74-75	B	01	1	1	I	P	10-12	03	17	36	D

continued

Rank	Environmental subindex			Social subindex			Economic subindex			Overall MLSDI c_1		
	PCA	PTA	MRMRB	PCA	PTA	MRMRB	PCA	PTA	MRMRB	PCA	PTA	MRMRB
59	B	74-75	37-39	94	94	94	B	37-39	18	36	17	A
60	36	36	51	18	18	L	51	18	77	50	50	37-39
61	17	17	36	L	L	50	37-39	51	37-39	03	03	17
62	D	D	B	50	50	78	03	03	87-88	23	37-39	36
63	37-39	24	17	B	B	18	O	O	51	37-39	23	23
64	24	37-39	D	A	A	A	87-88	87-88	A	A	A	50
65	51	51	24	01	01	01	93	93	O	B	B	51
66	23	23	23	78	78	B	A	A	01	B	B	19
67	20	20	20	02	02	02	01	01	93	01	51	01
68	19	19	19	61	61	61	50	50	50	19	19	B

Table A.16 Ranking of the economic objects in Statistical Classification of Economic Activities in the European Community (NACE) codes by the four composite measures and the three weighting methods in the German economy in 2016; see Table A.1 for denotation of section codes; MLSDI, Multilevel Sustainable Development Index; MRMRB, Maximum Relevance Minimum Redundancy Backward algorithm; PCA, Principal Component Analysis; PTA, Partial Triadic Analysis

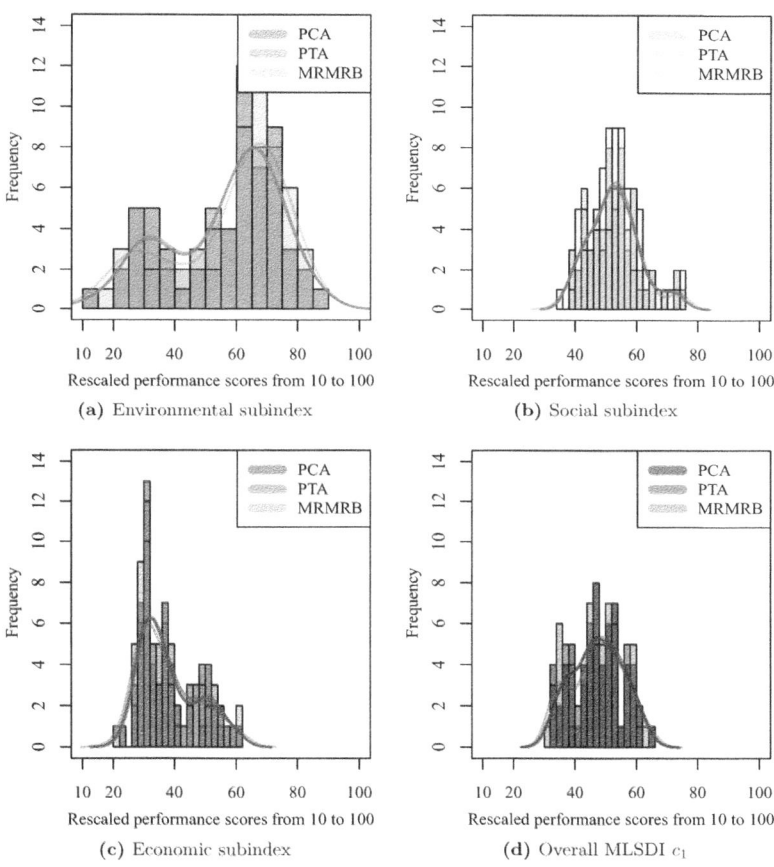

Figure A.3 Frequency distribution of the four composite measures by the three weighting methods in rescaled performance scores in the German economy in 2016; MLSDI, Multilevel Sustainable Development Index; MRMRB, Maximum Relevance Minimum Redundancy Backward algorithm; PCA, Principal Component Analysis; PTA, Partial Triadic Analysis

References

A4S. (2018). A4S knowledge hub: Guides. Retrieved November 21, 2019, from https://www.accountingforsustainability.org/content/a4s/corporate/en/knowledge-hub.html?tab1=guides

Aggarwal, C. C. (2017). *Outlier analysis* (2nd Ed.). Cham: Springer.

Aggarwal, C. C. & Sathe, S. (2015). Theoretical foundations and algorithms for outlier ensembles. *SIGKDD Explorations, 17*(1), 24–47. doi:10.1145/2830544.2830549

Aggarwal, C. C. & Sathe, S. (2017). *Outlier ensembles: An introduction.* Cham: Springer.

Agyeman, J. (2005). *Sustainable communities and the challenge of environmental justice.* New York: New York University Press.

AIChE & IfS. (2019). American Institute of Chemical Engineers (AIChE) Sustainability Index. Retrieved November 21, 2019, from https://www.aiche.org/ifs/resources/sustainability-index

Ajmal, M. M., Khan, M., Hussain, M. & Helo, P. (2018). Conceptualizing and incorporating social sustainability in the business world. *International Journal of Sustainable Development & World Ecology. 25*(4), 327–339. doi:10.1080/13504509.2017.1408714

Alcácer, V. & Cruz-Machado, V. (2019). Scanning the industry 4.0: A literature review on technologies for manufacturing systems. *Engineering Science and Technology, an International Journal, 22*(3), 899–919. doi:10.1016/j.jestch.2019.01.006

Allen, C., Metternicht, G. & Wiedmann, T. O. (2017). An iterative framework for national scenario modelling for the Sustainable Development Goals (SDGs). *Sustainable Development, 25*(5), 372–385. doi:10.1002/sd.1662

Allen, C., Metternicht, G. & Wiedmann, T. O. (2019). Prioritising SDG targets: Assessing baselines, gaps and interlinkages. *Sustainability Science, 14*(2), 421–438. doi:10.1007/s11625-018-0596-8

Almássy, D. & Pintér, L. (2018). Environmental governance indicators and indices in support of policy-making. In S. Bell & S. Morse (Eds.), *Routledge handbook of sustainability indicators* (Chap. 13, pp. 204–223). Abingdon: Routledge.

Amor-Esteban, V., Galindo-Villardón, M.-P. & García-Sánchez, I.-M. (2018). Useful information for stakeholder engagement: A multivariate proposal of an Industrial Corporate Social Responsibility Practices Index. *Sustainable Development, 26*(6), 620–637. doi:10.1002/sd.1732

Antheaume, N. (2004). Valuing external costs - From theory to practice: Implications for full cost environmental accounting. *European Accounting Review, 13*(3), 443–464. doi:10.1080/0963818042000216802

© The Author(s) 2021
C. Lemke, *Accounting and Statistical Analyses for Sustainable Development*, Sustainable Management, Wertschöpfung und Effizienz, https://doi.org/10.1007/978-3-658-33246-4

Antonini, C. & Larrinaga, C. (2017). Planetary boundaries and sustainability indicators: A survey of corporate reporting boundaries. *Sustainable Development*, *25*(2), 123–137. doi:10.1002/sd.1667

Aşıcı, A. A. (2013). Economic growth and its impact on environment: A panel data analysis. *Ecological Indicators*, *24*, 324–333. doi:10.1016/j.ecolind.2012.06.019

Atkinson, A. B. (2015). *Inequality: What can be done?* Cambridge: Harvard University Press.

Atkinson, G. D. (2000). Measuring corporate sustainability. *Journal of Environmental Planning and Management*, *43*(2), 235–252. doi:10.1080/09640560010694

Atkisson, A. & Hatcher, R. L. (2001). The Compass Index of Sustainability: Prototype for a comprehensive sustainability information system. *Journal of Environmental Assessment Policy and Management*, *3*(4), 509–532. doi:10.1142/S1464333201000820

BA. (2011). *Arbeitsmarkt in Zahlen Beschäftigungsstatistik: Schwerbehinderte Menschen in Beschäftigung 2008*. Nürnberg: Bundesagentur für Arbeit (BA).

BA. (2012). *Arbeitsmarkt in Zahlen Beschäftigungsstatistik: Schwerbehinderte Menschen in Beschäftigung 2009*. Nürnberg: Bundesagentur für Arbeit (BA).

BA. (2013). *Arbeitsmarkt in Zahlen Beschäftigungsstatistik: Schwerbehinderte Menschen in Beschäftigung 2010*. Nürnberg: Bundesagentur für Arbeit (BA).

BA. (2014a). *Arbeitsmarkt in Zahlen Beschäftigungsstatistik: Schwerbehinderte Menschen in Beschäftigung 2011*. Nürnberg: Bundesagentur für Arbeit (BA).

BA. (2014b). *Arbeitsmarkt in Zahlen Beschäftigungsstatistik: Schwerbehinderte Menschen in Beschäftigung 2012*. Nürnberg: Bundesagentur für Arbeit (BA).

BA. (2016a). *Arbeitsmarkt in Zahlen Beschäftigungsstatistik: Schwerbehinderte Menschen in Beschäftigung 2013*. Nürnberg: Bundesagentur für Arbeit (BA).

BA. (2016b). *Arbeitsmarkt in Zahlen Beschäftigungsstatistik: Schwerbehinderte Menschen in Beschäftigung 2014*. Nürnberg: Bundesagentur für Arbeit (BA).

BA. (2017). *Arbeitsmarkt in Zahlen Beschäftigungsstatistik: Schwerbehinderte Menschen in Beschäftigung 2015*. Nürnberg: Bundesagentur für Arbeit (BA).

BA. (2018). *Arbeitsmarkt in Zahlen Beschäftigungsstatistik: Schwerbehinderte Menschen in Beschäftigung 2016*. Nürnberg: Bundesagentur für Arbeit (BA).

BA. (2019). *Beschäftigte nach Wirtschaftszweigen (WZ 2008) (Zeitreihe Quartalszahlen) 2018*. Nürnberg: Bundesagentur für Arbeit (BA).

Bachmann, G. (2016). Science for sustainability - A societal and political perspective. In H. Heinrichs, P. Martens, G. Michelsen & A. Wiek (Eds.), *Sustainability science: An introduction* (Chap. 30, pp. 359–367). Dordrecht: Springer.

Bakkes, J. A., van den Born, G. J., Helder, J. C., Swart, R. J., Hope, C. W. & Parker, J. D. (1994). *An overview of environmental indicators: State of the art and perspectives*. Nairobi: United Nations Environment Programme (UNEP), Rijksinstituut voor Volksgezondheid en Milieu (RIVM).

Bansal, P. (2002). The corporate challenges of sustainable development. *Academy of Management Executive*, *16*(2), 122–131. doi:10.5465/AME.2002.7173572

Bansal, P. & Clelland, I. (2004). Talking trash: Legitimacy, impression management, and unsystematic risk in the context of the natural environment. *Academy of Management Journal*, *47*(1), 93–103. doi:10.2307/20159562

Bansal, P. & Song, H.-C. (2017). Similar but not the same: Differentiating corporate sustainability from corporate responsibility. *Academy of Management Annals*, *11*(1), 105–149. doi:10.5465/annals.2015.0095

Barnett, V. & Lewis, T. (1994). *Outliers in statistical data* (3rd Ed.). Chichester: John Wiley & Sons.

Barrios, E. & Komoto, K. (2006). Some approaches to the construction of a sustainable development index for the Philippines. *International Journal of Sustainable Development and World Ecology*, *13*(4), 277–288. doi:10.1080/13504500609469679

Bartelmus, P. (2018). Green accounting: Balancing environment and economy. In S. Bell & S. Morse (Eds.), *Routledge handbook of sustainability indicators* (Chap. 15, pp. 235–243). Abingdon: Routledge.

Barth, M. (2016). Teaching and Learning in Sustainability Science. In H. Heinrichs, P. Martens, G. Michelsen & A. Wiek (Eds.), *Sustainability science: An introduction* (Chap. 27, pp. 325–334). Dordrecht: Springer.

Bartlett, M. S. (1950). Tests of significance in factor analysis. *British Journal of Statistical Psychology*, *3*(2), 77–85. doi:10.1111/j.2044-8317.1950.tb00285.x

Bartlett, M. S. (1951). A further note on tests of significance in factor analysis. *British Journal of Statistical Psychology*, *4*(1), 1–2. doi:10.1111/j.2044-8317.1951.tb00299.x

Baumgartner, R. J. (2014). Managing corporate sustainability and CSR: A conceptual framework combining values, strategies and instruments contributing to sustainable development. *Corporate Social Responsibility and Environmental Management*, *21*(5), 258–271. doi:10.1002/csr.1336

Baumgartner, R. J. & Rauter, R. (2017). Strategic perspectives of corporate sustainability management to develop a sustainable organization. *Journal of Cleaner Production*, *140*(Part 1), 81–92. doi:10.1016/j.jclepro.2016.04.146

Beaujean, A. A. (2015). *Package 'BaylorEdPsych'*. Comprehensive R Archive Network (CRAN).

Beça, P. & Santos, R. (2010). Measuring sustainable welfare: A new approach to the ISEW. *Ecological Economics*, *69*(4), 810–819. doi:10.1016/j.ecolecon.2009.11.031

Becker, W., Saisana, M., Paruolo, P. & Vandecasteele, I. (2017). Weights and importance in composite indicators: Closing the gap. *Ecological Indicators*, *80*, 12–22. doi:10.1016/j.ecolind.2017.03.056

Bell, S. & Morse, S. (2008). *Sustainability indicators: Measuring the immeasurable?* (2nd Ed.). London: Earthscan.

Bell, S. & Morse, S. (2018). What next? In S. Bell & S. Morse (Eds.), *Routledge handbook of sustainability indicators* (Chap. 34, pp. 543–555). Abingdon: Routledge.

Bergman, L. (2005). CGE modeling of environmental policy and resource management. In *Handbook of environmental economics* (Chap. 24, Vol. 3, pp. 1273–1306). Amsterdam: Elsevier.

Berkhout, P. H., Muskens, J. C. & Velthuijsen, J. W. (2000). Defining the rebound effect. *Energy Policy*, *28*(6-7), 425–432. doi:10.1016/S0301-4215(00)00022-7

Biermann, F., Kanie, N. & Kim, R. E. (2017). Global governance by goal-setting: The novel approach of the UN Sustainable Development Goals. *Current Opinion in Environmental Sustainability*, *26-27*, 26–31. doi:10.1016/j.cosust.2017.01.010

Blankers, M., Koeter, M. W. & Schippers, G. M. (2010). Missing data approaches in eHealth research: Simulation study and a tutorial for nonmathematically inclined researchers. *Journal of Medical Internet Research*, *12*(5), e54. doi:10.2196/jmir. 1448

BMJV. (2019a). Sozialgesetzbuch Neuntes Buch: Rehabilitation und Teilhabe von Menschen mit Behinderungen - § 2 Begriffsbestimmungen. Retrieved November 21, 2019, from https://www.sozialgesetzbuch-sgb.de/sgbix/2.html

BMJV. (2019b). Verordnung über das Europäische Abfallverzeichnis. Retrieved November 21, 2019, from https://www.gesetze-im-internet.de/avv/

BMWi. (2019). *Gesundheitswirtschaft Fakten & Zahlen, Ausgabe 2018: Ergebnisse der Gesundheitswirtschaftlichen Gesamtrechnung*. Berlin: Bundesministerium für Wirtschaft und Energie (BMWi).

Boggia, A. & Cortina, C. (2010). Measuring sustainable development using a multicriteria model: A case study. *Journal of Environmental Management*, *91*(11), 2301–2306. doi:10.1016/j.jenvman.2010.06.009

Böhringer, C. & Jochem, P. E. (2007). Measuring the immeasurable - A survey of sustainability indices. *Ecological Economics*, *63*(1), 1–8. doi:10.1016/j.ecolecon. 2007.03.008

Bolcárová, P. & Kološta, S. (2015). Assessment of sustainable development in the EU 27 using aggregated SD index. *Ecological Indicators*, *48*, 699–705. doi:10.1016/j. ecolind.2014.09.001

Bolis, I., Morioka, S. N. & Sznelwar, L. I. (2017). Are we making decisions in a sustainable way? A comprehensive literature review about rationalities for sustainable development. *Journal of Cleaner Production*, *145*, 310–322. doi:10.1016/j.jclepro. 2017.01.025

Bond, A. & Morrison-Saunders, A. (2013). Challenges in determining the effectiveness of sustainability assessment. In A. Bond, A. Morrison-Saunders & R. Howitt (Eds.), *Sustainability assessment: Pluralism, practice and progress* (Chap. 3, pp. 37–50). London: Taylor & Francis.

Bond, A., Pope, J. & Morrison-Saunders, A. (2015). Introducing the roots, evolution and effectiveness of sustainability assessment. In A. Morrison-Saunders, J. Pope & A. Bond (Eds.), *Handbook of sustainability assessment* (Chap. 1, pp. 3–19). Cheltenham: Edward Elgar.

Bondarchik, J., Jabłońska-Sabuka, M., Linnanen, L. & Kauranne, T. (2016). Improving the objectivity of sustainability indices by a novel approach for combining contrasting effects: Happy Planet Index revisited. *Ecological Indicators*, *69*, 400–406. doi:10.1016/j.ecolind.2016.04.044

Bonin, H. (2019). Fachkräftemangel in der Gesamtperspektive. In K. Jacobs, A. Kuhlmey, S. Greß, J. Klauber & A. Schwinger (Eds.), *Pflege-Report 2019: Mehr Personal in der Langzeitpflege - Aber woher?* (Chap. 4, pp. 61–70). Berlin: Springer.

Boron, S. & Murray, K. (2004). Bridging the unsustainability gap: A framework for sustainable development. *Sustainable Development, 12*(2), 65–73. doi:10.1002/sd.231

Bosquet, B. (2000). Environmental tax reform: Does it work? A survey of the empirical evidence. *Ecological Economics, 34*(1), 19–32. doi:10.1016/S0921-8009(00)00173-7

Bossel, H. (1998). *Earth at a crossroads: Paths to a sustainable future.* Cambridge: Cambridge University Press.

Boström, M. (2012). A missing pillar? Challenges in theorizing and practicing social sustainability: Introduction to the special issue. *Sustainability: Science, Practice and Policy, 8*(1), 3–14. doi:10.1080/15487733.2012.11908080

Boulanger, P.-M. & Bréchet, T. (2005). Models for policy-making in sustainable development: The state of the art and perspectives for research. *Ecological Economics, 55*(3), 337–350. doi:10.1016/j.ecolecon.2005.07.033

Bourdakou, M. M., Athanasiadis, E. I. & Spyrou, G. M. (2016). Discovering gene re-ranking efficiency and conserved gene-gene relationships derived from gene co-expression network analysis on breast cancer data. *Nature Scientific Reports, 6*, 20518. doi:10.1038/srep20518

Bravo, G. (2014). The Human Sustainable Development Index: New calculations and a first critical analysis. *Ecological Indicators, 37*(Part A), 145–150. doi:10.1016/j.ecolind.2013.10.020

Bravo, G. (2018). Human Sustainable Development Index. In S. Bell & S. Morse (Eds.), *Routledge handbook of sustainability indicators* (Chap. 18, pp. 284–293). Abingdon: Routledge.

Brockwell, P. J. & Davis, R. A. (2016). *Introduction to time series and forecasting* (3rd Ed.). Basel: Springer.

Buch-Hansen, H. (2018). The prerequisites for a degrowth paradigm shift: Insights from critical political economy. *Ecological Economics, 146*, 157–163. doi:10.1016/j.ecolecon.2017.10.021

Bui, B. & de Villiers, C. (2018). Management control systems to support sustainability and integrated reporting. In C. de Villiers & W. Maroun (Eds.), *Sustainability accounting and integrated reporting* (Chap. 11, pp. 121–148). Abingdon: Routledge.

Bulmer, M. (1979). *Principles of statistics.* New York: Dover.

Cabeza Gutés, M. (1996). The concept of weak sustainability. *Ecological Economics, 17*(3), 147–156. doi:10.1016/S0921-8009(96)80003-6

Caldwell, R. (2003). Models of change agency: A fourfold classification. *British Journal of Management, 14*(2), 131–142. doi:10.1111/1467-8551.00270

Campbell, J. L. (2007). Why would corporations behave in socially responsible ways? An institutional theory of corporate social responsibility. *Academy of Management Review, 32*(3), 946–967. doi:10.5465/amr.2007.25275684

Carpenter, G. & White, P. (2004). Sustainable development: Finding the real business case. *Corporate Environmental Strategy, 11*(2), 51–56.

Carraro, C., Campagnolo, L., Eboli, F., Giove, S., Lanzi, E., Parrado, R., . . . Portale, E. (2013). The FEEM Sustainability Index: An integrated tool for sustainability assessment. In M. G. Erechtchoukova, P. A. Khaiter & P. Golinska (Eds.), *Sustainability appraisal: Quantitative methods and mathematical techniques for environmental performance evaluation* (Chap. 2, pp. 9–32). Berlin: Springer.

Carvalho, H., Govindan, K., Azevedo, S. G. & Cruz-Machado, V. (2017). Modelling green and lean supply chains: An eco-efficiency perspective. *Resources, Conservation and Recycling, 120*, 75–87. doi:10.1016/j.resconrec.2016.09.025

Cash, D. W., Clark, W. C., Alcock, F., Dickson, N. M., Eckley, N., Guston, D. H., . . . Mitchell, R. B. (2003). Knowledge systems for sustainable development. *Proceedings of the National Academy of Sciences, 100*(14), 8086–8091. doi:10. 1073/pnas.1231332100

Castellani, V., Piazzalunga, A. & Sala, S. (2013). Research findings and decision making: The case of renewable energy. *Environmental Sciences Europe, 25*(22). doi:10.1186/2190-4715-25-22

CBS & GNH Research. (2016). *A compass towards a just and harmonious society: GNH survey report.* Thimphu: Centre for Bhutan Studies (CBS), Gross National Happiness (GNH) Research.

Ceballos, G., Ehrlich, P. R., Barnosky, A. D., García, A., Pringle, R. M. & Palmer, T. M. (2015). Accelerated modern human- induced species losses: Entering the sixth mass extinction. *Science Advances, 1*(5), e1400253. doi:10.1126/sciadv.1400253

CEFIC. (2019). Responsible care. Retrieved November 21, 2019, from https://cefic.org/ our-industry/responsible-care/

Charmondusit, K., Phatarachaisakul, S. & Prasertpong, P. (2014). The quantitative eco-efficiency measurement for small and medium enterprise: A case study of wooden toy industry. *Clean Technologies and Environmental Policy, 16*(5), 935–945. doi:10.1007/s10098-013-0693-4

Charnes, A., Cooper, W. W. & Rhodes, E. (1978). Measuring the efficiency of decision making units. *European Journal of Operational Research, 2*, 429–444. doi:10.1016/ 0377-2217(78)90138-8

Chofreh, A. G. & Goni, F. A. (2017). Review of frameworks for sustainability implementation. *Sustainable Development, 25*(3), 180–188. doi:10.1002/sd.1658

Chowdhury, S. & Squire, L. (2006). Setting weights for aggregate indices: An application to the commitment to Development Index and Human Development Index. *Journal of Development Studies, 42*(5), 761–771. doi:10.1080/00220380600741904

Christie, I. & Warburton, D. (2001). *From here to sustainability: Politics in the real world.* London: Earthscan.

Clark, W. C. (2007). Sustainability Science: A room of its own. *Proceedings of the National Academy of Sciences, 104*(6), 1737–1738. doi:10.1073/pnas.0611291104

Clark, W. C., van Kerkhoft, L., Lebel, L. & Gallopín, G. C. (2016). Crafting usable knowledge for sustainable development. *Proceedings of the National Academy of Sciences, 113*(17), 4570–4578. doi:10.1073/pnas.1601266113

Clarkson, M. B. (1995). A stakeholder framework for analyzing and evaluating corporate social performance. *Academy of Management Review, 20*(1), 92–117. doi:10.2307/258888

Clean Energy Wire. (2019). "Dieselgate" - A timeline of Germany's car emissions fraud scandal. Retrieved November 21, 2019, from https://www.cleanenergywire.org/factsheets/dieselgate-timeline-car-emissions-fraud-scandal-germany

Clegg, S. R., Vieira da Cunha, J. & Pina e Cunha, M. (2002). Management paradoxes: A relational view. *Human Relations, 55*(5), 483–503. doi:10.1177/0018726702555001

Cobb, C., Halstead, T. & Rowe, J. (1995). If the GDP is up, why is America down? *Atlantic Monthly, 276*(4), 59–78.

Collins, L. M., Schafer, J. L. & Kam, C.-M. (2001). A comparison of inclusive and restrictive strategies in modern missing data procedures. *Psychological Methods, 6*(4), 330–351. doi:10.1037//1082-989X.6.4.330

Connelly, B. L., Certo, S. T., Ireland, R. D. & Reutzel, C. R. (2011). Signaling theory: A review and assessment. *Journal of Management, 37*(1), 39–67. doi:10.1177/0149206310388419

Conover, W. J. (1980). *Practical nonparametric statistics* (2nd Ed.). New York: John Wiley & Sons.

Cosijn, E. & Ingwersen, P. (2000). Dimensions of relevance. *Information Processing and Management, 36*(4), 533–550. doi:10.1016/S0306-4573(99)00072-2

Costanza, R. & Daly, H. E. (1992). Natural capital and sustainable development. *Conservation Biology, 6*(1), 37–46. doi:10.1046/j.1523-1739.1992.610037.x

Costanza, R., Daly, L., Fioramonti, L., Giovannini, E., Kubiszewski, I., Fogh Mortensen, L., ... Wilkinson, R. (2016). Modelling and measuring sustainable wellbeing in connection with the UN Sustainable Development Goals. *Ecological Economics, 130*, 350–355. doi:10.1016/j.ecolecon.2016.07.009

Costanza, R., Fioramonti, L. & Kubiszewski, I. (2016). The UN Sustainable Development Goals and the dynamics of well-being. *Frontiers in Ecology and the Environment, 14*(2), 59. doi:10.1002/fee.1231

Costanza, R., Fisher, B., Ali, S., Beer, C., Bond, L., Boumans, R., ... Snapp, R. (2007). Quality of life: An approach integrating opportunities, human needs, and subjective well-being. *Ecological Economics, 61*(2-3), 267–276. doi:10.1016/j.ecolecon.2006.02.023

Costanza, R., Hart, M., Kubiszewski, I., Posner, S. & Talberth, J. (2018). Lessons from the history of GDP in the effort to create better indicators of prosperity, well-being and happiness. In S. Bell & S. Morse (Eds.), *Routledge handbook of sustainability indicators* (Chap. 7, pp. 117–123). Abingdon: Routledge.

Costanza, R., Kubiszewski, I., Giovannini, E., Lovins, H., McGlade, J., Pickett, K. E., ... Wilkinson, R. (2014). Time to leave GDP behind. *Nature, 505*(7483), 283–285. doi:10.1038/505283a

Cover, T. M. & Thomas, J. A. (1991). *Elements of information theory*. New York: John Wiley & Sons.

CRAN. (2019). Package 'stats'. Comprehensive R Archive Network (CRAN). Retrieved November 21, 2019, from https://stat.ethz.ch/R-manual/R-devel/library/stats/html/00Index.html

Cubas-Díaz, M. & Martínez Sedano, M. Á. (2018). Measures for sustainable investment decisions and business strategy - A triple bottom line approach. *Business Strategy and the Environment*, *27*(1), 16–38. doi:10.1002/bse.1980

Cucek, L., Klemes, J. J. & Kravanja, Z. (2012). A review of footprint analysis tools for monitoring impacts on sustainability. *Journal of Cleaner Production*, *34*, 9–20. doi:10.1016/j.jclepro.2012.02.036

Curran, M. A. (1996). *Environmental life-cycle assessment*. New York: McGraw-Hill.

Custance, J. & Hillier, H. (1998). Statistical issue in developing indicators of sustainable development. *Journal of the Royal Statistical Society (Series A)*, *161*(3), 281–290. doi:10.1111/1467-985X.00108

Cuthill, M. (2010). Strengthening the "social" in sustainable development: Developing a conceptual framework for social sustainability in a rapid urban growth region in Australia. *Sustainable Development*, *18*(6), 362–373. doi:10.1002/sd.397

Dahl, A. L. (2012). Achievements and gaps in indicators for sustainability. *Ecological Indicators*, *17*, 14–19. doi:10.1016/j.ecolind.2011.04.032

Dahl, A. L. (2018). Contributions to the evolving theory and practice of indicators of sustainability. In S. Bell & S. Morse (Eds.), *Routledge handbook of sustainability indicators* (Chap. 3, pp. 42–58). Abingdon: Routledge.

Dahlmann, F., Stubbs, W., Griggs, D. & Morrell, K. (2019). Corporate actors, the UN Sustainable Development Goals and Earth system governance: A research agenda. *Anthropocene Review*, *6*(1-2), 167–176. doi:10.1177/2053019619848217

Daly, H. E. (1977). *Steady-state economics*. San Francisco: W. H. Freeman.

Daly, H. E. (1990). Toward some operational principles of sustainable development. *Ecological Economics*, *2*(1), 1–6. doi:10.1016/0921-8009(90)90010-R

Daly, H. E. (1991). *Steady-state economics* (2nd Ed.). Washington, D.C.: Island Press.

Daly, H. E. (1996). *Beyond growth: The economics of sustainable development*. Boston: Beacon Press.

Daly, H. E. (2005). Economics in a full world. *Scientific American*, *293*, 100–107. doi:10.1038/scientificamerican0905-100

Daly, H. E. & Cobb, J. B. (1989). *For the common good: Redirecting the economy toward community, the environment, and a sustainable future*. Boston: Beacon.

das Neves Almeida, T. A., Cruz, L., Barata, E. & García-Sánchez, I.-M. (2017). Economic growth and environmental impacts: An analysis based on a Composite Index of Environmental Damage. *Ecological Indicators*, *76*, 119–130. doi:10.1016/j.ecolind.2016.12.028

Dasgupta, P. (2010). Nature's role in sustaining economic development. *Philosophical Transactions of the Royal Society B: Biological Sciences, 365*(1537), 5–11. doi:10.1098/rstb.2009.0231

David, F. R. (2009). *Strategic management: Concepts and cases* (12th Ed.). Upper Saddle River: Pearson.

Davis, J. H., Schoorman, F. D. & Donaldson, L. (1997). Toward a stewardship theory of management. *Academy of Management Review, 22*(1), 20–47. doi:10.5465/amr.1997.9707180258

Davison, A. C. & Hinkley, D. V. (1998). *Bootstrap methods and their application.* Cambridge: Cambridge University Press.

de Bettignies, H.-C. & Lépineux, F. (2009). *Finance for a better world: The Shift toward sustainability.* Basingstoke: Palgrave Macmillan.

de Villiers, C. & Hsiao, P.-C. K. (2018). Integrated reporting. In *Sustainability accounting and integrated reporting* (Chap. 2, pp. 13–24). Abingdon: Routledge.

de Vos, J. M., Joppa, L. N., Gittleman, J. L., Stephens, P. R. & Pimm, S. L. (2015). Estimating the normal background rate of species extinction. *Conservation Biology, 29*(2), 452–462. doi:10.1111/cobi.12380

Decancq, K. & Lugo, M. A. (2013). Weights in multidimensional indices of wellbeing: An overview. *Econometric Reviews, 32*(1), 7–34. doi:10.1080/07474938.2012.690641

Deegan, C. (2002). Introduction: The legitimising effect of social and environmental disclosures - A theoretical foundation. *Accounting, Auditing & Accountability Journal, 15*(3), 282–311. doi:10.1108/09513570210435852

Demirtas, H., Freels, S. A. & Yucel, R. M. (2008). Plausibility of multivariate normality assumption when multiply imputing non-Gaussian continuous outcomes: A simulation assessment. *Journal of Statistical Computation and Simulation, 78*(1), 69–84. doi:10.1080/10629360600903866

Dempsey, N., Bramley, G., Power, S. & Brown, C. (2011). The social dimension of sustainable development: Defining urban social sustainability. *Sustainable Development, 19*(5), 289–300. doi:10.1002/sd.417

Destatis. (2009). *Mikrozensus: Bevölkerung und Erwerbstätigkeit - Stand und Entwicklung der Erwerbstätigkeit in Deutschland (Fachserie 1 Reihe 4.1.1) 2008.* Wiesbaden: Statistisches Bundesamt (Destatis).

Destatis. (2010a). *Input-Output-Rechnung im Überblick.* Wiesbaden: Statistisches Bundesamt (Destatis).

Destatis. (2010b). *Mikrozensus: Bevölkerung und Erwerbstätigkeit - Stand und Entwicklung der Erwerbstätigkeit in Deutschland (Fachserie 1 Reihe 4.1.1) 2009.* Wiesbaden: Statistisches Bundesamt (Destatis).

Destatis. (2011a). *Mikrozensus: Bevölkerung und Erwerbstätigkeit - Stand und Entwicklung der Erwerbstätigkeit in Deutschland (Fachserie 1 Reihe 4.1.1) 2010.* Wiesbaden: Statistisches Bundesamt (Destatis).

Destatis. (2011b). *Umwelt: Abfallentsorgung (Fachserie 19 Reihe 1) 2009.* Wiesbaden: Statistisches Bundesamt (Destatis).

Destatis. (2012a). *Finanzen und Steuern: Jährliche Körperschaftsteuerstatistik 2008.* Wiesbaden: Statistisches Bundesamt (Destatis).

Destatis. (2012b). *Umwelt: Abfallentsorgung (Fachserie 19 Reihe 1) 2010.* Wiesbaden: Statistisches Bundesamt (Destatis).

Destatis. (2012c). *Volkswirtschaftliche Gesamtrechnungen: Input-Output-Rechnung (Fachserie 18 Reihe 2) 2008.* Wiesbaden: Statistisches Bundesamt (Destatis).

Destatis. (2013a). *Finanzen und Steuern: Jährliche Körperschaftsteuerstatistik 2009.* Wiesbaden: Statistisches Bundesamt (Destatis).

Destatis. (2013b). *Finanzen und Steuern: Umsatzsteuerstatistik (Veranlagungen) (Fachserie 14 Reihe 8.2) 2008.* Wiesbaden: Statistisches Bundesamt (Destatis).

Destatis. (2013c). *Umwelt: Abfallentsorgung (Fachserie 19 Reihe 1) 2011.* Wiesbaden: Statistisches Bundesamt (Destatis).

Destatis. (2013d). *Volkswirtschaftliche Gesamtrechnungen: Input-Output-Rechnung (Fachserie 18 Reihe 2) 2009.* Wiesbaden: Statistisches Bundesamt (Destatis).

Destatis. (2014a). *Finanzen und Steuern: Jährliche Körperschaftsteuerstatistik 2010.* Wiesbaden: Statistisches Bundesamt (Destatis).

Destatis. (2014b). *Finanzen und Steuern: Umsatzsteuerstatistik (Veranlagungen) (Fachserie 14 Reihe 8.2) 2009.* Wiesbaden: Statistisches Bundesamt (Destatis).

Destatis. (2014c). *Mikrozensus: Bevölkerung und Erwerbstätigkeit - Stand und Entwicklung der Erwerbstätigkeit in Deutschland (Fachserie 1 Reihe 4.1.1) 2013.* Wiesbaden: Statistisches Bundesamt (Destatis).

Destatis. (2014d). *Umwelt: Abfallentsorgung (Fachserie 19 Reihe 1) 2012.* Wiesbaden: Statistisches Bundesamt (Destatis).

Destatis. (2015a). *Finanzen und Steuern: Gewerbesteuer (Fachserie 14 Reihe 10.2) 2010.* Wiesbaden: Statistisches Bundesamt (Destatis).

Destatis. (2015b). *Finanzen und Steuern: Jährliche Körperschaftsteuerstatistik 2011.* Wiesbaden: Statistisches Bundesamt (Destatis).

Destatis. (2015c). *Finanzen und Steuern: Umsatzsteuerstatistik (Veranlagungen) (Fachserie 14 Reihe 8.2) 2010.* Wiesbaden: Statistisches Bundesamt (Destatis).

Destatis. (2015d). *Mikrozensus: Bevölkerung und Erwerbstätigkeit - Stand und Entwicklung der Erwerbstätigkeit in Deutschland (Fachserie 1 Reihe 4.1.1) 2011.* Wiesbaden: Statistisches Bundesamt (Destatis).

Destatis. (2015e). *Mikrozensus: Bevölkerung und Erwerbstätigkeit - Stand und Entwicklung der Erwerbstätigkeit in Deutschland (Fachserie 1 Reihe 4.1.1) 2012.* Wiesbaden: Statistisches Bundesamt (Destatis).

Destatis. (2015f). *Mikrozensus: Bevölkerung und Erwerbstätigkeit - Stand und Entwicklung der Erwerbstätigkeit in Deutschland (Fachserie 1 Reihe 4.1.1) 2014.* Wiesbaden: Statistisches Bundesamt (Destatis).

Destatis. (2015g). *Volkswirtschaftliche Gesamtrechnungen: Input-Output-Rechnung (Fachserie 18 Reihe 2) 2010.* Wiesbaden: Statistisches Bundesamt (Destatis).

Destatis. (2016a). *Finanzen und Steuern: Gewerbesteuer (Fachserie 14 Reihe 10.2) 2011.* Wiesbaden: Statistisches Bundesamt (Destatis).

Destatis. (2016b). *Finanzen und Steuern: Jährliche Körperschaftsteuerstatistik 2012.* Wiesbaden: Statistisches Bundesamt (Destatis).

Destatis. (2016c). *Finanzen und Steuern: Umsatzsteuerstatistik (Veranlagungen) (Fachserie 14 Reihe 8.2) 2011.* Wiesbaden: Statistisches Bundesamt (Destatis).

Destatis. (2016d). *Finanzen und Steuern: Umsatzsteuerstatistik (Veranlagungen) (Fachserie 14 Reihe 8.2) 2012.* Wiesbaden: Statistisches Bundesamt (Destatis).

Destatis. (2016e). *Mikrozensus: Bevölkerung und Erwerbstätigkeit - Stand und Entwicklung der Erwerbstätigkeit in Deutschland (Fachserie 1 Reihe 4.1.1) 2015.* Wiesbaden: Statistisches Bundesamt (Destatis).

Destatis. (2016f). *Umwelt: Abfallentsorgung (Fachserie 19 Reihe 1) 2013.* Wiesbaden: Statistisches Bundesamt (Destatis).

Destatis. (2016g). *Umwelt: Abfallentsorgung (Fachserie 19 Reihe 1) 2014.* Wiesbaden: Statistisches Bundesamt (Destatis).

Destatis. (2016h). *Volkswirtschaftliche Gesamtrechnungen: Input-Output-Rechnung (Fachserie 18 Reihe 2) 2011.* Wiesbaden: Statistisches Bundesamt (Destatis).

Destatis. (2016i). *Volkswirtschaftliche Gesamtrechnungen: Input-Output-Rechnung (Fachserie 18 Reihe 2) 2012.* Wiesbaden: Statistisches Bundesamt (Destatis).

Destatis. (2017a). *Bevölkerung und Erwerbstätigkeit: Erwerbsbeteiligung der Bevölkerung - Ergebnisse des Mikrozensus zum Arbeitsmarkt (Fachserie 1 Reihe 4.1) 2016.* Nürnberg: Statistisches Bundesamt (Destatis).

Destatis. (2017b). *Finanzen und Steuern: Gewerbesteuer (Fachserie 14 Reihe 10.2) 2012.* Wiesbaden: Statistisches Bundesamt (Destatis).

Destatis. (2017c). *Finanzen und Steuern: Gewerbesteuer (Fachserie 14 Reihe 10.2) 2013.* Wiesbaden: Statistisches Bundesamt (Destatis).

Destatis. (2017d). *Umwelt: Abfallentsorgung (Fachserie 19 Reihe 1) 2015.* Wiesbaden: Statistisches Bundesamt (Destatis).

Destatis. (2017e). *Volkswirtschaftliche Gesamtrechnungen: Input-Output-Rechnung (Fachserie 18 Reihe 2) 2013.* Wiesbaden: Statistisches Bundesamt (Destatis).

Destatis. (2018a). *Finanzen und Steuern: Gewerbesteuer (Fachserie 14 Reihe 10.2) 2014.* Wiesbaden: Statistisches Bundesamt (Destatis).

Destatis. (2018b). *Finanzen und Steuern: Jährliche Körperschaftsteuerstatistik (Fachserie 14 Reihe 7.2) 2013.* Wiesbaden: Statistisches Bundesamt (Destatis).

Destatis. (2018c). *Finanzen und Steuern: Umsatzsteuerstatistik (Veranlagungen) (Fachserie 14 Reihe 8.2) 2013.* Wiesbaden: Statistisches Bundesamt (Destatis).

Destatis. (2018d). *Finanzen und Steuern: Umsatzsteuerstatistik (Veranlagungen) (Fachserie 14 Reihe 8.2) 2014.* Wiesbaden: Statistisches Bundesamt (Destatis).

Destatis. (2018e). *Umweltnutzung und Wirtschaft: Tabellen zu den Umweltökonomischen Gesamtrechnungen - Teil 2: Energie 2000-2016.* Wiesbaden: Statistisches Bundesamt (Destatis).

Destatis. (2018f). *Umweltnutzung und Wirtschaft: Tabellen zu den Umweltökonomischen Gesamtrechnungen - Teil 3: Anthropogene Luftemissionen 2018.* Wiesbaden: Statistisches Bundesamt (Destatis).

Destatis. (2018g). *Umweltnutzung und Wirtschaft: Tabellen zu den Umweltökonomischen Gesamtrechnungen - Teil 4: Wassereinsatz, Abwasser 2018*. Wiesbaden: Statistisches Bundesamt (Destatis).

Destatis. (2018h). *Volkswirtschaftliche Gesamtrechnungen: Inlandsproduktberechnung - Detaillierte Jahresergebnisse (Fachserie 18 Reihe 1.4) 2017*. Wiesbaden: Statistisches Bundesamt (Destatis).

Destatis. (2018i). *Volkswirtschaftliche Gesamtrechnungen: Input-Output-Rechnung (Fachserie 18 Reihe 2) 2014*. Wiesbaden: Statistisches Bundesamt (Destatis).

Destatis. (2019a). *Außenhandel: Rangfolge der Handelspartner im Außenhandel der Bundesrepublik Deutschland 2018*. Wiesbaden: Statistisches Bundesamt (Destatis).

Destatis. (2019b). *Finanzen und Steuern: Jährliche Körperschaftsteuerstatistik (Fachserie 14 Reihe 7.2) 2014*. Wiesbaden: Statistisches Bundesamt (Destatis).

Destatis. (2019c). *Produzierendes Gewerbe: Kostenstruktur der Unternehmen des Verarbeitenden Gewerbes sowie des Bergbaus und der Gewinnung von Steinen und Erden (Fachserie 4 Reihe 4.3) 2017*. Wiesbaden: Statistisches Bundesamt (Destatis).

Destatis. (2019d). *Umwelt: Abfallentsorgung (Fachserie 19 Reihe 1) 2016*. Wiesbaden: Statistisches Bundesamt (Destatis).

Destatis. (2019e). *Umweltökonomische Gesamtrechnungen: Umweltbezogene Steuern 2008-2016*. Wiesbaden: Statistisches Bundesamt (Destatis).

Destatis. (2019f). *Volkswirtschaftliche Gesamtrechnungen: Input-Output-Rechnung (Fachserie 18 Reihe 2) 2015*. Wiesbaden: Statistisches Bundesamt (Destatis).

Dickey, D. A. & Fuller, W. A. (1979). Distribution of the estimators for autoregressive time series with a unit root. *Journal of the American Statistical Association, 74*(366), 427–431. doi:10.2307/2286348

Dickey, D. A. & Fuller, W. A. (1981). Likelihood ratio statistics for autoregressive time series with a unit root. *Econometrica, 49*(4), 1057–1072. doi:10.2307/1912517

DiMaggio, P. J. & Powell, W. W. (1983). The iron cage revisited: Institutional isomorphism and collective rationality in organizational fields. *American Sociological Review, 48*(2), 147–160. doi:10.2307/2095101

dos Santos Gaspar, J., Cardoso Marques, A. & Fuinhas, J. A. (2017). The traditional energy-growth nexus: A comparison between sustainable development and economic growth approaches. *Ecological Indicators, 75*, 286–296. doi:10.1016/j.ecolind.2016.12.048

Dougherty, J., Kohavi, R. & Sahami, M. (1995). Supervised and unsupervised discretization of continuous features. *Proceedings of the 12th International Conference on Machine Learning*, 194–202. doi:10.1016/B978-1-55860-377-6.50032-3

Dower, N. (2004). Global economy, justice and sustainability. *Ethical Theory and Moral Practice, 7*(4), 399–415. doi:10.1007/s10677-004-2215-2

Dowling, J. & Pfeffer, J. (1975). Organizational legitimacy: Social values and organizational behavior. *Pacific Sociological Review, 18*(1), 122–136. doi:10.2307/1388226

Dragicevic, A. Z. (2018). Deconstructing sustainability. *Sustainable Development, 26*(6), 525–532. doi:10.1002/sd.1746

Dray, S., Dufour, A.-B. & Thioulouse, J. (2018). *Package 'ade4'*. Comprehensive R Archive Network (CRAN).

Dustmann, C., Fitzenberger, B. & Zimmermann, M. (2018). Housing expenditures and income inequality. *ZEW Discussion Paper*, (18), 048. doi:10.2139/ssrn.3289094

Dyllick, T. & Hockerts, K. (2002). Beyond the business case for corporate sustainability. *Business Strategy and the Environment*, *11*(2), 130–141. doi:10.1002/bse.323

Ebert, U. & Welsch, H. (2004). Meaningful environmental indices: A social choice approach. *Journal of Environmental Economics and Management*, *47*(2), 270–283. doi:10.1016/j.jeem.2003.09.001

EC. (2018). *Action plan: Financing sustainable growth*. Brussels: European Commission (EC).

EC, IMF, OECD, UN & World Bank. (2009). *The system of national accounts 2008*. New York: European Commission (EC), International Monetary Fund (IMF), Organisation for Economic Co-operation and Development (OECD), United Nations (UN), World Bank.

Eccles, R. G., Ioannou, I. & Serafeim, G. (2014). The impact of corporate sustainability on organizational processes and performance. *Management Science*, *60*(11), 2835–2857. doi:10.1287/mnsc.2014.1984

EEA. (2018). *Trends and projections in Europe 2018: Tracking progress towards Europe's climate and energy targets*. Luxembourg: European Environment Agency (EEA).

Efron, B. & Tibshirani, R. (1993). *An introduction to the bootstrap*. New York: Chapman & Hall.

Egels-Zandén, N. & Wahlqvist, E. (2007). Post-partnership strategies for defining corporate responsibility: The business social compliance initiative. *Journal of Business Ethics*, *70*(2), 175–189. doi:10.1007/s10551-006-9104-7

Elkington, J. (1997). *Cannibals with forks: The triple bottom line of 21st century business*. Oxford: Capstone.

Elkington, J. (2018). 25 years ago I coined the phrase "Triple Bottom Line." Here's why it's time to rethink it. *Harvard Business Review*.

Enders, C. K. (2010). *Applied missing data analysis*. New York: Guilford Press.

Engert, S., Rauter, R. & Baumgartner, R. J. (2016). Exploring the integration of corporate sustainability into strategic management: A literature review. *Journal of Cleaner Production*, *112*(Part 4), 2833–2850. doi:10.1016/j.jclepro.2015.08.031

Epstein, P. R., Buonocore, J. J., Eckerle, K., Hendryx, M., Stout, B. M., Heinberg, R., ... Glustrom, L. (2011). Full cost accounting for the life cycle of coal. *Annals of the New York Academy of Sciences*, *1219*(1), 73–98. doi:10.1111/j.1749-6632.2010.05890.x

Escrig-Olmedo, E., Muñoz-Torres, M. J., Fernández-Izquierdo, M. Á. & Rivera-Lirio, J. M. (2017). Measuring corporate environmental performance: A methodology for sustainable development. *Business Strategy and the Environment*, *26*(2), 142–162. doi:10.1002/bse.1904

Esty, D. C. (2018). Measurement matters: Toward data-driven environmental policy-making. In S. Bell & S. Morse (Eds.), *Routledge handbook of sustainability indicators* (Chap. 31, pp. 494–506). Abingdon: Routledge.

Esty, D. C. & Emerson, J. W. (2018). From crises and gurus to science and metrics: Yale's Environmental Performance Index and the rise of data-driven policymaking. In S. Bell & S. Morse (Eds.), *Routledge handbook of sustainability indicators* (Chap. 5, pp. 93–102). Abingdon: Routledge.

Eurostat. (2008a). *Manual of supply, use and input-output tables*. Luxembourg: European Communities.

Eurostat. (2008b). *NACE Rev. 2: Statistical classification of economic activities in the European Community*. Luxembourg: European Communities.

Eurostat. (2013). *European system of accounts: ESA 2010*. Luxembourg: European Union (EU).

Eurostat. (2018). *Sustainable development in the European Union: Monitoring report on progress towards the SDGs in an EU context*. Luxembourg: European Union (EU).

Eurostat. (2019a). Business expenditure on R&D (BERD) by NACE Rev. 2 activity [rd_e_berdindr2]. Retrieved February 12, 2019, from https://appsso.eurostat.ec. europa.eu/nui/show.do?dataset=rd_e_berdindr2&lang=en

Eurostat. (2019b). House price index (2015 = 100) - Quarterly data [prc_hpi_q]. Retrieved July 18, 2019, from https://appsso.eurostat.ec.europa.eu/nui/show.do?dataset= prc_hpi_q&lang=en

Eurostat. (2019c). Statistics explained: Thematic glossaries. Retrieved November 21, 2019, from https://ec.europa.eu/eurostat/statistics-explained/index.php/ Thematic_glossaries

Eurostat. (2019d). Total R&D personnel and researchers in business enterprise sector by NACE Rev. 2 activity and sex [rd_p_bempoccr2]. Retrieved February 12, 2019, from http://appsso.eurostat.ec.europa.eu/nui/show.do?dataset=rd_p_bempoccr2& lang=en

Ewing, B. R., Hawkins, T. R., Wiedmann, T. O., Galli, A., Ercin, A. E., Weinzettel, J. & Steen-Olsen, K. (2012). Integrating ecological and water footprint accounting in a multi-regional input-output framework. *Ecological Indicators, 23*, 1–8. doi:10. 1016/j.ecolind.2012.02.025

Fath, B. D. & Cabezas, H. (2004). Exergy and Fisher information as ecological indices. *Ecological Modelling, 174*(1-2), 25–35. doi:10.1016/j.ecolmodel.2003.12.045

Fernandez-Feijoo, B., Romero, S. & Ruiz, S. (2014). Effect of stakeholders' pressure on transparency of sustainability reports within the GRI framework. *Journal of Business Ethics, 122*(1), 53–63. doi:10.1007/s10551-013-1748-5

Field, A. (2009). *Discovering statistics using SPSS* (3rd Ed.). London: Sage.

Figge, F. & Hahn, T. (2004). Sustainable value added - Measuring corporate contributions to sustainability beyond eco-efficiency. *Ecological Economics, 48*(2), 173–187. doi:10.1016/j.ecolecon.2003.08.005

Finnveden, G., Hauschild, M. Z., Ekvall, T., Guinée, J., Heijungs, R., Hellweg, S., ... Suh, S. (2009). Recent developments in life cycle assessment. *Journal of Environmental Management*, *91*(1), 1–21. doi:10.1016/j.jenvman.2009.06.018

Finnveden, G. & Moberg, Å. (2005). Environmental systems analysis tools - An overview. *Journal of Cleaner Production*, *13*(12), 1165–1173. doi:10.1016/j.jclepro.2004.06.004

Finnveden, G. & Östlund, P. (1997). Exergies of natural resources in life-cycle assessment and other applications. *Energy*, *22*(9), 923–931. doi:10.1016/S0360-5442(97)00022-4

Folke, C., Biggs, R., Norström, A. V., Reyers, B. & Rockström, J. (2016). Social-ecological resilience and biosphere-based sustainability science. *Ecology and Society*, *21*(3), 41. doi:10.5751/ES-08748-210341

Freeman, R. E. (1984). *Strategic management: A stakeholder approach*. Marshfield: Pitman.

Freeman, R. E. (2010). *Strategic management: A stakeholder approach*. Cambridge: Cambridge University Press.

Frugoli, P. A., Villas Bôas de Almeida, C. M., Agostinho, F., Giannetti, B. F. & Huisingh, D. (2015). Can measures of well-being and progress help societies to achieve sustainable development? *Journal of Cleaner Production*, *90*, 370–380. doi:10.1016/j.jclepro.2014.11.076

Galbreath, J. (2009). Building corporate social responsibility into strategy. *European Business Review*, *21*(2), 109–127. doi:10.1108/09555340910940123

Galbreath, J. (2010). Drivers of corporate social responsibility: The role of formal strategic planning and firm culture. *British Journal of Management*, *21*(2), 511–525. doi:10.1111/j.1467-8551.2009.00633.x

Gallego-Álvarez, I., Galindo-Villardón, M.-P. & Rodríguez-Rosa, M. (2015). Evolution of sustainability indicator worldwide: A study from the economic perspective based on the X-STATICO method. *Ecological Indicators*, *58*, 139–151. doi:10.1016/j.ecolind.2015.05.025

Galli, A., Weinzettel, J., Cranston, G. & Ercin, A. E. (2013). A footprint family extended MRIO model to support Europe's transition to a one planet economy. *Science of the Total Environment*, *461-462*, 813–818. doi:10.1016/j.scitotenv.2012.11.071

Galli, A., Wiedmann, T. O., Ercin, A. E., Knoblauch, D., Ewing, B. R. & Giljum, S. (2012). Integrating ecological, carbon and water footprint into a "footprint family" of indicators: Definition and role in tracking human pressure on the planet. *Ecological Indicators*, *16*, 100–112. doi:10.1016/j.ecolind.2011.06.017

Gallopín, G. C. (1997). Indicators and their use: Information for decision-making. In B. Moldan, S. Billharz & R. Matravers (Eds.), *Sustainability indicators: A report of the project on indicators of sustainable development* (Chap. 1, pp. 13–27). Chichester: John Wiley & Sons.

Gao, J. & Bansal, P. (2013). Instrumental and integrative logics in business sustainability. *Journal of Business Ethics*, *112*(2), 241–255. doi:10.1007/s10551-012-1245-2

García-Sánchez, I.-M., das Neves Almeida, T. A. & de Barros Camara, R. P. (2015). A proposal for a Composite Index of Environmental Performance (CIEP) for countries. *Ecological Indicators, 48,* 171–188. doi:10.1016/j.ecolind.2014.08.004

Gasparatos, A. & Scolobig, A. (2012). Choosing the most appropriate sustainability assessment tool. *Ecological Economics, 80,* 1–7. doi:10.1016/j.ecolecon.2012.05.005

Geels, F. W. (2002). Technological transitions as evolutionary configuration processes: A multi-level perspective and a case study. *Research Policy, 31*(8-9), 1257–1274. doi:10.1016/S0048-7333(02)00062-8

George, D. & Mallery, P. (2005). *SPSS for Windows step by step: A simple guide and reference (12.0 Update)* (5th Ed.). Boston: Pearson.

Gerlach, J. N., Legler, B. & Ostwald, D. A. (2018). *Gesundheitswirtschaft Fakten und Zahlen: Handbuch zur Gesundheitswirtschaftlichen Gesamtrechnung mit Erläuterungen und Lesehilfen.* Berlin: Bundesministerium für Wirtschaft und Energie (BMWi).

Giannetti, B. F., Agostinho, F., Villas Bôas de Almeida, C. M. & Huisingh, D. (2015). A review of limitations of GDP and alternative indices to monitor human wellbeing and to manage eco-system functionality. *Journal of Cleaner Production, 87,* 11–25. doi:10.1016/j.jclepro.2014.10.051

Giannetti, B. F., Bonilla, S. H., Silva, C. & Villas Bôas de Almeida, C. M. (2009). The reliability of experts' opinions in constructing a composite environmental index: The case of ESI 2005. *Journal of Environmental Management, 90*(8), 2448–2459. doi:10.1016/j.jenvman.2008.12.018

Gibson, C. C., Ostrom, E. & Ahn, T. (2000). The concept of scale and the human dimensions of global change: A survey. *Ecological Economics, 32*(2), 217–239. doi:10.1016/S0921-8009(99)00092-0

Giljum, S., Burger, E., Hinterberger, F., Lutter, S. & Bruckner, M. (2011). A comprehensive set of resource use indicators from the micro to the macro level. *Resources, Conservation and Recycling, 55*(3), 300–308. doi:10.1016/j.resconrec.2010.09.009

Gjølberg, M. (2009). Measuring the immeasurable? Constructing an index of CSR practices and CSR performance in 20 countries. *Scandinavian Journal of Management, 25*(1), 10–22. doi:10.1016/j.scaman.2008.10.003

Gladwin, T. N., Kennelly, J. J. & Krause, T.-s. (1995). Shifting paradigms for sustainable development: Implications for management theory and research. *Academy of Management Review, 20*(4), 874–907. doi:10.2307/258959

Glaser, G. (2012). Base Sustainable Development Goals on science. *Nature, 491*(7422), 35. doi:10.1038/491035a

Godos-Díez, J. L., Fernández-Gago, R. & Martínez-Campillo, A. (2011). How important are CEOs to CSR practices? An analysis of the mediating effect of the perceived role of ethics and social responsibility. *Journal of Business Ethics, 98*(4), 531–548. doi:10.1007/s10551-010-0609-8

Goldstein, M. & Uchida, S. (2016). A comparative evaluation of unsupervised anomaly detection algorithms for multivariate data. *PLoS One, 11*(4), e0152173. doi:10.1371/journal.pone.0152173

Gond, J.-P., Grubnic, S., Herzig, C. & Moon, J. (2012). Configuring management control systems: Theorizing the integration of strategy and sustainability. *Management Accounting Research, 23*(3), 205–223. doi:10.1016/j.mar.2012.06.003

Grabisch, M., Marichal, J.-L., Mesiar, R. & Pap, E. (2009). *Aggregation functions.* Cambridge: Cambridge University Press.

Greco, S., Ishizaka, A., Tasiou, M. & Torrisi, G. (2019). On the methodological framework of composite indices: A review of the issues of weighting, aggregation, and robustness. *Social Indicators Research, 141*(1), 61–94. doi:10.1007/s11205-017-1832-9

Greene, W. H. (2003). *Econometric analysis* (5th Ed.). Upper Saddle River: Prentice Hall.

GRI. (2016). *Consolidated set of GRI sustainability reporting standards.* Amsterdam: Global Reporting Initiative (GRI).

GRI. (2019). GRI standards download center. Retrieved November 21, 2019, from https://www.globalreporting.org/standards/gri-standards-download-center/

GRI & UNGC. (2018a). *An analysis of the goals and targets.* Amsterdam: Global Reporting Initiative (GRI), United Nations Global Compact (UNGC).

GRI & UNGC. (2018b). *Integrating the SDGs in corporate reporting: A practical guide.* Amsterdam: Global Reporting Initiative (GRI), United Nations Global Compact (UNGC).

GRI, UNGC & WBCSD. (2015). *SDG compass: The guide for business action on the SDGs.* Amsterdam: Global Reporting Initiative (GRI), United Nations Global Compact (UNGC), World Business Council for Sustainable Development (WBCSD).

GRI, UNGC & WBCSD. (2017). *SDG compass annex: Linking the SDGs and GRI.* Amsterdam: Global Reporting Initiative (GRI), United Nations Global Compact (UNGC), World Business Council for Sustainable Development (WBCSD).

Griggs, D., Stafford-Smith, M., Gaffney, O., Rockström, J., Öhman, M. C., Shyamsundar, P., . . . Noble, I. (2013). Sustainable Development Goals for people and planet. *Nature, 495*(7441), 305–307. doi:10.1038/495305a

Griggs, D., Stafford-Smith, M., Rockström, J., Öhman, M. C., Gaffney, O., Glaser, G., . . . Shyamsundar, P. (2014). An integrated framework for Sustainable Development Goals. *Ecology and Society, 19*(4), 49. doi:10.5751/ES-07082-190449

Grinsted, A., Ditlevsen, P. & Hesselbjerg, J. (2019). Normalized US hurricane damage estimates using area of total destruction, 1900-2018. *Proceedings of the National Academy of Sciences,* 1–5. doi:10.1073/pnas.1912277116

Grubbs, F. E. (1969). Procedures for detecting outlying observations in samples. *Technometrics, 11*(1), 1–21. doi:10.1080/00401706.1969.10490657

Gusmão Caiado, R. G., de Freitas Dias, R., Veiga Mattos, L., Gonçalves Quelhas, O. L. & Leal Filho, W. (2017). Towards sustainable development through the perspective of eco-efficiency - A systematic literature review. *Journal of Cleaner Production, 165,* 890–904. doi:10.1016/j.jclepro.2017.07.166

Hacking, T. & Guthrie, P. (2006). Sustainable development objectives in impact assessment: Why are they needed and where do they come from? *Journal of Environmental Assessment Policy & Management*, *8*(3), 341–371. doi:10.1142/S1464333206002554

Hacking, T. & Guthrie, P. (2008). A framework for clarifying the meaning of triple bottom-line, integrated, and sustainability assessment. *Environmental Impact Assessment Review*, *28*(2-3), 73–89. doi:10.1016/j.eiar.2007.03.002

Hadi, A. S., Rahmatullah Imon, A. & Werner, M. (2009). Detection of outliers. *WIREs Computational Statistics*, *1*(1), 57–70. doi:10.1002/wics.6

Haerdle, W. K. & Simar, L. (2012). *Applied multivariate statistical analysis* (3rd Ed.). Berlin: Springer.

Haffar, M. & Searcy, C. (2018). Target-setting for ecological resilience: Are companies setting environmental sustainability targets in line with planetary thresholds? *Business Strategy and the Environment*, *27*(7), 1079–1092. doi:10.1002/bse.2053

Hahn, R. (2013). ISO 26000 and the standardization of strategic management processes for sustainability and corporate social responsibility. *Business Strategy and the Environment*, *22*(7), 442–455. doi:10.1002/bse.1751

Hahn, R. & Kühnen, M. (2013). Determinants of sustainability reporting: A review of results, trends, theory, and opportunities in an expanding field of research. *Journal of Cleaner Production*, *59*, 5–21. doi:10.1016/j.jclepro.2013.07.005

Hahn, T. & Figge, F. (2011). Beyond the bounded instrumentality in current corporate sustainability research: Toward an inclusive notion of profitability. *Journal of Business Ethics*, *104*(3), 325–345. doi:10.1007/s10551-011-0911-0

Hahn, T., Figge, F., Pinkse, J. & Preuss, L. (2010). Trade-offs in corporate sustainability: You can't have your cake and eat it. *Business Strategy and the Environment*, *19*(4), 217–229. doi:10.1002/bse.674

Hahn, T., Figge, F., Pinkse, J. & Preuss, L. (2018). A paradox perspective on corporate sustainability: Descriptive, instrumental, and normative aspects. *Journal of Business Ethics*, *148*(2), 235–248. doi:10.1007/s10551-017-3587-2

Hahn, T., Pinkse, J., Preuss, L. & Figge, F. (2015). Tensions in corporate sustainability: Towards an integrative framework. *Journal of Business Ethics*, *127*(2), 297–316. doi:10.1007/s10551-014-2047-5

Hajer, M., Nilsson, M., Raworth, K., Bakker, P., Berkhout, F., de Boer, Y., . . . Kok, M. (2015). Beyond cockpit-ism: Four insights to enhance the transformative potential of the Sustainable Development Goals. *Sustainability*, *7*(2), 1651–1660. doi:10.3390/su7021651

Hák, T., Janoušková, S. & Moldan, B. (2016). Sustainable Development Goals: A need for relevant indicators. *Ecological Indicators*, *60*, 565–573. doi:10.1016/j.ecolind.2015.08.003

Hall, D. M., Feldpausch-Parker, A., Peterson, T. R., Stephens, J. C. & Wilson, E. J. (2017). Social-ecological system resonance: A theoretical framework for brokering sustainable solutions. *Sustainability Science*, *12*(3), 381–392. doi:10.1007/s11625-017-0424-6

Han, J., Kamber, M. & Pei, J. (2012). *Data mining: Concepts and techniques* (3rd Ed.). Waltham: Morgan Kaufmann.

Hanley, N. (2000). Macroeconomic measures of "sustainability". *Journal of Economic Surveys, 14*(1), 1–30. doi:10.1111/1467-6419.00102

Hanley, N., Moffatt, I., Faichney, R. & Wilson, M. (1999). Measuring sustainability: A time series of alternative indicators for Scotland. *Ecological Economics, 28*(1), 55–73. doi:10.1016/S0921-8009(98)00027-5

Hansmann, R., Mieg, H. A. & Frischknecht, P. (2012). Principal sustainability components: Empirical analysis of synergies between the three pillars of sustainability. *International Journal of Sustainable Development and World Ecology, 19*(5), 451–459. doi:10.1080/13504509.2012.696220

Harangozo, G., Csutora, M. & Kocsis, T. (2018). How big is big enough? Toward a sustainable future by examining alternatives to the conventional economic growth paradigm. *Sustainable Development, 26*(2), 172–181. doi:10.1002/sd.1728

Hart, S. L. (1995). A natural-resource-based view of the firm. *Academy of Management Review, 20*(4), 986–1014. doi:10.2307/258963

Hart, S. L. & Dowell, G. (2011). A natural-resource-based view of the firm: Fifteen years after. *Journal of Management, 37*(5), 1464–1479. doi:10.1177/0149206310390219

Harvey, A. C. (1989). *Forecasting, structural time series models and the Kalman filter.* Cambridge: Cambridge University Press.

Häyhä, T., Lucas, P. L., van Vuuren, D. P., Cornell, S. E. & Hoff, H. (2016). From planetary boundaries to national fair shares of the global safe operating space - How can the scales be bridged? *Global Environmental Change, 40*, 60–72. doi:10.1016/j.gloenvcha.2016.06.008

Holden, E., Linnerud, K. & Banister, D. (2014). Sustainable development: Our common future revisited. *Global Environmental Change, 26*, 130–139. doi:10.1016/j.gloenvcha.2014.04.006

Holden, E., Linnerud, K. & Banister, D. (2017). The imperatives of sustainable development. *Sustainable Development, 25*(3), 213–226. doi:10.1002/sd.1647

Honaker, J., King, G. & Blackwell, M. (2011). Amelia II: A program for missing data. *Journal of Statistical Software, 45*(7), 1–54. doi:10.18637/jss.v045.i07

Honaker, J., King, G. & Blackwell, M. (2018). *Package 'Amelia'.* Comprehensive R Archive Network (CRAN).

Hood, C. & Margetts, H. Z. (2007). *The tools of government in the digital age.* Basingstoke: Palgrave Macmillan.

Hopwood, B., Mellor, M. & O'Brien, G. (2005). Sustainable development: Mapping different approaches. *Sustainable Development, 13*(1), 38–52. doi:10.1002/sd.244

Hörisch, J., Freeman, R. E. & Schaltegger, S. (2014). Applying stakeholder theory in sustainability management: Links, similarities, dissimilarities, and a conceptual framework. *Organization and Environment, 27*(4), 328–346. doi:10.1177/1086026614535786

Hueting, R. & de Boer, B. (2018). Environmental sustainable national income, an indicator. In S. Bell & S. Morse (Eds.), *Routledge handbook of sustainability indicators* (Chap. 14, pp. 224–234). Abingdon: Routledge.

Hughes, R. A., White, I. R., Seaman, S. R., Carpenter, J. R., Tilling, K. & Sterne, J. A. (2014). Joint modelling rationale for chained equations. *BMC Medical Research Methodology, 14*, 28. doi:10.1186/1471-2288-14-28

Huppes, G. & Ishikawa, M. (2005). Eco-efficiency and its terminology. *Journal of Industrial Ecology, 9*(4), 43–46. doi:10.1162/108819805775247891

Husted, B. W. & de Jesus Salazar, J. (2006). Taking Friedman seriously: Maximizing profits and social performance. *Journal of Management Studies, 43*(1), 75–91. doi:10.1111/j.1467-6486.2006.00583.x

IASB. (2018). *International Financial Reporting Standards (IFRS)*. London: International Accounting Standards Board (IASB).

ICSU & ISSC. (2015). *Review of targets for the Sustainable Development Goals: The science perspective*. Paris: International Council for Science (ICSU), International Social Science Council (ISSC).

IIRC. (2013). *The international IR framework*. London: International Integrated Reporting Council (IIRC).

IISD. (1997). *Assessing sustainable development: Principles in practice*. Winnipeg: International Institute for Sustainable Development (IISD).

ILO. (2013). *Decent work indicators: Guidelines for producers and users of statistical and legal framework indicators* (2nd Ed.). Geneva: International Labour Organization (ILO).

Isil, O. & Hernke, M. T. (2017). The triple bottom line: A critical review from a transdisciplinary perspective. *Business Strategy and the Environment, 26*(8), 1235–1251. doi:10.1002/bse.1982

Jabareen, Y. (2009). Building a conceptual framework: Philosophy, definitions, and procedure. *International Journal of Qualitative Methods, 8*(4), 49–62. doi:10.1177/160940690900800406

Jackson, T. (2009). *Prosperity without growth: Economics for a finite planet*. London: Earthscan.

Jahn, T., Bergmann, M. & Keil, F. (2012). Transdisciplinarity: Between mainstreaming and marginalization. *Ecological Economics, 79*, 1–10. doi:10.1016/j.ecolecon.2012.04.017

Jakulin, A. & Bratko, I. (2004). Quantifying and visualizing attribute interactions: An approach based on entropy, 1–30. arXiv: cs/0308002 [abs]

James, G., Witten, D., Hastie, T. & Tibshirani, R. (2013). *An introduction to statistical learning with applications in R*. New York: Springer.

James, P., Magee, L., Scerri, A. & Steger, M. (2015). *Urban sustainability in theory and practice: Circles of sustainability*. Abingdon: Earthscan.

Janoušková, S., Hák, T. & Moldan, B. (2018). Relevance - A neglected feature of sustainability indicators. In S. Bell & S. Morse (Eds.), *Routledge handbook of sustainability indicators* (Chap. 30, pp. 477–493). Abingdon: Routledge.

Jarek, S. (2015). *Package 'mvnormtest'*. Comprehensive R Archive Network (CRAN).

Jennings, P. D. & Zandbergen, P. A. (1995). Ecologically sustainable organizations: An institutional approach. *Academy of Management Review, 20*(4), 1015–1052. doi:10.2307/258964

Jensen, M. C. & Meckling, W. H. (1976). Theory of the firm: Managerial behavior, agency costs and ownership structure. *Journal of Financial Economics, 3*(4), 305–360. doi:10.1016/0304-405X(76)90026-X

Jerneck, A., Olsson, L., Ness, B., Anderberg, S., Baier, M., Clark, E., ... Persson, J. (2011). Structuring sustainability science. *Sustainability Science, 6*(1), 69–82. doi:10.1007/s11625-010-0117-x

Jesinghaus, J. (2018). How evil is aggregation? Lessons from the dashboard of sustainability. In S. Bell & S. Morse (Eds.), *Routledge handbook of sustainability indicators* (Chap. 26, pp. 392–406). Abingdon: Routledge.

Johnson, E. (2012). *Sustainability in the chemical industry*. Dordrecht: Springer.

Jolliffe, I. T. (2002). *Principal component analysis* (2nd Ed.). New York: Springer.

Joshi, D. K., Hughes, B. B. & Sisk, T. D. (2015). Improving governance for the post-2015 Sustainable Development Goals: Scenario forecasting the next 50 years. *World Development, 70*, 286–302. doi:10.1016/j.worlddev.2015.01.013

Kaiser, H. F. (1960). The application of electronic computers to factor analysis. *Educational and Psychological Measurement, 20*(1), 141–151. doi:10.1177/001316446002000116

Kaiser, H. F. (1970). A second generation little jiffy. *Psychometrika, 35*(4), 401–415. doi:10.1007/BF02291817

Kaiser, H. F. (1974). An index of factorial simplicity. *Psychometrika, 39*(1), 31–36. doi:10.1007/BF02291575

Kajikawa, Y., Ohno, J., Takeda, Y., Matsushima, K. & Komiyama, H. (2007). Creating an academic landscape of sustainability science: An analysis of the citation network. *Sustainability Science, 2*, 221–231. doi:10.1007/s11625-007-0027-8

Kallis, G., Kostakis, V., Lange, S., Muraca, B., Paulson, S. & Schmelzer, M. (2018). Research on degrowth. *Annual Review of Environment and Resources, 43*(1), 291–316. doi:10.1146/annurev-environ-102017-025941

Kalman, R. E. (1960). A new approach to linear filtering and prediction problems. *Journal of Basic Engineering (Series D), 82*(1), 35–45. doi:10.1115/1.3662552

Kates, R. W. (2015). Sustainability and sustainability science. In J. D. Wright (Ed.), *International encyclopedia of the social & behavioral sciences* (2nd Ed., pp. 801–806). Oxford: Elsevier.

Kates, R. W., Clark, W. C., Corell, R. W., Hall, J. M., Jaeger, C. C., Lowe, I., ... Svedin, U. (2001). Sustainability science. *Science, 292*(5517), 641–642. doi:10.1126/science.1059386

Kelley, J. G. & Simmons, B. A. (2015). Politics by number: Indicators as social pressure in international relations. *American Journal of Political Science, 59*(1), 55–70. doi:10.1111/ajps.12119

Kemp, R. (1994). Technology and the transition to environmental sustainability: The problem of technological regime shifts. *Futures*, *26*(10), 1023–1046. doi:10.1016/0016-3287(94)90071-X

Kerschner, C. (2010). Economic de-growth vs. steady-state economy. *Journal of Cleaner Production*, *18*(6), 544–551. doi:10.1016/j.jclepro.2009.10.019

King, A. A. & Lenox, M. J. (2000). Industry self-regulation without sanctions: The chemical industry's responsible care program. *Academy of Management Journal*, *43*(4), 698–716. doi:10.5465/1556362

Kohavi, R. & John, G. H. (1997). Wrappers for feature subset selection. *Artificial Intelligence*, *97*(1-2), 273–324. doi:10.1016/S0004-3702(97)00043-X

Köhler, J., Geels, F. W., Kern, F., Markard, J., Onsongo, E., Wieczorek, A., ... Wells, P. (2019). An agenda for sustainability transitions research: State of the art and future directions. *Environmental Innovation and Societal Transitions*, *31*, 1–32. doi:10.1016/j.eist.2019.01.004

Kojadinovic, I. (2005). Relevance measures for subset variable selection in regression problems based on k-additive mutual information. *Computational Statistics & Data Analysis*, *49*(4), 1205–1227. doi:10.1016/j.csda.2004.07.026

KPMG. (2017). *The road ahead: The KPMG survey of corporate responsibility reporting.* Zurich: KPMG International.

Krajnc, D. & Glavič, P. (2005). A model for integrated assessment of sustainable development. *Resources, Conservation and Recycling*, *43*(2), 189–208. doi:10.1016/j.resconrec.2004.06.002

Kroonenberg, P. M. (1983). *Three-mode principal component analysis.* Leiden: DSWO Press.

Kubiszewski, I., Costanza, R., Franco, C., Lawn, P. A., Talberth, J., Jackson, T. & Aylmer, C. (2013). Beyond GDP: Measuring and achieving global genuine progress. *Ecological Economics*, *93*, 57–68. doi:10.1016/j.ecolecon.2013.04.019

Kucuk, S. U. & Krishnamurthy, S. (2007). An analysis of consumer power on the internet. *Technovation*, *27*(1-2), 47–56. doi:10.1016/j.technovation.2006.05.002

Kuznets, S. (1934a). National Income, 1929-1932. *National Bureau of Economic Research*, *49*, 1–12.

Kuznets, S. (1934b). *National Income, 1929-32.* Washington, D.C.: United States Government Printing Office.

Landrum, N. E. & Ohsowski, B. (2018). Identifying worldviews on corporate sustainability: A content analysis of corporate sustainability reports. *Business Strategy and the Environment*, *27*(1), 128–151. doi:10.1002/bse.1989

Lang, D. J., Wiek, A., Bergmann, M., Stauffacher, M., Martens, P., Moll, P., ... Thomas, C. J. (2012). Transdisciplinary research in sustainability science: Practice, principles, and challenges. *Sustainability Science*, *7*(Supplement 1), 25–43. doi:10.1007/s11625-011-0149-x

Laplume, A. O., Sonpar, K. & Litz, R. A. (2008). Stakeholder theory: Reviewing a theory that moves us. *Journal of Management*, *34*(6), 1152–1189. doi:10.1177/0149206308324322

Latouche, S. (2009). *Farewell to growth*. Cambridge: Polity Press.

Lawn, P. A. (2003). A theoretical foundation to support the Index of Sustainable Economic Welfare (ISEW), Genuine Progress Indicator (GPI), and other related indexes. *Ecological Economics, 44*(1), 105–118. doi:10.1016/S0921-8009(02)00258-6

Leach, M., Raworth, K. & Rockström, J. (2013). Between social and planetary boundaries: Navigating pathways in the safe and just space for humanity. In *World social science report: Changing global environments* (Chap. 6, pp. 84–89). Paris: United Nations Educational, Scientific and Cultural Organization (UNESCO).

Lemke, C. & Bastini, K. (2020). Embracing multiple perspectives of sustainable development in a composite measure: The Multilevel Sustainable Development Index. *Journal of Cleaner Production, 246*, 118884. doi:10.1016/j.jclepro.2019.118884

Levin, J. (1965). Three-mode factor analysis. *Psychological Bulletin, 64*(6), 442–452. doi:10.1037/h0022603

Lewis, M. W. (2000). Exploring paradox: Toward a more comprehensive guide. *Academy of Management Review, 25*(4), 760–776. doi:10.2307/259204

Leys, C., Ley, C., Klein, O., Bernard, P. & Licata, L. (2013). Detecting outliers: Do not use standard deviation around the mean, use absolute deviation around the median. *Journal of Experimental Social Psychology, 49*(4), 764–766. doi:10.1016/j.jesp.2013.03.013

Li, M., Wiedmann, T. O. & Hadjikakou, M. (2019). Towards meaningful consumption-based planetary boundary indicators: The phosphorus exceedance footprint. *Global Environmental Change, 54*, 227–238. doi:10.1016/j.gloenvcha.2018.12.005

Li, T., Zhang, H., Yuan, C., Liu, Z. & Fan, C. (2012). A PCA-based method for construction of composite sustainability indicators. *International Journal of Life Cycle Assessment, 17*(5), 593–603. doi:10.1007/s11367-012-0394-y

Lim, S. S., Allen, K., Dandona, L., Forouzanfar, M. H., Fullman, N., Goldberg, E. M., ... Zonies, D. (2016). Measuring the health-related Sustainable Development Goals in 188 countries: A baseline analysis from the Global Burden of Disease Study 2015. *Lancet, 388*(10053), 1813–1850. doi:10.1016/S0140-6736(16)31467-2

Linnenluecke, M. K. & Griffiths, A. (2010). Corporate sustainability and organizational culture. *Journal of World Business, 45*(4), 357–366. doi:10.1016/j.jwb.2009.08.006

Little, R. J. (1988). A test of missing completely at random for multivariate data with missing values. *Journal of the American Statistical Association, 83*(404), 1198–1202. doi:10.1080/01621459.1988.10478722

Little, R. J. & Rubin, D. B. (2002). *Statistical analysis with missing data* (2nd Ed.). Hoboken: John Wiley & Sons.

Liu, J., Gelman, A., Hill, J., Su, Y.-S. & Kropko, J. (2014). On the stationary distribution of iterative imputations. *Biometrika, 101*(1), 155–173. doi:10.1093/biomet/ast044

Ljung, G. M. & Box, G. E. (1978). On a measure of lack of fit in time series models. *Biometrika, 65*(2), 297–303. doi:10.2307/2335207

Lock, I. & Seele, P. (2017). Theorizing stakeholders of sustainability in the digital age. *Sustainability Science, 12*(2), 235–245. doi:10.1007/s11625-016-0404-2

Loorbach, D. A. (2007). *Transition management: New mode of governance for sustainable development*. Utrecht: International Books.

Loorbach, D. A. (2010). Transition management for sustainable development: A prescriptive, complexity-based governance framework. *Governance, 23*(1), 161–183. doi:10.1111/j.1468-0491.2009.01471.x

López, M. V., Garcia, A. & Rodriguez, L. (2007). Sustainable development and corporate performance: A study based on the Dow Jones Sustainability Index. *Journal of Business Ethics, 75*(3), 285–300. doi:10.1007/s10551-006-9253-8

López, R. E. & Figueroa, E. B. (2016). On the nexus between fiscal policies and sustainable development. *Sustainable Development, 24*(4), 201–219. doi:10.1002/sd.1622

Lozano, R. (2008). Envisioning sustainability three-dimensionally. *Journal of Cleaner Production, 16*(17), 1838–1846. doi:10.1016/j.jclepro.2008.02.008

Lozano, R. (2015). A holistic perspective on corporate sustainability drivers. *Corporate Social Responsibility and Environmental Management, 22*(1), 32–44. doi:10.1002/csr.1325

Magee, C. L. & Devezas, T. C. (2017). A simple extension of dematerialization theory: Incorporation of technical progress and the rebound effect. *Technological Forecasting and Social Change, 117*, 196–205. doi:10.1016/j.techfore.2016.12.001

Maletič, M., Maletič, D., Dahlgaard, J. J., Dahlgaard-Park, S.-M. & Gomišček, B. (2014). Sustainability exploration and sustainability exploitation: From a literature review towards a conceptual framework. *Journal of Cleaner Production, 79*, 182–194. doi:10.1016/j.jclepro.2014.05.045

Markard, J., Raven, R. & Truffer, B. (2012). Sustainability transitions: An emerging field of research and its prospects. *Research Policy, 41*(6), 955–967. doi:10.1016/j.respol.2012.02.013

Maroun, W. (2018). Consequences of reporting. In C. de Villiers & W. Maroun (Eds.), *Sustainability accounting and integrated reporting* (Chap. 9, pp. 90–100). Abingdon: Routledge.

Maslow, A. H. (1943). A theory of human motivation. *Psychological Review, 50*(4), 370–396. doi:10.1037/h0054346

Maslow, A. H. (1972). *The farther reaches of human nature*. Harmondsworth: Penguin Books.

Maslow, A. H. (1987). *Motivation and personality* (3rd Ed.). New York: Harper & Row.

Max-Neef, M. A., Elizalde, A. & Hopenhayn, M. (1991). *Human scale development: Conception, application and further reflections*. New York: Apex Press.

Maxime, D., Marcotte, M. & Arcand, Y. (2006). Development of eco-efficiency indicators for the Canadian food and beverage industry. *Journal of Cleaner Production, 14*(6-7), 636–648. doi:10.1016/j.jclepro.2005.07.015

Mayer, A. L. (2008). Strengths and weaknesses of common sustainability indices for multidimensional systems. *Environment International, 34*(2), 277–291. doi:10.1016/j.envint.2007.09.004

McGrath, M. (2019). Climate change: Bigger hurricanes are now more damaging. Retrieved November 21, 2019, from https://www.bbc.com/news/science-environment-50380431

McGreavy, B. & Kates, R. W. (2012). Interview with Robert Kates, pathfinder in sustainability science. *Maine Policy Review, 21*(1), 14–21.

McGregor, J. A. & Pouw, N. (2017). Towards an economics of well-being. *Cambridge Journal of Economics, 41*(4), 1123–1142. doi:10.1093/cje/bew044

McLachlan, G. J. & Krishnan, T. (1997). *The EM algorithm and extensions.* New York: John Wiley & Sons.

McWilliams, A. & Siegel, D. S. (2011). Creating and capturing value: Strategic corporate social responsibility, resource-based theory, and sustainable competitive advantage. *Journal of Management, 37*(5), 1480–1495. doi:10.1177/0149206310385696

Meadowcroft, J. (1997). Planning for sustainable development: Insights from the literatures of political science. *European Journal of Political Research, 31*(4), 427–454. doi:10.1111/1475-6765.00324

Meadowcroft, J. (2011). Engaging with the politics of sustainability transitions. *Environmental Innovation and Societal Transitions, 1*(1), 70–75. doi:10.1016/j.eist.2011.02.003

Mebratu, D. (1998). Sustainability and sustainable development: Historical and conceptual review. *Environmental Impact Assessment Review, 18*(6), 493–520. doi:10.1016/S0195-9255(98)00019-5

Menegaki, A. N. & Ozturk, I. (2013). Growth and energy nexus in Europe revisited: Evidence from a fixed effects political economy model. *Energy Policy, 61*, 881–887. doi:10.1016/j.enpol.2013.06.076

Menegaki, A. N. & Tiwari, A. K. (2017). The Index of Sustainable Economic Welfare in the energy-growth nexus for American countries. *Ecological Indicators, 72*, 494–509. doi:10.1016/j.ecolind.2016.08.036

Meng, C., Zeleznik, O. A., Thallinger, G. G., Kuster, B., Gholami, A. M. & Culhane, A. C. (2016). Dimension reduction techniques for the integrative analysis of multi-omics data. *Briefings in Bioinformatics, 17*(4), 628–641. doi:10.1093/bib/bbv108

Meyer, J. W. & Rowan, B. (1977). Institutionalized organizations: Formal structure as myth and ceremony. *American Journal of Sociology, 83*(2), 340–363. doi:10.1086/226550

Meyer, P. E. (2008). *Information-theoretic variable selection and network inference from microarray data.* Brussels: de l'Université Libre de Bruxelles (Département d'Informatique).

Meyer, P. E., Kontos, K., Lafitte, F. & Bontempi, G. (2007). Information-theoretic inference of large transcriptional regulatory networks. *Journal on Bioinformatics and Systems Biology, 2007*(1), 79879.

Meyer, P. E., Lafitte, F. & Bontempi, G. (2008). minet: A R/Bioconductor package for inferring large transcriptional networks using mutual information. *BMC Bioinformatics, 9*, 461. doi:10.1186/1471-2105-9-461

Meyer, P. E., Lafitte, F. & Bontempi, G. (2019). *Package 'minet'*. Comprehensive R Archive Network (CRAN).

Meyer, P. E., Marbach, D., Roy, S. & Kellis, M. (2010). Information-theoretic inference of gene networks using backward elimination. *International Conference on Bioinformatics & Computational Biology (BIOCOMP)*.

Missimer, M., Robèrt, K. H. & Broman, G. (2017a). A strategic approach to social sustainability - Part 1: Exploring the social system. *Journal of Cleaner Production, 140*(Part 1), 32–41. doi:10.1016/j.jclepro.2016.03.170

Missimer, M., Robèrt, K. H. & Broman, G. (2017b). A strategic approach to social sustainability - Part 2: A principle-based definition. *Journal of Cleaner Production, 140*(Part 1), 42–52. doi:10.1016/j.jclepro.2016.04.059

Mistler, S. A. & Enders, C. K. (2017). A comparison of joint model and fully conditional specification imputation for multilevel missing data. *Journal of Educational and Behavioral Statistics, 42*(4), 432–466. doi:10.3102/1076998617690869

Moldan, B. & Dahl, A. L. (2007). Challenges to sustainability indicators. In T. Hák, B. Moldan & A. L. Dahl (Eds.), *Sustainability indicators: A scientific assessment* (Chap. 1, pp. 1–24). Washington, D.C.: Island Press.

Moldan, B., Janoušková, S. & Hák, T. (2012). How to understand and measure environmental sustainability: Indicators and targets. *Ecological Indicators, 17*, 4–13. doi:10.1016/j.ecolind.2011.04.033

Montiel, I. & Delgado-Ceballos, J. (2014). Defining and measuring corporate sustainability: Are we there yet? *Organization and Environment, 27*(2), 113–139. doi:10.1177/1086026614526413

Moritz, S. (2018). *Package 'imputeTS'*. Comprehensive R Archive Network (CRAN).

Morley, B. (2012). Empirical evidence on the effectiveness of environmental taxes. *Applied Economics Letters, 19*(18), 1817–1820. doi:10.1080/13504851.2011.650324

Müller, K., Holmes, A., Deurer, M. & Clothier, B. E. (2015). Eco-efficiency as a sustainability measure for kiwifruit production in New Zealand. *Journal of Cleaner Production, 106*, 333–342. doi:10.1016/j.jclepro.2014.07.049

Murphy, K. (2012). The social pillar of sustainable development: A literature review and framework for policy analysis. *Sustainability: Science, Practice, and Policy, 8*(1), 15–29. doi:10.1080/15487733.2012.11908081

Nardo, M., Saisana, M., Saltelli, A., Tarantola, S., Hoffman, A. & Giovannini, E. (2008). *Handbook on constructing composite indicators: Methodology and user guide*. Paris: Organisation for Economic Co-operation and Development (OECD).

National Weather Service. (2019). Hurricane Dorian - September 6, 2019. Retrieved November 21, 2019, from https://www.weather.gov/mhx/Dorian2019

NEF. (2012). *The Happy Planet Index: 2012 Report - A global index of sustainable well-being*. London: New Economics Foundation (NEF).

Ness, B., Urbel-Piirsalu, E., Anderberg, S. & Olsson, L. (2007). Categorising tools for sustainability assessment. *Ecological Economics, 60*(3), 498–508. doi:10.1016/j.ecolecon.2006.07.023

Neumayer, E. (2010). *Weak versus strong sustainability*. Cheltenham: Edward Elgar.

Nie, Y., Lv, T. & Gao, J. (2017). Co-evolution entropy as a new index to explore power system transition: A case study of China's electricity domain. *Journal of Cleaner Production*, *165*, 951–967. doi:10.1016/j.jclepro.2017.07.122

Nilsson, M., Griggs, D. & Visback, M. (2016). Map the interactions between Sustainable Development Goals. *Nature*, *534* (7607), 320–322. doi:10.1038/534320a

Novo, A. A. & Schafer, J. L. (2015). *Package 'norm'*. Comprehensive R Archive Network (CRAN).

O'Neill, D. W., Fanning, A. L., Lamb, W. F. & Steinberger, J. K. (2018). A good life for all within planetary boundaries. *Nature Sustainability*, *1*, 88–95. doi:10.1038/s41893-018-0021-4

Odum, H. T. (1996). *Environmental accounting: EMERGY and environmental decision making*. New York: John Wiley & Sons.

OECD. (2016). *Better policies for 2030: An OECD action plan on the Sustainable Development Goals*. Paris: Organisation for Economic Co-operation and Development (OECD).

OECD. (2017). *How's life? Measuring well-being*. Paris: Organisation for Economic Co-operation and Development (OECD).

Ogata, K., Inoue, S., Ueda, A. & Yagi, H. (2018). The functional differentiation between the International Integrated Reporting Council (IIRC) and the Global Reporting Initiative (GRI) in the sphere of sustainability reporting. In K.-H. Lee & S. Schaltegger (Eds.), *Accounting for sustainability: Asia pacific perspectives* (Chap. 11, pp. 261–279). Cham: Springer.

Oh, S.-H. & Lee, Y.-J. (1994). Effect of nonlinear transformations on correlation between weighted sums in multilayer perceptrons. *IEEE Transactions on Neural Networks*, *5*(3), 508–510. doi:10.1109/72.286927

Oxford Dictionaries. (2018a). Definition of "ecology". Oxford University Press. Retrieved November 21, 2019, from https://en.oxforddictionaries.com/definition/ecology

Oxford Dictionaries. (2018b). Definition of "environment". Oxford University Press. Retrieved November 21, 2019, from https://en.oxforddictionaries.com/definition/environment

Oxford Dictionaries. (2018c). Definition of "prosperity". Oxford University Press. Retrieved November 21, 2019, from https://en.oxforddictionaries.com/definition/prosperity

Oxford Dictionaries. (2018d). Definition of "prosperous". Oxford University Press. Retrieved November 21, 2019, from https://en.oxforddictionaries.com/definition/prosperous

Parris, T. M. & Kates, R. W. (2003). Characterizing and measuring sustainable development. *Annual Review of Environmental Resource*, *28*(1), 559–586. doi:10.1146/annurev.energy.28.050302.105551

Partidário, M. R. (1999). Strategic environmental assessment - Principals and potential. In J. Petts (Ed.), *Handbook of environmental impact assessment: Volume 1* (Chap. 4, pp. 60–73). Oxford: Blackwell.

Patterson, M., McDonald, G. & Hardy, D. (2017). Is there more in common than we think? Convergence of ecological footprinting, emergy analysis, life cycle assessment and other methods of environmental accounting. *Ecological Modelling*, *362*, 19–36. doi:10.1016/j.ecolmodel.2017.07.022

Pawlowski, C. W., Fath, B. D., Mayer, A. L. & Cabezas, H. (2005). Towards a sustainability index using information theory. *Energy*, *30*(8), 1221–1231. doi:10.1016/j.energy.2004.02.008

Pearce, D. W. & Atkinson, G. D. (1993). Capital theory and the measurement of sustainable development. *Ecological Economics*, *8*(2), 103–108. doi:10.1016/0921-8009(93)90039-9

Pearce, D. W., Hamilton, K. & Atkinson, G. D. (2001). Valuing nature. In E. C. V. Ierland, J. van der Straaten & H. Vollebergh (Eds.), *Economic growth and valuation of the environment: A debate* (Chap. 9, pp. 211–224). Cheltenham: Edward Elgar.

Pearson, K. (1901). LIII. On lines and planes of closest fit to systems of points in space. *Philosophical Magazine (Series 6)*, *2*(11), 559–572. doi:10.1080/14786440109462720

Peng, H., Long, F. & Ding, C. (2005). Feature selection based on mutual information: Criteria of max-dependency, max-relevance and min-redundancy. *IEEE Transactions on Pattern Analysis and Machine Intelligence*, *27*(8), 1226–1238. doi:10.1109/TPAMI.2005.159

Perez-Batres, L. A., Miller, V. V. & Pisani, M. J. (2011). Institutionalizing sustainability: An empirical study of corporate registration and commitment to the United Nations Global Compact guidelines. *Journal of Cleaner Production*, *19*(8), 843–851. doi:10.1016/j.jclepro.2010.06.003

Petts, J. (1999a). *Handbook of environmental impact assessment: Volume 1*. Oxford: Blackwell.

Petts, J. (1999b). *Handbook of environmental impact assessment: Volume 2*. Oxford: Blackwell.

Pezzey, J. (1992). *Sustainable Development Concepts: An economic analysis*. Washington, D.C.: World Bank.

Piketty, T. (2014). *Capital in the twenty-first century*. Cambridge: Harvard University Press.

Pinar, M., Cruciani, C., Giove, S. & Sostero, M. (2014). Constructing the FEEM Sustainability Index: A Choquet integral application. *Ecological Indicators*, *39*, 189–202. doi:10.1016/j.ecolind.2013.12.012

Pintér, L., Hardi, P., Martinuzzi, A. & Hall, J. (2012). Bellagio STAMP: Principles for sustainability assessment and measurement. *Ecological Indicators*, *17*, 20–28. doi:10.1016/j.ecolind.2011.07.001

Pintér, L., Hardi, P., Martinuzzi, A. & Hall, J. (2018). Bellagio STAMP: Principles for sustainability assessment and measurement. In S. Bell & S. Morse (Eds.), *Routledge handbook of sustainability indicators* (Chap. 2, pp. 21–41). Abingdon: Routledge.

Pollesch, N. L. & Dale, V. H. (2015). Applications of aggregation theory to sustainability assessment. *Ecological Economics, 114*, 117–127. doi:10.1016/j.ecolecon.2015.03.011

Pollesch, N. L. & Dale, V. H. (2016). Normalization in sustainability assessment: Methods and implications. *Ecological Economics, 130*, 195–208. doi:10.1016/j.ecolecon.2016.06.018

Pope, J., Bond, A., Hugé, J. & Morrison-Saunders, A. (2017). Reconceptualising sustainability assessment. *Environmental Impact Assessment Review, 62*, 205–215. doi:10.1016/j.eiar.2016.11.002

Porritt, J. (2007). *Capitalism as if the world matters*. Abingdon: Earthscan.

Pradhan, P., Costa, L., Rybski, D., Lucht, W. & Kropp, J. P. (2017). A systematic study of Sustainable Development Goal (SDG) interactions. *Earth's Future, 5*(11), 1169–1179. doi:10.1002/2017EF000632

Prescott-Allen, R. (2001). *The wellbeing of nations: A country-by-country index of quality of life and the environment*. Washington, D.C.: Island Press.

Rajsekhar, D., Singh, V. P. & Mishra, A. K. (2015). Multivariate drought index: An information theory based approach for integrated drought assessment. *Journal of Hydrology, 526*, 164–182. doi:10.1016/j.jhydrol.2014.11.031

Ramanathan, R. (2003). *An introduction to data envelopment analysis: A tool for performance measurement*. New Delhi: Sage.

Rametsteiner, E., Pülzl, H., Alkan-Olsson, J. & Frederiksen, P. (2011). Sustainability indicator development - Science or political negotiation? *Ecological Indicators, 11*(1), 61–70. doi:10.1016/j.ecolind.2009.06.009

Ramos, T. B. & Caeiro, S. (2010). Meta-performance evaluation of sustainability indicators. *Ecological Indicators, 10*(2), 157–166. doi:10.1016/j.ecolind.2009.04.008

Ramos, T. B., Caeiro, S. & Joanaz de Melo, J. (2004). Environmental indicator frameworks to design and assess environmental monitoring programs. *Impact Assessment and Project Appraisal, 22*(1), 47–62. doi:10.3152/147154604781766111

Ramos, T. B. & Moreno Pires, S. (2013). Sustainability assessment: The role of indicators. In S. Caeiro, W. Leal Filho, C. Jabbour & U. M. Azeiteiro (Eds.), *Sustainability assessment tools in higher education institutions: Mapping trends and good practices around the world* (Chap. 5, pp. 81–100). Cham: Springer.

Randers, J., Rockström, J. & Stoknes, P.-E. (2019). Achieving the 17 Sustainable Development Goals within 9 planetary boundaries. *EarthArXiv*. doi:10.31223/OSF.IO/XWEVB

Rässler, S., Rubin, D. B. & Zell, E. R. (2013). Imputation. *WIREs Computational Statistics, 5*(1), 20–29. doi:10.1002/wics.1240

Raworth, K. (2012). *A safe and just space for humanity: Can we live within the doughnut?* Oxford: Oxfam International.

Raworth, K. (2017). A doughnut for the Anthropocene: Humanity's compass in the 21st century. *Lancet Planetary Health, 1*(2), e48–e49. doi:10.1016/S2542-5196(17)30028-1

Rees, W. E. & Wackernagel, M. (1999). Monetary analysis: Turning a blind eye on sustainability. *Ecological Economics, 29*(1), 47–52. doi:10.1016/S0921-8009(98)00079-2

Reid, D. (1997). *Sustainable development: An introductory guide.* London: Earthscan.

Reyers, B., Stafford-Smith, M., Erb, K.-H., Scholes, R. J. & Selomane, O. (2017). Essential variables help to focus Sustainable Development Goals monitoring. *Current Opinion in Environmental Sustainability, 26-27*, 97–105. doi:10.1016/j.cosust.2017.05.003

Rip, A. & Kemp, R. (1998). Technological change. In S. Rayner & E. L. Malone (Eds.), *Human choice and climate change* (Chap. 6, pp. 327–399). Columbus: Battelle Press.

RobecoSAM. (2018a). *Corporate sustainability assessment companion.* Zurich: RobecoSAM.

RobecoSAM. (2018b). *Corporate sustainability assessment: Criterion weights.* Zurich: RobecoSAM.

RobecoSAM. (2018c). CSA Methodology. RobecoSAM. Retrieved November 21, 2019, from https://www.robecosam.com/en/csa/csa-resources/csa-methodology.html

RobecoSAM. (2019). DJSI index family. Retrieved November 21, 2019, from https://www.sustainability-indices.com/index-family-overview/djsi-index-family.html

Rockström, J., Steffen, W. L., Noone, K., Persson, Å., Chapin III, F. S., Lambin, E., ... Foley, J. (2009a). A safe operating space for humanity. *Nature, 461*(24), 472–475. doi:10.1038/461472a

Rockström, J., Steffen, W. L., Noone, K., Persson, Å., Chapin III, F. S., Lambin, E., ... Foley, J. (2009b). Planetary boundaries: Exploring the safe operating space for humanity. *Ecology and Society, 14*(2), 32.

Rockström, J. & Sukhdev, P. (2014). From MDGs to SDGs: Transition to a development paradigm of human prosperity within a safe operating space on Earth. *Input to the 11th session of the UN Open Working Group on Sustainable Development Goals.*

Rogge, N. (2012). Undesirable specialization in the construction of composite policy indicators: The Environmental Performance Index. *Ecological Indicators, 23*, 143–154. doi:10.1016/j.ecolind.2012.03.020

Roser, M. & Ortiz-Ospina, E. (2019). Global extreme poverty. Retrieved November 21, 2019, from https://ourworldindata.org/extreme-poverty#is-the-world-on-track-to-end-extreme-poverty-by-2030

Rotmans, J. (2002). Scaling in integrated assessment: Problem or challenge? *Integrated Assessment, 3*(2-3), 266–279. doi:10.1076/iaij.3.2.266.13572

Rotmans, J., Kemp, R. & van Asselt, M. (2001). More evolution than revolution: Transition management in public policy. *Foresight, 3*(1), 15–31. doi:10.1108/14636680110803003

Royston, J. P. (1982). An extension of Shapiro and Wilk's W test for normality to large samples. *Journal of the Royal Statistical Society (Series C), 31*(2), 115–124. doi:10.2307/2347973

Rubin, D. B. (1976). Inference and missing data. *Biometrika, 63*(3), 591–592. doi:10. 1093/biomet/63.3.581

Rubin, D. B. (1987). *Multiple imputation for nonresponse in surveys.* New York: John Wiley & Sons.

Ruf, B. M., Muralidhar, K. & Paul, K. (1998). The development of a systematic, aggregate measure of corporate social performance. *Journal of Management, 24*(1), 119–133. doi:10.1177/014920639802400101

S&P Dow Jones Indices. (2018). *Dow Jones Sustainability Indices: Methodology.* New York: S&P Dow Jones Indices.

S&P Dow Jones Indices. (2019). *Float adjustment: Methodology.* New York: S&P Dow Jones Indices.

Saaty, T. L. (1980). *The analytic hierarchy process.* New York: McGraw-Hill.

Saaty, T. L. (2001). Fundamentals of the analytic hierarchy process. In D. L. Schmoldt, J. Kangas, G. A. Mendoza & M. Pesonen (Eds.), *The analytic hierarchy process in natural resource and environmental decision making* (Chap. 2, pp. 15–36). Dordrecht: Springer.

Sachs, J. D. (2012). From Millennium Development Goals to Sustainable Development Goals. *Lancet, 379*(9832), 2206–2211. doi:10.1016/S0140-6736(12)60685-0

Saisana, M. & Philippas, D. (2012). *Sustainable Society Index (SSI): Taking societies' pulse along social, environmental and economic issues: The Joint Research Centre audit on the SSI.* Luxembourg: European Union (EU).

Saisana, M., Saltelli, A. & Tarantola, S. (2005). Uncertainty and sensitivity analysis techniques as tools for the quality assessment of composite indicators. *Journal of the Royal Statistical Society, 168*(2), 307–323. doi:10.1111/j.1467-985X.2005. 00350.x

Sala, S., Ciuffo, B. & Nijkamp, P. (2015). A systemic framework for sustainability assessment. *Ecological Economics, 119*, 314–325. doi:10.1016/j.ecolecon.2015.09. 015

Sala, S., Farioli, F. & Zamagni, A. (2013). Progress in sustainability science: Lessons learnt from current methodologies for sustainability assessment (Part 1). *International Journal of Life Cycle Assessment, 18*(9), 1653–1672. doi:10.1007/s11367-012-0508-6

Saling, P., Kicherer, A., Dittrich-Krämer, B., Wittlinger, R., Zombik, W., Schmidt, I., ... Schmidt, S. (2002). Eco-efficiency analysis by BASF: The method. *International Journal of Life Cycle Assessment, 7*(4), 203–218. doi:10.1007/bf02978875

Saltelli, A. & Annoni, P. (2010). How to avoid a perfunctory sensitivity analysis. *Environmental Modelling and Software, 25*(12), 1508–1517. doi:10.1016/j.envsoft. 2010.04.012

Saltelli, A., Ratto, M., Andres, T., Campolongo, F., Cariboni, J., Gatelli, D., ... Tarantola, S. (2008). *Global sensitivity analysis: The primer.* Chichester: John Wiley & Sons.

Saltelli, A., Tarantola, S., Campolongo, F. & Ratto, M. (2004). *Sensitivity analysis in practice: A guide to assessing scientific models.* Chichester: John Wiley & Sons.

SASB. (2018). SASB standards. Sustainability Accounting Standards Board (SASB). Retrieved November 21, 2019, from https://www.sasb.org/standards-overview/

Schafer, J. L. (1997). *Analysis of incomplete multivariate data*. Boca Raton: Chapman & Hall.

Schafer, J. L. & Graham, J. W. (2002). Missing data: Our view of the state of the art. *Psychological Methods, 7*(2), 147–177. doi:10.1037//1082-989X.7.2.147

Schafer, J. L. & Olsen, M. K. (1998). Multiple imputation for multivariate missing-data problems: A data analyst's perspective. *Multivariate Behavioral Research, 33*(4), 545–571. doi:10.1207/s15327906mbr3304_5

Schäfer, J. & Strimmer, K. (2005). An empirical Bayes approach to inferring large-scale gene association networks. *Bioinformatics, 21*(6), 754–764. doi:10.1093/bioinformatics/bti062

Schaltegger, S., Beckmann, M. & Hansen, E. G. (2013). Transdisciplinarity in corporate sustainability: Mapping the field. *Business Strategy and the Environment, 22*(4), 219–229. doi:10.1002/bse.1772

Schaltegger, S. & Hörisch, J. (2017). In search of the dominant rationale in sustainability management: Legitimacy- or profit-seeking? *Journal of Business Ethics, 145*(2), 259–276. doi:10.1007/s10551-015-2854-3

Schaltegger, S. & Sturm, A. (1989). *Ökologieinduzierte Entscheidungsprobleme des Managements: Ansatzpunkte zur Ausgestaltung von Instrumenten*. Basel: Wirtschaftswissenschaftliches Zentrum, Universität Basel.

Schiermeier, Q. (2018). Droughts, heatwaves and floods: How to tell when climate change is to blame. *Nature, 560*(7716), 20–22. doi:10.1038/d41586-018-05849-9

Schmalwasser, O. & Weber, N. (2012). Revision der Anlagevermögensrechnung für den Zeitraum 1991 bis 2011. *WISTA - Wirtschaft und Statistik, 11*(3), 933–947.

Schmidt-Traub, G., Kroll, C., Teksoz, K., Durand-Delacre, D. & Sachs, J. D. (2017a). National baselines for the Sustainable Development Goals assessed in the SDG index and dashboards. *Nature Geoscience, 10*, 547–555. doi:10.1038/NGEO2985

Schmidt-Traub, G., Kroll, C., Teksoz, K., Durand-Delacre, D. & Sachs, J. D. (2017b). Supplementary information to: National baselines for the Sustainable Development Goals assessed in the SDG index and dashboards. *Nature Geoscience, 10*, Supplement. doi:10.1038/NGEO2985

Schneider, F., Martinez-Alier, J. & Kallis, G. (2011). Sustainable degrowth. *Journal of Industrial Ecology, 15*(5), 654–656. doi:10.1111/j.1530-9290.2011.00388.x

Searcy, C. (2012). Corporate sustainability performance measurement systems: A review and research agenda. *Journal of Business Ethics, 107*(3), 239–253. doi:10.1007/s10551-011-1038-z

Seghezzo, L. (2009). The five dimensions of sustainability. *Environmental Politics, 18*(4), 539–556. doi:10.1080/09644010903063669

Seyfang, G. & Haxeltine, A. (2012). Growing grassroots innovations: Exploring the role of community-based initiatives in governing sustainable energy transitions. *Environment and Planning C: Government and Policy, 30*(3), 381–400. doi:10.1068/c10222

Shaker, R. R. (2015). The spatial distribution of development in Europe and its underlying sustainability correlations. *Applied Geography, 63*, 304–314. doi:10.1016/j.apgeog.2015.07.009

Shaker, R. R. (2018). A mega-index for the Americas and its underlying sustainable development correlations. *Ecological Indicators, 89*, 466–479. doi:10.1016/j.ecolind.2018.01.050

Shannon, C. E. (1948). A mathematical theory of communication. *Bell System Technical Journal, 27*(3), 379–423. doi:10.1002/j.1538-7305.1948.tb01338.x

Shapiro, S. S. & Wilk, M. B. (1965). An analysis of variance test for normality (complete samples). *Biometrika, 52*(3/4), 591–611. doi:10.2307/2333709

Shevchenko, A., Lévesque, M. & Pagell, M. (2016). Why firms delay reaching true sustainability. *Journal of Management Studies, 53*(5), 911–935. doi:10.1111/joms.12199

Siew, R. Y. (2015). A review of corporate sustainability reporting tools (SRTs). *Journal of Environmental Management, 164*, 180–195. doi:10.1016/j.jenvman.2015.09.010

Singh, R. K., Murty, H. R., Gupta, S. K. & Dikshit, A. K. (2012). An overview of sustainability assessment methodologies. *Ecological Indicators, 15*(1), 281–299. doi:10.1016/j.ecolind.2011.01.007

Skouloudis, A., Isaac, D. & Evaggelinos, K. (2016). Revisiting the national corporate social responsibility index. *International Journal of Sustainable Development and World Ecology, 23*(1), 61–70. doi:10.1080/13504509.2015.1099121

Smith, A., Voß, J.-P. & Grin, J. (2010). Innovation studies and sustainability transitions: The allure of the multi-level perspective and its challenges. *Research Policy, 39*(4), 435–448. doi:10.1016/j.respol.2010.01.023

Spaiser, V., Ranganathan, S., Swain, R. B. & Sumpter, D. J. (2017). The sustainable development oxymoron: Quantifying and modelling the incompatibility of Sustainable Development Goals. *International Journal of Sustainable Development and World Ecology, 24*(6), 457–470. doi:10.1080/13504509.2016.1235624

Spangenberg, J. H. (2011). Sustainability science: A review, an analysis and some empirical lessons. *Environmental Conservation, 38*(3), 275–287. doi:10.1017/S0376892911000270

Spangenberg, J. H. (2015). Indicators for sustainable development. In M. R. Redclift & D. Springett (Eds.), *Routledge international handbook of sustainable development* (Chap. 20, pp. 308–322). Abingdon: Routledge.

Spangenberg, J. H. (2017). Hot air or comprehensive progress? A critical assessment of the SDGs. *Sustainable Development, 25*(4), 311–321. doi:10.1002/sd.1657

Spence, M. (1973). Job market signaling. *Quarterly Journal of Economics, 87*(3), 355–374. doi:10.2307/1882010

Sperber, D. & Wilson, D. (1999). *Relevance: Communication and cognition* (2nd Ed.). Oxford: Blackwell.

Steenbergen, M. R. & Jones, B. S. (2002). Modeling multilevel data structures. *American Journal of Political Science, 46*(1), 218–237. doi:10.2307/3088424

Steffen, W. L., Richardson, K., Rockström, J., Cornell, S. E., Fetzer, I., Bennett, E. M., ... Sörlin, S. (2015). Planetary boundaries: Guiding human development on a changing planet. *Science*, *347*(6223), 736–746. doi:10.1126/science.1259855

Stern, N. (2015). *Why are we waiting? The logic, urgency, and promise of tackling climate change*. Cambridge: MIT Press.

Stevens, S. S. (1946). On the theory of scales of measurement. *Science*, *103*(2684), 677–680. doi:10.1126/science.103.2684.677

Stiglitz, J. E. (2002). Information and the change in the paradigm in economics. *American Economic Review*, *92*(3), 460–501. doi:10.1257/00028280260136363

Stiglitz, J. E., Sen, A. & Fitoussi, J.-P. (2009). *Report by the Commission on the Measurement of Economic Performance and Social Progress (CMEPSP)*. Paris: CMEPSP.

Stineman, R. W. (1980). A consistently well-behaved method of interpolation. *Creative Computing*, *6*, 54–57.

Stoknes, P. E. & Rockström, J. (2018). Redefining green growth within planetary boundaries. *Energy Research and Social Science*, *44*, 41–49. doi:10.1016/j.erss.2018.04.030

Stokstad, E. (2015). Sustainable goals from UN under fire. *Science*, *347*(6223), 702–703. doi:10.1126/science.347.6223.702

Stumpf, K. H., Baumgärtner, S., Becker, C. U. & Sievers-Glotzbach, S. (2015). The justice dimension of sustainability: A systematic and general conceptual framework. *Sustainability*, *7*(6), 7438–7472. doi:10.3390/su7067438

Stumpf, K. H., Becker, C. U. & Baumgärtner, S. (2016). A conceptual structure of justice - Providing a tool to analyse conceptions of justice. *Ethical Theory and Moral Practice*, *19*(5), 1187–1202. doi:10.1007/s10677-016-9728-3

Suchman, M. C. (1995). Managing legitimacy: Strategic and institutional approaches. *Academy of Management Review*, *20*(3), 571–610. doi:10.5465/amr.1995.9508080331

Tangen, S. (2005). Analysing the requirements of performance measurement systems. *Measuring Business Excellence*, *9*(4), 46–54. doi:10.1108/13683040510634835

Tay, L. & Diener, E. (2011). Needs and subjective well-being around the world. *Journal of Personality and Social Psychology*, *101*(2), 354–365. doi:10.1037/a0023779

Taylor, C. (1989). *Sources of the self: The making of the modern identity*. Cambridge: Cambridge University Press.

Testa, F., Miroshnychenko, I., Barontini, R. & Frey, M. (2018). Does it pay to be a greenwasher or a brownwasher? *Business Strategy and the Environment*, *27*(7), 1104–1116. doi:10.1002/bse.2058

Therivel, R. & Partidário, M. R. (1996). *The practice of strategic environmental assessment*. London: Earthscan.

Thioulouse, J. & Chessel, D. (1987). Les analyses multi-tableaux en écologie factorielle - I de la typologie d'état à la typologie de fonctionnement par l'analyse triadique. *Acta Oecologica, Oecologia Generalis*, *8*(4), 463–480.

Thioulouse, J., Simier, M. & Chessel, D. (2004). Simultaneous analysis of a sequence of paired ecological tables. *Ecology, 85*(1), 272–283. doi:10.1890/02-0605

Todorov, V. I. & Marinova, D. (2011). Modelling sustainability. *Mathematics and Computers in Simulation, 81*(7), 1397–1408. doi:10.1016/j.matcom.2010.05.022

Togtokh, C. (2011). Time to stop celebrating the polluters. *Nature, 479*(7373), 269. doi:10.1038/479269a

Togtokh, C. & Gaffney, O. (2010). 2010 Human Sustainable Development Index. Our World. Retrieved November 21, 2019, from https://ourworld.unu.edu/en/the-2010-human-sustainable-development-index

Torre, A. & Zuindeau, B. (2009). Proximity economics and environment: Assessment and prospects. *Journal of Environmental Planning and Management, 52*(1), 1–24. doi:10.1080/09640560802504613

Trapletti, A., Hornik, K. & LeBaron, B. (2018). *Package 'tseries'*. Comprehensive R Archive Network (CRAN).

Triantaphyllou, E. (2000). *Multi-criteria decision making methods: A comparative study.* Dordrecht: Springer.

Tseng, M.-L., Lim, M. K. & Wu, K.-J. (2018). Corporate sustainability performance improvement using an interrelationship hierarchical model approach. *Business Strategy and the Environment, 27*(8), 1334–1346. doi:10.1002/bse.2182

Tucker, L. R. (1964). The extension of factor analysis to three-dimensional matrices. In N. Frederiksen & R. P. Abelson (Eds.), *Contributions to mathematical psychology* (Chap. 4, pp. 110–127). New York: Holt, Rinehart & Winston.

Tucker, L. R. (1966). Some mathematical notes on three-mode factor analysis. *Psychometrika, 31*(3), 279–311. doi:10.1007/BF02289464

Tukey, J. W. (1977). *Exploratory data analysis.* Reading: Addison-Wesley.

Turner II, B. L., Clark, W. C., Kates, R. W., Richards, J. F., Mathews, J. T. & Meyer, W. B. (1990). *The Earth as transformed by human action: Global and regional changes in the biosphere over the past 300 years.* Cambridge: Cambridge University Press, Clark University Press.

Turner II, B. L., Kasperson, R. E., Matson, P. A., McCarthy, J. J., Corell, R. W., Christensen, L., ... Schiller, A. (2003). A framework for vulnerability analysis in sustainability science. *Proceedings of the National Academy of Sciences, 100*(14), 8074–8079. doi:10.1073/pnas.1231335100

Turner, M. G., Dale, V. H. & Gardner, R. (1989). Predicting across scales: Theory development and testing. *Landscape Ecology, 3*(3/4), 245–252. doi:10.1007/BF00131542

Uhlman, B. W. & Saling, P. (2010). Measuring and communicating sustainability through eco-efficiency analysis. *Chemical Engineering Progress, 106*(12), 17–29.

Ulanowicz, R. E., Goerner, S. J., Lietaer, B. & Gomez, R. (2009). Quantifying sustainability: Resilience, efficiency and the return of information theory. *Ecological Complexity, 6*(1), 27–36. doi:10.1016/j.ecocom.2008.10.005

Ulrich, H. (2001). *Das St. Galler Management-Modell.* Bern: Paul Haupt.

UN. (2018). *Global indicator framework for the Sustainable Development Goals and targets of the 2030 agenda for sustainable development.* New York: United Nations (UN).

UN. (2019a). Sustainable Development Goal indicators website. United Nations (UN). Retrieved November 21, 2019, from https://unstats.un.org/sdgs/

UN. (2019b). Sustainable development knowledge platform: Sustainable Development Goals. United Nations (UN). Retrieved November 21, 2019, from https://sustainabledevelopment.un.org/sdgs

UN. (2019c). *World economic situation prospects.* New York: United Nations (UN).

UNCED. (1992). *Report of the United Nations Conference on Environment and Development (UNCED).* Rio de Janeiro: United Nations (UN).

UNCHE. (1972). *Report of the United Nations Conference on the Human Environment (UNCHE).* Stockholm: United Nations (UN).

UNCSD. (2012). *Report of the United Nations Conference on Sustainable Development (UNCSD).* Rio de Janeiro: United Nations (UN).

UNDP. (1990). *Human development report.* New York: United Nations Development Programme (UNDP).

UNEP. (2010). *Green economy: Developing countries success stories.* Geneva: United Nations Environment Programme (UNEP).

UNEP. (2011). *Towards a green economy: Pathways to sustainable development and poverty eradication.* Nairobi: United Nations Environment Programme (UNEP).

UNFCCC. (1998). *Kyoto Protocol to the UNFCCC.* Kyoto: United Nations Framework Convention on Climate Change (UNFCCC).

UNGA. (2000). *United Nations millennium declaration.* New York: United Nations General Assembly (UNGA).

UNGA. (2015). *Transforming our world: The 2030 agenda for sustainable development.* New York: United Nations General Assembly (UNGA).

Valente, M. (2012). Theorizing firm adoption of sustaincentrism. *Organization Studies, 33*(4), 563–591. doi:10.1177/0170840612443455

Vallance, S., Perkins, H. C. & Dixon, J. E. (2011). What is social sustainability? A clarification of concepts. *Geoforum, 42*(3), 342–348. doi:10.1016/j.geoforum.2011.01.002

van de Kerk, G. & Manuel, A. R. (2008). A comprehensive index for a sustainable society: The SSI - The Sustainable Society Index. *Ecological Economics, 66*(2-3), 228–242. doi:10.1016/j.ecolecon.2008.01.029

van de Kerk, G., Manuel, A. R. & Kleinjans, R. (2014). *Sustainable Society Index: SSI-2014.* The Hague: Sustainable Society Foundation.

van den Bergh, J. C. (2009). The GDP paradox. *Journal of Economic Psychology, 30*(2), 117–135. doi:10.1016/j.joep.2008.12.001

van den Bergh, J. C. (2011). Environment versus growth - A criticism of "degrowth" and a plea for "a-growth". *Ecological Economics, 70*(5), 881–890. doi:10.1016/j.ecolecon.2010.09.035

van der Byl, C. A. & Slawinski, N. (2015). Embracing tensions in corporate sustainability: A review of research from win-wins and trade-offs to paradoxes and beyond. *Organization and Environment, 28*(1), 54–79. doi:10.1177/1086026615575047

van Buuren, S. (2007). Multiple imputation of discrete and continuous data by fully conditional specification. *Statistical Methods in Medical Research, 16*(3), 219–242. doi:10.1177/0962280206074463

van Buuren, S. (2012). *Flexible imputation of missing data.* Boca Raton: Chapman & Hall.

van Buuren, S., Brand, J. P., Groothuis-Oudshoorn, C. G. & Rubin, D. B. (2006). Fully conditional specification in multivariate imputation. *Journal of Statistical Computation and Simulation, 76*(12), 1049–1064. doi:10.1080/10629360600810434

van Poeck, K., Læssøe, J. & Block, T. (2017). An exploration of sustainability change agents as facilitators of nonformal learning: Mapping a moving and intertwined landscape. *Ecology and Society, 22*(2), 33. doi:10.5751/ES-09308-220233

Vavik, T. & Keitsch, M. M. (2010). Exploring relationships between universal design and social sustainable development: Some methodological aspects to the debate on the sciences of sustainability. *Sustainable Development, 18*(5), 295–305. doi:10.1002/sd.480

Verfaillie, H. A. & Bidwell, R. (2000). *Measuring ecoefficiency: A guide to reporting company performance.* Geneva: World Business Council for Sustainable Development (WBCSD).

Vermeulen, W. J. (2018). Substantiating the rough consensus on concept of sustainable development as point of departure for indicator development. In S. Bell & S. Morse (Eds.), *Routledge handbook of sustainability indicators* (Chap. 4, pp. 59–90). Abingdon: Routledge.

von Hippel, P. T. (2005). Mean, median, and skew: Correcting a textbook rule. *Journal of Statistics Education, 13*(2), 1–13. doi:10.1080/10691898.2005.11910556

Waas, T., Hugé, J., Block, T., Wright, T., Benitez-Capistros, F. & Verbruggen, A. (2014). Sustainability assessment and indicators: Tools in a decision-making strategy for sustainable development. *Sustainability, 6*(9), 5512–5534. doi:10.3390/su6095512

Wackernagel, M., Galli, A., Hanscom, L., Lin, D., Mailhes, L. & Drummond, T. (2018). Ecological footprint accounts: Principles. In S. Bell & S. Morse (Eds.), *Routledge handbook of sustainability indicators* (Chap. 16, pp. 244–263). Abingdon: Routledge.

Wackernagel, M. & Rees, W. E. (1996). *Our ecological footprint: Reducing human impact on the Earth.* Gabriola Island: New Society.

Wallis, A. M. (2006). Sustainability indicators: Is there consensus among stakeholders? *International Journal of Environment and Sustainable Development, 5*(3), 287–296. doi:10.1504/IJESD.2006.010898

Wang, Q., Yuan, X., Zhang, J., Gao, Y., Hong, J., Zuo, J. & Liu, W. (2015). Assessment of the sustainable development capacity with the entropy weight coefficient method. *Sustainability, 7*(10), 13542–13563. doi:10.3390/su71013542

Watanabe, S. (1960). Information theoretical analysis of multivariate correlation. *IBM Journal of Research and Development, 4*(1), 66–82. doi:10.1147/rd.41.0066

WCED. (1987). *Report of the World Commission on Environment and Development (WCED): Our common future.* Oxford: Oxford University Press.

Weaver, P. M. & Rotmans, J. (2006). Integrated sustainability assessment: What is it, why do it and how? *International Journal of Innovation and Sustainable Development, 1*(4), 284–303. doi:10.1504/IJISD.2006.013732

Weitz, N., Carlsen, H., Nilsson, M. & Skånberg, K. (2018). Towards systemic and contextual priority setting for implementing the 2030 agenda. *Sustainability Science, 13*(2), 531–548. doi:10.1007/s11625-017-0470-0

White, M. A. (2013). Sustainability: I know it when I see it. *Ecological Economics, 86*, 213–217. doi:10.1016/j.ecolecon.2012.12.020

Whiteman, G., Walker, B. & Perego, P. (2013). Planetary boundaries: Ecological foundations for corporate sustainability. *Journal of Management Studies, 50*(2), 307–336. doi:10.1111/j.1467-6486.2012.01073.x

Wiek, A., Ness, B., Schweizer-Ries, P., Brand, F. S. & Farioli, F. (2012). From complex systems analysis to transformational change: A comparative appraisal of sustainability science projects. *Sustainability Science, 7*(Supplement 1), 5–24. doi:10.1007/s11625-011-0148-y

Wiek, A. & Weber, O. (2014). Sustainability challenges and the ambivalent role of the financial sector. *Journal of Sustainable Finance and Investment, 4*(1), 9–20. doi:10.1080/20430795.2014.887349

Wijethilake, C. (2017). Proactive sustainability strategy and corporate sustainability performance: The mediating effect of sustainability control systems. *Journal of Environmental Management, 196*, 569–582. doi:10.1016/j.jenvman.2017.03.057

Witjes, S., Vermeulen, W. J. & Cramer, J. M. (2017). Assessing corporate sustainability integration for corporate self-reflection. *Resources, Conservation and Recycling, 127*, 132–147. doi:10.1016/j.resconrec.2017.08.026

Wood, D. J. (1991). Corporate Social Performance Revisited. *Academy of Management Review, 16*(4), 691–718. doi:10.2307/258977

World Weather Attribution. (2018). Heatwave in northern Europe, summer 2018. Retrieved November 21, 2019, from https://www.worldweatherattribution.org/attribution-of-the-2018-heat-in-northern-europe/

WSSD. (2002). *Report of the World Summit on Sustainable Development (WSSD).* Johannesburg: United Nations (UN).

WTO. (2018). *Mainstreaming trade to attain the Sustainable Development Goals.* Lausanne: World Trade Organization (WTO).

Wu, J. & Wu, T. (2012). Sustainability indicators and indices: An overview. In C. N. Madu & C.-H. Kuei (Eds.), *Handbook of sustainability management* (Chap. 4, pp. 65–86). Singapore: World Scientific.

WWF. (1998). *Living planet report.* Gland: World Wide Fund for Nature (WWF).

Yang, Y. & Webb, G. I. (2003). On why discretization works for naive-Bayes classifiers. In T. D. Gedeon & L. C. Che Fung (Eds.), *Advances in artificial intelligence: 16th*

Australian conference on artificial intelligence (Chap. 37, pp. 440–452). Berlin: Springer.

Yang, Y. & Webb, G. I. (2009). Discretization for naive-Bayes learning: Managing discretization bias and variance. *Machine Learning, 74*(1), 39–74. doi:10.1007/s10994-008-5083-5

Yoon, K.-S. P. & Hwang, C.-L. (1995). *Multiple attribute decision making: An introduction.* Thousand Oaks: Sage.

Young, H. P. (1995). *Equity: In theory and practice.* Princeton: Princeton University Press.

Yu, L. & Liu, H. (2004). Efficient feature selection via analysis of relevance and redundancy. *Journal of Machine Learning Research, 5,* 1205–1224.

Yucel, R. M. (2011). State of the multiple imputation software. *Journal of Statistical Software, 45*(1), v45/i01.

Zelený, M. (1982). *Multiple criteria decision making.* New York: McGraw-Hil.

Zhang, B., Bi, J., Fan, Z., Yuan, Z. & Ge, J. (2008). Eco-efficiency analysis of industrial system in China: A data envelopment analysis approach. *Ecological Economics, 68*(1-2), 306–316. doi:10.1016/j.ecolecon.2008.03.009

Zhang, Y., Yang, Z. & Li, W. (2006). Analyses of urban ecosystem based on information entropy. *Ecological Modelling, 197*(1-2), 1–12. doi:10.1016/j.ecolmodel.2006.02.032

Zhou, P., Ang, B.-W. & Poh, K.-L. (2006). Comparing aggregating methods for constructing the composite environmental index: An objective measure. *Ecological Economics, 59*(3), 305–311. doi:10.1016/j.ecolecon.2005.10.018

Zhou, P., Ang, B.-W. & Poh, K.-L. (2007). A mathematical programming approach to constructing composite indicators. *Ecological Economics, 62*(2), 291–297. doi:10.1016/j.ecolecon.2006.12.020

Zhou, P., Fan, L.-W. & Zhou, D.-Q. (2010). Data aggregation in constructing composite indicators: A perspective of information loss. *Expert Systems with Applications, 37*(1), 360–365. doi:10.1016/j.eswa.2009.05.039

Zuo, X., Hua, H., Dong, Z. & Hao, C. (2017). Environmental Performance Index at the provincial level for China 2006-2011. *Ecological Indicators, 75,* 48–56. doi:10.1016/j.ecolind.2016.12.016

The manufacturer's authorised representative in the EU is Springer
Nature Customer Service Centre GmbH, Europaplatz 3, 69115 Heidelberg,
Germany. If you have any concerns regarding our products, please
contact ProductSafety@springernature.com

Printed and bound by CPI Group (UK) Ltd, Croydon, CR0 4YY
24/04/2026
02096335-0005